THE BUTTERFLY AND THE SERPENT
ESSAYS IN PSYCHIATRY, RACE AND RELIGION

THE BUTTERFLY AND THE SERPENT

ESSAYS IN PSYCHIATRY, RACE AND RELIGION

Roland Littlewood

FREE ASSOCIATION BOOKS / LONDON / NEW YORK

Published in 1998 by
Free Association Books Ltd
57 Warren Street, London W1P 5PA
and 70 Washington Square South,
New York, NY 10012–1091

ISBN 1 85343 399 3 hardback; 1 85343 400 0 paperback

A CIP catalogue record for this book is available
from the British Library.

Designed, typeset and produced for
Free Association Books Ltd by
Chase Production Services, Chadlington, OX7 3LN
Printed in the EC by J.W. Arrowsmith Ltd, Bristol

Contents

Acknowledgements

I am grateful to my editors, and publishers for permission to reprint the following:

Anthropology and Psychiatry: An Alternative Approach (*British Journal of Medical Psychology*, 1980, **53**, 213–225); The Antinomian Hasid (*British Journal of Medical Psychology*, 1983, **56**, 67–78); The Individual Articulation of Shared Symbols (*Journal of Operational Psychiatry*, 1984, **15**, 17–24); From Vice to Madness: The Semantics of Naturalistic and Personalistic Understandings in Trinidadian Local Medicine (1988, *Social Science and Medicine*, **27**:2, 129–148); An Indigenous Conceptualization of Reactive Depression in Trinidad (*Psychological Medicine*, 1985, **15**, 275–281); The Imitation of Madness: The Influence of Psychopathology upon Culture (*Social Science and Medicine* 1984, **19**, 705–715); Putting Out The Life: From Biography to Ideology Among the Earth People (In *Anthropology and Autobiography*, ed. J. Okely and H. Callaway, Routledge 1992;), embodiment and religious innovation: and historical instance (In *Religion and Psychiatry*, 1996, ed. D. Bhugra, London, Routledge); The Effectiveness of Words: Religion and Healing Among the Lubavitch of Stamford Hill (with Simon Dein, 1995, *Culture, Medicine and Psychiatry*, **19**, 339–383); The Butterfly and the Serpent: Culture, Psychopathology and Biomedicine (with Maurice Lipsedge, 1987, *Culture, Medicine and Psychiatry*, **11**, 289–335); Against Pathology: The New Psychiatry and Its Critics (*British Journal of Psychiatry* (1991, **159**, 696–702); Jungle Madness: Some Observations on Expatriate Psychopathology (*International Journal of Social Psychiatry*, 1985, **31**:3, 194–197); Thaumaturgy to Human Potential: The King's Evil Revisited (*British Medical Anthropology Review*, 1996, **3**:2, 1–4); From Demonic Possession to Multiple Personality – and Back Again: The Contents of Consciousness and Pathology (1994, Inaugural Lecture UCL Press: a fuller account was published by the Royal Anthropological Institute as an occasional paper); Verticality as the Idiom for Mood and Disorder: A Note on an Eighteenth Century Representation (*British Medical Anthropology Review*, 1994, **2**:1, 44–48).

Preface

The invitation to republish some earlier papers prompts thoughts, not only of vanity, but of their relevance some years after. These essays are contributions to cultural psychiatry: that is, they are concerned with how patterns of illness recognised by psychiatrists may be mapped against the perspectives of social anthropology. This is not to say that what medicine takes as biological is necessarily to be understood solely as society's construction, but that issues of social classification and power, and of human agency within the limits of possibility made available by a biology and a culture, have necessarily to be taken into account.

The title of the collection is taken from a paper by Maurice Lipsedge and myself presented in 1987, and reprinted here, which proposes a model of Western psychiatric illness developed from anthropological approaches to spirit possession; this might justifiably be considered emblematic of the book in its reversal of the usual procedures of clinical psychiatry which generally takes Western illness as the real entity, with analogous patterns in non-Western societies as simply variants or confusions. I propose here the contrary: it is less that spirit possession is a sort of hysteria than that hysteria is – in some sense – spirit possession. The order of the chapters follows in large measure my own intellectual trajectory: from epidemiological psychiatry to the recognition of social classification and cultural meanings, and thence to the ambiguities of reconciling what have usefully been described as the 'naturalistic' and 'personalistic' modes of thinking; here biomedicine and social anthropology. I hope that this might still remain useful. While some of these papers appeared as contributions to now occluded debates, I think they stand alone reasonably well. They were written primarily for psychiatrists interested in culture, and for medical anthropologists interested in psychiatry and religion; the intention in republication is that there may be something here for a wider readership. I am grateful to Simon Dein and Maurice Lipsedge for their agreement to allowing joint papers to be reprinted. A certain difficulty has been occasioned by the different referencing system of the original journals: here numerical referencing to a list of references for each chapter has been retained, but name and date references have been referred to a cumulative bibliography for the whole book.

vii

'Anthropology and psychiatry', the first paper, deals with what for me were earlier influences on psychiatry from anthropology which did not follow from the conventional 'culture and personality' – that is psychoanalytical – perspective. Already, I had doubts about the universality of psychoanalysis and preferred an approach derived from the more empirical public recognition and use of symbols. Like the second paper, 'The antinomian Hasid', it argues for the utility of a binary system of classification for ethnic minority groups in Western societies; the type of analysis we find congenial reflects the original subject matter – psychiatric delusion or culturally normative symbolism. The next paper details the difference between social psychiatry and cultural psychiatry ('ethnopsychiatry'), and describes the value of symbolic inversion in an existing rather sparse system of dual classification as a means of gaining richness and diversity. My debt here to the 'Oxford structuralists' (and their enthusiasms for binary symbolism) will be evident, as is that to Victor Turner and Ioan Lewis.

'Against pathology' is a reply to certain medical critics of my earlier work who saw a 'cultural' approach as legitimising pathology: instead I argue the determination of meaning and of abnormality are fairly independent procedures; the use of a term like 'pathology' is a social and political process. The same chapter is also a clarification of approach, pointing out the difference between what was to become the 'British' approach and that of Arthur Kleinman's 'new cross-cultural psychiatry' in the United States.

'Jungle madness' is a short (and light-hearted?) contribution to a meeting on expatriate stress disorder. The next two papers deal with Trinidadian, West Indian, understandings of mental illness in the context of colonialism and gender disparity. 'From vice to madness' is a broad overview of how concepts of madness fit with ideas about ill health in the context of certain ideas about Caribbean values, including history and ethnicity, particularly what is generally called respectability versus reputation. The paper on tabanka illustrates one example in more detail: tabanka is simultaneously a contextual mood state related to relations between men and women, a joke, and a path from normal functioning to insanity. The 'imitation of madness' paper deals again with the relationship between individual insanity and normative social institutions, but suggests that occasionally they may be inherently connected: in certain situations what might otherwise be seen as mad and valueless may be rewarded by a society and incorporated as a worthwhile social innovation, not a new idea. It is suggested however that this is a rare process and perhaps limited to periods of social crisis and to certain types of society. A possible instance from my fieldwork in Trinidad is described – the Earth People

– as well as the antinomian model in Judaism to which I have referred earlier. 'Putting out the life' describes the Earth People in more detail, looking at the relationship between the founder, Mother Earth, and the processes which convert her life experiences into a new social order.

The paper on 'verticality' briefly looks at how a physical metaphor is transformed into a normative reading of mood – in contemporary psychiatry and in one of Hogarth's engravings. 'Moments of creation' concerns another metaphor, physical birth, and how it might be understood rather differently by men and women: female prophets often use a more connected idiom of parturition to describe their relationship to their followers, men favouring a more abstracted idiom of creation at a distance. The 'effectiveness of words' deals more exactly with what we mean by a metaphor in a situation where what may initially strike us as metaphorical usage is physically intended by the participants in what may otherwise be seen as 'ritual' healing.

The title paper follows, arguing that the model which underlies Western psychiatric disorder is that of spirit possession, and the article on multiple personality disorder proposes that the parallel may be even closer than first appears. The last paper suggests that the value of the illnesses of a British princess can be understood as charismatic rather than monarchical power (following the old model of the monarch's two bodies). Physical and social, the two bodies run through most of the papers here. Contrary to much of recent medical social science, I propose that the physical cannot be reduced to the 'socially constructed' alone. While we should be wary of ignoring the political uses of the physical, we cannot reduce all our knowledge of the physical to the ideological alone.

In a number of papers, some reprinted here, I have argued rather for a procedural dualism: we can understand ourselves and the world as a consequence of cause and effect processes, generally independent of, but potentially accessible to, human awareness – the naturalistic or scientific mode of thought. We can also understand the same matters personalistically – as the motivated actions of volitional agents employing such characteristically human attributes as intention, representation, narration, self-awareness, inter-subjectivity, identification, deceit and shame. And whilst Euro-Americans conventionally allocate one or other area of interest to the naturalistic or the personalistic, perhaps even objectifying them as separate domains (such as nature : culture :: brain : mind), we can apply either mode of thought to any phenomenon. The self may be a machine, the natural world may be personified. Psychiatric considerations of such phenomena as self-harm (symptom of depressive illness? intention to die?)

or myalgic encephalomyelitis (disease process? malingering?), like medico-legal debates on criminal responsibility (mad? bad?), continually slip between one and the other, for only one mode can be correct at any one time. Neither can be demonstrated as true, nor false: we always live with the two options.

As Plato put in the *Timaeus*, 'the world came about as a combination of reason and necessity'. But combined how? In certain areas – anthropology and psychiatry, but also medical jurisprudence, cognitive science, ethology and the sociology of knowledge – the practical problems of reconciling causation and volition become especially salient. As in the Hegelian or Marxist emergence of mind, in phrenology, phenomenology and psycho-analysis, in sociobiology and in contemporary neuropsychology and the philosophy of mind, these generally reduce one position to the other as prior and essential: whether in ontology, in epistemology or, usually, in both. These are not essays on scientific rationality and I do not wish to detail here current attempts to resolve the antinomy, but rather to take it as an inescapable ambiguity in our everyday life and thence in expert practice.

1 Anthropology and Psychiatry: An Alternative Approach[*]

The subject matter of this paper is transcultural psychiatry. The suggestion made here is that transcultural psychiatry is characterized not by its subject matter but by its methods. This assumes that mental illness is not only a function of such objective indices as social class or the availability of services, but of the considerably less tangible idea of the unique experience of being a member of a particular society: a society with its own characteristic web of economic constraints, social relations and beliefs. This web or culture is mediated by particular symbols which exist at all levels of analysis and which bind the society together. Transcultural psychiatry is concerned with these symbols. It is concerned not only with aetiology and epidemiology but with meaning. To put it another way: the relation between trans-cultural psychiatry and social psychiatry is that between anthropology and sociology.

Anthropology, psychology and psychiatry

The initial focus of this paper is upon relations between anthropology and the psychological sciences. This is followed by consideration of the possible relevance for psychiatry of the more recent developments of that branch of anthropology which has deliberately tried to exclude personal experience. Pioneers in anthropology and psychology such as Rivers and Seligman did not clearly separate the two fields. Physiological, psycho-logical and sociological explanations were used in both. Concepts of social symbols were derived from neurology (Mauss, 1979), and for McDougall and Wundt social experience could be explained by indi-vidual psychology. In European anthropology this approach was criti-cized by Durkheim (1901) and to 'psychologize' in the social sciences became unorthodox if not disreputable (Lewis, 1977).

Under the banner of 'Culture and personality', psychoanalysis in the United States appeared to offer a mode of explanation that bridged

---

[*] First published in the *British Journal of Medical Psychology* (1980)

normal and abnormal, the society and the individual. General psychiatry merely offered anthropology a series of special cases – possession states and the culture-bound syndromes. A recent appeal for a rapprochement between psychiatry and anthropology indeed implies that what psychiatry has to offer is psychoanalysis (Lewis, 1977). Freud had suggested that culture itself was the resolution of Oedipal conflicts, that religion was an illusion and that religious rituals were comparable to obsessional acts. Psychoanalytical anthropology maintained that adult culture was intelligible in terms of the needs and experiences of individuals. Society like individuals had defence mechanisms; warfare was associated with early feeding patterns; societies were characterized by terms such as paranoid or obsessional derived from individual psychopathology, and religious movements were interpreted as the socialization of psychosis (Jones, 1916; Benedict, 1935; Mead, 1949; La Barre, 1970; Devereux, 1978). Culture and personality reduced sociology to psychology; societies were *explained* by the experience of individuals and social symbols were *explained* as the result of intrapsychic conflict. The problem of the comparability in different societies of such isolated items as personality traits, defence mechanisms and repressed conflicts was largely ignored. It was assumed that similarity between individual fantasies in one society and social norms in another was somehow an explanation. Typical of these difficulties was the long-standing debate on the mental health of the shaman. Solutions which suggested that the shaman was abnormal in relation to a pan-human norm but normal in relation to a particular society (Devereux, 1970) merely replaced the idea of primitive societies by that of sick societies. Tribal peoples, like psychotics, children and our own ancestors, were supposed to operate a less disguised symbolism with a minimum of secondary process thinking.

Psychoanalytical anthropology found it difficult to distinguish between real and nominal emotion (in for example mourning rituals); roles were perceived as though they were affective responses. The function of social symbol and ritual was equated with their genesis in the individual. The question of the autonomy within the social sphere of symbols and how society manipulates symbols was ignored. Because individual experiences were assumed to be similar everywhere, symbols were deemed to be invested with a meaning independent of their social context and relationship with other symbols. In short, psychoanalysis solved the relations between psychology and anthropology by confounding them. It offered a model, not of sociology but of socialization. Its successes were perhaps in showing the strains on individuals in particular societies and in suggesting how social change may be generated in individual experience (Kluckhohn, 1944). If psychoanalysis had postulated how conflict arises between instinctual forces and society, its application in anthropology reduced the latter to the fulfilment of individual needs, generating an endless series of circular reductions.

The Durkheimian perspective

The alternative and dominant social anthropology in Britain and France derives from Durkheim: 'whenever a social phenomenon is directly explained by a psychological phenomenon we may be sure that the explanation is false' (Durkheim, 1901). For Durkheim's school – the *Année Sociologique* – the symbols by which we think are reflections, not of individual experience, but of the social order. If they do serve individual needs it is only by their effect on the whole society. 'The main function or effect of a central belief system is to inculcate, to make compulsive, the pivotal concepts, moral, cognitive and other, of that society' (Gellner, 1978). Given an initial competence, symbols are acquired as a language, a language whose themes but not concerns are drawn from the physical world; the organization of the universe reflects the organization of society and the integrity of the physical body reflects that of the body politic (Durkheim & Mauss, 1963; Douglas, 1966). This approach has proved successful in dealing with existing institutions such as witchcraft without recourse to theories of projection or compensation (cf. Evans-Pritchard, 1937 and Kluckhohn, 1944). If witchcraft beliefs are nightmares, then they are the standardized nightmares of the community derived from economic and political concerns (Wilson, 1951).

Although some ethnographers like Malinowski attempted to incorporate Durkheim's position into a perspective in which symbol and ritual serve individual needs, most workers proceeded to examine the social system independently of the individual. Durkheim had difficulty in describing how individuals acquired symbols and resorted to a quasi-physiological explanation in which heightened receptivity was triggered by heightened social interaction. Such was their dislike of psychological explanation that the *Année Sociologique* frequently tied biology directly to sociology without the mediation of psychology (e.g. Mauss, 1979). There were still residues of psychology: Radcliffe-Brown (1952) suggested that kinship could be the extension of family sentiments (cf. Needham, 1962). An 'inconstant disciple' of Durkheim, Lévi-Strauss assumes, with George Kelly, that we are primarily motivated to make sense of our situation (Lévi-Strauss, 1966, 1968). The direct use of psychological or psychiatric theories is still however regarded as an admission of failure and 'the rather limited fruits which [transcultural psychiatry] as so far produced merely provide for British social anthropology additional confirmation of the undesirability of all liaisons of this sort' (Lewis, 1977). Attempts to reintroduce such psychiatric concerns as possession states into a Durkheimian framework have generally proved unsuccessful (Douglas, 1970).

If symbols are social, and independent of individual needs, then their autonomous functioning and interrelations can be studied as an intellectual system. Lévi-Strauss suggests that symbols* do not in themselves correspond to a particular concept or concepts, but that the relations between symbols stand for the relations between concepts (Lévi-Strauss, 1968, ch. 2). For 'the simple-minded Freudian' (Leach, 1973), long objects represent penises and round ones vaginas; for the structuralist, the relation of penis to vagina is that of male to female and that of long to round. Social systems of classification are then normally polythetic and not monothetic. Symbols are only meaningful inasmuch as they are members of sets. Lévi-Strauss has suggested that many societies utilize a symbolic system of binary oppositions which are amenable to a series of transformations. By bypassing individual experience and by studying meaning and not function he claims we are examining the fundamental characteristics of the mind (Lévi-Strauss, 1966). The relations between such symbols, and their transformations in myth and ritual, can articulate a whole series of tensions, between men and women, parents and children, residence and inheritance (Turner, 1967). Signification is not fixed and different symbols may have contradictory significance at different levels.

If we wanted to apply this approach to the question of why in many societies the mentally ill are considered as akin to saints (or geniuses), we would not look for the overlap in our conceptual terms (the percentage of insane saints), but see how the two concepts might have a similar symbolic significance in relation to other cultural concerns. One type of symbolic transformation is that involved in inversions such as saturnalia and transvestism (Bateson, 1958; Needham, 1963, 1977; Leach, 1973). 'Prescribed' insane behaviour in certain societies may be the inversion of normally acceptable behaviour (Schooler & Caudill, 1964). A psychiatric explanation of the Plains Indians'

---

* There is little agreement in semiology as to the definition of sign, symbol, signal, and so on. An elementary guide is found in Leach (1976). 'Symbol' is here used very generally for that which stands for (signifies) another by human choice, as both metaphor and metonym. The terms 'structural anthropology' and 'symbolic classification' are employed rather loosely to refer to recent work in a Durkheimian tradition by Lévi-Strauss, Leach and Needham.

Berdache (Devereux, 1937) might be that it legitimates biologically determined sexual tendencies, but we are left with the questions of why such institutions are not universal (and why indeed the recognition of homosexual tendencies is not universal) and how they relate to the web of social, economic and ritual concerns in different societies. The recognition of mental illness or homosexuality or multiple births as distinct ontological entities suggests they articulate certain fundamental problems of the whole community.

In many ways psychoanalytical and Durkheimian anthropology answer different questions: the former offers a theory of socialization and change, the latter a theory of social behaviour, belief and ritual. Before looking at the relevance for psychiatry of the insights of structural anthropology I must briefly deal with certain problems. We are likely to be looking at a heterogeneous industrial society in which symbols overdetermined with a wealth of nuances appear uncommon. For us social life and religion are less likely to be associated than in the small-scale communities with prescriptive marriage customs in which structural anthropology has proved so fruitful (Needham, 1963).

Certain groups within society are dominant and control access to and use of the social symbols. If a particular binary system such as culture/nature or male/female articulates a range of social concerns and the principle is somehow located within the social system (Needham, 1962), then as psychiatrists and psychologists we may wonder whether it is also located in the perception of the individual as an individual (do he or she see themselves as located within one part of a duality or merely as 'insiders' as opposed to outsiders – those in the other half?) or whether the structure is merely a tool of analysis located externally to the participants (Lévi-Strauss, 1968, ch. XV). Anthropologists like psychiatrists do not always clearly separate (i) informants' statements, (ii) observed behaviour, (iii) conceptual models of the observer (Turner, 1967).

Members of cultural minority groups in a society (women, children, ethnic and sexual minorities, the mentally ill) have to use the majority culture to articulate their concerns (Ardener, 1972). Even if temporary disharmony is a treatable dislocation between the individual and the symbolic order (Lévi-Strauss, 1968, ch. X; Turner, 1967), there is still the problem of permanent minorities. The 'dominant model may impede the free expression of alternative models of the world which subdominant groups may possess and perhaps may even inhibit the very generation of such models. Groups dominated in this sense find it necessary to structure their world though the model (or models) of the dominant group, transforming their own model as best they can in terms of the received ones'

(Ardener, 1975). Their use of the dominant symbolism is likely to be 'rickety and cumbersome' (Ardener, 1975). Symbolic classification then makes certain cognitive assumptions about society as a whole but ignores the affective participation of individuals and groups. The distinction of symbols from other signs is however by their affective component. We shall consider later how public symbols acquire their characteristic sense of urgency for the individual.

A related question to that of constituent groups within a society is the extent to which different but related societies share the same set of cultural assumptions. These may often represent a continuum, wherein the boundary of a particular cultural system is drawn more or less arbitrarily. Structural anthropology has looked at neighbouring communities which share a common set of rituals and beliefs but in which these bear an inverted relationship to each other (Lévi-Strauss, 1977, ch. XIII). There is often an interpenetration of related symbolic systems, historically associated and which change their relations, together with individuals moving from one to the other.

If the cultural symbols by which we articulate our existence are the dominant ideas, how can an alternative perspective be generated? Or indeed how can social change occur? If we cannot demonstrate how society habitually generates new alternatives, we are left, like the psychoanalytical anthropologists (La Barre, 1970), with explanations of insanity as innovation. (Whilst innovations are possible through mental illness – the pioneers of the 19th century anti-slavery movement among the American Quakers appear to have been insane [Davis, 1966] – they seem to be rare.) It is possible that dominant modes of perception are primarily used when the fundamental concerns of a society are being ritually articulated (Bloch, 1977). It is part of the present thesis that they also come to the fore when the fundamental concerns of small groups or individuals are being threatened (Weinstein, 1962).

Understanding and explaining

This paper includes an attempt to understand the experience of a psychotic person by looking at the discrepancy between her personal experience and the modes of social classification open to her. The emphasis is on understanding not explaining; an empathic approach can however offer some prediction of events and formulate testable hypotheses (Jaspers, 1962). Even though I am principally using a model in which cultural symbols reflect the social order, I am not reducing psychology or psychiatry to sociology, but merely extending the commonplace notion that life is lived within the constraints of a particular society. In the splendid words of Mary Douglas: 'Physical nature is masticated and driven through the cognitive meshes to satisfy social demands for clarity which compete with logical demands for consistency' (Douglas, 1973). Public symbols articulate private concerns. Healing in small-scale societies is the relocation of the individual to bring his or her experience in line with social norms by the symbolic integration of social and psychological (Turner, 1967). Lévi–Strauss has even suggested that situating physiological problems in social space can facilitate physiological healing but it is difficult to see this as a specific process (Lévi-Strauss, 1968, ch. X).

We shall take into account (in a way structural anthropology does not, e.g. Needham, 1977) the relation between individual experience and the dominant symbolism. We frequently find that there is a convergence between psychoanalytical and sociological explanations of specific sets of symbols which might seem a little strange given their differing theory and approach (Richards, 1956; Lévi-Strauss, 1968, ch. IX; Devereux, 1978; Mauss, 1979). The symbolism of hair for example often appears to be related to overt or proscribed sexuality (Leach, 1958). This is not to imply with the psychoanalyst that the origins and functions of private and public symbolism are identical. Turner (1967) has suggested that the convergence occurs because every public symbol has both a conscious public (ideological) pole and an unconscious private (sensory) pole. The society uses the public pole for social concerns by activating the powerful personal relevance of the private pole. Public symbols may thus use overt sexuality in an undisguised form which would be difficult to predict from a psycho-analytical position (cf. Jones, 1916 and Leach, 1958). The power of symbolism is not necessarily derived from the resolution of personal conflicts (Rivers, 1920). 'When the structure of a certain type of phenomenon does not lie at a great depth, it is more likely that some kind of model, standing as a screen to hide it, will exist in the collective consciousness ... Conscious models are not intended to explain the phenomenon but to perpetuate it' (Lévi-Strauss, 1968, ch. XV). If the use of symbols is a function of social processes, their meaning for the anthropologist, as for the psychiatrist, is latent, indeed hidden (Douglas, 1973). They are the products of contradictions, not in the mind, but in society.

An approach to emotional experience that follows the linguistic determinism of what is generally known as the Sapir–Whorf hypothesis (that emotional experience is largely dependent on an affective lexicon, e.g. Leff, 1973) is thus likely to prove inadequate (Lévi-Strauss, 1968, ch. V). The individual does not have available all the subtle variations of expression open to him in his culture in the form of a lexicon or grid. Even language is not a nomenclature but a series of relations between signified and signifier (Saussure, 1916). If we look at the underlying structure of linguistic categories they appear not as a totally relativistic grid but as similar in different cultures (Ardener, 1971). We cannot compare grids of perception in different societies independently of the historical relations between them or the social context of language. In polite daily conversation the Victorians appeared to have no word for that part of the body lying between the 'throat' and the 'limbs', and divided the intervening space with these two words, but it seems unlikely that they were not aware of the existence of thorax and abdomen. Addition of the linguistic subdivisions of an area do not necessarily amount to the same as a description of the whole area: a generalized concept of 'Roman uncle' derived from addition of avunculus (mother's brother) and patruus (father's brother) is of little significance. A structural approach will continually return us to relationships not entities, and mediate between the reduction of psychology to sociology, and of sociology to psychology.

If we have considered the psychological and sociological properties of symbols, what of the underlying neurophysiology? Psychiatrists, unlike anthropologists, cannot take the brain as an invariable 'given'. We can conceive of mental illnesses as located along a spectrum between those best defined in organic terms (such as the symptomatic psychoses) and those best defined in social or interpersonal terms (parasuicide, the culture-bound syndromes, cf. Schneider, 1959). Even at the organic pole, psychiatric disorder has still to be articulated in a common symbolism: it is difficult to see white mice in delirium tremens without a concept of mice. In fact, like the hallucinatory experiences of South American Indians (Harner, 1973), such a grossly altered state of consciousness might be that *most* conducive to cultural patterning ('consensual validation'). This is comparable to Bleuler's (1924) two-level approach to schizophrenic symptoms. Nonfocal symptoms after head injury such as delusions and confabulations appear related to individual personal preoccupations as modulated by cultural symbols; these are used in the sense of what they personally connote rather than what they abstractly denote (Weinstein, 1962). It is not a question of organic versus social, but how society uses the organic and vice versa. The biological fact of cerebral laterality may provide the basic symbolism of a whole society (Needham, 1977). If understanding rather than explaining appears more relevant at the social and personal, rather than the organic, pole of mental illness, it is because our interventions here are necessarily verbal.

The following case history exemplifies the view that public symbols can articulate both social and individual concerns and that confusion between the two systems not surprisingly results in psychologically and socially abnormal behaviour. Concern is not with the personal symbolic productions of psychosis, but with psychosis located in the public system of symbols. This is not to deny that the former occur, notably in schizophrenia. The present approach differs from the traditional structuralist position (e.g. Needham, 1977) in introducing and examining the experience of the individual, by looking at diachronic and synchronic variations in symbolic classification, and by examining a system of dual classification in which the original significance of the relations becomes lost and the elements become monothetic groups rather than a series of polythetic terms. The concrete application of our systems of classification can result in a lack of flexibility and is characteristic of periods when psychological and social integrity are threatened. A minority group is likely to be more conservative and less flexible in its use of a dominant set of symbols (Ardener, 1971).

Case study: Beatrice Jackson

Beatrice Jackson is the 34 year old daughter of a black Jamaican Baptist minister. Her parents were both the children of tobacco labourers who attributed their modest financial success to an unswerving religious faith and a righteous life amidst a sinful and depraved world. Family life was strict: self-control and a horror of sensual indulgence were daily stressed to Beatrice and her older brother and sister. Mrs Jackson died when Beatrice was 8 and she was brought up by her mother's sister who came to join the household, a hard embittered woman whose own marriage had broken down and whose strictness with the children sometimes disturbed even the pastor. Daily life was a continual battle against the evil forces which swirled around the virtuous family. At home and school Beatrice was quiet and self-effacing, working hard and methodically, but more and more frequently lost in day-dreams about the elegant ladies of old London who filled her history books.

To become a full member of the congregation to which her father was minister one had to be 'born again', and be publicly accepted by the whole congregation in a testimony of repentance and a demonstration of the spirit of Christ within. As befitted the children of the minister, her siblings were 'born again' when they were only 13, the precocious children of a proud parent. By the age of 18 Beatrice had not yet testified and was causing anxiety to her family. Her obvious indifference to spiritual matters and the reluctance with which she attended prayer meetings contrasted with her pleasure in displaying a new frock at the church picnics and in the admiring glances of boys. Her aunt repeated her warnings of demonic temptation and her father forbade her to go out unless she was escorted by her sister. The family atmosphere became strained. The next Easter service, however, 'the Lord used her tongue' and she declared herself reborn into the army of the righteous. Her father was relieved, the atmosphere at home improved and her aunt found less occasion to chastise her.

Soon after this the family agreed to send her on a typing course, after which, with some parental misgivings, she was able to fulfil her dreams and came to England. She found accommodation with a family friend in Notting Hill and soon afterwards started work in a local travel agent. She was not disappointed in London and, joining a local church, and making friends, proceeded to enjoy herself. Her letters home did not mention her difficulties with the church which did not accord her the affection and respect she demanded. Nor did she mention that she married when she was 21 until after a baby was born the following year.

Her husband was killed in an accident at work before she was able to visit Jamaica with him. Her family's letters clearly showed they were worried about her. Her aunt even hinted that she doubted that Beatrice had ever been married at all. Her sister visited London the next year and reported back to Jamaica that it was unlikely that Beatrice had been married. Her father sent a letter indicating that she should cease to think of herself as being his daughter: communication between England and the Caribbean ceased.

Over the next 10 years Beatrice's dream turned sour. She lost her job and could only find work in a dress factory in another part of the city. Her friends went away. Lonely and depressed, she reproached her family for the difficulties in which she found herself. She didn't blame the British whom in fact she admired and envied more than ever. Life centred around her son John with whom she spent all her non-working time. An Irish girl at work introduced her to the local Catholic church, whose solemnity and ritual contrasted with the rather austere furnishing of her old church.

Beatrice and John lived in three rooms in a house in East London. The front room was carefully decorated; spotlessly clean, it was filled with glass fronted cabinets full of china, cut glass and artificial flowers, whilst the papered walls were hung with framed religious pictures and a photograph of the Queen. John was not allowed in this room which was reserved for the rare visitor. The other rooms were a small bedroom for John and the kitchen where she slept. Even when I got to know her well Beatrice never let me see the two back rooms, insisting they were dirty, although glances through the half-opened door suggested the reverse. One day when she was about 30 she was talking to a West Indian neighbour in the 'front' room when a quarrel started. Beatrice got angry and told the neighbour to leave.

Over the next few days she became uneasy: something was wrong with her front room. It had become polluted and disturbed. As this feeling did not go away Beatrice called in her Catholic priest who rather reluctantly sprinkled some holy water about and said a prayer. Beatrice was not satisfied and demanded a full-scale exorcism. He refused nor was he very impressed when a rather agitated Beatrice told him that her neighbour, who came from St Lucia, was a witch, and that she, Beatrice, was being persecuted because she was an outstandingly religious woman: 'If God choose you, Satan don't let go.' Dissatisfied with his help, Beatrice left the church, confiding in me later that the priest was not a 'white priest but black inside'.

She now received news that her father had died in Jamaica and began to feel guilty, constantly ruminating over her past life. She developed pain in her womb and, at her request, a gynaecologist performed a small vaginal operation. The pains continued however and, after further appointments, she persuaded the doctor to perform a hysterectomy, removing her womb and 'clearing all that away' as she put it. The pains now shifted to her back and the irritated gynaecologist referred 'this hysterical woman' back to her general practitioner. She continued to ask for further operations which she felt would remove the trouble.

Last year, after the Notting Hill carnival in London, her son John who was now aged 13, returned home with an alarming story. Angry and upset, he told her of fighting between young West Indians and police. He talked in a way which Beatrice found new and disturbing: he told her that he thought the police had deliberately attacked the young blacks. Using ideas he had been introduced to that day he told her that the immigrants had to stick together against white racialism. Beatrice, horrified by his rejection of the British, argued with him, trying to insist that the fighting at the carnival was the fault of the blacks who should have obeyed the police. West Indians should know better than to fight with the police. Tearfully the two went to bed, their argument unresolved.

Next morning, Beatrice's neighbours called the police after finding her naked on her balcony shouting down into the street that God had told her to kill herself. Taken to a nearby psychiatric hospital she fought with the police, talking incoherently but at times could be understood to say that her son was not hers because he was black, that God was telling her to have sex with her social worker and that black people were ugly although *she* was not as she was not black. Three days later she was less upset and told me that she had been made to come into hospital by Satan as a punishment. She could still feel him inside her wrestling with her spirit. All was going to turn out well, however, as she was now surrounded by God.

On the ward it became apparent that Beatrice was much more attached to the white nurses and doctors than to the coloured ones, frequently hugging and caressing them. She kept getting into arguments with the West Indian staff, refusing to carry out for them requests which she readily agreed to if asked by a white nurse. She enjoyed being in hospital, quickly became attached to the ward routine and announced her intention of becoming a nursing aide when she was completely recovered. She even tried to organize the patients who wanted to see the doctor in a queue 'as a sign of respect' instead of the comparatively informal approach encouraged. In any disagreement between staff and patients she invariably sided with the staff and eventually the other patients refused to talk to her. She complained of recurrent back pain and told me she wanted to stay in hospital 'till the operation'. She avoided the more relaxed atmosphere of occupational therapy, group therapy and informal meetings whilst feeling more comfortable in the more medical and structured atmosphere of the ward. Informal approaches left her angry and feeling neglected and she took it as a slight if in meetings the doctor refused the largest chair which she had reserved for him.

The world of Beatrice Jackson

Beatrice quite literally sees the world in black and white terms. Everything is either one or the other. Blackness appears to represent West Indians in general but also sin, sexual indulgence and dirt. Whiteness by contrast is associated with quite different qualities, with a white skin, with religion, purity and renunciation. Black and white are often seen as referring to two opposing universes. In Christianity white stands for purity and joy, whilst black represents hatred and evil. Brides and angels are dressed in white; black by contrast signifies devils, darkness and mourning: evil people are 'blackhearted'. However, we also use black/white in apparently quite a different context when we refer to skin pigmentation and, by implication, ethnic group. It is perhaps not entirely a coincidence that Christianity, primarily the religion of whites, values white as signifying desirable qualities. After the abolition of slavery missionaries in the Caribbean preached this Christianity to the black ex-slaves.

By being born again into Christianity, the despised blacks were able to 'become white inside' even though it was of course physically impossible for them to become white in reality, or indeed for them to enter the economically powerful class to which the white planters and officials belonged. By experiencing the European Christ within and by adopting Christianity, together with the virtues of obedience and patience, the blacks were offered a chance to become white in fantasy. Christianity, of course, stressed that the purity within was infinitely more worth while than such mundane satisfactions as power or social advantage.

A lighter coloured skin and its association with European supremacy is still a highly valued social asset in countries where many people trace descent from both Europe and Africa (such as in the Caribbean or Brazil) (Fanon, 1952; Henriques, 1953). Class and colour are intimately linked, although they may be represented, not by a conscious black/white symbolism or working-class/middle-class distinction, but by the less obvious 'outside/inside' which articulates concepts of class, 'slave culture'/'white culture', illegitimate/legitimate, manual/white collar, immoral/moral and even the linked idea of the type of sanitary facilities (Austin, 1979). Black and white taken separately do not of course always bear this symbolic resonance but the paired distinction black/white does. In other societies the black/white distinction often carries the association of mundane/holy (Berlin & Kay, 1969; Ardener, 1971), and black can also represent luck, luxury, fertility and humanity (Turner, 1967; Goody, 1977). Terms may operate differently in particular societies.

The social value of white physical attributes in the Caribbean is attested to by pages of advertisements in popular magazines for skin lightening creams and hair straighteners. To the extent that it was possible blacks tried to become white in a physical sense. Religion provided a less realistic but more attainable mode of becoming white.

Beatrice's family also saw the world in sharply divided terms. They considered themselves an oasis of purity in a sinful world. They had only succeeded in a material way by their righteousness in repelling the temptations represented by the Devil. The rigid distinction of the world into spheres of black and white reflected the physical impossibility of black becoming white, although the adoption of 'white' values could, as with the Jacksons, occasionally lead to a modest approximation to a European standard of living. Early confusion for Beatrice between the material benefits of being white (elegance, respect and fine clothes) and white as renunciation and austerity was solved by her religious experience. This allowed her to be accepted again by the congregation and her family, and also gave her greater freedom. For her family the battle between good and evil was fought out on her body. The spiritual and material consummation could only be gained at the cost of sexual renunciation. Beatrice does not succeed in becoming 'white inside' and later feels part of her is still black, locating the trouble quite clearly in her sex organs. Her carnal feelings are in conflict with that part of her which seems to have managed to become white. The only solution is to remove her womb.

Her rigid distinction between physical experience on one hand and socially approved behaviour on the other extends to her house. The part reserved for visitors is seldom used, untouched and peaceful, religious and patriotic, occupied by unused furniture. The rooms of her physical existence, of her cooking and eating and washing, and of her son, she claims are 'dirty'. The balance between the two is upset by the argument with her (black) neighbour in the (white) room. The clear categories are confused, the boundaries become ambiguous. She attempts to restore the balance with the white priest. He fails, either because he does not perform the necessary expurgation, or because he tries to discredit her ideas. Just as Beatrice has tried to become white he changes too: he becomes 'black inside'.

Because she moves to Britain and tries to become white in a more real way, Beatrice's system of symbols is upset by the real world. It becomes clear that being white inside does not automatically result in becoming white socially. She deals with the discrepancies which arise in various ways. She emphasizes the importance of 'internal colour' so that the respected whites may, as individuals, be spiritually black: this helps explain why all white people do not conform to expectations. She denies the social reality of her situation and attempts to confront it on a symbolic level. Although concealing from her certain political realities, this device is adaptive. She is able to continue working and successfully bring up her son.

This strategy is however threatened by her son's statements about his encounter with the police. To her astonishment John says that all the police, the representatives of white society, are bad. He challenges her complicated system with the simple statement that all blacks, by virtue of their skin, are treated unfairly, whatever personal efforts they may make and whatever their morals. His views appear to shatter the precarious balance she has just achieved and, in a rather confused period, she repudiates her son altogether and actually perceives herself as having a white skin. The complexity of her system has eventually failed to cope with external reality and, in a simple restatement of her black/bad, white/good dichotomies, she identifies herself both ethnically and morally with the white/good side. This is too much at variance with the experience of others. In other words Beatrice has become insane. She is admitted to a psychiatric hospital. To prove useful her symbolism needs continued validation: the social reality it mirrors must continue: when it does not, her system collapses.

Beatrice never discards altogether her original ideas. They are continually restated in new form. In the course of her admission to hospital she returns to the view that whites are somehow superior and that by correct conduct she can become allied with them. Recovering from her psychotic episode she explains that it was due to the (black) Devil. Although her illness was in many ways a more desperate restatement of her essential dichotomies, it enables her to partially satisfy her wish to become part of the white system. Being part of a hospital system in which most of the doctors happened to be white and the nurses black, gave her another chance of becoming white by identifying with the doctors.

Even though she continually restates the black/white dichotomy, her position becomes increasingly maladaptive on each occasion. By seeing the Catholic priest as black, she eschews the social resources of the church. Her views even when she is in hospital are in direct opposition to those of the only person she is close to, her son.

Coming to Britain, Beatrice uses her symbolic system in a variety of settings: in terms of physical illness, in a religious context and, when these fail, as a mental patient. Each time her private worries are clarified by adopting a particular role: as a sinner, a patient with abdominal pain or as a psychotic. Each of these roles has enabled her to communicate her difficulties in a form reasonably accessible to other people and also to provide her with a particular type of social support. Each change of status has involved new adjustments, new expectations by others, new obligations but also new rights. Beatrice approached the medical profession twice. On the first occasion she saw a gynaecologist, on the second a psychiatrist. The events leading up to the psychotic episode seem a more accurate assessment of her situation than trying to place all her difficulties in her womb. Her mental illness is, however, more socially disruptive, refers to and involves other people, compared with her original formulation in terms of her body alone.

If anything is constant in her adaptation it is not Beatrice's own problems but the way she tends to see them. Initially she has to reconcile her own pleasure with family obligations and later, her own sexual needs with her unmarried state and her beliefs about white social norms, her enthusiastic acceptance of white society with the reality of it and her idealization of white people's motives with her son's political view. In trying to come to terms with these difficulties she continues to use her symbolic system in an increasingly concrete way.

To help Beatrice make a more accurate and possibly more satisfactory adjustment requires interference with this way of seeing the world. We can help her conceive of black and white as relative descriptive categories which she has used because of her background, rather than as absolute entities. This is, of course, difficult – we are asking Beatrice to discard one of the few things which has stayed constant in a changing and confusing world.

We can help her differentiate between black and white in religious and political senses and suggest to her that part of her difficulties lie in confusing them. It is possible that as her categories become more relative and less absolute, Beatrice will be able to accept ambivalance and conflict both in herself and in society. She may be able to accept that conflict is in fact inevitable. Psychotherapy will of course also be concerned with the significance of her symbols in relation to the therapeutic situation (Myers, 1977).

Conclusions

That public symbols serve private concerns, rather than the reverse, is not to say individuals are passive vehicles of the dominant symbolic classification. They experience, choose and act, sometimes in a crisis using a less flexible mode of the dominant ideology, but sometimes creating a new end. No attempt has been made to exhaust the examination of the single case. We might profitably look, for instance, at Beatrice's confusion between instrumental and expressive signs, a confusion characteristic of both paranoia and witchcraft beliefs (Leach, 1976); we should be able to produce a more satisfactory account of the concurrence of these two phenomena than the psychoanalytical idea of projection (e.g. Kluckhohn, 1944). Can we make any predictions from a single case? It is likely that if aspects of Beatrice's experience mirror to any extent that of the black community in Britain, they are likely, as her son is doing, to move towards 'ethnic redefinition': a self-definition in response to prejudice that is non-pejorative but which nevertheless uses the attitudes of the majority culture (Sartre, 1948). This appears to be happening with the Rastafarian movement and we seem to be seeing a shift from women to men as the principal bearers of black culture. From the psychiatric perspective, it seems likely that acute psychotic reactions of the type Beatrice experienced will become less common and be replaced by depressive reactions.

It was earlier suggested that transcultural psychiatry is character-ized not by its subject matter but by its methods. As in anthropology, these methods may most easily have been evolved when an observer is looking at a society other than his own, but they are in no way limited to 'exotic' societies. The present perspective is not useful solely in relation to ethnic and cultural minorities (but see Okely, 1975). It is relevant to the description of emotional experience in different classes, between the sexes, or in situations of social mobility or cultural change. In the example used here the history of the symbolic system is well known: Beatrice's two black/white modes have not evolved independently or innocently (Fanon, 1952; Jordan, 1968). Points of transition between different symbolic systems are likely to reveal a good deal about the fundamental social building blocks which underlie both (Turner, 1967).

Transcultural psychiatry must move beyond mere translations of emic/etic categories and examine their interrelations more carefully. The application to psychiatry of some of the insights of the *Année Sociologique* and its successors will enable us to progress beyond the simple pathogenic/pathoplastic distinction without resort to psychodynamic hypotheses. If transcultural psychiatry is to offer more than answers to a series of 'when is a delusion not a delusion' questions, it needs to pay greater attention to the methodology of anthropology, semiology and the sociology of knowledge, and not just to their conclusions.

2 The Antinomian Hasid*

In opposition to the statistical epidemiology of social psychiatry, ethnopsychiatry is concerned with abnormal mental states or abnormal behaviour within the context of culture. It attempts to understand how the abnormal individual reconstructs his personal identity and social role by using the ideas which are available to him. The approach is similar whether we conceive of the abnormality as a displacement which is primarily physiological (Birnbaum, 1923), psychological (Devereux, 1978) or social (Turner, 1964). Like delusions, the acceptable positions offered by a culture may be a reflection or exaggeration of the normal or they may conform to an accepted deviant type: even inappropriate behaviour has a pre-existing social meaning. The individual who fails to meet certain criteria of normality in one position may be forced to accept another. Such a position may be an inversion of the normal – frequently that appropriate to the opposite sex (Devereux, 1978). At times the position adopted may be only implicit in the culture and not generally recognized by the members. For the psychiatrist, approaching the community from the outside, it is frequently difficult to decide how abnormal the individual is within the context of his culture.

This sort of situation has been studied under the rubric of 'deviancy theory'. Using this primarily sociological construction, it is however difficult to describe how the individual actually reconstructs his particular position in relation to his available ideas. In its study of 'symbolic inversion' social anthropology offers us an appropriate theory and methodology (Littlewood, 1980). The example I shall discuss concerns a young member of a Jewish sect – the Hasidim. The uncertainty of his community as to whether or not he is insane mirrors the position he has adopted, a position enmeshed in the historical development of the group.

The Hasidic community

The physical appearance of Hasidic men is familiar from the paintings of Marc Chagall: long beards and side curls, black caftan or suit,

*First published in the *British Journal of Medical Psychology* (1983)

fringed undershirt and broad brimmed hat. The women wear conservative British clothes with their hair cropped short under a wig. Yiddish speaking refugees from Eastern Europe, the Hasidim of north London are skilled workers in the fur and diamond trades and in the knitwear industry or small retailers to other orthodox Jews.

From the outside, Hasidic homes, gathered together in a group of streets, are not distinctive: the life of the community is directed inwards. Whilst there is frequent correspondence, travel and intermarriage between the London community and members in Antwerp and New York, there is no contact with the neighbouring *Goyim* (non-Jews) beyond essential economic transactions. To assimilated Jews and Goyim the community appears as a self-imposed ghetto with no desire either to integrate or to return to East Europe. Unlike most British Jews (70 per cent of whom work on the Sabbath – Kupfermann, 1976), Hasidic residence, family life, activities, and education are strictly determined by the religious law and its commentaries (the Talmud). Conversation, eating, bathing, excretion and sex are practised in conformity with established ritual. Life is constantly lived within the constraints of a rigid system of classification and a rejection of secular culture. The community's schools teach a religious fundamentalism and evolution is denied. For most Hasidim there is no television or radio and entertainment is always religious – the celebration of the Sabbath and the annual festivals and the retelling of the innumerable tales of the lives, wit and teaching of saintly *Zadikim*. Nothing outside the community can be considered entirely wholesome. If a member converts to Christianity funeral prayers are offered: to leave is spiritual death.

Hasidim have preserved intact much of the prewar culture of the *shtetl* (the Eastern European Jewish village community described in the stories of Isaac Bashevis Singer) with its close association of the human and the supernatural. Many still accept the efficacy of talismans and exorcisms against possession by the wandering dead or by devils born out of men's 'wasted seed'. Mothers guard their children against the evil eye and against Adam's first wife, the demon Lilith. Ritual transgressions may bring disaster to the whole community, visit sickness or misfortune on the individual, or even rebirth in a non-human form.

As in all variants of Judaism men are dominant in religious life. They conduct the services in the prayer house; women, if they attend at all, are concealed behind a partition. From an early age boys and girls learn to avoid each other, for male and female domains are always distinct. Whilst a girl's interest is directed towards the home, her brother is encouraged to spend long hours in religious study. Initially he learns by rote but later gains considerable freedom for disputation with other scholars. Whilst human conduct must conform to the divine law, this is open to the varied interpretations of older men whose authority is their knowledge. A man gains more respect by such wisdom than he does by lineage, age or wealth. After marriage he continues to study for a few years supported by his father-in-law before he turns to earning a living.

The ideal man is thin, pale and emaciated from extensive study. A woman by contrast should be plump, ruddy and with large breasts. 'The only wisdom of a woman is in her sewing'. She is less intelligent, eager for adornment and quarrelsome – almost non-Jewish in her qualities (Zborowski & Herzog, 1962). Her role is that of guardian of home and family; by her care in this she safeguards the ritual purity of the men through whom alone she can hope for spiritual salvation. She is particularly praised for her preparation of food: 'The ideal son is one on whom you can endlessly urge food with no danger that he will ever seem to need it'. Relations between mother and son are regarded as close and highly charged: 'When a man marries he gives his wife a contract and his mother a divorce'.

Sex roles and religious life are tied together in the symbolism of everyday experience. *Kosher* is a term which can be applied variously to food, clothes, non-menstruating women, books and ideas. The geography of prayer house, home, room, clothes and body are all carefully ordered. The head is the most sacred part of the body: it is always covered and a child's face is never slapped; the father as head of the household, sits at the head of the table and eats the head of the Sabbath fish; children picture God as a large disembodied head. Feet are the opposite pole – they are associated with dirt and death – and corpses are always picked up by the feet. The body must always be correctly ordered in space: children are taught that if they kick backwards with their right foot they are cursing their father, with the left their mother.

The Law gives specific instructions for all daily activities but also, through a complex numerology employing the numerical value of letters, cardinal numbers (the number of good or bad deeds, gifts, objects, alms) and ordinal numbers (number of a text or family order), it encloses the social and physical worlds in a tight intellectual network. There is no act or event, good or bad, which does not have a place. Indeed it can be said that Hasidim have no secular life.

Although adhering strictly to the accepted body of Jewish Law and tradition, Hasidim differ from other orthodox Jews in two characteristic features: the cultivation of ecstasy and the role of the dynastic male leader the *Rebbe* or Zadik. The movement was developed by wandering preachers among the small Jewish communities of Poland in the 18th century. The preachers or Zadikim emphasized the presence of God in all creation and in all human activity: every person however humble could communicate with Him through ecstatic prayer or contemplation. Hasidim originally used intoxicants and tobacco and turned somersaults in their prayers and there is still encouragement of a practical mysticism which delights in the joys of shouting, singing, clapping and dancing in the prayer houses, punctuated by trembling and rapturous prayer.

The movement spread rapidly during a period of economic crisis and endemic antisemitism despite fierce opposition from other orthodox Jews. In 1939 perhaps half of the eight million Jews in Eastern Europe were associated with Hasidism. The vast majority died in Nazi concentration camps. The many different groups which have survived in England, Belgium and America have varied traditions but each is characterized by the reverence paid to the Rebbe. The life of the community is rooted in him as mediator with the external world.

Surrounded by a constant crowd of attendants and petitioners, he literally holds court for his awed followers who follow his advice and orders without question. Often considered to be the incarnation of a Biblical prophet he has the power of foretelling misfortune and of healing infertility and disease, and he performs daily miracles through the talismans he distributes. Many Rebbes claim to alter the course of world events. During the heightened excitement of communal meals the food he leaves on his plate is distributed to his eager followers, after which he may offer homilies in a joyful trance-like state. Despite his disclaimers to the contrary the Rebbe's powers are regarded as personal rather than derived from God. Hasidim consult him on important and on trivial matters – how and when to travel, which job to take, whether to divorce, whether to invest in a particular project, whom their children should marry, which doctor to consult. Some orthodox Jews (for whom the Rabbi is only a teacher however gifted) view Hasidic Rebbes with distaste – 'the wretched ringleaders of a widely spread delusion' (Schechter, 1970). For most Jews however, the Hasidim are a continued guarantee of the permanence of East European Jewish culture and their 'naïveté' is regarded with affectionate amusement.

Case study: Mordechai Mandelbaum

Mordechai Mandelbaum was born in a Displaced Persons' Camp in Germany in 1946. In a situation where children were extremely uncommon, his parents devoted a considerable portion of their rations to their son. The only child among the remnants of Hungarian Hasidim in the camp, his birth appeared as a portent for the future. The Mandelbaums came to Britain and joined their community in London; all their relatives had died in the concentration camps. Two daughters were born and the father found work in a local knitwear factory owned by another orthodox Jew.

Mordechai's education followed the traditional pattern of *cheder* and then *yeshiva*, where he learned to analyse the Talmud and how to reconcile the apparent contradictions in the sacred texts. He was not particularly gifted and failed to live up to his father's hopes that he would become a respected scholar. Eventually the Rebbe arranged a marriage to a Hasidic girl in Antwerp. Mordechai met his father-in-law's criteria of family reputation and orthodox practice and, at the age of 26, started work for the first time helping in the family workshop. A year later he returned to London with the marriage dissolved for non-consummation. To his worried parents Mordechai was unusually quiet and preoccupied, unable to concentrate on study and failing to earn a living helping in his father's factory.

Two years after the divorce Mordechai was taken to the local psychiatric hospital on the advice of his Rebbe. His anxious mother explained that as a result of extreme fasting his weight had fallen to six stones: 'he should eat – he should be healthy'. Mordechai was not eating at all on Mondays and Thursdays and little in between, even on the Sabbath. He was spending up to 20 hours each day in the study house and standing for long periods in the *mikveh* – the bath for religious purification. Family meals were a battle as he firmly refused to eat without giving a reason. His mother alternatively cajoled and wept whilst his father appeared strangely unconcerned.

In appearance Mordechai was a typical Hasid: thin and pale with a straggling beard, restrained and laconic, avoiding eye or body contact. He said his mother was mistaken in her belief that he was *meshugeh* (insane). He was deferential but supercilious, returning my questions in the manner of a Jewish joke: 'Why aren't you eating?' – 'I should eat more?'; 'You don't say much.' – 'I should talk a lot?' He refused to talk about religion or his marriage, gazing past into the distance.

The immediate psychiatric concern was to determine the abnormality of his behaviour relative to the community. His refusal to eat and apparent distortion of perceived body image suggested the possibility of anorexia nervosa. However, given the importance of food in the Jewish family – 'the rejection of food is the rejection of loved ones ... Children attempt to coerce parents by refusing to eat' (Zborowski & Herzog, 1962) – his actions might not be particularly unusual. Depression was a possibility given the Hasidic injunctions against its overt display: 'melancholy is a great hindrance to God's service' (Weisel, 1978). Diagnostic specula-tion was confused by subsequent events. The group's Rebbe became sick and died. Some weeks later Mordechai was found apparently eating a bacon sandwich and his behaviour became more bizarre, culminating in sexual advances to his mother.

Given the strict Hasidic rules on the preparation and consumption of food, obtained only from other community members to ensure it is *glat kosher* (extra kosher), the division of kitchen space and utensils into milk and meat sections and the careful sweeping of leaven bread from the house at Passover, together with pork being the most basic of all food prohibitions, the idea of a Hasid eating bacon was like a bad Goyish joke. As for sex with his mother, as in most societies the very idea was totally monstrous, possibly even more so for a community so sexually restricted that men, wearing skull cap and prayer shawl, pray during intercourse which is performed through a hole in a sheet during the period of the menstrual cycle when the wife is ritually pure. In fact Mordechai had done the two things which were virtually inconceiv-able. The rest of the time he remained quiet, still praying for long periods and refusing to explain his actions.

The starting point for the analysis we are going to offer is that some men in the community were undecided as to whether Mordechai was really meshugeh. Psychiatrists are familiar with the concepts of the sick shaman or the holy madman – occasions when a community does not make our distinction between sainthood and insanity. But such a concept is alien to Judaism: Old Testament prophets were discredited by being called insane (Rosen, 1968). Physical health implies mental and spiritual health (Singer, 1976). An orthodox Rabbi, visiting the hospital and finding Mordechai praying against the east wall of the psychiatric ward, in great indignation tried to have his prayer shawl taken away. Insanity and spirituality are quite different categories. If he was truly religious Mordechai could not be insane.

We have seen how Mordechai Mandelbaum's behaviour was at variance with the external features of community life. If we are to try to understand his actions better it will be necessary to examine the internal structure of Hasidic culture. We can approach this best by looking at how the sect developed within the context of Judaism.

Mystics and messiahs

The origins of Hasidism have been closely tied to the Jewish mystical tradition and to certain claimants to messiahship whose advent shook the foundations of European Jewry in the 17th and 18th centuries

(Scholem, 1954). The exile of the Jews from Palestine at the beginning of the Christian era resulted in the dispersion of a single self-contained community from its own land into a series of complementary relationships with Christian and Islamic communities. The rabbinical tradition preserved much of the original culture and elaborated it into the Law which defined the boundaries between Jew and non-Jew and explained the separation from the historic land as a temporary interlude until the messianic redemption.

The traditional view of the Messiah was of a conquering king who would re-establish the historical kingdom of David and Solomon by the apocalyptic destruction of the old world. Alternatively he was pictured as the suffering and rejected servant who held a message for the gentiles. For others the exile was a metaphor for personal alienation from God and the promised redemption was purely spiritual.

These ideas are all found in the Kabbalah, the medieval mystical system spread throughout the Jewish world by those Iberian Jews who before fleeing had been forcibly converted to Christianity (Scholem, 1978). Like Christian mysticism it emphasized a near-pantheism: God was in all Nature including Man. The failure to recognize this hidden divinity and reliance on the external Law alone had resulted in a disharmonious world. One tradition suggested that the Messiah would only come when the existence of the community was threatened by internal sin and external violence. Some believed the Messiah would only come when Man had deliberately entered into the sinful world to release the divine sparks hidden there. The Kabbalah used the natural symbols of human morphology and sexual relations to illustrate the structure of the universe and its various conjunctions and oppositions: for example, the part of God concealed in the world was conceptualized as female.

The only large-scale Jewish messianic movement since Jesus was that led by Sabbatai Svi and his followers in the 17th and 18th centuries (Scholem, 1971, 1973). Sabbatai's declaration of messiahship and his eventual apostasy caused reverberations in Jewry which echo till this day.

With the development of capitalism and the birth of the centralized nation state, the traditional Jewish accommodation in Eastern Europe began to fail (Katz, 1961). Deprived of the support of Catholic feudal lords, the Jews were open to repeated pogroms by the Polish peasantry and the neighbouring Cossacks. The physical identity of East European Jewry was threatened by assimilation and attrition: massacre and forced conversion accounted for perhaps half a million Polish Jews in the 1640s.

Sabbatai Svi, a devout young scholar, engaged in frequent fasts, endless ritual purifications and all-night prayer, punctuated by periods of elation and depression. After two marriages, which ended in divorce for non-consummation, he began to engage in increasingly antinomian behaviour – breaking the Law for the value inherent in this act. A kabbalistic tradition had asserted that as the Messiah had to redeem evil he was in some measure evil himself and Sabbatai offered a new prayer: 'Praised be Thee O Lord who permits the forbidden' (Scholem, 1973).

There is a certain amount of evidence that Sabbatai Svi was manic-depressive (Scholem, 1973). Extreme apathy and withdrawal alternated with periods of infectious elation and enthusiasm, restlessness and refusal to eat or sleep, practical jokes and flights of apparent nonsense. Jewish mystics already used high/low to refer to nearness to/absence from God. (In prayer Hasidim still tie a band round the body to separate the upper spiritual part from the lower profane half.) Sabbatai employed this spatial metaphor to explain his moods as religious experience: 'high' was associated with religious ecstasy, 'low' with self-doubt. For Hasidim depression is still conceptualized as isolation from God (Wiesel, 1978). In contemporary manic-depressive patients who have religious preoccupations it is usual for these to be associated with the manic state alone but not universally so: a Jewish patient of mine when manic became a fervent evangelical Christian (of the 'Jews for Jesus' persuasion) whilst when depressed he was tortured by gloomy religious ruminations on the implications of his apostasy. (See Winstanley, 1973 for a Calvinist instance.) The acceptance by Sabbatai's disciples of his interpretation of his manic-depression and their own emulation of it is an example of what has been termed *pathomimesis*; if epilepsy for instance is believed to be of supernatural origin, then the presence of divinity may be signalled by fits, whether we regard them as physiological or dissociative.

Expelled by the local Rabbis, Sabbatai Svi was proclaimed Messiah by a disciple. The movement spread rapidly among the whole Jewish world from Asia to England: in London Jewish merchants left their business in expectation of the millennium. Sabbatianism was characterized by miracles, prophecies, mass visions, states of possession and ecstatic confession and penance, fasts to death and self-burial. Sabbatai invented new ceremonies and fantastic titles: days of ritual mourning became days of rejoicing. The Law was deliberately subverted and Sabbatai married a prostitute to unite himself with the female aspect of the deity. He encouraged free love, nudity and incest: if the messianic age could only be ushered in by sin the people must sin. The overturning of the Law was particularly attractive to the Iberian Jews who had been forcibly baptized as Christians whilst retaining a private Jewish identity: Sabbatianism legitimated their apostasy (Bulka, 1979).

Within a year Sabbatai Svi was arrested by the Sultan for sedition, had converted to Islam under pain of death and was pensioned off under house arrest. Most followers abandoned him in this ultimate rejection of Judaism and returned to traditional rabbinical teachings but for others his apostasy was the ultimate messianic sacrifice: 'The Lord was but veiled and waiting'. A few followed him to Islam and some converted to Christianity. Many continued as apparently orthodox Jews, conducting Sabbatian rites in secret and making obscure reference in apparently orthodox writings to their private convictions. As an organized body of belief the movement soon died away, but in the 18th century a Sabbatian, Jacob Frank, proclaimed himself Messiah, claiming to end the Law so the Kingdom of God could emerge in innocence. A few Sabbatian sects continued with their secret sexual initiations until the 1920s possibly even up to the 1970s (Scholem, 1978). Many leading Rabbis were accused (sometimes with good reason) of Sabbatian leanings.

Sabbatai Svi and Sigmund Freud

It has been suggested that the attack on the Law by the Sabbatians both reflected and precipitated the development of modern secular Judaism (Scholem, 1954). Freed from traditional religious constraints the method of criticism and argument perfected in the ghetto was harnessed to the development of modern rationalist thought. Psychoanalysis has been regarded by David Bakan (1958) as a later stage of the same process. Freud himself stated that analysis could only have evolved out of Judaism (Robert, 1974). He was atypically reluctant to apply his ideas in one particular area: on the death of a Zionist colleague he wrote that 'Jewishness ... was inaccessible to any analysis so far' (quoted in Robert, 1974). Ellenberger (1970) suggests that the origins of the Oedipus complex lie in the experience of antisemitism, whilst for Kafka the revolt against the father in psychoanalysis was not against the father *per se* but the revolt of the assimilated Jew against the Jewishness of his father (Robert, 1974). For castration read circumcision. Whether we accept that Freud consciously identified himself with Sabbatai Svi as Bakan suggests, it is true that Freud was Hasidic in origin and we can find certain kabbalistic themes in psychoanalysis: sex and knowledge as interchangeable metaphors; the transcendance of the social world by sex with the celestial mother; the return of the repressed; renunciation and sublimation; the significance behind the apparently random association of ideas in dreams, jokes and parapraxes; the master–pupil relationship and mastery through experience. For Freud then the concept of the libido was perhaps a metaphor for certain social relations, a point he came close to accepting before he died (Freud, 1938). If his ultimate concerns were cultural he was using the available medical symbolism offered by his education and the physical symptoms of his hysterical patients. By accusing hysterics of projecting psychological themes onto their bodies, Freud was projecting his own social themes onto a hypothetical psychology. If, as most British psychiatrists believe, hysteria is best regarded as a social phenomenon, patients and doctor were not dissimilar to the Australian aborigines described by Lévi-Strauss: 'The total system of social relations, itself bound up with a system of the universe, can be projected onto the anatomical plane' (Lévi-Strauss, 1968). If Sabbatianism was primarily concerned with articulating the relations between Jew and Gentile, then one of its successors, Hasidism, used its themes to recreate the ghetto wall, whilst the other, psychoanalysis, attempted to end the ghetto by universalizing the principles of Jewish mysticism, principles evolved during a period of forced assimilation. The Jew as analyst was less vulnerable to antisemitism that the Jew as Lawgiver (Bakan, 1958).

The Hasidic resolution

If some Sabbatians used the contravention of the Law as a bridge to the secular society, others incorporated the messianic reality and antinomianism into the orthodox rabbinical tradition. The exact relation of Sabbatian messianism to the Hasidic movement remains controversial. Hasidism has been described as a 'neutralisation of messianic elements into mainstream Judaism' (Scholem, 1954) and as 'a dialectical synthesis' of the two (Bakan, 1958). It appears to have crystallized out of the mystical–pietist groups influenced by Sabbatai Svi: many early leaders were ex-Sabbatians and utilized some of his ritual changes whilst opponents condemned it as a continuation of the heresy (Scholem, 1954).

Let us look again at the characteristics which differentiate modern Hasidism from the rabbinical tradition – the personal religious experience and the role of the Zadik. Hasidic texts to the present day include endless injunctions against excessive asceticism as these practices continued (Buber, 1948; Mintz, 1968). To avoid military service which would have prevented them carrying out their rituals, Hasidim fasted to near starvation and mutilated themselves. They also fasted for purely religious reasons: as recently as 1957 a Rebbe declared that 'a man who serves God in eating [observing the dietary laws] does so at mealtimes only, whilst a man who fasts does so all the time'. Hasidim study the Kabbalah with its cryptic references to the nature of evil. Judaism has always emphasized the neutralization rather than the rejection of evil: sorrow is necessary for joy, evil for good. The Hasidim take this attitude further: 'The subversion of the Torah is its true fulfilment'; 'Great is sin committed for its own sake'. Evil is not to be avoided but sublimated so that the scattered parts of God can be finally united. In the last even Jesus may be redeemed (Mintz, 1968).

The descent into evil to 'raise the sparks of divinity' is dangerous: it is easy to go down and not return. The descent is reserved for the Rebbe alone (Dresner, 1974). He has other characteristics of the Sabbatian messiah – charisma and supernatural power. Some contemporary Hasidim privately believe that their leader is the Messiah (Mintz, 1968). As mediator between Hasid and Goy he is in constant contact with evil; the select few must interact with sin to preserve the rest (Dresner, 1974). Hasidic tales are full of references to inversion of the Law by the Rebbes – always motivated and always with a deeper purpose beyond the Law and beyond its inversion (Buber, 1948). It is as if the Rebbe were so pure he could sin with impunity; he alone could eat pork without contamination. In practice he does not and indeed usually conforms to all traditional observances. But his saintliness is gained only by association with sin (Bulka, 1979).

To summarize our argument – the Jewish exile was legitimated by the traditional Law and the future messianic redemption. When the accommodation was threatened in the early modern period an active messianic movement rejected the Law and introduced the supernatural redemption into the real world. The frustration of the active messianic impulse resulted in a return to an orthodoxy constantly threatened by antisemitism and assimilation. Hasidism internalizes active messianism within the traditional framework whilst Zionism endeavours to create the millennium without the Messiah. Each solution – rabbinical orthodoxy, Sabbatianism, Hasidism or Zionism – is concerned with the preservation of the ethnic group as a distinct entity and each offers a solution to the changing relations with the non-Jewish majority.

Symbolic inversion and individual displacement

In a community with a rigid system of social and symbolic classification, social change and intellectual coherence are obtained by *inverting* the symbolic order. Such inversions include those in which a whole community is turned upside down temporarily and those in which certain individuals – innovators, leaders, the mentally ill, women, sexual deviants – can occupy a permanently inverted position (Littlewood, 1980).

The analysis we have offered shows a progression from an example of the first type of inversion which is located in historical time (Sabbatai Svi) to one of the second located in the permanent social order (the Zadik). The Hasidim, in spite of fluctuating messianic expectations, live like some other enclosed ethnic minorities in Britain (Calley, 1965) in a continuous Biblical present. The Zadik sees across space and time and he may be the incarnation of a prophet; life is organized around cyclical festivals; children are named after the dead and take on part of their personality; the dead remain in other ways – as ghosts, in dreams and in visions (Poll, 1962; Zborowski & Herzog, 1962; Mintz, 1968; Kupfermann, 1976).

The Hasidic tradition contains the opposing principles of the rabbinical Law and its inversion, Sabbatian antinomianism: the Law can be inverted for greater ends by select individuals at certain carefully controlled times and the licence to invert it is only gained by its conspicuous observance at all other times. Whether we see Hasidism primarily as a continuation of Sabbatian messianism or as a reaction against it, it appears to be an accommodation of certain active messianic elements within orthodoxy: the emphasis on the Law is simultaneously present with the possibility of inverting it. The two principles – Law and antinomianism – persist together in a dynamic balance which provides a remarkably consistent pattern of culture. This balance articulates the relationship of Zadik to follower, male to female and Hasid to the outside world. Each element possesses its meaning only by its relationship to the other.

Antithetical social principles may be represented in different social or biological groups but together they offer a system in which the individual can negotiate his own positions (Littlewood, 1982). Although wealth and learning are regarded by Hasidim as opposing principles it is recognized that wealth can make a life of study possible. The West Indian man who attempts to gain respectability without first having achieved its polar opposite – reputation – is regarded as being pretentious (Wilson, 1973). What is significant is not total identity with one element of a paired set but the appropriate articulation of their relationship: for Mordechai the embarrassment and confusion which met his clumsy use of the bipolar set resulted in a solution external to the community – psychiatric hospitalization. Using the conception of binary oppositions (and Jewish society has frequently been characterized as dualistic – Freud, 1938; Zborowski & Herzog, 1962; Mintz, 1968; Kupfermann, 1976), we can emphasize the importance, not of the elements or sets in themselves, but of the relationships between them:

$$\frac{\text{Observance of the Law (mitsva)}}{\text{Violation of the Law (aveyreh)}} = \frac{\text{Jew}}{\text{Goy}} = \frac{\text{Sacred}}{\text{Profane}} = \frac{\text{Hasid}}{\text{Jew}} = \frac{\text{Male}}{\text{Female}} =$$

$$\frac{\text{Learned (sheyn)}}{\text{Simple (prost)}} = \frac{\text{Adult}}{\text{Child}} = \frac{\text{Zadik}}{\text{Hasid}} = \frac{\text{Ascetic}}{\text{Desire}} = \frac{\text{Ecstasy}}{\text{Ritual}} = \frac{\text{Sin for its own sake}}{\text{Observance of the Law}}$$

This generates of course a polythetic rather than a monothetic system of classification (Needham, 1975). The relation between the first and the last paired set is the same *in this context*, whilst if taken in isolation they would appear to be inverted: the later sets presume the existence of the sets to their left. Other cultures may have a similar set, Sane/Insane, but Hasidim perceive mental illness not as a clear inversion, but as a distortion. Since Pinel and Esquirol psychiatry has tended to see insanity as the inversion of rationality. This accounts for our puzzlement when the Hasidic community do not regard Mordechai as 'holy but insane'. For European psychiatry the *morbus classicus* is schizophrenia with its obvious opposition, Sane/Insane, whilst for the Jewish community it is perhaps manic-depressive psychosis yielding the obvious set, High/Low, a set Sabbatai Svi had included in the series above.

Complementarity: Modes of interpretation and diagnoses

Mordechai's behaviour is certainly less at variance with his culture than we originally might have supposed and we can now understand the reluctance of the community to discredit his actions by unequivocally declaring him insane. We have then an unsuccessful young Hasid, a failure in terms of study, family life and work, who was born at a time of extreme crisis for his community, a crisis associated with the revival of messianic hopes (Mintz, 1968). He structures his experience through the available symbolic system – his behaviour is both deviant and legitimate. He first aligns himself within the tradition of extreme asceticism and religious observance. After the death of his Rebbe (who proclaimed the imminence of the Messiah) Mordechai follows the Zadik into ritualized sin. In practical terms he has no chance of becoming leader – the Rebbe is usually dynastic and, as leaders elsewhere in conditions of relative calm, is not conspicuously unusual. Whether in a situation of community crisis, such as that 30 years earlier, he could have become a leader is uncertain (cf. Littlewood, 1980); Mordechai does not conform to the ideal pattern of the Rebbe: evil can only be redeemed by joy but he himself is a morose and solitary man.

His actions can be seen as both instrumental – an attempt to increase his status in the community – and as intellectual – an attempt to make sense of the events of his life. His reticence to make any overt messianic identification in the absence of clear encouragement is in accordance with other Jewish messianic claimants (Scholem, 1971). We have suggested that the development of Jewish culture is in part a reflection of relations with non-Jews and we can interpret Mordechai's attempts to eat pork and commit incest in these terms; following his denial of the central role of the Jewish mother by refusing her food, his attempted incest with her ('pouring oil on olives' in the Law) is a denial of the separate reality of the community.

What conclusions can be drawn for psychiatric practice? It is sometimes only with difficulty that psychotic beliefs and behaviour can be distinguished from normative values – for delusions must of course be derived from, and bear a relation to, culturally standardized beliefs (Weinstein, 1962). It has been suggested that although certain *beliefs* may be normative – symbolic statements about social life – to *act* as if they were literally true is psychotic (Spiro, 1969): the Martian psychiatrist who studies our own society may well conclude that although a belief in telepathy may be not uncommon, to actually be in telepathic communication with someone is schizophrenic. Mordechai however does not act upon his presumptive beliefs with delusional intensity: like Sabbatai Svi he awaits some external validation of his ambiguous position.

That there appears to be some support for Mordechai's position from the Hasidim certainly suggests that he is not psychotic. For even when beliefs are idiosyncratic and contrary to empirical reality we do not regard them as delusions if they are validated by the community. However an enclosed group which has a changing relationship to the wider society may be uncertain as to what is currently normative or may penalize 'regressive' cultural patterns as psychotic (Littlewood & Lipsedge, 1982). In such situations we can certainly not assume that all members of the enclosed group are equally socialized into identical modes of expressing and redressing individual displacement.

One solution is to look at the *type of interpretation* necessary to give us an understanding of Mordechai's position. Conventionally psychiatry suggests we can interpret psychoses in two ways. (i) In reactive psychoses and situational reactions the delusions and hallucinations are intelligible with some knowledge of the individual's everyday common-sense world and by placing ourselves in his particular position (Fish, 1962). Frequently the psychosis can be interpreted as a development of the previous personality given the specific precipitating situation (Jaspers, 1962). (ii) In spite of occasional suggestions that delusions are elaborations or anticipations of an overt and dominant cultural perspective (Weinstein, 1962; Murphy, 1967), it is generally accepted that schizophrenic experiences can only be interpreted by using psychodynamic, more specifically psychoanalytic, theories (for example, Freud, 1911; Federn, 1952; Laing, 1959).

I have suggested elsewhere (Littlewood, 1982; Littlewood & Lipsedge, 1982) that there is a third possibility which we can conceive of as intermediate between these two and one which is particularly relevant to the culturally standardized patterns of behaviour usually referred to as the 'culture-bound syndromes': reactions which have a problem-solving nature for the dislocated individual and which are at the same time tacitly accepted sanctioned communications for the social group, serving to cement its unity both at the ideological level and in terms of social relations. The alternative position offered to the individual, whether as witch, transexual or victim of involuntary possession, is frequently an inversion of the accepted pattern – a standardized communal nightmare which nevertheless expresses the dislocated individual's new situation and which is integrated back into culture at a high order beyond everyday common-sense knowledge. This third mode of interpretation endeavours to understand such reactions, as we have done in this paper, by employing the methods and theories of social anthropology, particularly those of cognitive and structural anthropology.

In changing situations we cannot be certain that culture-bound syndromes (at best a rather loose idea) will maintain their traditional form although their function may appear to remain unchanged (cf. Rawnsley & Loudon, 1964); they may become modified to form 'syndromes of culture contact'. The present approach – what we might term 'ethnopsychiatric analysis' – can still provide a useful perspective as it is not limited to bounded societies (Littlewood, 1980). Additionally most cultures already contain within themselves an internal model of other societies, a model with which the abnormal individual – whether zadik or psychotic – may align himself (Littlewood & Lipsedge, 1982).

As with psychoanalytic explanations, we cannot expect that an interpretation of this type will be in accord with the common-sense everyday reality of the community, for 'conscious models are not intended to explain the phenomenon but to perpetuate it' (Lévi-

Strauss, 1968). Psychiatric criteria like the Present State Examination which only look at the overt cultural context may perceive such reactions as more idiosyncratic than they are. In Mordechai's case, an expressed identification with the Messiah would have been denied by the community and a PSE rating would have suggested he had religious delusions and hence a putative diagnosis of mania (Catego class M+).

The social roots of Mordechai's experience do not preclude our attempting another alternative explanation in a different domain – psychodynamics. Unless logically incompatible or contradictory, different modes of understanding are both legitimate and indeed necessary (Devereux, 1978). The purely sociological approach we have adopted may help us perceive the meaning of Mordechai's actions but it will not explain why this particular individual acted as he did; we have symbols without sentiments (Lewis, 1977). Mechanisms such as inversion (ethnopsychiatric description) and reaction formation (psychodynamic description) are complementary but they are not identical. Our three modes of understanding may nevertheless be arranged hierarchically:

Individual position	Minimal mode of interpretation necessary
(a) Reactive psychosis	Empathy with situation in terms of everyday reality
(b) 'Culture-bound psychosis'	Ethnopsychiatric analysis of (latent) cultural themes
(c) Schizophrenia	Psychodynamic analysis

They provide a heuristic approach through which in a particular instance we can attain a general category of diagnosis. Whilst psychodynamic theory can illuminate both reactive psychoses and culture-bound syndromes, we can achieve one type of understanding of the individual's experience without it; not so with schizophrenia for, although the schizophrenic experience is derived from everyday reality and latent cultural themes, understanding of them alone cannot provide an understanding of schizophrenia. (Whether we feel that existing psychoanalytic interpretations actually do so is not the point: without some type of psychodynamic interpretation there can be no pretence at understanding.)

If we conclude by moving for a moment beyond the heuristic, we have a corollary which may illuminate the continuing (Torrey, 1980) question of the universality of schizophrenia. If all idiosyncratic experiences in a community can be understood without recourse to psychodynamics then schizophrenia does not occur in that society. We might note, not entirely unseriously, that at one time Freud thought that individuals who could interpret dreams without the benefit of psychoanalytic theory must be schizophrenic (Freud, 1914).

3 The Individual Articulation
of Shared Symbols[*]

A problem for psychiatrists, particularly when working with patients from different cultures, is the distinction between personal experiences and those shared assumptions which are held in common with other members of a society. The traditional approach of general psychiatry has been to use a model in which the individual is represented as a universal type whose personal differences are manifest through a surrounding 'envelope' of culture. By contrast, social anthropology suggests that individual experiences can only be understood as themselves part of the culture. This raises a difficulty for the psychiatrist who is concerned primarily with individual patterns. Cultures are specific and limited ways of perceiving the world, patterns of belief and behaviour articulated by symbols, and ultimately are tied to a particular political system. Individuals adhere to a set of common understandings because these are perceived as a tangible reality in the form of every day experience. How then can an individual perspective be articulated? In this paper I look at one of the commonest modes of symbolic classification, that of binary classification, and consider how the individual can utilize the relationship between elements to negotiate crises and life events.

Social Psychiatry and Ethnopsychiatry

There are two rather different ways in which we can look at cultural questions in psychiatry. *Social psychiatry* is concerned with the frequency of patterns of psychopathology defined in universal terms: the quantification of cultural events which have been translated into the supposedly culture-free language of psychiatry. We explain these patterns as variable associations with such traditional biological and sociological indices as genetic predisposition, organic pathology, sex or class membership, stress, solidarity, or status striving. The second approach – that of transcultural psychiatry proper or *ethnopsychiatry* –

* First published in the *Journal of Operational Psychiatry* (1984)

utilizes the concepts of normality and abnormality held by a particular community. It is concerned with the relationship between public and private symbolism and how the individual conceives of his or her personal situation given the intellectual tools available. It attempts to explain how these tools, whether they are systems of magic or medicine, religion or psychology, reflect the physical environment of the community and its political organization. It looks in particular at how the overt disharmonies between individuals and society may be resolved in certain new functional roles; many of these have been termed 'culture-bound syndromes' but the approach is similar whether the disharmonies are regarded by psychiatry as primarily physical or social in origin (1).

Both approaches are essential and complementary. The former models itself on the procedures of the physical sciences, the latter on those of the humanities. Ethnopsychiatry conceives of a society less as coping with biological universals than as imposing its own particular meanings on the natural world. While the dominant concern of social psychiatry is with explaining, that of ethnopsychiatry is with understanding (2): the first is characterized by metonymy and formal logic, the second additionally by metaphor and analogy.

As I have previously demonstrated with particular instances (3, 4), ethnopsychiatry offers us an alternative to psychoanalytic or biological determinism by regarding psychopathology, not as a particular individual's state of mind at a given time or as Nature thinly disguised, but as a cultural datum with complex linguistic, political, and historical determinants. It approaches the mind through the examination of shared cultural categories of thought and action rather than through the statistical study of individuals. It is non-psychological in that the symbols which articulate both public and private concerns are regarded not as the products of individual experience and motivation, however generalized, but primarily as the ordering and reflection of social organization: 'they lie outside the boundaries of the individual organism as such *in that intersubjective world* of common understandings into which all human individuals are born, in which they pursue their separate careers, and which they leave persisting behind them after they die' (5, my emphasis).

Natural Symbols and the Social Order

In operating within environmental constraints, using available technical knowledge, and coping with relations with other groups, every society employs an appropriate social organization and ideology. In doing so it imposes its own set of meanings on the every day physical world – meanings which are common to all its members. Social concerns are thus embodied in the raw material of the available experiences of the individual: birth, childhood, sex, parenthood and death (6, 7); the production and consumption of food (8); the organization of space and the experience of time (9, 10, 11, 12); physical and mental illness (13, 14); dreams and other altered states of consciousness (15). There are comparatively few sources for such 'natural symbols' and it is not surprising that one of the most pervasive is the morphology and functioning of the human body (6, 16, 17), perhaps because (and here we are in agreement with psychoanalysis) a child is introduced initially into human society by constraints upon its body and because of the powerful personal resonances of bodily experience.

Natural symbols provide a series of formal homologies, and occasionally direct isomorphisms (9), between the social order and the appearance of the world to the individual. Ethnic minorities such as the Jews, constantly faced with the threat of assimilation and the need to guard the boundaries and exits of the body politic, may thus be concerned with the boundaries, entrances and exits of the body physical, through the prohibition of certain foods, the practice of circumcision or rituals and prayers involving washing and excretion (16). 'Blessed be Thou, O Lord Our God, King of the Universe, Who has created us with orifices and openings.' The intellectual *organization* of such symbols may associate cultural concerns of quite a varied order. To take an example common to all societies – the physical difference between the two sexes may relate occupations, attitudes, social groups, foods, clothes, animals, domestic space, and local geography, all of which are perceived as characteristically male or female in some way (18, 19). We represent this conventionally as a:b::c:d::e:f and so on, so that, for example, the relationship of man to woman may parallel that of horse to cow, and garden to kitchen. The division of the whole social and physical world into male and female domains does not however inevitably create an inflexible system: the classification of any element in this way always depends on *its relation to other elements* and at times we find inversions of the normal pattern, paradoxes which can only be resolved by implicitly relying on concepts of a higher order beyond simple dualism, although this may not be apparent to the participants. The world of the Hasidic Jew is perceived as dual so that male:female::husband:wife::sacred:profane (4). The Sabbath, which we might expect to be male by opposition to the profane week, is however female by its opposition to the religious community which 'embraces' it (20).

Symbols serve to perpetuate society, not to explain it (21, 23). Their daily experience ensures that the social order is perceived as reality, not metaphor. We ourselves find it notoriously difficult to distinguish the biological facts of male and female sex from the social facts of masculinity and femininity: although we appreciate that the latter are somewhat derived from the former, in a given situation we are often uncertain as to which is which and we justify the gender distinctions of society by recourse to a hypothetical biology.

The success of a particular symbolic system demands that all participants alike should be ignorant of its origin and function (22, 23). While certain individuals or groups benefit disproportionately from a symbolic system which seems to reflect their interests or world view in particular, they themselves are not conscious of the origin of that symbolism any more than the dominated 'cultural minority'. While a 'dominant symbolism' of this type may be an effective mode of social control, it is no conscious conspiracy or manipulation.

Psychiatrists have traditionally regarded the *cultural* couvade (the complex of behaviour in certain tribal societies in which the male undergoes a ritual childbirth as his wife delivers a child) as the generalization of a series of individual reactions engendered in anxiety, the couvade *syndrome* (in which men, typically separated from their pregnant wives by their occupation, develop abdominal pains at the time of childbirth). Anthropologists have disputed this and called attention to the public meaning of ritual couvade. We could say that the couvade syndrome is a demonstration of paternity in a particular situation, that it is in fact a reaction located within a *public* set of meanings (16). The putative psychological state as explanation is redundant.

A sociological approach of this type suggests that the private experiences of individuals themselves can only be realized through the organization of a public symbolism which the experiences both reflect the legitimate (23). This is not to suggest that the individual can be reduced to the statistics of a positivist sociology, but that cultural principles are inevitably coded in a symbolic classification that is represented simultaneously in social organization and personal psychology. Indeed, our customary distinction between psychology and sociology may itself be a distinction which we can locate in cultural and historical time – an 'emic' rather than an 'etic' distinction. To consider psychological and sociological explanations as independent but parallel (24) neglects the fact that psychologies such as behaviourism or psychoanalysis already contain their own implicit sociology.

To take some examples from our own discipline: it is difficult to elaborate theories which contravene the natural symbols which articulate medical psychology – metaphors which are frequently drawn from the passage of the individual through life (for example, growth, maturity, mental and moral retardation, regression, degeneration) or from our experience of bodies in space (tension, stability, balance, displacement, transference, projection). Indeed, a common conceptualization of psychiatric illness is that of a (pathogenic) physical mould which passively fills up with (pathoplastic) material; form versus content (1, 25).

Moving beyond the surface differences of such competing systems as the various sects and schools of religion, psychotherapy, and social control (22, 26, 27), we frequently find certain preoccupations and symbolic organization common to all the variants. Contemporary theories of mental illness, social deviance, and education may all have originated in a similar organization of individuals in social and architectural space, an organization which simultaneously explains aetiology and prescribes remedies (27). Psychodynamic theories in particular tend to follow earlier pre-scientific metaphors of this type. The analytic explanation of witchcraft (projection) simply reverses the direction of perceived causality – from bewitched to bewitcher rather than from witch to victim. Both witches and the mentally ill subvert the dominant rationality (28). While complex concepts must perhaps ultimately be described in terms of physical metaphors, one consequence is that even in scientific discourse disparate social and personal situations are likely to be perceived in similar ways and thus inevitably appear related (29). An alternative methodology, such as we are pursuing here, is to look directly at such metaphors. To what extent are they shared between subject and observer? What are the origins of a particular analogy and its limitations?

Dual Classification

The commonest mode of symbolic classification is dual – the division of the world into two distinct and opposed spheres. For ethnic minorities like the Hasidim, who are politically dominated by another group, or for societies dependent on two distinct modes of production, dual classification is a persuasive option. It is, however, also common in contemporary political and scientific discourse: church/state, capitalism/communism, particles/waves, mind/body, cognition/affect (or head/heart), individual/society, reality principle/pleasure principle. Binary classification frequently organizes 'folk' medical systems; among medical patients in London for instance the Cold/Fever distinction articulates oppositions of Nature/Culture and Responsibility/Chance

(30). Scientific discourse, however, conceives of the whole folk system as in opposition to itself: disease/illness, etic/emic, and thus perhaps our original distinction, social psychiatry/ethnopsychiatry.

In word association tests antonyms are the most frequent responses (31) and they produce equivalent loadings in personal construct theory (32). Whilst the tendency to divide the universe into two opposed domains has an undeniable intellectual elegance, its origins may lie in physical experience in a gravitational field (up/down), in sexual life (male/female), in the bilateral symmetry of the human body (right/left), or in some more universal structuring. The same logical structures seem to be present in grammar and social life (33). Both the psychologist Kelly ('all constructs follow the dichotomous form') and the anthropologist Lévi-Strauss (who adapted his theory of cognitive oppositions from the phonetic oppositions of the linguist Jakobson) point out the similarity between intellectual processes and the logical oppositions (1/0) of contradictory terms found both in neuronal activity and the cybernetic model based on electronic valves (21, 32).

In other words, the structuring of the intellect parallels the structuring of the natural world, perhaps not surprisingly if the natural world can only be conceived of through the intellect, itself part of that world (34). Women have been associated with the left of the body and men with the right, both by scientific reasoning (which is typically metonymic) and by symbolic reasoning (metaphoric). It has been suggested that women are characteristically skilled at the functions represented in the right cerebral hemisphere and men with those of the left (35), and that communities which employ a system of binary classification associate woman, the 'non-logical' partner, with the left of the body (36). As the right hemisphere and thus the left hand side of the body is particularly associated with paralogical (metaphoric) modes of thought and the left with logical (metonymic) modes, we find that the origin of our metaphor-metonym distinction may itself be either metaphoric or metonymic!

Thus, although the symbolic system participates in and reflects the social order, it is not simply a function of it. Conversely the social order which we have described almost as if it were independent of the mind must itself follow the possibilities of human thought (21). While the particular natural symbols chosen may vary from one community to another and articulate particular modes of production, their organization reflects certain universal human abilities such as the recognition of homology, analogy, and binary opposition. As Judah Loew, the 'Rabbi of Prague' (whom legend credits with the creation of Golem), pointed out in the sixteenth century, 'oppositions' may be of various logical types (37): they may be contraries (male/female), correlatives (superior/inferior), or simply presence or absence of some characteristic (light/dark) (38). Innovations, if they are to gain legitimacy, can be made only within certain intellectual limits: ultimate validation, however, may depend on social changes which the new symbolic variants reflect or participate. Millennial movements like Sabbatianism or the Earth People of Trinidad may initially make external political change meaningful for the individual but the continued dynamic of the movement's thinking offers a potential vehicle for transcending or controlling this change (39).

The Individual's Use of Symbolic Classification

The concern of the ethnopsychiatrist is of course not just to understand a person's culture but to interpret that person's individual attitudes and actions. The use of an approach derived from social anthropology presents us with an immediate problem. The study of symbolic classification originated when anthropologists looked at the ideology of homogeneous, bounded, small-scale communities with prescriptive marriage systems and a close formal relationship between social and symbolic organization. Can we apply it to personal experience in these societies or, indeed, in urbanized, literate, and pluralistic societies? Does the personal relevance or the common fund of symbols differ for each individual? Individuals can only construct their personal reality in terms of the dominant culture: their 'nature' is always a socially appropriated nature. The very idea of a shared public symbolism suggests that they have little room to manoeuvre inside it to explore their private predicament. What of the case of migrants moving from one total system to another? Must we perceive them as suspended in between two separate cultures or is there some way in which the premigration culture already contains some procedure for dealing with this situation – a sort of internal model of the world outside the community (3, 4)?

Even small-scale communities may contain more than one cultural principle. The whole society itself may oscillate over time between two contrasted principles of social organization, each of which has its own pattern of belief and action such as democracy and hierarchy (40). Each set of patterns is, however, always present in the culture, even if one is currently dominant, and the relationship between the two articulates daily life. In one West African community then are simultaneously two quite different principles of social organization and inheritance; one passes through the father and is concerned with residence while the other is traced through the mother and is concerned with property and with the settlement of disputes (41). In a similar way the dual organization of certain South American Indian societies seems to be cut across by a series of linear age-grades but these are integrated into dual structure through serial oppositions, alternate years aligning with one or another of the two social divisions (42). In both communities, the individual is a member of two systems at the same time and can employ either as suitable. He plays off his role in one against his role in the other.

Even when symbolic elements are tightly enmeshed in distinct biological groups they may offer to the individual (who has fixed membership in one group) some flexibility with which to negotiate crises and life-events – but only within certain limits. The leader or *zadik* of a Jewish Hasidic group is male. One group, unusually, had a female *zadik*: as Hasidic life rigidly separates male and female domains she had to become a 'classificatory' male and, alone of the women in the community, was in most respects treated as a man (20, 43). As the customary male/female distinction was embodied principally in the natural symbols of sexual relationships, however, she was unable to continue as *zadik* after she married.

In some communities a man's failure to be acceptably aggressive may result in adoption of a quasi-female status such as the American Indian *berdache* (24). In a similar way, in contemporary Britain, because the masculine/feminine distinction is still articulated most fundamentally by heterosexual coitus, the male homosexual (the 'sexual invert' of psychiatry) becomes in some measure feminine. We can distinguish between 'active' and 'passive' homosexual subgroups, a distinction paralleling the customary male/female one (and variously glossed as *insertor/insertee* by sociologists for the male homosexual, and *butch/fem* in the traditional lesbian argot):

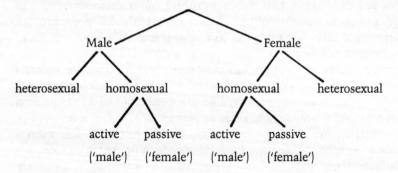

In contrast to the situation found in scientific classifications (32), we find that the same differentiating principle (male/female) may articulate different levels of differentiation – a:b::b1:b2. We can expect, then, that in situations such as prisons where women are absent, men who are heterosexual on the outside will be active rather than passive homosexuals on the inside (Jackson, in 44). Similarly a male transexual is unlikely to be the 'active' sexual partner. However in Gay Liberation and the Women's Movement we find 'a diffuse, polymorphous and non-focused sexuality which transcends the genital definition of male and female roles' (17). In the last few years it has thus become possible for a man to be homosexual without being 'effeminate'. Indeed, in America, the six 'sexes' can be identified sartorially, although the four homosexual classes have still to define themselves by differing combinations of traditional male and female apparel (34). Homosexual men may thus wear a single earring on the left (female) side.

In the Caribbean there are two contrasted principles: *respectability* (characterized by chastity, legal marriage, education, church attendance, imported goods, hierarchy, and affluence) and *reputation* (represented by sexual prowess, cohabitation, seductive technique, drinking parties, home produce, democracy, and poverty) (45). Respectability and reputation are located in the female/male, middle-class/working-class, white/black social divisions. A person of either sex or class may, however, act in accordance with either principle: indeed, a working-class black man must first gain reputation and then, if he can increase his wealth, gradually shifts into the respectability mode. The two principles themselves however remain antithetical.

It is always the constant articulation of the relationship between symbols that determines life for an individual in a particular culture, irrespective of membership of one or other social division in which these symbols are rooted (21). While in many societies women may take over a man's role in certain situations, the relationship between the sexes remains the same: if men are traditionally farmers (or bus drivers) and women housekeepers, women can only become farmers when men are at war (a:b::b1:b2 again). Such a relationship may also represent a particular society's relationship with the external world – the black/white distinction for rural Caribbean communities and the Jew/Gentile distinction for the Hasidim. As West Indian women are identified with 'white' values in the community (45) and Jewish women have 'non-Jewish' attributes (20), each community already contains within itself a model of the outside world. In both cases this is represented in women (who are less 'sartorially marked' than men (34). It is thus perhaps more easy for women as individuals to migrate to another culture: 'ethnic redefinition' – the reaffirmation of the premigration identity – is a characteristically male procedure. While the Jewish woman can assimilate however, the black woman is still constrained by her biology (3).

In many languages 'eat' is a common synonym for male sexual activity and both anthropologists and psychoanalysts have recognized that cooking and copulation are frequently complementary modes. Traditionally both are regarded as provided by women for men (male:female::consumer:producer) but in industrial societies they are in part commercialized. In the form of restaurants and prostitution they continue to exist in close proximity (as in the London district of Soho). In the Chinese and other cultural revolutions these have together been singled out as targets for reform. Industrialization involves the transfer of women's domestic tasks to specialized male workers (8). True of restaurants but not, for obvious reasons, of prostitution, this accounts in part for the ambiguous role of the prostitute and her anomalous labour status.

Inversion and Catharsis – Anthropology and Psychiatry

Where dominant sets of oppositions of this type exist they can be overturned in certain specific contexts. The term *symbolic inversion* is conventionally given to this turning of the habitual 'upside-down' (44). *Symbolic opposition* is more appropriate to describe the given system (38), but inversion, as a spatial metaphor, conveys the physical sense of overturning so characteristic of the participants' experience in this type of situation.

We can distinguish two major patterns on inversion with which the individual can align himself and thus generate an alternative perspective and identity:

(1) Those in which the whole community is *temporarily* turned upside-down. The Jewish messianic leader Sabbatai Zevi 'took over items of Jewish tradition ... but stood them on their head' (46). We find total inversions in such institutions as Carnival, the Roman Saturnalia, Lords of Misrule, sanctioned alcoholic binges, cultural revolutions and successful millennial movements, the serving of Christmas dinners by doctors to their patients, the periodic rituals of rebellion of certain societies, and, indeed, in culture-bound syndromes (1, 44, 47, 48, 49, 50). These inversions of hierarchy (or countercultures) can only continue as such for a short time for, if everything continues upside-down, it of course eventually becomes the right way up.

Temporary inversions may be of a recurrent nature. Male life in the area of North London where I live is dominated by two sets of oppositions: activity (work/leisure) and class (white collar/blue collar, represented in indigenous British/Irish groups). Movement from work to leisure is signalled each day in the middle class by changing to less formal clothes (T-shirt and jeans) while the working class wear suits and ties to attend pub or church. The external model for leisure is thus the opposing group's work role.

(2) Inversions which are *permanent* are characteristic only of certain individuals in the community. These are frequently members of such non-dominant groups as women, ethnic and sexual minorities, religious sects or the mentally ill (3). The cultural minority are defined against the majority. Typical behaviour in East European Jewish communities often derived its significance by simply being the opposite of the behaviour of the surrounding Gentiles (2). Conversely, assimilated French Jews made a deliberate attempt to act in direct opposition to the ascribed stereotype of the antisemite (51). 'Black' behaviour in the Caribbean is the reverse of 'white' behaviour (45). As 'black' is associated with evil in Christianity, Mother Earth, the founder of the Caribbean Earth People, a black millennial sect, identifies herself with the Biblical Devil (39). As God is 'good' she defines herself as 'bad', the primordial and natural attribute of the universe, the meaning of which has been inverted by the whites and their God. Recognizing that everyday language reflects ideology, the Earth People make other conscious inversions – left for right and so on.

As we have seen in the case of British homosexuals, a dominant system of symbolic classification may leave the individual no choice but to identify his position with the group whose attributes most resemble his own in some particular, an ascribed rather than an achieved identification. European psychology defined the mentally ill, children, and non-Europeans in identical terms as closer to nature (29) but also equated witchcraft with mental illness (28). Similarly in some tribal communities both witches and the mentally ill are represented as physically upside down (36). Although members of the inverted group are normally despised they may rarely (as with the schizophrenic of antipsychiatry) be consciously seen as completing the complementary harmony on behalf of the whole community. The Haitian *hungan* who is respected for his ability to invoke spirits is regarded as homosexual (52), because his sexual invasion complements his professional inversion of the natural order. As Zulu ancestor spirits return through their 'daughters', a man who becomes possessed by them becomes a transvestite (53): in this patrilineal and highly patriarchal society, male:female::jural:religious.

Explanations have been offered by observers of symbolic inversion from three apparently diverse perspectives, the psychological, the sociological, and the cognitive.

Psychological

In this perspective, *psychological* interpretations emphasize the release of the repressed, as elaborated by psychoanalytic and literary theory (54). It may be regarded as a 'reaction formation' of the socialized individual to the recognition of his physiological drives (55). There may be a conscious cultural elaboration of some type of catharsis or discharge of tension to restore equilibrium, usually associated with a quantifiable conception of sin or emotion which can penetrate boundaries. We can find examples in the various Jewish rituals of the scapegoat, excretion before prayer, the treatment of illness by enema, or the 'purging' of the house at Passover (20). Theories of catharsis in drama, following Aristotle, stress the resonance of the dramatic role with the personal experiences of actor and audience (54); in extreme situations actor and audience may together run *amok* in the deviant role (5).

Smith and Apter's Reversal Theory suggests that individuals may at different times be in opposed and equally valid 'metamotivational states', such as conformist/negativistic, goal orientated/playful (31). As against a psychology predicated on an invariate personality, it regards 'negative' and 'gratuitous' behaviour as primary. The theory is principally concerned with underlying states or mind rather than meanings but it suggests a mechanism by which an individual may switch systems in situations of frustration, satiation, or external contingency. A particular symbolic set may be associated with opposing motivations: a man undressing in public may be deliberately contravening the norm or may be aligning himself with the nudist ideal; he may move from one position (naked) to the other (nude) while his external behaviour remains the same. The theory fails, however, to explain the continued recognition of the cultural dominance of Clothed to Naked for the committed nudist. Reversal theory suggests that religious innovation may lie in individuals who, while in the logical goal-directed (telic) state, take up solutions elaborated in the analogic, playful (paratelic) state, solutions to problems for which there can be no telic solution: metaphor becomes reality. It situates the old question of pathomimesis (the psychopathological origin of cultural innovation) in a broader context: psychopathology becomes one of a number of paratelic modes – play, daydreaming, fantasy, art (31). The deliberate contravention of tradition by manic-depressive millennial leaders frequently has a playful 'negativism' about it although their followers usually accept the doctrines in a logical relic mode (39): 'yesterday's liminal becomes today's stabilized' (56).

What of psychological therapies? The most appropriate tool for the individual enmeshed in the type of problems we have been discussing would appear to be some type of cognitive therapy, particularly George Kelly's Personal Construct Theory. There are, however, some fundamental differences in approach. Kelly's suggestion (52) that the individual is constantly able to choose different dichotomous variables which offer 'greater possibility of extension ... making more and more of life's chances' ignores the fact that any culture is precisely a negation of such freedom. In contrast to the free-thinking, free-floating, idealized individual of construct theory, making free choices in a pluralistic world independently of other constraints, we would maintain that in the most important areas – sexuality, life-style, and occupation – Western life is still lived through a 'non-rational' symbolic organization (glossed half-seriously by Sahlins (34) as *La Pensée Bourgeoise*). Indeed, Kelly himself can be seen as a representative of a particular individualistic tradition which plays down the social rootedness of our constructs. Like reversal theory, personal construct theory implies that culture can be regarded best as the outcome of a statistical trend in individual choice (and thus we could theoretically carry out a multivariate analysis of individual constructs to attain 'higher order' cultural values). As we have seen, individuals may reverse their normal 'values' or define themselves in opposition to social norms, less stepping out of the stream than reversing its flow. 'Negativism' may imply inversions which are still part of the shared symbolic matrix. Our main quarrel with personal construct theory, however, is its difficulty in construing analogic patterns; Kelly (32), tells us that the notion of sex is not appropriate when talking about 'time of day'. By contrast we would suggest that frequently male:female::day:night.

Sociological

Inversion is presented by a culture as the only alternative to the established order and, since it is both temporary and allowed only in specific ritual contexts (or limited to a powerless minority), it reaffirms the boundaries of control and thus cements the existing system (47). While orthodox Jews are usually forbidden to play cards or get drunk, these activities are tolerated or even deliberately encouraged on two specific days in the year; similarly the blood of humans or animals is scrupulously avoided at all times except at circumcision when indeed it might actually be sucked (20). In communities where the idea of cannibalism is totally repugnant, the homicide may be purified by ritual ingestion of the deceased's liver (8). Inversion marks a principle by following constrained contravention of it: the tiresome sexuality of the office party is less the relaxing of the code (by which daily occupation precludes sexual overtures) than an affirmation of it. If religion reflects and validates the social order, its otherworldly authority may be reinforced by controlled logical inversions; among the East African Gurage, women of the traditionally despised Fuga minority mediate ritual for Gurage men, as do Fuga men for Gurage women (57). Alternatively, inversion, paralleling reversal theory, may be merely one phase of the alternation between two equally necessary cultural modes (40).

Both the psychological and sociological groups of theories are functional and, hence, static. They emphasize the homeostasis of a given system: inversion is either the catharsis of undesirable elements or the passage between two equivalent and co-existing systems.

Cognitive

Inversions are useful intellectual tools and enlarge the potential conceptual repertoire (56). The antinomian individual who contravenes the norm gives unity to a simple bipolar system (58). Although oppositions may be our dominant mode of symbolic ordering, their inversion provides the basis for change. The apparent paradox is resolved at a higher implicit level (to use the usual spatial metaphor); simple oppositions thus become the means by which a more sophisticated and radical conceptualization may be attained (44). The Messiah, whether Jesus or Sabbatai Zevi, who fulfils the spirit of the Law by breaking it in practice, generates a more universal law (39). The Earth People, like Rastafarians, invert the usual black/white stereotypes but in this act gain the potential to transcend ethnic stereotypes altogether. In the words of William Blake, 'I must destroy the Negation, to redeem the Contraries'. The homosexual offers a conception of sexuality which is no longer located in morphological opposition, and for the radical dialectician 'The fight will be won when the obscene symbiosis of opposites is broken' (Marcuse, quoted in 17).

The anthropologist Victor Turner (56), like reversal theorists, concentrates on the liminal point at which paradigms change. Rather than seeing their coming into being simply as an immediate inversion of prior principles, he looks at the period in which symbols and social structures become dissolved in a symbolic return of the individual to childhood (unsocialized) status. This period of antistructure, free and fertile, may generate a counterstructure. Symbols are a relationship between public ideology and private experience and the separation of the two is thus frequently experienced as liberation or as anomie. If, as psychoanalysis suggests, male and female identities are achieved by denying public recognition to certain biological attributes ('repressing the female in ourselves' for men), it is not surprising that many characteristics of the inverted state are those appropriate to the opposite sex: public symbolism is disengaged from one interpretation of personal biology and retied in a fresh way.

These various types of explanations then are not mutually exclusive. If catharsis is accepted as a valid social and psychological mechanism it can be regarded as one way in which cultural institutions replicate their concern in each member – a natural metaphor through which ideologies are made real to the individual and through which they may, at times, be transcended.

References

1 Littlewood R, Lipsedge M, Culture-Bound Syndromes, in *Recent Advances in Clinical Psychiatry 5*, edited by K. Granville Grossman. Edinburgh: Churchill Livingstone, 1984

2 Jaspers K, *General Psychopathology*. Manchester: Manchester University Press, 1962

3 Littlewood R, Anthropology and Psychiatry – An Alternative Approach. *Brit J Med Psychology* 53:213–225, 1980. See Chapter 1.

4 Littlewood R, The Antinomian Hasid. *Brit J Med Psychology* 56:67–78, 1983. See Chapter 2.

5 Geertz C, Religion as a Cultural System, in *Anthropological Approaches to the Study of Religion*, edited by M. Banton. London: Tavistock, 1966

6 Hertz R, *Death and the Right Hand*. Aberdeen: Aberdeen University Press, 1960

7 La Fontaine JS, *Sex and Age as Principles of Social Differentiation*. London: Academic Press, 1978

8 Goody J, *Cooking, Cuisine and Class*. Cambridge: Cambridge University Press, 1982

9 Durkheim E, Mauss M, *Primitive Classification*. London: Routledge, 1903

10 Hubert H, Mauss M, *Etude sommaire de la representation du temps dans la religion et la magie*. Paris: Alcan, 1929

11 Evans-Pritchard EE, *The Nuer*. Oxford: Oxford University Press, 1940

12 Leach E, Two Essays Concerning the Symbolic Representation of Time, in *Rethinking Anthropology*. London: Athlone, 1961

13 Weinstein, EA, *Cultural Aspects of Delusion*. New York: Free Press, 1962

14 Sontag S, *Illness as Metaphor*. London: Allen Lane, 1979

15 Furth PT, *Flesh of the Gods*. London: Allen and Unwin, 1972

16 Douglas M, *Implicit Meanings*. London: Routledge and Kegan Paul, 1975

17 Benthal J. Polhemus T (eds), *The Body as a Medium of Expression*. Harmondsworth: Penguin, 1975

18 Harris O, Complementarity and Conflict: An Andean View of Women in *Sex and Age at Principles of Social Differentiation*, edited by JS La Fontaine. London: Academic Press, 1978

19 Hugh-Jones C, Food for Thought: Patterns of Production and Consumption in Pira-Parana Society, in *Sex and Age as Principles of Social Differentiation*, edited by JS La Fontaine. London: Academic Press, 1978

20 Zborowski M & Herzog E, *Life is with People: The Culture of the Stetl*. New York: Schocken, 1962

21 Levi-Strauss C, *Structural Anthropology, vol 2*. London: Allen Lane, 1977

22 Berger PL, *The Social Reality of Religion*. London: Faber, 1969

23 Douglas M, *Rules and Meanings*. Harmondsworth: Penguin, 1973

24 Devereux G, *Ethnopsychoanalysis*. Berkeley: University of California Press, 1978

25 Birnbaum K, The Making of a Psychosis: the Principles of Structural Analysis in Psychiatry, in *Themes and Variations in European Psychiatry*, ed. by SH Hirsch, M Shepherd. Bristol: John Wright, 1923

26 Reiff P, *The Triumph of the Therapeutic*. Harmondsworth: Penguin, 1973

27 Foucault M, *Discipline and Punish*. Harmondsworth: Penguin, 1979

28 Spanos NP, Witches in the history of psychiatry: a critical analysis and an alternative conceptualization. *Psychol Bulletin* P5, 417–439, 1975

29 Littlewood R & Lipsedge M, *Aliens and Alienists*. Harmondsworth: Penguin, 1982

30 Helman CG, 'Feed a Cold, Starve a Fever': Folk models of infection in a European suburban community. *Culture Medicine Psychiatry*, 2:107–137, 1978

31 Apter MJ, *The Experience of Motivation: The Theory of Psychological Reversals*. London: Academic Press, 1982

32 Kelly GA, *The Psychology of Personal Constructs*. New York: Norton. 1955

33 Harré R & Secord PF, *The Explanation of Social Behaviour*. Oxford: Blackwell, 1972

34 Sahlins M, *Culture and Practical Reason*. Chicago: University Chicago Press, 1976

35 Ornstein R, *The Nature of Human Consciousness*. New York: Viking, 1974

36 Needham R, *Right and Left*. Chicago: University Chicago Press, 1977

37 Sherwin BL, *Mystical Theology and Social Dissent: The Life and Works of Judah Loew of Prague*. London: Associated University Presses. 1982

38 Needham R, Reversals. Henry Myers Lecture. Royal Anthropological Institute, 1980

39 Littlewood R, The Imitation of Madness: the influence of psychopathology upon culture. *Soc Sci Medicine*. See Chapter 8.

40 Leach E, *Political Systems of Highland Burma*. London: Bell, 1954

41 Forde D, Double Descent among the Yako, in *African Systems of Kinship and Marriage*. edited by AR Radcliffe-Brown, D Forde. Oxford: Oxford University Press, 1950

42 Maybury-Lewis D (ed.), *Dialectical Societies: The G and Bororo of Central Brazil*. Cambridge: Harvard University Press, 1979

43 Mintz JR, *Legends of the Hasidim*. Chicago: University Chicago Press. 1968

44 Babcock BA, *The Reversible World: Symbolic Inversion in Art and Society*. Cornell University Press, 1978

45 Wilson PJ, *Crab Antics*. New Haven: Yale University Press. 1973
46 Scholem GC, *The Messianic Idea in Judaism*. London: Allen & Unwin, 1971
47 Gluckman M, *Rituals of Rebellion in South-East Africa*. Manchester: Manchester University Press, 1962
48 Hill C, *The World Turned Upside Down*. London: Temple Smith. 1972
49 Kupfere HJ, A case of sanctioned drinking: the Rupert's House Cree. *Anthropological Quarterly*, October 198–203, 1979
50 Lee RLM, Structure and antistructure in the culture-bound syndromes: The Malay Case. *Culture Medicine Psychiatry* 5:233–248, 1981
51 Sartre JP, *Antisemite and Jew*. New York: Schocken, 1948
52 Metraux A, *Voodoo*. Oxford: Oxford University Press, 1959
53 Ngubane H, *Zulu Medicine*. London: Academic Press, 1977
54 Scheff TJ, *Catharsis in Healing, Ritual and Drama*. Berkeley: University of California Press, 1979
55 Freud A, *The Ego and the Mechanisms of Defense*. London: Hogarth, 1937
56 Turner V, *Dramas, Fields and Metaphors*. Ithaca: Cornell University Press, 1974
57 Shack WA, *The Gurage: People of the Ensete Culture*. Oxford: Oxford University Press, 1966
58 Peacock JL, *Rites and Modernization: Symbolic Aspects of Indonesian Proletarian Drama*. Chicago: University Chicago Press, 1968

4   Against Pathology:
The New Psychiatry and Its Critics*

> We predicate of the thing what lies in the method of
> representation. Impressed by the possibility of a comparison,
> we think we are perceiving a state of affairs of the highest
> generality. (Wittgenstein, 1958: 105)

The new approach to psychiatric knowledge which has developed
under the influence of social anthropology over the last decade has
produced a critique of existing comparative psychiatry, but it has also
been concerned with the status of psychiatric theory and practice in all
contexts. Thus, some have preferred simply the term 'the new
psychiatry' rather than 'the new cross-cultural psychiatry' (Littlewood,
1990a). While its workers have adopted a variety of perspectives, from
the Marxist to the post-modern, one particular idea which appears to
have occasioned some difficulty for psychiatrists is the suggestion that
our very notion of 'pathology' might be usefully abandoned.[1]

For some, it seems that this is simply a return to the 'anti-
psychiatry' of the Counterculture in the 1960s and 1970s (Leff, 1990a,
b). Certainly we can trace some analogies – indeed influences – but in
many respects the current argument is quite different. The new
approach is less a return to what may be termed the 'humanistic
tradition' within psychiatry – the conviction that psychiatric diagnoses
inappropriately match our lived experience unless they become
self-fulfilling through social power – than a concern with how this type
of humanism, or any other position, is associated with our research
procedures and our social context. As a 'meta-psychiatry' – an
investigation into how psychiatry is itself constructed – it does not
make any necessary assumptions about correct therapeutic procedures
in themselves. The clinical positions adopted take a variety of forms,
from the expressly political to the psychodynamic (Littlewood, 1980;
Chrisman & Maretzki, 1982; Taussig, 1987; Kleinman, 1988).

The problem is not just that the ambitious extension of psychiatric
categories outside their original context may be inappropriate, ethno-

*First published in the *British Journal of Psychiatry* (1991)

centric, or worse, but that this inapplicability brings into focus some problems with the epistemological status of these categories themselves: in particular their collection together under some such unifying rubric as 'psychopathology'. For the Counterculture critics of psychiatry, psychopathology was simply an application of the biomedical project outside its proper frame of reference – biological disease (Cooper, 1967; Ingelby, 1981). A similar position is that of the psychoanalyst Szasz (1961) or the sociologist Goffman (1971), who both equate psychiatric illness with brain disease alone, or the essayist Sontag (1979), who argues similarly for the 'reality' of physical disease in a world to be truly understood through biology as against its extension as a rhetorical trope, or those who have examined how the idiom of 'pathology' has been used to characterise social dissent or ethnicity (Podrabinek, 1980; Deleuze & Guattari, 1984; Gilman, 1985; Miller & Rose, 1986; Müller-Hill, 1988). As it is a social practice, the debates on what properly constitutes the subject matter of psychiatry have been bound up with the question of its social power and legitimacy as an institution. Not surprisingly, solutions to the question 'what is mental illness?', perhaps the defining question of psychiatry, have for 30 years simply been subsumed under an 'anti-psychiatric' or a 'pro-psychiatric' position, Sedgwick (1982) perhaps excepted.

What the 'new psychiatry' proposes is something arguably more radical: whether the idiom of pathology and disease in any system of understanding – psychological, sociological or even biological – always enables us to understand the phenomena in question; not just 'pathology as lesion' but any restricted, if heuristic, focus on 'problem' or 'malfunction', developmental, physiological or functional.(2)

In claiming to be a biomedical discipline, psychiatry has been vulnerable because its area of interest encompasses not only the experiential and behavioural correlates of abnormal cerebral processes, but also patterns of individual response which may be understood more immediately in terms of gender or political antagonisms, points of development in the individual life history or family cycle, or even social crises (Littlewood, 1990a). We seldom find central or 'general' theories in psychiatry, for it is even more obviously a social practice than the supposedly 'pure' scientific disciplines. Attempts to produce a unifying schema have either had to jettison much of the traditional area of interest and develop others (as has psychoanalysis) or else have been so unwieldy as to constitute a procedure rather than anything one can call a theory (as does Meyer's psychobiological approach).

While psychiatry has drawn, at different times, on virtually every available discipline from ethology to biophysics, from existential philosophy to narratology, its most consistent frame of reference has been that of medicine. The biomedical paradigm presumes that we can, independently of our favoured explanations, start from conventional distinctions between aetiology, pathology (whether qualitative entity or quantitative process), and treatment. Indeed it seems difficult to envisage a system of medical practice which does not.

It was the 'old transcultural psychiatry' which suggested there could be some problems here.(3) Certain local categories of illness which were fitted into the psychiatric nosology turned out to be mythical tales, statements of collective ideologies, not everyday experiences. Others seemed on closer examination to be moral values, or even patterns of relationships between colonial psychiatrists and subject peoples. In the case of what psychiatry pathologised as 'possession states' in non-industrialised societies, it became difficult to distinguish adventitious social events from individual experience and from the collective response. Are individuals who become possessed demonstrating an illness, are they enacting a social drama on behalf of the community, or is the possession to be understood as a healing process (Littlewood & Lipsedge, 1987)? Is possession a symptom or a treatment? Or both? A process or an event? What were understood by Europeans as calendrical 'rituals' – socially standardised and collective practices – among the colonised peoples disappeared under the impact of imperialism and industrialisation: in many cases there was a concomitant appearance of more individualised patterns, closer to something doctors could interpret as 'neurosis', but which demonstrated similar themes to the earlier rituals (Littlewood, 1990b). Were the collective ceremonies now to be understood as social support whose absence precipitated illness? If so, what was the aetiology of the illness? Or was there a more intimate relationship between the two? Was colonisation pathogenic? Or did it reframe the whole social field so that the very idiom of conflict became one of pathology (Swartz, 1989)? Could one answer such questions by using a framework similar to that of natural science? What types of analysis could examine how such social forms are manifest in the individual?

A related, but contrary, problem occurs in the reinvention of 'ritual healing' within the women's movement, where psychopathologies identified with women (pre-menstrual tension, eating disorders, agoraphobia, overdoses) are reframed from individual pathologies into active attempts at political or spiritual revitalisation and resistance (Teish, 1985; Adler, 1986). A similar process has occurred among once colonised peoples (Sidel, 1973; Jilek, 1982; Shook, 1985). What is happening when existing patterns of psychopathology characteristic of individual relations within a community become emblematic of the totality of relations between communities (Ngui, 1969)?

A wide range of subdominant communities have higher rates of psychiatric illness than the dominant groups (Rip, 1973; Scheper-Hughes, 1979; Jilek, 1982; Adebimpe, 1984; Swartz, 1989; Sachdev, 1990). Can we still employ an individual focus and simply say that they have 'more stress' or 'less support', given that dominant Western groups have pathologised (and thus individualised) the very context within which what might otherwise be resistance is expressed (Deleuze & Guattari, 1984)? Are pathology and the perception of ethnicity (or gender) really independent constructs which can be correlated, or does the very notion of pathology become internalised as part of personal self-hood (Scheper-Hughes, 1979; Fisher, 1985; Littlewood & Lipsedge, 1987; Littlewood, 1987), so that psychopathology and collective response are themselves part of the same process (Fanon, 1965)? If so, can a non-dialectical and statistical approach that ignores volition disentangle them?

Social scientists themselves have used an idiom of 'social pathology' to collect together undesirable patterns of activity among marginal or oppressed groups (Wootton, 1959; Rip, 1973). While the 'truly pathological [is] defined to include all those actions on the prevention of which public money is spent' (Wootton, 1959, p. 14), this perspective more usually employs a functionalist model of society in which 'it' becomes a homeostatic organism by analogy with the physiological body, a perspective which of course places a primacy on the notion of society as a harmonious whole, ignoring questions of social change, oppression, unequal power, and conflict. Like the physical body, the body politic is subject to imbalances, malfunctions and invasions (Foucault, 1973). In the extreme case, society becomes prey to cancer, invasion and decay (Sontag, 1979).

My argument up to this point is unexceptional (e.g. Wing, 1978); it would simply seem to argue for a more restricted definition of 'pathology', away from the problematic social arena to situations where we find relatively invariate biological abnormalities, perhaps to what our translation of Kurt Schneider (1959) terms 'coarse brain disease' or at least to 'constituent characteristics [that] can be defined without recourse to social phenomena' (Wing, 1978, p. 22). The problem is perhaps merely one of powerful metaphors extended too far. That the experience of physical suffering is so ubiquitous, so overwhelming and painful, so demanding of resolution, makes it an apt vehicle for a variety of 'ills' experienced as dangerous. The biological assumptions through which psychiatry employs the idiom of pathology have a powerful natural ('objective') status and can serve to legitimate or initiate a variety of social control procedures, reinforced by the coercive power which treatment demands; for once we recognise a disease, our everyday understanding of sickness is that it presumes the imperative for treatment.

What 'the new psychiatry' argues is that such an extended (weak) notion of disease is no more – or less unreasonable than our restricted (strong) use of it in biological medicine. Both are 'figurative', both are 'real'. They are grounded alike in our assumptions as embodied social beings. Since the 17th century, Western thought has employed a distinction between a human world of agency and a natural world of causal necessity. 'Pathology' in the strong (biological) sense is to be located as a pattern existing in the natural world as 'disease', independent of our knowledge of it. It is 'real'. It is 'there'. It is experientially manifest to us through 'illness', depending on our bodily states, values, expectations, and the possibility of action, but it appears directly observable through the procedures of natural science.

Psychiatry remains marginal within medicine precisely because it fails to achieve this in the same way as the other medical specialties. This is not through historical bad luck, but because psychiatry is constituted by this inability; it is a residual area of clinical practice in which success leads to the rapid transfer of the particular disease entity into the body of knowledge of another specialty, as happened with general paralysis of the insane and thyrotoxicosis. Psychiatry is a residual discipline, dealing, it is true, with the behavioural and experiential correlates of our disease, but it is also marked by an absence – the absence of a neat one-to-one correspondence between illness and disease (and thus between patient's and doctor's explanatory models). The attempt to reaffirm such a one-to-one model within psychiatry itself seems to make some sense through employing the form/content distinction (Littlewood, 1990a) but becomes unhelpful in the margins of psychotic or non-psychotic patterns (Kleinman, 1987) where a multiplicity of factors confound any neat one-to-one causal linear relationship. The categories of psychosis remain polythetic, each sharing many of its characteristics with the others (Kendell, 1975). 'Pathology' is a measure of difference: both between the normal and the abnormal, and between pathologies themselves. While this difference, or singularity, is the defining feature, it by no means follows that defining features have a determining role in the sequence of preceding events, as we tend to assume when weighing the significance of Schneider's first-rank symptoms against depression in a case of schizophrenia (Littlewood, 1990a).

If 'pathology' in the strong sense is to be understood as some sort of undesirable state of affairs in the natural world, independent of any necessary human apperception, although its personal consequences are potentially unpleasant, how is this undesirability conceived? We have a variety of choices between entities, processes and events, between functional balance (whether psychological, social or physiological), anatomical change, evolutionary and developmental processes, ideal norms of health or autonomy, or simply the cause of our experience of suffering (see Long, 1965; Kendell, 1975; Sedgwick, 1982; Canguilhem, 1989 for partial reviews). The conceptualisations themselves are not, however, given by the subject matter but are selected within a particular clinical and historical context. A particular pathology may be understood as all of them. But they are not arbitrary tropes: they return us to the personal experience of illness, to everyday pain and disability. (Such experiences are themselves socially constructed in that 'pain', for instance, is not necessarily perceived as an illness or indeed as an unalloyed evil.) As Leff (1990b) puts it, the aim of our medical diagnosis is to alleviate immediate suffering, and psychiatric research then should be 'practical' (Leff, 1990a).

Doubtless a post-modernist would welcome this frank acknowledgement that it is social action that characterises the subject of psychiatry. The new psychiatry would hardly quarrel with the notion that, as embodied social beings, we bring to our afflictions an urgency and certain powerful assumptions which are shared with our fellows. And that we are compelled to act: to be 'practical'. And psychiatry is a practice.

I propose to take here a more conventional view, that we can still make an attempt to attain some more distanced knowledge of social and biological phenomena. The question is not the ultimate value of biological data, but the choice of frame through which to generate and interpret them: how independent this frame is of social institutions with their own need for categorical action. What is questionable is whether our current methodological individualism invariably leads to the most satisfactory procedures for comparing illness experience in different situations and at different times, and for understanding the relationship between what we arbitrarily limit as causation, experience, classification, and therapy. Is our practical distinction between these always helpful? The objection is less the old one that psychiatry is simply only biomedical in its thinking but rather that it is too socially embedded in the sense that it cannot examine its own institutional assumptions, and mistakes the particular for the universal, what it can conveniently examine for alternative constructions of the phenomenon. It is not that such embedded (and embodied) human actions are somehow invalid, but merely that they cannot have the particular level of generality we claim without our examining their social construction itself.

If the questions are indeed heuristic, where does the notion of 'pathology' (in either a strong or a weak sense) usefully get us? Does it provide some practical constraints on the limits of the phenomenon which we could study and alter, defining 'it' as a phenomenon? Certainly. Does it give some notion that the phenomenon is ultimately undesirable? This hardly seems necessary unless we feel unable to act without assuming our therapeutic or penal procedures must have the power of contraverting some almost inevitable, natural order of things. Through identification and extension we recognise 'pathology' in animals akin to ourselves (hence veterinary medicine) but the limits of our sympathy fade when applied to unicellular organisms. Are phages the 'diseases' of sick bacteria? In what environment can *Treponema pallidum* develop most fruitfully? The idiom is absurd because our idea of disease is so radically rooted in our personal concerns.(4)

Does this anthropocentrism matter? Would we lose if medical theory became comparative ecology, independent of our compelling human interests? While the implications are in part moral, a more neutral perspective can ask certain new questions about any theme within that area of interest which we conventionally call 'psychopathology'. One is the distinction between aetiology and pathology, which becomes more problematic because of the loss of the immediate frame, as in the vexed question of distinguishing *stress* from *stressor* (Littlewood, 1990a), or of neurotic illness in its social context from the therapies elaborated within the same context (Littlewood & Lipsedge, 1987). Were Charcot's hysterics suffering from an illness, a treatment, or a lifestyle (Eisenberg, 1977)? Were they 'suffering', 'enacting' or 'representing' (Littlewood & Lipsedge. 1987)? Was Charcot? What are the criteria by which we distinguish? Karl Kraus' acerbic declaration that 'psychoanalysis is a symptom of the sickness it claims to cure' may be seen to have a wider generality: if our focus on illness has shifted to examining undesirable limitations on an increasingly Cartesian indexical and autonomous self which is given in advance of its external relations (Gaines, 1982), then the therapies derived are manifestations of the same historical shift.

How then do we take the suggestion that 'psychosis may generate alternative world views which at times become more generally accepted' (Littlewood, 1984): a resurrection of 'Laing's assertion that schizophrenia is not a break-down but a break-through' (Leff, 1990a)? My point is that from a more distanced perspective, schizophrenia is neither. To say that one or the other *is* true is equally arbitrary, depending not on the biological or social data in themselves but on a particular culturally embedded point of view. Schizophrenia, like left-handedness or dyschromic spirochaetosis, can be perceived in a variety of ways depending on our own frame of reference, our personal identification and sympathies, our compelling social urgencies. 'Break-through' and 'break-down' are equally political positions constrained by their particular powers of social representation. This is not to deny that from the clinical perspective schizophrenia is a biosocial phenom-enon, relatively invariate across cultures, and whose local meaning is generally undesirable (Horwitz, 1982). But potential meanings do not necessarily follow the biomedical paradigm, for meaning is not a phenomenon of the natural world but, biologically speaking, arbitrary. If the experiences of schizophrenia are taken on occasion as meaning-ful then they are meaningful in that context. If they are not, then they are not. Leff's example, the Counterculture, in fact failed to institu-tionalise social patterns in which schizophrenia could be a valid experience (for a poignant instance see Vonnegut, 1976). Particularly in periods of rapid social change it does seem that meaning may be placed on experiences which recall those which at other times would be perceived as insane (Littlewood, 1984, 1987). Occasionally, we find situations in which everyday insanity is consistently recognised as especially meaningful, although these seem to be rare (Morris, 1985), while the 'fey' or the 'touched' can certainly be taken as the authentic (Scheper-Hughes, 1979; Fisher, 1985; Robins, 1986).

Deafness and sign language provide a powerful contemporary instance. There is a biological difference certainly, but we have recently seen a dramatic shift from perceiving deafness as a defect state, as simply a failure or an absence, to a recognition that signing has a validity as a communication in itself (Lane, 1988; Sachs, 1989). *Signing* is not some compensatory pantomime of spoken languages, nor does it follow their syntactical structures. Like them, it is powerfully expressive, with its own particular subtleties and meta-phors, spatial representations of agency or of pronouns, and not least its own dreams.

The allocation of meaning to everyday madness has a long history, not restricted to the antipsychiatrists, and which I have reviewed elsewhere (Littlewood, 1984, 1987). Indeed, in the form of psychobiog-raphy and psychohistory, it has frequently featured in the evening interests of psychiatrists themselves, as a rather Romantic interpreta-tion of 'creativity' sometimes known as the 'Napoleon's glands view of history': St Paul was epileptic, Van Gogh psychotic, and so forth. In literary criticism this sort of causality is criticised as the 'biographical fallacy'. What I am suggesting here is something rather different, not 'biological causality' but (in Steven J. Gould's phrase) 'biological potentialism'. The meanings that are placed on natural phenomena as they appear to us, whether these meanings are disease or creativity, are by no means determined by the phenomenon itself.

Sociological data and biological data are not exclusive yet additive categories (cf. Leff, 1990a), but the workings of procedures: not places but maps. Nor can we reduce one to the other; each is inescapable and equally valid, producing a vital dialectic within Western thought, whether couched in the style of interpretation versus explanation, human agency versus causal necessity, the humanities versus the natural sciences. Attempts to fuse them into a single system – whether it be psychoanalysis or sociobiological psychiatry – work by a sleight of hand whose elusive simplicity palls after a few passes. Madness is not merely a literary trope, nor can human society be predicated on neurophysiology.

None of this argument is especially novel in those cross-disciplinary studies which take the human potential for sociality and culture itself as both a biologically and a historically given attribute (Ingold, 1989). By contrast, for psychiatrists the only alternative to reductionism seems to be to regard humans as biology plus society, as genes topped up with culture. This mistakes the nature of biology as much as that of culture. Biology is a discipline, a social procedure, a way of examining what is going on in the field in which organic forms are perceived, not a type of stuff.(5)

If the modern scientific project attempts a perspective which is independent of a particular observer's point of view at a particular place and time, then the abandonment of 'pathology' is exemplary. The attempt to exclude social meaning and context from psychiatric theory itself does not automatically render our discipline value free and universal. Indeed the reverse.

Notes

1   This short paper is in partial reply to published and personal correspondence following an earlier review (Littlewood, 1990a; Leff, 1990a; *British Journal of Psychiatry*, 1990, **157**, 294–297; **158**, 575–576). While this appears to have raised a number of queries, I have restricted myself here to clarifying its position on 'pathology'.

2   'Functional', still the distinguishing attribute of psychiatry as opposed to neurology (Hill, 1964; Bynum, 1985; Reynolds, 1990), has a somewhat vague but characteristic status in psychiatry, usually referring to psychoses without gross structural changes, yet whose patterns of abnormality are presumed to have an eventually demonstrable biological origin (Schneider, 1959). My use of 'functional' here is more conventional. It refers to the activity of parts of a delineated pattern or process which is recognised as integral to the coherence of some whole (Parsons, 1952). Once dominant in the social sciences, functionalism has been criticised for its inability to model historical change, external influence, conflict within the system, or to allow for personal motivation. Similar problems arise in biology with

'fitness', and with 'adaptation' (Lewontin, 1983) which is used in psychiatry to refer to patterns which may well be socially functional but which primarily maintain the coherence and state of the individual. (The social sciences may term this also as 'functional', here coming close to the psychologist's notion of 'need' (Firth, 1957).) The point is not whether a particular model or frame is 'true' but whether it is the most useful at any point in the development of a discipline to understand the phenomena of interest (Littlewood & Lipsedge, 1987). Does the methodological individualism of psychiatric theory inhibit our understanding of the 'individual'? Does the frame we have chosen generate results which merely replicate the experimental design? Ultimately the answer to such questions is aesthetic and socially pragmatic, not methodological nor given by the data.

3   Cognate questions to those of synchronic (comparative) psychiatry arise with tracing continuity diachronically (historically). Has hysteria 'changed into' other patterns (Littlewood & Lipsedge, 1987)? What has to change before we agree we are talking of a different entity?

4   At one level we are ourselves historically constituted by 'disease', not only in that we share certain nucleotide sequences with bacteria, but because contemporary humans are determined through millennia of epidemics in which each generation of survivors constitute our ancestors. (Survival is in part a function of antigenic complementarity, while the correlates of one identified pathology may of course be the decreased likelihood of another.) As pathologies are not processes distinct from ourselves, so neither is biology merely the domain which we share with animals (Ingold, 1986), nor is the natural environment some unaltered and neutral ground (Lewontin, 1983).

5   The interested reader may wish to consult the following references for the general approach: Bourdieu (1977), Hundert (1989), Leary (1990), Lewontin (1983), and Mayr (1982).

5   Jungle Madness*

A common conclusion in the many studies on migration and mental health is that migration for clear-out economic reasons seems to result in better mental health than when carried out for purely 'personal' reasons. While expatriates may find themselves working abroad officially for reasons of state or commercial policy, there are still the questions of personal motivation, whether these are merely a desire for promotion or (bearing in mind that many expatriates go to the Third World) what we may gloss as the 'lure of the exotic'. It will be useful to consider that the expatriate experience is always orientated to two poles; (i) absence from home and (ii) the environment and political context of the place of sojourn and the nature of relations with local people. Psychopathological reactions historically described by doctors emphasised the separation from home.

Scanning the medical literature produced during the period of European colonialism, it is clear that the major interest was in physical rather than in psychological distress.(1) *Nostalgia* had been recognised during the Thirty Years War amongst soldiers who had little prospect of leave but it was soon found in travellers and the socially isolated and rootless.(2) Symptoms included dejection, fever, palpitations and anxiety. The only successful treatment was to return home. Each episode was brought on by memories of home. Nostalgia was last observed during the American Civil War, after which it appears to have been replaced by biological conceptions more compatible with 19th century medicine.

Neurasthenia had been described by Beard in the early 19th century as 'chronic physical and mental lassitude' with depression, anergia, anomie and difficulty in concentration. Treatment was physical and included rest cures, diet, massage and galvanic stimulation. *Tropical Neurasthenia* appears to have been the predominant cause for the invaliding home of a fifth of the employees of the Anglo-Persian Oil Company in the 1920s.(3) A British Medical Associations symposium suggested it could be caused by the heat of the sun, stagnant air, atonic dyspepsia or over-indulgence in dinner parties, alcohol and bridge. A psychologist, Culpin, criticised this

* First published in the *International Journal of Social Psychiatry* (1985)

aetiology and suggested a different one: 'generally unable to make ends meet for some reason or other; suffering, in many cases, loneliness and lack of congenial society; envious of others; disappointed over promotion; with ambition thwarted. Living amidst a native population causes him annoyance at every turn, because he has never troubled to understand its language and its psychology. From early morn to dewy eve he is in a state of unrest – ants at breakfast, flies at lunch, and termites at dinner, with a new species of moth every evening in his coffee. Beset all day by a sodden heat, whence there is no escape, and the unceasing attentions of the voracious insect world, he is driven to bed by his lamp being extinguished by the hordes which fly by night, only to be kept awake by the reiterated cry of the brain-fever bird or the local chorus of frogs. Never at rest! Always an on-guardedness!'.(4)

Culpin decided that the most vulnerable individuals were the idealists who avoided cocktail parties and fraternised excessively with the local population. He introduced psychological screening of potential expatriates and reduced repatriation from 20% to 4% within five years.

Whilst something about unofficial attitudes can be gleaned from policy statements such as those of Lord Lugard,(5) we can learn much from popular fiction and imaginative literature.(6) Somerset Maugham's 'Outstation' immortalised Warburton, the colonial official who endeavoured to recreate his London life among the natives of Borneo: 'He liked their courtesy and their distinguished manners, their gentleness and their sudden passions. He knew by instinct exactly how to treat them. He had a genuine tenderness for them. But he never forgot that he was an English gentleman, and he had no patience with the white man who yielded to native customs. He made no surrenders!' (7)

Warburton is joined in his outstation by Cooper, a vulgar lower-middle class junior administrator:

'I always dress for dinner.'

'Even when you're alone?'

'Especially when I'm alone,' replied Warburton, with a frigid stare.

'When I lived in London I moved in circles in which it would have been just as eccentric not to dress for dinner every night as not to have a bath every morning. When I came to Borneo I saw no reason to discontinue so good a habit. For three years during the war I never saw a white man. I never omitted to dress on a single occasion on which I was well enough to come to dinner. You have not been very long in this country; believe me, there is no better way to maintain the proper pride which you should have yourself. When a white man surrenders in the slightest degree to the influences that surround him he very soon loses his self-respect, and when he loses his self-respect you may be quite sure the natives will soon cease to respect him'.(8)

Warburton is in fact only the son of a tradesman and has created a fantasy of his past life in Britain. He conceives a dislike of his vulgar colleague and, unable to appreciate the roots of his anger, effectively arranges to have him killed by the locals, who thus enact his stereotype of them. It is perhaps significant to note that, like Warburton, the expatriate (and the anthropologist and the psychiatrist) is often marginal in his own society.

The stereotype of the tropics was of course an indolent, languorous, too beautiful island with mysterious and primitive passions seething below the surface. For the expatriate who resisted their embrace the tropics placed him in a conflict. At times the pressures of social isolation, sexual frustration and alcohol led him to outbursts of aggression, popularly known as 'Jungle Madness' in which after periods of brooding, depression and increasing suspiciousness, the individual would run amok like the natives. Cawte (9) describes a number of hospitalised cases of 'flight into the wilderness' ('going bush' or 'going troppo') in which they appear to be solutions to previous difficulties 'at home'. This is a pattern which we would now call an acute psychotic reaction, reminiscent of what the Americans called 'three day battle-field schizophrenia,' or the 'aliens' paranoid reaction' described in Britain in the 1930s among linguistically isolated domestic servants.(10, 11) A recent example of this is perhaps the Irish soldier who, whilst on United Nations duty in Lebanon, killed his colleagues and was found wandering around in a dazed state.

We have then various possibilities of identity or balance between the two poles: adherence to home norms and a recreation of home, or else dangerous adherence to the fantasy of the tropics ('going native'): the 'cold' and the 'hot' solutions. The missionaries appeared to be in a particularly difficult situation in having close contact with the local culture but with the aim of dominating it, transcending and then transforming it. A paper in the British Medical Journal in 1913 suggested that missionaries in China had a greater incidence of mental illness than those in Africa: the explanation given was that in China the missionaries confronted a powerful intact culture, confident of its own values, whilst in Africa the missionaries were closely identified with the dominant imperialism.(12) The Jesuit missionaries in China were in particular criticised for their adoption of Chinese clothes, language and customs.(13)

I think a similar conflict of values is still to be found among teachers on overseas programmes. The missionary/teacher relationship to their work is well shown in another quotation from Maugham:

'We had no one to help us. We were alone, thousands of miles from any of our people, surrounded by darkness. When I was broken and weary she (his wife) would put her work aside and take the Bible and read to me till peace came and settled upon me like sleep upon the eyelids of a child, and when at last she closed the book, she'd say: "We'll save them in spite of themselves." And I felt strong again in the Lord, and I answered: "Yes, with God's help I'll save them. I must save them."

'You see, they were so naturally depraved that they couldn't be brought to see their wickedness. We had to make sins out of what they thought were natural actions. We had to make it a sin, not only to commit adultery and to lie and thieve, but to expose their bodies and to dance and not come to church. I made it a sin for a girl to show her bosom and a sin for a man not to wear trousers.' (14)

Again we have an encapsulated white enclave 'surrounded by darkness'. In this story. 'Rain', the frigid missionary is seduced by the tempestuous languor of his environment into sexual relations with the prostitute he is trying to reform.

The expatriate group who have gone most 'native' are of course the anthropologists. On initial observation they appear to have few psychiatric difficulties, perhaps surprising given the total isolation from colleagues, the loneliness and frequent boredom of ethnography. It may be that these reactions are the very tool of investigation. The anthropologist, of course returns from 'the field' to write up his work and gain a doctorate, so that activity 'out there' is not an end in itself. The stresses on even the most committed anthropologist are well shown in the diary of Malinowski, one of the founders of intensive fieldwork.(15)

One of the most ethical dilemmas for the anthropologist is the traditional lack of commitment to the people he is working amongst, a point frequently cited by Third World governments.(16) There may be conflicts between the needs of the local people and the central government who often regard the locals as an embarrassing anachronism; particularly in Latin America, anthropological support for land registration by the locals is a highly politicised question. There may still be an over-emphasis on the romantic aspects of fieldwork and the American anthropologist Margaret Mead has been recently taken to task for her work in Samoa in which she appears to have sought an idealised adolescence of sexual freedom.(17)

I have at present an anthropologist in psychotherapy who is addicted to fieldwork. Whilst time 'in the field' is usually restricted to two years, he has managed to spend eight in a rural area of Africa; he feels uneasy in Britain and has difficulty relating to British social institutions and lifestyle.

Fieldwork findings may not be politically acceptable and recently an American anthropologist has been dismissed from his PhD programme for publishing data about compulsory abortion in rural China. There can be more problems of this type for the anthropologist than for the commercial expatriate whose loyalty lies primarily to his company which devises its own particular relationship with foreign governments.

The old exotic stereotypes probably still motivate the expatriate. Commercial supplements in *The Times* published for the use of international companies still emphasise the traditional triad of sexuality, atavism and absence from conventional restraints.[18] The two poles – home and the country of sojourn – generate a variety of relations, compromises and encapsulated ideals. There seem to be four general modes of adaption: (i) Warburton's retention of an idealised home; (ii) Jungle Madness ('going troppo'); (iii) The missionary position, close to the locals but with the aim of transforming them; (iv) The anthropoligist's planned and sanctioned 'going native'.

The expatriate does not exist in a vacuum; he has to establish contacts with the local population which are likely to be sexual, political and moral. How does the expatriate situate his own identity within the wider political issues? It may be relevant to note that the major reason President Reagan gave for the invasion of Grenada was the presence there of American expatriates.[19]

References

1 Andrew Balfour and Henry H. Scott, *Health Problems of the Empire.* London: Collins, 1924
2 Gregory Rosen, Nostalgia: a 'forgotten' psychological disorder, *Psychol. Med.*, **1**. 340–5, 1975
3 Millais Culpin, Neurasthenia in the Tropics, *The Practitioner.* **85**, 146–54, 1953. (I am indebted to Dr Stephen Mackeith for his kindness in bringing the work of Culpin to my attention)
4 H.S. Stannus, (*Trans. Roy. Soc. Trop. Med. Hyg.* **20**, 327, 1926/7) cited by Culpin.
5 Brian Street, *The Savage in Literature.* London: Routledge and Kegan Paul, 1975
6 F.D. Lugard, *The Dual Mandate in British Tropical Africa.* Edinburgh: Blackwood, 1929
7 Somerset Maugham, The Outstation in *Collected Short Stories*, Vol. 4 p. 347. Harmondsworth: Penguin, 1963
8 Ibid, p. 340.
9 John Cawte, *The Visions of the White Man*, in '*Medicine is The Law*' (Cawte). Honolulu: University of Hawaii Press, 1974
10 Georges Devereux, *Mohave Ethnopsychiatry and Suicide.* Washington: Smithsonian Institute, 1961

11 F.F. Kino, Refugee psychoses in Britain: Alien's paranoid reaction, *J. Ment. Sci.* 97, 589–94, 1951
12 G.B. Price, Discussion on the causes of invaliding from the tropics, *BMJ.*, ii. 1290–7, 1913
13 Owen Chadwick, *The Reformation.* Harmondsworth: Penguin, 1964
14 Somerset Maugham, Rain in *Collected Short Stories* Vol. 1. p. 19. Harmondsworth: Penguin, 1963
15 Bronislaw Malinowski, *A Diary in the Strict Senses of the Term.* New York: Harcourt Brace, 1967
16 Andrew Stathern, Research in Papua New Guinea: Cross-currents of Conflict. *Roy. Anthrop. Instit. News* 58, 4–10, 1983
17 Derek Freeman, *Margaret Mead and Samoa. The Making and the Unmaking of an .Anthropological Myth.* Harvard University Press, 1982
18 *The Times,* Following the Lovers on Dodo Island, in *Mauritius Supplement,* London, 24 October, 1983
19 *The Times* London, 26 October, 1983

6   From Vice to Madness:
The Semantics of Naturalistic
and Personalistic Understandings
in Trinidadian Local Medicine*

Local knowledge of the area of human experience which biomedicine terms *psychopathology* may employ a variety of different understandings ranging from those akin to an empirical cause and effect interpretation of everyday 'physical' illness, to those including the manifest intentions of individuals or unknowable ultra-human agencies. Following Foster (1) we can gloss the first as 'naturalistic' – involving physical processes shared with other natural phenomena in a purely somatic domain independently of human consciousness, law governed and predictable – and the second as 'personalistic', including such fundamentally human characteristics as meanings, ends and motivations.

Broadly speaking, the professionalisation of health care in Western medicine has endorsed naturalistic explanations: the influence and resources of biomedicine are reflected in the extent to which the notion of *madness* becomes transformed into *psychopathology* or *mental illness*; in the translation of what Horwitz (2) terms the basic incomprehensibility of madness into a systematised disease entity.(3) On its coat tails a variety of unwanted practices and experiences, including inappropriate use of psychoactive substances, persistent anti-social behaviour, certain sexual practices, transient dysphorias and interpersonal conflicts, may be subsumed under the explanations of biomedicine. Here medicalisation competes uneasily with personalistic and voluntaristic explanations, producing an uncertain margin where such categories as addiction, parasuicide, abnormal personality, eating disorders, pseudo-disease and factitious illness slide in and out of the biomedical domain.(4)

The two types of explanation offered by Creoles in Trinidad for somatic illness and madness appear to offer clear examples of the

*First published in *Social Science and Medicine* (1988)

naturalistic and personalistic paradigms. Local exegesis affirms that there is no association whatsoever between the causes of physical sickness and madness: the professional notion of 'mental illness' is regarded as a misnomer for a situation beyond the knowledge and treatments of doctors. Attempts to place the two in a unified frame of knowledge are met with derision: 'Man, sickness is a body thing that come to you own senses; the mad ai' have right senses ... Sickness can cure but once you mad, always mad.' As Lawrence Fisher notes, in West Indian societies there is a striking popular salience of madness – in general conversation, gossip, tales, calypsos and literature.(5) The madman is a ubiquitous cultural figure. His presence has not however been matched by any systematic scholarly examination of popular Afro-Caribbean conceptualisations of madness or of their social construction. Anthropological literature merely records the most commonly stated symptoms and the causes of madness, typically 'spirits', replicating in the local ethnomedicine the tacit empiricist theory of biomedicine (6, 7; for example 8–14). Beliefs about madness float freely like the spirits, independent of context. One thing is however clear from the comparative literature: there appears to have been a developing autonomy of the spirits: once not so distinct from human faculties the spirits are now perceived as independent entities. (8, 11, 15, 16) Not only are they external to the human personality, they are increasingly withdrawing from the vicinity of human society altogether. As one of my Trinidadian informants put it:

> Time of the older heads, it have spirit all about place make you sick. But not again. It have electric an' spirit can' take that again! Maybe you see them in the bush and thing they frighten (of) electric. Spirit can' take the machine. Perhaps it the light now.

It would be tempting to take this analytically and conclude that industrialisation is incompatible with a theory that somatic sickness may be induced by malevolent external beings. Shifts from a personalistic to a naturalistic theory of disease are however not likely to be a simple function of the means (or indeed the mode) of production, but of complex local psychologies of self-hood, autonomy and locus of control, reflecting perhaps the local popularity and power of biomedical intervention.(17)

Whilst an idiom of spirit intrusion may still occasionally structure transient psycho-social stresses in Trinidad,(12) the spirits rarely appear now in everyday life except perhaps as folkloric representations in carnival or the annual Best Village Competition. But there is one area of human distress which has not yielded to purely mechanistic explana-

tions – that of madness. Whilst, in the absence of any developed ethnopsychiatry of Western Europeans, we may doubt whether 'popular' Western notions of madness are especially biomedical (and biomedicine has
failed to produce any convincing interpretation of madness), an idiom of
malevolent spirit intrusion is rarely invoked. With a relatively high
standard of living for a Third World country (so that many Trinidadians
indignantly deny that they are part of the Third World), Trinidad has an
extensive network of modern medical care encompassing the whole
country; full time popular healers are rare and a literate, lively and well-
informed post-colonial society has access to cinema, television and
newspapers. Its cultural references and expectations are those offered by
the United States.

Why do the spirits linger still? It may be argued that in one area
medicine has not delivered the goods: that it has failed to effectively treat
the local madmen who remain a common feature of the rural and urban
community – and therefore an explanation of madness which places it in
the biomedical domain is unconvincing. Madness is unintelligible because the spirits are unintelligible. However, rather than employ an explanation which, recalling nineteenth century anthropology, relegates
the ultra-human to a residual domain as yet unexplicated by science, I
suggest in this paper that the local epistemology and semantics of everyday physical distress (bush medicine) do share some meanings with
those of madness. Both articulate aspects of Creole identity, history and
social organisation. Contrary to the immediate local exegesis, there is
not a total rupture between naturalistic theories of physical sickness and
the personalistic theories of madness. As Evans-Pritchard pointed out 50
years ago, naturalistic ('how?') and personalistic ('why') understandings
are not incompatible alternative answers to the same question.(18) An
egalitarian individualistic Creole ideology prescribes voluntaristic and
personalistic interpretations for a variety of antisocial behaviours – the
vices – which are no more medicalised than is madness. A vice carried to
its extreme is madness, providing one cognitive path between the variant
possibilities of everyday behaviour and what on the surface is regarded as
fixed and inexplicable. Shared intersubjective meanings are drawn upon
by individuals to construct and understand undesirable behaviour and
experience. Whilst my interpretation is unambiguously cognitive and
structural, rather than processual,(6, 19) it will be apparent from my
examples that here, as elsewhere, the negotiation of medical knowledge
by actors, relatives, neighbours and professionals, is more interactive
and pragmatic than the elicited local exegesis would immediately suggest, utilising a variety of apparently contradictory explanations according to the status and personal history of the identified individual, and
shaped by the unfolding events.

Pinnacle Village

The West Indian island of Trinidad lies in the Orinoco delta a few miles from Venezuela. Colonised by the Spanish until its capture by the British in 1797, it was largely ignored by Spain but a few French planters settled with their African slaves to grow sugar in the lower areas to the west along the Caroni River. Apart from some sense of French cultural identity, Trinidad's history is typical of the English-speaking Caribbean: the development of sugar plantations; the emancipation of the slaves followed by indentured immigration from India in the latter part of the nineteenth century; the collapse of the price of cane sugar, economic stagnation and Imperial neglect; increasing local participation in government and the establishment of trade unions, culminating in internal self-government. The governing parties have been pro-Western and social democratic, confirmed in power through parliamentary elections since independence in 1962. Approximately half the population are Asians (usually called Indians), while the Afro-Caribbean *Negroes* or *Africans* include a substantial minority of Venezuelan origin (*Spanish*). The term *Creole* refers to the shared local working-class culture of Africans and Europeans; in practice 'Creoles' are Afro-Caribbeans. Virtually the whole population speaks 'Trinidad English', but many older villagers also speak French Creole (*Patois*) or Spanish and the local English is peppered with Creole idiom. I spent 14 months in 'Pinnacle Village' on the North Coast, with a further period of 2 months in Belmont, a working-class district in the capital Port of Spain. Both areas have a predominantly Afro-Caribbean population and Creole culture (16, 20–22) with similar conceptualisations of health and sickness.

Pinnacle is a village of 447 people, lying along the coastal road surrounded by bush. Most of its inhabitants have small *estates* growing *ground provision*. Money enters the village economy from the sale of fish, copra, nutmeg, cocoa and coffee, but principally from wages earned elsewhere and also from pensions and casual road work (*10 days*). About half of the people born in Pinnacle have left it for Port of Spain or Canada. The only middle-class professionals in the village are the 3 teachers who board there during the school terms.

As elsewhere in the anglophone Caribbean, social organisation is orientated to long or short term dyadic relationships and to a certain replaceability of kin roles. Local 'kinship groups' are not corporate but loose local descent groups or centred around the individual and the household. Sexual partnerships usually correspond to household groups and an adult woman and her children are supported by men in most instances, typically by her *church-married* husband or current partner. A father provides for his children whether he is resident with their mother or not. Women, like men, engage in subsistence agricultural work and cash crops but it is usually the men who can obtain paid work away from the household. Ownership of land is historically associated with freedom, economic independence and, to a lesser extent, status. The ideal union is the 'nuclear family' with church marriage but this pattern is more typical of the wealthier, the older and those of Venezuelan origin. Compared with Jamaica, more couples in Trinidad marry and do so at a younger age,(20) particularly in Pinnacle where the commonly described Afro-Caribbean pattern of 'serial monogamy' is less common and less likely to be considered an acceptable option. However cohabitation and extra-residence unions are flexible and easily entered into and ended. Inheritance of land is equally to all children and if women have land, buildings or other property, these are owned separately from those of their spouse.

Middle class Trinidadian opinion, like that of the local women, suggests that men are relatively peripheral to the working class household: village men dispute this. Both sexes agree however that a child's relationship with its mother is more important and enduring than that with the father. The publically accepted ideal of family organisation and life style is that of the white middle class of Britain or the United States; it is recognised in Pinnacle that women as a whole conform more closely to this ideal in their values and behaviour than do men, although, as with marriage, men tend to adopt these respectable values as they become older or wealthier They are then more likely to attend Mass like the women. Nearly every villager is a nominal Catholic although they tend to adhere to an informal eclectic Christianity recalling Anglicanism, but incorporating Biblical fundamentalism. Most villagers have also attended Spiritual Baptist (Shouter) meetings at some time.

Bush Medicine

The rural medical practice of the Creoles of African descent is locally known as *bush medicine*. *Bush* includes the leaves, flowers, shoots, barks and roots of a variety of plants, frequently used in conjunction with commercial oils, essences and waxes. These medicinal plants are grown around the house yards or are easily available in the forest or cocoa estates surrounding the villages. Every villager has a working knowledge of some bush and most adults can describe the properties of between 30 and 100. In Pinnacle Village I obtained a list of 125, together with other home remedies manufactured from fruit or other foods.(23) Whilst everyone has their favourites and there is no single overarching theory of classification or therapeutic efficacy, a core of about 20 common plants are known to every villager and are in common use. Men are believed to know more about bush than women, and they treat themselves when working in the bush.

Physical illness has a *natural* cause and the choice of a particular bush is empirical and pragmatic, depending on past experience or local availability. A bush found on one occasion to be ineffectual for the treatment of a complaint is soon discarded in favour of another recommended or supplied by a neighbour. There is little theoretical relationship between the efficacy of a bush and its shape, locality or other characteristics. Bush is never sold in country areas but is freely offered or exchanged: there are no professional herbalists, as in other parts of the Caribbean,(24) although some *older heads* are recognised as particularly knowledgeable.

Sickness and bush are not regarded as anything especially mysterious. They are part of the everyday order. 'Every sickness have its own bush', although, in practice, the same bush may treat different conditions, and any sickness has a variety of plant remedies. Sickness is caused by weather, climate, conditions of work, an imbalance in the hot–cold system of the body or the neglect of some other health precaution. Bush medicine is regarded as valued traditional knowledge and its ready availability in the Village is cited frequently to demonstrate the superiority of rural Creole life over that in *town* (Port of Spain) or in the United States.

If possible, bush is used in preference to pharmaceuticals especially by men:

> since the tablets come into being I ai' take them on. My tablets is bush. Bush is more effective. Every bush has its work. Every bush suppose to be a medicine but I don't know them all. Long time people know all. Now the older heads know a little but the younger none.

Sickness treated by the doctor and that cured by bush are the same and the 'new' sicknesses attributable to modern life – *sugar* (diabetes) and *high* (blood) *pressure* are also susceptable to bush medicine. Pharmaceuticals are held to contain the active ingredients of a bush but prepared in a more potent, and thus more dangerous, form. It is appropriate to use bush first and the doctor who visits the village every few weeks is only resorted to if bush fails. His tablets too are used pragmatically, inspected, tasted and exchanged, often taken concurrently with bush. A particular sickness can be prevented by taking small quantities of the bush normally used to treat it.

Hot and cold

Most sicknesses with their corresponding bush, and also foods, are interpreted in a binary hot–cold system of classification. In Trinidad whilst heat is an 'intrinsic quality' (25) there is a close association between the subjective experience of heat, both physiological and environmental, and the classification of illness or medicine.(26) Thus many hot conditions involve inflammation. They include blows (*bless, lash, coups*), measles (*pya*), cough (*tuss*), *labse* (abscess, cancer), venereal disease (*runnings, coulant*), abortion (*drop baby*), toothache (*malda*), sore (*bobo*), constipation (*corstive*), and rashes (*heats, gracelles, buttons challay*) Hot–cold systems of traditional medicine are found extensively in Latin America and the Caribbean; their origin has usually been taken as Hispanic (Graeco–Arab) but a case has been made out for an autonomous Amerindian hot–cold system.(27)

The natural course of life increases one's heat particularly through physical labour and exercise, especially pounding coffee, but also through remaining too long in the sun, sleeping, burns, cooking, eating most foods, violence, snake bites, menstruation and contact with menstrual blood, pregnancy and childbirth, and sex. To relax is to *cool*, to *chill*, to *lime*; to feel non-specifically unwell is to be *on fire*. As sexual activity is particularly *heating*, as is dancing, it is not surprising that the annual carnival is a hot time. To say that arguments, sex, music and carnival are *hot* is not only to speak metaphorically but to assert that, when engaged in them, one's body is actually physically heated, with possible risks to one's health. Too rapid a passage from hot to cold (drinking ice water after baking) may cause a 'cold' (*fwiday* or *lawim*) which may then develop into pneumonia or a fever (*fievre*). In view of the body's tendency to *catch a fire* and become heated in the course of daily life, it is advisable to take a periodic *cooling* for 3 days – an infusion (*tea*) of a mixture of cooling bushes. By promoting diuresis or sweating, cooling returns the body to a less heated state. Cooling is a prophylactic measure rather than a treatment, and the bushes chosen may be those used generally to make morning *tea*, the first meal of the day; a cooling used to be known as *refraichement* (refreshment). However, if one is feeling sluggish or unwell in a non-specific way or otherwise 'feeling a heat', a cooling is recommended, and particular cooling bushes are also used for treating named hot sicknesses. Cooling is not a 'tonic'; it does not add anything to a deficient body but enables a body laden with heat to discharge it. The cathartic element is reinforced by backing up the cooling with a purge (28) on the third day which helps reduce heat still further and also rids the body of other harmful substances, whether ingested from the environment or produced in the course of normal functioning.

The Trinidadian hot/cold system is not a simple 'humoural' one in which constitutional balance must be retained by treating a bodily state of deviation in one direction with its complement: it is distinctly 'cathartic'. Cooling and purges takes heat out rather than going in to counteract it by opposite properties. They 'clean the blood'. An extension of the use of purges to remove heat is their use in heavy doses to induce abortion. Purges themselves are classified as hot. Less commonly, hot foods are taken to treat a cold but there is the danger of passing too rapidly from hot to cold, and external applications of heating substances – *soft candle* (tallow) or rum are preferable.(29) A related cathartic idiom is that of *gas*. Gas is produced in the stomach by eating too late after a previous meal and it can be felt there after a heavy meal. Gas is dangerous for it can travel anywhere in the body, causing functional disability or pain, or, if it rises to the head, death. It must be released by belching or breaking wind, a process which is aided by various aromatic local bushes or peppermint water which 'go about to find the gas'.

The use of bush is mundane and pragmatic, an instance of what has been termed the 'according' ethos of Trinidadian society in which there are few absolute values and everything depends on the circumstances.(21, 30) Norms are statistical rather than prescriptive. Older men do maintain that, to be efficacious, some bushes have to be picked at certain phases of the moon; this is simple empirical knowledge, not any type of conjuration; although dreams may reveal the location of an efficacious bush, diagnosis is always based on somatic signs and symptoms. The moon, the sea and the earth (and, according to some, work capacity and the menstruation of women) are in harmony. Particular phases of the moon are associated with growth in plants and animals, the tides and the presence of fish, though, in practice little attention is paid to the moon unless a crop of ground provision or a previously successful bush are not up to their usual quality.

Bush medicine appears then a 'naturalistic' rather than a 'personalistic' system. Its efficacy does not depend on the individual's state of mind, personality, behaviour or their interaction with others except in as much as these lead to a changed relationship between the body and the rest of nature. There seems little explicit overlap between bush medicine and the local personalistic systems of affliction which we can gloss for the moment as 'ultra-human' and 'psychopathological'. *Pacro* (oyster) water or the bark from the *bois banday* improve sexual performance, not by acting as a stimulant to desire, but by inducing penile erection. Whilst madness may be said to be hot, it cannot be treated with bush. Conversely, *obeah* (sorcery) does not cause physical *sickness* directly but may increase vulnerability.(31) Dressler, in contemporary St Lucia, makes a distinction between 'naturalistic' bush and 'personalistic' obeah.(32) Although Simpson in the 1950s placed Trinidadian bush and obeah together as a single system he did not describe how choices of treatment are made and his collection is essentially a set of 'recipes'.(33) It is likely that obeah and bush were once more closely associated as empirical practices, and obeah has become more personalistic through church influences coming increasingly to resemble European 'witchcraft'.

The two systems of active sorcery; *obeah* and *high science*, both associated primarily with men, are dangerous, undesirable and secret.(34) Obeah can be opposed by counter-obeah, the use of *guards* (talismans) or by the powers of the Catholic Church. Bush medicine is largely ineffectual against it. *Maljo*,(35) by contrast, like other variants of the evil eye, is involuntary envy which causes *blight*, a failure to develop in children, plants or livestock. An involuntary act by the sender who is born with the power, maljo is treated either with bathing in an infusion of the same type of bush as used to treat other physical diseases, by prayers, or by requesting the offending agent to remove the blight. Maljo thus appears intermediate between naturalistic and personalistic understandings.

Similarly, in the area of what we may gloss as 'psychopathology', both *madness* (approximating to the psychiatrist's 'psychosis') and *malkadi* ('epilepsy') are principally regarded as the consequence of obeah and are manifested by altered behaviour. *Doltishness* ('mental handicap', 'senility') is taken as a failure to develop physically or as a process of bodily decay, whilst it may be the consequence of obeah, a fright to the pregnant woman or physical trauma. Madness and malkadi (36) are distinct ruptures with everyday life whilst doltishness is only a variant: 'Always he distract. He ai' mature. He backwards, he bend down so. It ai' a sickness, it ai' catching.' In the elderly, 'some doltish depending on their inside sickness. It ai' just your age. What else besides? Grinding (worrying) makes you doltish.'

We can provisionally tabulate our different patterns as naturalistic (N) or personalistic (P) (Fig. 1).

Figure 1

	Effects	Aetiology	Treatment
Bush, physical illness	N	N	N
Maljo	N	N?	N/P
Doltishness	N	N/P	–
Madness, malkadi	P	P	P
Obeah	P	P	P

Madness

Madness is called *folie* in Creole (as in standard French); it is also known as *crazy, offkey, off the head, loco, kinky, head not right, ai' right dey, not collective*. It is characterised by continued unintelligible behaviour usually involving violence:

> They would do something opposite to your sense: so we style them mad people. Something unusual in madness but they selves ai' know they mad. They climb a pole; go in water; they feel they bathe when it have sun; they out of memory – they don't know what they do; they just pick up a cutlass and chop someone, or pick up a baby and dash them in road; cuss; lie down in the centre of the road; always do strange things other don't do: take he clothes and bum it up: burn house; launch boat and go out by heself.

Other mad actions which are commonly cited are eating *fig* (banana) skin, garbage and raw food; walking around naked; touching people who pass; walking in the hot sun in the middle of the road; staring at the sun or the stars; failing to recognise people; refusing to bathe or accept the help of others. One villager, Thomas, who had been in St

Ann's, the psychiatric hospital in Port of Spain, for many years, was discharged home to be visited at intervals by a nurse who gave him injections of depot neuroleptics. Any initial sympathy for Thomas on his return was rapidly forfeited by his ungracious behaviour. His brother built him a small wooden house on family land 'but he just mash it down'. When I was in the village Thomas had stripped his hut of its walls for firewood for cooking and it consisted of a leaky roof, the house posts and some floorboards. He was given old clothes at intervals but could often not be persuaded to wear them. Thomas was seldom seen in the village, usually disappearing into the nearby bush or greeting any passerby with surly and unintelligible mutters.

The *madman* is best avoided. Talking to him is not going to change anything. He will not be grateful for anything you do and you may get hurt so 'pass by a next way for some say it do rub off on you'. (37) He is regarded as living in a private world of his own.

'They laugh so, just by themselves. Tell them howdy and they ai' tell you. If you carry on a conversation, they on a different (one).' Madmen say things which are manifestly untrue. If they maintain 'I just walk here from Tobago' (the island to the north which can be seen from Pinnacle Village), are they deliberately lying or just deluded? 'These imaginations they put it on a real side. From the time it reality, you sick.'

The *madman* is loud, boisterous, erratic and potentially explosive. (38) His most frequently mentioned characteristic is violence: 'They just do anything that get in their way.' Stories circulate in Trinidad about violence in St Ann's and I repeatedly heard one about 'this madman a few years back take a knife and stab the boy in the next bed'. Other patterns of behaviour may seemingly resemble madness: 'A child behave as if it mad but it ai' mad.' The confusion of the madman is distinguished from that of one who is *bazody* (dizzy); one becomes bazody in the crowds of Port of Spain, particularly during Carnival; or when one has frights or continued worries as when 'you don' know what you' wife doing'; with *low pressure*, or after a blow on the head. The bazody person soon recovers and the state, although it may be associated briefly with bizarre behaviour, is always intelligible on the basis of immediate precipitants. Drunkenness (*sou*) is also akin to madness 'When you runs a drunk you do similar things, you part mad.' The drunkard however can always be recognised by his staggering gait and slurred speech: 'The mad must walk straight, they just do funny things. He has a different expression on his face – he look kind of wild. Mad person's eyes got wide and staring you, staring you; if they sit down nice, all of a sudden they want to make a sudden grip.' One villager says that mad people may walk like drunks and that it could be difficult to tell the difference initially unless you know them: 'They kind of off-balance like a drunk, they walk too fast.'

Respectability and Reputation

Afro-Caribbean societies have been frequently described as ideologically dualistic. An egalitarian working-class and male-orientated notion of *reputation* is contrasted with *respectability* which is associated with church marriage, middle-class and White values, education, social hierarchy and chastity, and is represented most typically in women. (39) *Reputation* is represented by the footloose 'circumstance-orientated' man, pragmatic and democratic, drinking in the rum shop and (in theory) pursuing comparatively indiscriminate sexual adventures. Wilson and Austin suggests that *respectability* represents social stratification reflecting the colonial and post-colonial society with its close relationship of class and colour, whilst *reputation* is the response to this, an active affirmation of the ascribed working-class and 'Black' values. Both sexes move towards respectability if they get richer, more educated or as they marry lighter skinned partners. It is a goal, not a norm. Marriage for the man is to move away from 'circumstance-orientated' reputation towards *tibourg* (petit bourgeois) respectability; its economic obligations are assumed half-reluctantly: 'Why buy cow when I get milk free?'

Wilson employs analytically the local terms found in the island of Providencia. In Jamaica a similar ideology of class is known as *inside–outside* which refers simultaneously to education, geographical space (the home), marital status (church, marriage and legitimacy) and dominant social values. Although in Trinidad *respectability* is used in the Providencian sense, the opposed value is not called *reputation* but by the disparaging (and sometimes defiant) terms *nigger ways*, *worthlessness* or *no behaviour*. Wilson emphasises the Providencian respectability–reputation bipolarity as against the usual anthropology of the Caribbean which was centred in the household (and thus on the female), generating a 'matricentric' (respectable) focus to the whole local ideology, leaving male concerns ideologically as well as geographically peripheral and residual. Respectability in Providencia is less an ideal abstract value than an available goal. However in other Caribbean islands, including Trinidad, the respectable goal appears more firmly established in local values than is its polar opposite *worthlessness*, which appears to be defined by, and relative to, the respectable pole, itself ultimately rooted in the external White (planter/bourgeois/American) values. Unlike *reputation* in Providencia, it is difficult to see extra-household, intermale relations in Pinnacle Village as having a very autonomous existence: they are regarded by both sexes as subsidiary, secondary to the more highly valued respectability. Whilst a society in which everyone is respectable is a goal to be imagined and worked for by most Pinnacle villagers, a society characterised by universal worthlessness would be considered just a mess. This may reflect a greater influence in the village of respectability as demonstrated by the numbers of Black Spanish.

Respectability is precarious, always dependent on an adequate income. Not a fixed status in Pinnacle, it is recognised publically by relatively reserved public behaviour and an avoidance of inappropriate familiarity. A respectable person is one who respects others in public, particularly those themselves respectable or otherwise powerful – 'you got to respect a police man' because they can do you harm if you don't. Older men may maintain that a man's respectability is actually enhanced by outside sexual relations if you avoid *confusion* with your wife and do not neglect her. This they maintain was the practice of the old White French Creoles: 'You' wife now she come more on the White side and you satisfy you' nature with a Black girl.'

An egalitarian 'zero sum' model of economic relationships is critical of self-advancement and always alert to failure: 'The higher monkey climb the more he expose himself.' The pregnancy of Julia, the daughter of a fisherman but now one of the village teachers, who was *friending* with a married policeman, was the occasion for unconcealed delight in the Pinnacle rum shops; the monkey's exposure is determined by the higher standards imposed as you move up; the risks of failing to live up to them are consequently greater. To adopt the outward signs of respectability (frequent church attendance, straightened hair, 'good English' or an affectation of superiority), too soon or without possessing a reliable income, is to be considered pretentious, *béké negre* (black white). Colour, class and behaviour are, inside the community, flexible and *according* notions. Most Pinnacle villagers have both African and European ancestry; whilst the more African villagers are generally referred to as *dark* or as *black*, and *black* is often used as synonymous with *worthless* or *bad* (as in *bad hair*: curly hair), one may be a *nigger* or *worthless* because of one's behaviour even with a light skin (*red* or *high colour with no curl*). Similarly the term *béké negre* refers both to those who imitate White ways and to those just born with *high colour* or those with *half-tone* (vitiligo). 'Bad' is not simply a term of disapprobation; it is used to celebrate periodic disorder and *bacchanal, free up* oneself, a self-mocking suspension of the values of respectability, similar to its use among Black Americans.(40) 'Bad' implies energy, force and nature:

'too bad' may be glossed as 'extremely': 'he got a giant case of the hots. Eh Papa! He love she too bad.' Wilson describes this egalitarian ideology by a local expression, 'crab antics'; as crabs try to climb out of a crab barrel they are pulled down by others so the top of the barrel can be safely left off. (A single crab in an open barrel escapes.) This, particularly male, ideology is articulated by an extensive local repertoire of *picong* (satire), institutionalised in the calypso, which represents 'a lower class view point, or a Negro viewpoint, or a male viewpoint'. (21, p. 203; 41)

The madman is described as characteristically male. His attributes – disorder, semi-nudity, his preference for bush as opposed to his house, his potential for violence – all recall the image offered by respectable people of the poorer working-class man. Fisher suggests that the popular notion of the madman is an ironical but hopeless, internalised self-image, one rooted in the identity which the White has ascribed to the Black, a caricature of Wilson's *reputation*. (5, 15, 42) The respectable person's image of the madman recalls that of the Rasta: indeed, for many middle-class West Indians, the Rasta is dismissed as 'mad'. 'The wider society associated Rastafarianism with madness ... The process of becoming a Rastafarian is still regarded as one of mental deterioration and the more modern embrace of the creed by young educated high school and university graduates is seen as an urgent matter for the psychiatrist'. (43) As Ras Tafari can be taken as an achieved reassertion of those values which Whites have ascribed historically to Blacks, it is not surprising that many of the younger psychiatric patients in St Ann's have adopted dreadlocks and Rasta idiom. If madness and the *natty* (nutty) *dread* are associated, then the active adoption of Ras Tafari by the madman is a reassertion of an otherwise devalued identity. Rastas themselves have a more sympathetic attitude to madness than other Trinidadians, frequently emphasising that it is the consequence of social *pressure*.(44)

Knowledge of Madness

Madness is a state of being. It is not a sickness which happens 'to' you: you 'are' a madman. However, when questioned on the possibility, some villagers say there may be a disturbance of the brain or head, the controlling organ which 'operate the whole body; if it ai' function normally you get mad or thing like that'. Most maintain that madness is present everywhere in the body as it is caused by a spirit. If a madman waves his arm the spirit is in the arm. Even those who advance the (immediate) 'head' theory always also offer a similar (remote) 'spirit' aetiology. The causes of madness advanced by every villager are spirits and obeah.

Spirits are a heterogeneous group of beings, including, depending on the informant, the powers of the Shango cult, African ancestors, the fallen angels of the Bible, the spirit guides of the Shouter Baptists (or more rarely those of European *high science*). They cause madness by entering the body when sent by another as part of malevolent obeah (usually jealous neighbours or disappointed lovers), or if returned to the sender when the prospective victim has a *guard*, or as the result of a failed conjuration: 'I saw man running naked through the cemetery screaming, "Alright, alright, I sorry I bother you." He went mad for truth a few days later.' Spirits may occasionally be sent by God or a Catholic priest as a punishment or revenge on the individual or his family but they are not part of the Christian pantheon.

Madness is described as an all or nothing condition, total and effectively untreatable: 'Once mad always mad.' The madman when identified, must be taken to St Ann's by the police. This is for public safety not for treatment as there is nothing the doctors can do. Even madness caused by a spirit, the usual cause, cannot be removed without God's rare intercession. Madness has a discrete identifiable cause; even informants who advocate a 'pass down in family' theory (which is usually attributed to obeah on the part of an ancestor) feel that the affected individual needs more than a predisposition: 'you ai' born with a weak brain; it have to have something make you mad.'

In practice, when describing actual instances in Pinnacle, a more complex set of interpretations is offered by villagers which do link madness to personality, life-style and coping mechanisms. Madness in a friend may be the consequence of *pressure*, *grinding* or types of studiation other than science, or of *tabanka* or vices. Head injuries also are occasionally mentioned. In addition, we can distinguish between 'weak' (denotative, metaphorical) and 'strong' (connotative, diagnostic) uses of the terms *mad* and *doltish*; any individual acting in a stupid or inappropriate way may be called 'mad' or 'doltish' without suggesting they are really insane or mentally handicapped. When there is any doubt the terms *mad for truth*, *mad like hell* or *madmad* ('really mad') are used. Eccentricity or behaviour out of character may be termed *mad* but never *madmad* unless it leads to violence:

(a) 'My aunt "mad". She always talk to herself. She can't hear any other noise at all! She talk like foreign language, I don't know how she do it. Tante talk Spanish, Patois, Congo, she call the names.'

(b) 'My uncle "mad" once. He was to stand for compère (godfather) to my sister and he just go and drop his suit in latrine! He climb up house without a ladder. That really crazy. They tie him with rope and pull him down.'

The term *pressure* refers simultaneously to the subjective pressures of paid employment, poverty, worries and the pace of town life but also to *high blood* or *high pressure*, understood variously as over-rich blood, the recording on the doctor's plethysmograph or blood moving up to one's head.(45) 'Pressure come as a new thing but now it common in the world. It have blood thickened and heated so it can' flow too good. Once it in you, if you get vex it raise.' Low pressure is experienced as weakness and thus stout beer, used as a *build up*, may cause high pressure.

Pressure like heat or gas is used to explain everyday fluctuations in well-being. It may be caused by the use of fertilisers on the land. Some villagers say pressure is hot and can be relieved by cooling teas. Pressure builds up like heat or gas and has to be released but here the catharsis is usually interpersonal; worries and anger should be ventilated and not retained inside by studying them, grinding away. Otherwise they cause high pressure and possibly madness: 'Inside here does eat people.' If one has angry feelings against another they should be freely expressed, at any rate in theory: in practice one runs the risk of being accused of gossip (*mauvay lang*) or stirring up trouble (*comess*) (46): 'I was going to answer but Rupert say she ignorant (badly behaved). "Don' answer, it make enemy." But I have to tell she! Better than keep inside you and worry worry.' All strong feelings including one's *nature* (sexual drive) should be released lest they cause pressure. 'Cooling it' is not, as in British English, suppressing an emotion but avoiding pressure by relaxation, by *liming*. Bad news may cause madness through pressure because it is sudden and overwhelming: 'It have a woman in Blanchisseuse an' they come and tell she the man (her husband) drown off Tobago. An' she bawl an' she carry on. An' she crazy for truth. They take she up to the mental.'

Whilst most villagers employ a rich lexicon of personality and 'psychological states',(47) only pressure, and its related notions studiation, grinding, and tabanka, offers an accepted but rare pathway from everyday life to madness which involves an internalised set of mental attitudes or physiological processes. The more respectable villagers, who read the newspapers are familiar with a 'modern' pattern of behaviour, known as *nerves mashup* or *nervous breakdown*, typical of woman and characterised by a quieter picture: 'They look shaky like, they can' think. They don' say strange things, they don' go to lash. To my mind it don' come like a madness.' Nerves mashup are an extension of normal transient moods or personality and are seldom the occasion for special remark. They are hardly to be identified as a discrete state, let alone a disease.(48)

Studiation, like pressure, is a polysemous term, referring to the study of high science, but also to any undesirable habit ('they study meanness and commonness') and especially to excessive concentration on any subject, notably books (49): 'You overpower with pressure of study. We have young people at school an' they can' take it a next time. You overlearn an' you brain too light, it worry you head.' Theological speculation, a favourite village activity, is dangerous: 'scripture hell of a thing, it send you mad.'

Studiation madness is described as rather different from the otherwise undifferentiated picture of madness: it is characterised by social withdrawal (*selfish*), aloofness, emotional distance and ultimately total self-absorption. Some villagers in Pinnacle feel that the European – supercilious and self-centred – has become like that through books: the White temperament is, as it were, studiation madness spread out thin!

Studiation madness is not however described as cold in the hot–cold system of classification although madness is, to an extent, hot: as we move to more consciously metaphorical ('weak') uses classification, they become increasingly distinct from the intrinsic ('strong') use of the classification:

	Hot	Cold	
	Burn	Chill	
	Fever	Coconut water	
'Strong use'	Pepper	Cooling	
	Hot bush	Liming	
	Sex, etc		
	Grinding		Limit of usual
			application of
			hot–cold system
	Rum	Beer	
'Weak use'	Madness	Studiation	
	Africans	Whites	

Whilst local ideology in the Caribbean is certainly dualistic (White-:Black:: respectability:reputation:: female:male:: inside:outside), the hot–cold system of bush only interdigitates with this and cannot be said to form a single unified theory with it. The cool of the liming male villager is at one end of the respectability–reputation dichotomy, the cool of the White is at the other; the latter are to an extent so cool that the hot–cold perturbations of everyday life (fieldwork, pressure) do not affect them (Fig. 2).

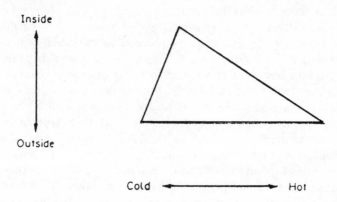

Inside

Outside

Cold ← → Hot

Figure 2

The most severe form of *grinding* is *tabanka*. It occurs 'when you wife left and you take it on, keep study it.' It particularly affects a man when his wife deserts him and goes to live with another man. It is said to be most common among those formally married in church and among nurses and school-teachers – *békés negres* who aspire to White and middle-class values and life-style. While symptoms include a 'heavy heart' (lassitude, anorexia, stomach contractions, insomnia and a loss of interest in work or social life), the tabanked male is characterised by wandering about or remaining alone at home, continually turning over in his mind angry thoughts of the faithless one, *grinding*.(50) 'They don' do anything to pass off studiation, they drink, they smoke, they ai' eat, often they ai' coming home. They concentrate on how they was before. You broken down; it does take an effect on you body also; from brain to body; according as the brain function the body deteriorate to an extent; you not eating, you not drinking, you not sleeping, everywhere you turn you thinking.' Tabanka is caused not by the act of leaving, but by the victim's response to it: 'Once you take it on you get tabanka. If you don' take it on you ai' get tabanka.'

I have argued elsewhere (51) that tabanka, like studiation madness, is an occasion for local hilarity because it ridicules economical and psychological investment in another person when one lives in a precarious and ultimately individualistic world. It is not a critique of the values of fidelity or respectability when appropriate, but of a snobbish assumption of them by people who can ultimately not sustain them. Tabanka mocks the masquerade of respectable ideas and reaffirms the tyranny of individual physiology and accident in the face of unsuccessful attempts at rigid social structures which are no longer *according* to circumstances.

The victim of tabanka is encouraged by a few close friends to forget the faithless one lest grinding proceed to madness, and to turn his interests to fresh attachments: 'Every day is fishing day, not every day is catching day.' The consequences of tabanka can include death from accidents while drunk and the loss of work: 'you drink to keep off studies. It act on the brain: you drink it out, you cast it out, you taking away thoughts.' If unresolved it can lead to murder or suicide: 'it happen to nearly every man in Trinidad. You hear man poison self? It tabanka. A man hang on tree? It tabanka.' Unresolved tabanka progresses to madness (52) and Pinnacle people believe that there is a special ward for victims in the psychiatric hospital: 'It have this boy die through grief. He die in mental. He quiet, you take food into the house an' he throw it away.' Another villager had been 'mad once but that wear out from him, then the girl leave him an' he get crazy again.' He is now madmad.

Both personalistic and naturalistic systems of Creole medicine employ a common idiom in the therapeutic efficacy of what we may gloss as 'cartharsis', the expulsion of something undesirable to return to a balanced state. We find it in the notions of heat, gas, pressure, grinding and tabanka. It is recognised in the national institution of the annual Carnival. 'It amazing what we Trinis put up with an' don' explode. But come Carnival it jus' baccanal'.(53) In fêting 'you free up you self, you ai' got pressure, no one looking at you.' Carnival is a hot time and Trinidadians respond good-humouredly, in picong and calypso, to the Ministry of Health posters which start appearing each year after Christmas advising prophylaxis against venereal disease and 'carnival babies'.

Mary Douglas suggests that societies with 'weak social control' have weak bodily control and no elaboration of a cathartic theory or the use of purgatives.(54) On looking within Afro-Caribbean societies it would be difficult to regard them as employing 'strong social controls'. If, however, we take a wider view of the West Indies as part of the European political system with its particular relationship between Black and White, established in slavery and continuing through colonialism and after, it is difficult to see what 'stronger social controls' there might be than allocation of social privilege and resources according to immutable skin colour, reflected locally in the ironies of the respectability–reputation system. Trinidadians themselves explicitly see Carnival and their own 'tendency' to fêting as an explanation of their national characteristics, as opposed to Bajans who are 'uptight and lickerish' always trying to imitate Whites, or Jamaicans who have responded by prickly sensitivity and anger. By contrast 'we is a Carnival people', laidback, phlegmatic and balanced, a position endorsed by the local psychiatrists.(55, 56)

Vices

Alcohol and *ganja* (cannabis) use may lead to madness like other *vices*. (57) We may gloss vice as 'addiction', a fixed behaviour pattern, initially chosen freely by people because it is pleasurable, although it may be harmful to them or others, and which becomes increasingly difficult to resist until they are controlled by it and eventually destroyed.

Thiefing is a vice and becomes increasingly difficult to stop when a victim *lights a candle* (or *prays*) on you, a form of sorcery permissible because it involves the use of a Catholic candle and prayers to God against the unknown thief, although some villagers say it works automatically without God acting and on a 'named' thief, in which case it comes close to obeah. God may intervene independently with similar consequences but some suggest, in a more 'psychological' theory, that stealing itself has an effect on the thief, compelling him to engage in it with fewer precautions against detection until he *get spoil* – he is caught or becomes mad: 'Their hand fast, they can' see without taking.' The compulsion to repeat stereotyped acts is also found in the vices of high science and obeah, when, eventually, a spirit one has sent returns or else God decides that enough is enough. After a spirit sent by the Roseau family onto the young son of a neighbour (who had stolen some washing) was deflected back by a carefully placed *guard*, 'the father go like he drive truck all over, the mother act like cocoa picker and she daughter like she a sewing machine.' (The Roseaus maintained that they had not sent a spirit but had lit a candle on an unknown thief and the neighbour who was the thief had responded with obeah.)

Rare behaviours which are vices and which may end in madness include being a male or female homosexual, a *mamapoule* or a *zami*; (58) sodomy with people or animals (*bulla* or *bugger*); or sexual relations within the prohibited limits of affinity.(59) On the whole spirits or witch-like transformations do not engage in sexual activity

with the exception of the *gumboglissay*, a type of air-borne incubus.
(60) Not all inappropriate sexual behaviours are vices. Thus a shy
young fisherman who annoyed the village women by stealing their
underclothes was just seen as lonely and socially inept. Nevertheless
public pressure led him to leave Pinnacle. Rape was unknown in the
village and was regarded as an unacceptable extension of normal
sexual behaviour not a vice. When I asked if there were any other
vices, a few suggestions were offered including sex with children and
the sadistic beating of members of the family. Persistent lying,
quarrelling, making *comess*, gambling at *whe-whe*, bad talking,
atheism (usually associated with *science*), smoking and laziness are
not really vices but they are often dismissed as such in the heat of
argument, in a 'weak' usage. (Taken together, in consistent antisocial
behaviour which does not produce any long term advantages for the
individual, they may constitute vice.)

Vices then are patterns of behaviour and personality which are
regarded generally as socially unacceptable but intelligible on the basis
of human personality. Alcohol and ganja use, although they are the
most frequently volunteered vices after obeah, at least by the more
respectable villagers, are rather different. Apart from three families
who are *Seven Days* (Adventists), no one regards moderate rum
drinking as a vice in the strong sense. On the contrary, as we shall see,
it is a welcome lubricant to village life. It is excessive drinking as
determined by its social consequences which is a vice and can thus
lead to madness. Any smoking of ganja (as opposed to using it in bush
tea) is a vice according to the tibourgs and more respectable women.
Not so say the young men, although they agree it can send you mad if
'you can' take it'. Similarly heavy drinkers believe that rum can cause
madness if 'you got a weak head'. Whilst vices may be cited as moral
offences, they are usually criticised as rendering normal social life
impossible or as contraventions of the natural fitness of things: 'I feel
man should be man and woman woman. The way you made. This
kind of filthiness (homosexuality) is a bad thing because God make a
partner for you. I don't like it, they dress and speak like a woman'. (61)

In theory no particular personality is more liable to a vice. It is the
sort of thing anybody may be tempted to do in a weak moment. If one
has a vice one should keep it secret for to flaunt it publically suggests it
is further advanced and is taking you over. Nevertheless, accusations
of vice are directed against those who are worthless and might already
have another vice. Baptist *mourning*, which is said to lead to madness
is attributed by non-Baptists to rum: 'It the drink make them so.' Any
sexual vice leads to private accusations of obeah. Both are known by
the general term of *filthiness* (*nasty ways*) which is *worthlessness*

taken further. *'Interference'* denotes both obeah and sexual vice. A whole family, through past misdeeds or obeah may be liable to vices, in which case they are known as *blighted*, the same term which is given to the victims of maljo, although here suggesting an inherited tendency to engage in obeah, thieving and other *filthiness*, the whole complex inexorably moving to general incest and insanity.(62) (To be *spoil* is a type of blight but one in which the affected individual is more clearly personally responsible.) If your father was mad, *ran a drunk* or had a reputation for science, you are regarded as that much more vulnerable and thus suspect. As with any specific vice, a blight on a family or individual may simultaneously be taken as divine punishment and as the inevitable working out of a current vice.

Suzanne, a *doltish* young woman, is called a 'cooler for men': she has frequent casual relationships with the more worthless men of Pinnacle Village who visit her at night when drunk. She is popularly rumoured to have born her first child, Andrew, to her own father. This is confirmed by Andrew's slow development. Suzanne herself is maintained to have been the result of a union between her mother and

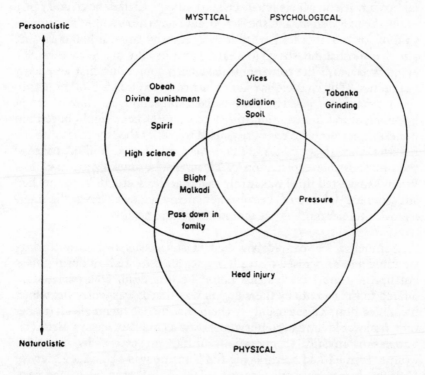

Figure 3

her mother's father, a scientist, and 'she lie plenty, deceitful ... she got fits too'. Vices both generate madness and doltishness and are caused by them, forming a constraining circle of addiction in which vice is relentlessly pursued to increasingly self-punishing ends beyond free choice.(63)

We are now in a position to examine the relationships between the elements of the indigenous medical system as they interact in madness, making our somewhat arbitrary distinctions in the analytical categories of 'psychological', 'mystical' and 'physical' (Fig. 3).

Whilst in theory *obeah* and spirits are the usual interpretation offered of madness and malkadi the other theories may also be employed simultaneously. Persistent antisocial behaviour so persistent as to constitute a vice – stealing or violence – may be regarded as an attenuated form of madness, reminiscent of the psychiatrist's 'psychopathic personality'. 'It ai' just a vice. He ai' really bad. He ai' exactly what you call mad. It come as what we call half-way crack.' The ascription of madness is negotiated subtly, pragmatically. It is always *according*. To take three instances:

(a) 'An' my friend Marcelline been start talk queer like she go crazy. An' I take she to a woman and she say, 'It have one throw something in you' yard. It for you' mother but it hit you'. An' the girl still half crazy an', after her mother die, she go to mental, but she cure in a few weeks. She ai' crazy because she got cure. It have been something that an enemy put on her.' The speaker had later married Marcelline's brother.(64) In theory, madness caused by obeah is fixed and cannot be removed except by supernatural intervention; the doctor's treatment would have been useless. The complete recovery is used to justify the fact that although her friend had to go to St Ann's she was not madmad, and the obeah is the only possible explanation of an otherwise unexpected madness. When I suggested this I was firmly told that the doctor didn't 'cure' her, she 'got cure' (recovered) because her enemy had withdrawn the interference after her mother, the intended victim, had died.

(b) Samuel, a 19-year-old boy died in *status epilepticus* from longstanding and recognised malkadi. I was called to see him during Mass but by the time I reached his house he was dead. One explanation offered to his parents by the villagers was that it was *worm fits* which had killed him. To say openly to them that he had had malkadi (rather than fits) would have been unsympathetic as malkadi always carries an unpleasant mystical connotation, unlike fits caused by intestinal worms. Samuel had been having fits since he was 12 and a variety of anticonvulsants from the General Hospital in Port of Spain had been only partially effective in reducing them. Whilst he was alive these attempts were derided by the other villagers: 'Samuel don' have what you term fits His arm (during them) strong like you can move it. It a spirit.' Nevertheless they agreed that they would start by taking their child to the doctor in similar circumstances. However 'good doctor should say 'ai' sickness, go to priest'.' Why was there a spirit on Samuel? Some suggested that it was a punishment for obeah by someone in the family. His father had twice had fits. 'Something happen in that family for true: they use to have a shop an' it go suddenly.' At his funeral this was insinuated to the visiting Catholic priest by a villager who was famed for her mauvaylang. He ignored her suggestion. Samuel's mother had previously flirted with Pentecostalism, and another explanation was that her son had become ill either as divine punishment or because a spirit had passed over her during some exorcism. 'He get spoil.' The Pentecostal theory was generally accepted by the villagers because they were resentful that since her return to the Catholics she remained associated with the more charismatic wing (influenced by the Archbishop in town and very 'American' and social) and, like some other light skinned Spanish in Pinnacle maintained a rather reserved demeanour. She and her husband were economically relatively successful and had built a concrete house somewhat away from the rest of the village, near the cemetery which overlooks Pinnacle River (which occasioned further gossip about things seen at night). They had bought another house and planned to open a 'club', a novelty in Pinnacle. Samuel himself was not accused; a quiet and sickly but friendly boy, he could not be regarded as the initiator of any mystical unpleasantness. Although theories of a turned spirit were generally discussed at the wake on the evening of his death no mention of this was made directly to his family for fear of hurting their feelings. In spite of their move to respectability and their Spanish ancestry, Samuel's parents are accepted as generous and good-humoured, quite simply the most pleasant people in the village. To accuse them too openly or too consistently of filthiness would be so inappropriate as to rebound on the speaker, giving rise to further discussion as to why he should be so knowledgeable on that particular subject. The theory offered in the course of the illness by the family's friends, that pzasm could be a natural sickness which may 'pass down in the family', was eventually accepted as one consensus public explanation at the wake, together with a suggestion that an old woman who had died 100 days before 'was lonely and she came back to take the boy.'

(c) Jules is a heavy drinking shopkeeper born in Tobago, who is rumoured to use high science to attract customers (his prices were the highest in Pinnacle). His sister church-married a Spanish who owned a van and was herself the Village's only Jehovah's Witness. Her son Augustin thus carried a rather weighted past: science, foreign origin, Jehovah's Witnesses, prosperity on both sides of the family, and the rather ambiguous Spanish connection (associated it is true both with church-going and strong family-centred respectable values, but also with the secret and potentially dangerous prayers against maljo). Augustin was always worthless. He *thiefed*. He didn't join in the fishing (not that he was often invited) but occasionally made a trip down coast alone to pick copra from the now abandoned family estate. Most of the time he sat around the village liming with the local Rastas who came from poorer backgrounds than he did, smoking ganja and idly trading picong with passers-by. He became increasingly withdrawn and could be seen talking to himself although, when questioned, he turned queries aside in a reasonable though surly way, occasionally offering fatuous jokes. One day. in a rather confused state, he attacked one of the villagers with a cutlass, was arrested and eventually taken to St Ann's Hospital on the other side of the island. Diagnosis there, as reported back, was ganja madness. Pinnacle opinion was unanimous, and was voiced more openly than in the case of Samuel: Augustin was blighted and was clearly being punished both on his own behalf and because his uncle *mounted* the goods in his store forcing the purchaser to return to shop there again and again. This compulsion was mirrored in the blight: 'He going crazy, with ganja again an' again. It have a thing on that family. Someone mouth on them and now he can' stop.' Augustin's mother was furious at these hints but did not respond, standing on her dignity as a respectable villager who alone was sure of God's message of salvation. She shared her hurt feelings with the only outsider available, myself: 'He had an ear infection in his childhood and was born before his time (premature). Since then he can' stop stealing. I don' know if he killed someone yet but if he do he sorry after and say "Mam – I didn't mean to do it".' At the same time as seeking exculpation for his behaviour through his having a disease and thus not being immediately responsible, she tried to persuade me that he was not mad anyway because there was a motivation for his violence: 'He only do it to this man who get him vex.' Augustin himself attributed the episode to ganja and at his mother's urging, took to hawking fruit round the village from a basket. As this is overpriced and the community anyway prefer to exchange rather than sell their own fruit, Augustin's blighted reputation is not diminished. Clement, who sold him the *ganja* says he is not madmad, only a little *light headed*; if he was mad he could not now be selling fruit at a profit.

Rum

Whilst obeah and science are vices more rumoured than practiced, the vices of ganja smoking and drunkenness are not uncommon. All men in Pinnacle apart from the Seven Days drink rum,(65) with an average consumption of about 8 units of alcohol per day. Some may drink only 1 or 2 glasses once a week and the most is about 2 bottles per day.(66) At periods of fêting – weddings, wakes, Christmas, saints days – consumption goes up considerably. Most men will drink at some time in the rum shop (a partitioned off portion of the general store), but the more respectable men prefer to drink at home when a visitor comes round to call, except during communal fêting. The more worthless villagers are likely to drink sitting by the roadside or even walking about carrying a bottle in their hand. If a man is engaged in continued agricultural or road work it is acceptable for him to take a bottle with him but the preferred alternative is to wait until work is completed when he can repair to the rum shop with his friends. Drinking and fishing do not go together, in part because rum is hot and if spilt may disturb the (cold) sea, but more pragmatically because fishing is dangerous and requires all the concentration one has. Even when mending their nets fishermen do not drink by the harbour but move up the hill into the shadow of the church. Whilst rum is transported by *canot* (boat) to a beach some miles away for the annual Mass and fête for the Virgin of the Sea, it is not drunk in the canot. By contrast there is an affinity between rum and the land. A libation was once poured into the open grave and when men are together and slightly drunk a portion of rum may still be poured onto the ground in a rather self-conscious tribute to the ancestors.

Women, as one might expect from their association with respectable *inside* values, seldom drink outside the home and almost never in the rum shop. Many of them do not drink at all except at Christmas, and they prefer imported fortified wines or home-made fruit wines to rum. Rum is for men. 'Rum is macho' as the commercial poster puts it.(67) As men get older and have demonstrated their responsibilities, heavier drinking becomes more acceptable. Whilst a 20-year-old man when drunk is disgusting, really worthless, the spectacle of a drunken man of 80 if he is otherwise respectable is a guarantee that he is not too *social*, that he remembers he is only a poor fisherman.

Drinking is more acceptable as the day goes on; whilst a shot of rum first thing in the morning is an effective prophylactic against a wet day in the *cocoa*, communal drinking is for later, when the day's labour is over. Solitary drinking, the prophylactic nip excepted, is not approved of inside the village. To drink alone, whether one is male or female, is a vice, a sign that rum has taken one over. When drinking, either in the house or in the shop, a bottle is provided by one person for all and a glass for each. After the invitation 'Make you self easy now', everybody helps themselves when they want but at a tempo carefully in tune with the occasion and with the other drinkers: a *lickerish* man is one who pours himself too soon or too large a tot (generally known as a *coolie shot* in tribute to the supposed heavy drinking of the Trinidadian Asians). Men visiting men, and less often women visiting women, may drink; to offer a single visitor of the opposite sex a drink implies a sexual invitation.

Why do men drink? Rum is praised for its effect in lightening mood, in enhancing relaxation after work, for improving sociability, for lowering inhibitions,(68) for helping ease *pressure* and in a controlled way easing social tensions. Drinking is a measure of reciprocity, of obligations remembered and discharged, a measure of trust. Thoughts otherwise private are ventilated under its influence: a man must choose his companions. His personality and his respectability can be determined by his behaviour in the rum shop. Drinking is a skill which requires balance. The *social* standoffish man declines the bottle too early. The worthless one anticipates the others; he is too *forward*. The effects of drinking depend on the weather, on activity and on personality ('Some born strong for rum'). They may be simply unpredictable: 'One day he drink a whole two bottles and next day he drink a little shot an' it act on him. He drunk like that.' (The terms 'drink' and 'drunk' are used as in International English.)

I found that when men got drunk they tended to engage in abstruse theological debate. They became maudlin and sentimental, professing endless friendship and talking about how much people respected them. A common theme was their own death, how much people would remember them: 'They fight to carry my coffin, man!' The more worthless ones tended to start fights over trivia, usually involving their *amour propre*. The more respectable villagers usually remained quiet. In other words alcohol tended to exaggerate social characteristics which were already present: this is in accordance with the beliefs of the heavier drinkers. By contrast, the respectable opinion was that rum put something (undesirable) into one which was not there previously: 'like the spirit have a spirit, it take you over now.'

Rum is good for health. A glass early in the morning 'clears the body' or 'draws out' a pain. Taken internally it may prevent a chill, whilst if one has an incipient cold (*fwiday*) the application of rum externally. often rubbed in with tallow, can prevent it developing, according to the hot/cold system. To drink alcohol is to *fire one*. The standard Trinidadian rum, amber like other Eastern Caribbean rums, is sometimes rated as moderately hot; hence 'The cold you take after drinking is the worse cold.' Rum is thus useful for counteracting a cold but would not be appropriate for using as a cooling. The extra-distilled (white) *puncheon rum* is more clearly hot and thus particularly good as medicine; it is sold in small bottles for this purpose. Puncheon is seldom drunk for relaxation: its potency and hence heat turns it into an occasional medicine for 'Hot liquor mash you nerves.' Rum is manufactured commercially by state-licenced companies; to distill one's own rum (*moonshine*, *bubash* or *mountain dew*) is illegal without an expensive licence and is no longer worth the risk; the still can be detected from a distance by its smell, cane is not plentiful in Pinnacle and commercial rum is relatively cheap anyway: a bottle costs about the same as a day's food if purchased locally or a quarter of an unskilled workers daily wage When available, moonshine, as hotter and more 'natural', is more effective than commercial rum as a medicine. It is supposed to increase sexual performance in men: 'You punch that cunt all night – man, you don' stop!' Rum is usually taken before a meal, occasionally with it. Local theory is divided on the advisability of this: some say you must never drink rum with food; some say you must always drink rum with food; some that you must avoid sweet food when drinking. Rum is not itself a 'food' or 'tonic' (69) although stout, often mixed with eggs, is used to build up a pregnant or parturant woman, a *nashy* child or elderly person after an illness. 'It ai' a medicine, it just a build up.' Stout is seldom drunk socially in the village in spite of a national advertising campaign. Lager beer which is much more expensive (a small bottle costs the same as about 4 large glasses of rum) is becoming more popular although associated particularly with fêtes and is more common in town. Beer in town is drunk ice-cold and its increasing popularity is undermining the hot/cold classification of alcohol: plenty of hot and tired people drink ice-cold beer without obviously suffering from the sudden transition from a heated to a cold state! By convention rum is seldom mixed with water, coconut water or juice because of the admixture of hot and cold The mixed drink rum punch, popular in town, is derided as *social* but also as dangerous (70): 'It give you gas.' Mixed drinks make one drunk quicker and are to be avoided for that reason; no one says they drink to get drunk. Another theory is that rum should not be diluted because it then stays longer in the body and slowly poisons the system. Treatment for an *overhang* is 3 more tots of rum or fish liver oils or Andrew's Liver Salts.

Whisky, imported and vastly more expensive than rum, is a drink for special occasions or for demonstrating superior social status or wealth without appearing pretentious. It is said to be the drink par excellence for Whites who come from a cold country and have a colder bodily and emotional constitution.(71) Whisky is regarded as more heated than rum because it is believed to be stronger; potency and heat are associated. By contrast the African, living in Trinidad, a hot country, has a hotter constitution, and hence rum, a less hot drink is more appropriate. Europeans however are to an extent outside the local system of classification; they can wear shorts or bikinis without any opprobrium attaching to them, and they can mix their drinks hot with cold without anything disastrous happening.(72) The hot/cold system as applied to race and alcohol is not then carthartic although constitution must be matched with its opposite. However the hot/cold classification of alcohol is not taken that seriously and many villagers, particularly the women, suggest it is merely the rationalisation offered by heavy drinkers for not taking anything other than neat rum. It is only partly applied to women for instance who (unless sexually aroused) are less *hot* than men and following the 'converse theory' of alcohol and constitution, should have more heated drinks than do men: they do take wine (hotter than rum) but not whisky (hotter still). As children are hot, however, it is appropriate that they should have cooling drinks, particularly coconut water or juice. Women do seem to use stout cathartically together with a purge to induce an abortion. As I understood it, the reasoning here is that 'building up' a woman after childbirth requires stout, and the abortion is analogous with child-birth; some notion maybe of one hot thing replacing or displacing another. The purge itself is however classified as hot and is used after childbirth to clean away 'the blood and thing' which is also hot.

There is no sickness in Pinnacle approximating to 'alcoholism'. Rum is potentially dangerous because when drunk one may have accidents: 'You drunk an' you can' tell what the France happen to you.' One may act in a hasty way which is later regretted, or if grinding, one may, like the tabanked man, be suddenly tempted to do away with oneself. Rum may make one underestimate real dangers, a state known as *bwavo dangay*. 'Excessive' rum drinking is only a vice when it is recognised to lead to habitual violence, to neglect of one's family or to poverty. In addition 'some say when you mother or father drink you get stupidy or twist.' A man who often *runs a drunk* may be called a *rummy*. He has a vice not a sickness. He is initially responsible for his condition. If madness ensues it is because of all the other implicit elements in vice: blight, obeah and so forth. Heavy rum consumption, which by itself does not have a separate name, is to be deplored because it is part of vice, offending against the general fitness of things. Heavy drinkers say that you only become mad if you are not strong enough to take the rum; if you are free from other difficulties you can drink as much as you want, apart from the risks of consequent accident or poverty. No women in the village are regarded as having a vice for rum; criticism of their drinking is limited to suggestions that, like Suzanne, they let themselves be persuaded by men to have a drink to facilitate casual sexual encounters.

Ganja

How long *Cannabis sativa* (73) has been smoked in Trinidad is unclear. The Pinnacle villagers say that until the 1940s its use as tobacco was restricted to the Indians who smoked it in a *chillum* or clay pipe and that it then spread to the Creoles who preferred to roll up the dried leaves as a *spliff*.(74) Until the recent government clampdown on its use by Rastas, it was openly grown in the houseyards along with other bush. Ganja tea was hot, unlike most other bush teas and was used for colds and chest complaints such as asthma, and they are resentful of the Rastas for having indirectly deprived them of one of their most useful remedies. Ganja (*weed, herb*) is now grown illicitly in clearings in the bush or on the margins of the forested Crown Lands which look down onto the sea from the Northern Range of mountains. Leaves and twigs are stripped from the plants which grow up to 6 ft, and are then dried for smoking. The majority of local ganja is probably taken to town for sale. Who does this is not a matter of polite conversation: though the discrete consumption of it around the village is not of great interest to the police, large scale selling out of the area would (theoretically) attract their notice.

Whilst most male villagers have smoked at some time, regular consumption is restricted to the more worthless young men between the ages of 14 and 30, especially the group who wear dreadlocks and profess nominal adherence to Ras Tafari. Smoking is carried out among a few together when a single spliff is passed round. Little attempt is made to avoid detection but decorum suggests that the main streets of the village are not used. Older fishermen, church married with regular employment, occasionally smoke, usually on the paths which lead into the bush or on the quiet side of the church. As with alcohol, no one smokes alone, except for the two Rastas who are building a *batchy* hut in the bush (to be near a plentiful supply of ganja as the Pinnacle matrons are wont to sniff). Perhaps because it is illegal, ganja is sold inside the village and not freely exchanged like other bush. An outraged grandmother of my acquaintance complained indignantly that she had to pay a Rasta to get some to make tea for her asthma. The usual cost of a spliff is equivalent to about 2 glasses of rum or a packet of cigarettes. Ganja is now part of the money economy of the village; it is seldom given as a gift and even those who grow it themselves make a point of buying it, perhaps to give the impression in public that they are not growers. Whilst refusing alcohol marks one as pretentious and *social*, it is acceptable that young men may refuse ganja when it is offered by their friends.(75)

The reasons offered for smoking are not cathartic. Nothing is 'let out'. Ganja is calm and meditative whilst alcohol is social and tension relieving. Ganja should not be smoked when you have pressure. It is an aid to concentration and contemplation, called *meditation* by the Pinnacle Rastas. Even though smoking is communal the heightened experience is diffused through minimal talk. Visions are not sought and no one reported them.(76) If pressed, some smokers classify ganja as *cool* but not *cold*. On the *older heads'* classification of bush, ganja is very hot (treatment for chills such as *azma*) and that is why, say some, it may lead to madness. The habitual smokers, orientated to a rather diffuse Rasta philosophy, say it cannot send you mad unless you are already *confuse* and are not able to take the *reasoning* which ganja facilitates. They suggest the real antecedents of madness lie in the pressure of *social* life, striving continually for elusive goals. They agree however with the obeah theory of madness, less with the idea of blight as it overlaps with worthless behaviour. Nevertheless they believe that Augustin (page 139) should not smoke because he 'ai' have the head for it'. To mix rum and ganja is dangerous.

This is the theory, probably deriving in part from the more consciously 'Jamaican' Ras Tafari of Port of Spain. In practice, the worthless young men who use ganja habitually nearly all also drink rum and many also try other drugs *to build a head* or *high*: a rather non-specific and indiscriminate use of psycho-active substances to produce a radically altered sensorium, including the use of *Datura strammonium*.(77) 'Building a head' implies a state of confusion and the term is used disparagingly by villagers to describe the vice of heavy rum drinking. Pinnacle ganja smokers refer back to the use of the plant in bush medicine and, combining it with Rasta ideas on the *herb*, recommend it for its health preserving properties, although there is no elaborate theory of therapeutic action as in Jamaica.(78) Ganja is believed to aid work through concentrating the mind and strengthening the body against the elements.

To use it to improve your sexual performance is a mistake: 'You smoke to fuck alright but you don' want sex a next time.' Ganja tea is not considered to have an effect on the head, nor is it regarded as a vice or a potential cause of madness by anybody.

The occasional ganja smokers, all men and some successful fishermen and cultivators, agree it facilitates meditation and has work enhancing properties.(79) Many maintain a loosely mystical attachment to the land, saying they prefer to go into the bush to sit and think on Sundays rather than attend Mass. They suggest that modern life is 'too crucial to the flesh', that much sickness is caused by agricultural chemicals and that, with the extraction of oil in Trinidad, the land is turning dry and arid. These ideas are developed to a greater extent by a new religious movement, the Earth People, who have established a settlement 10 miles away from the village. The leader of this community, Mother Earth, combines Rasta, Shouter Baptist and Shango themes in an earth-revering 'natural' religion.(16, 80) The Earth People use ganja in a similar way to Jamaican Ras Tafari, particularly the men. In Trinidad ganja smoking remains firmly identified with males. No woman in Pinnacle smokes apart from a few girls who live with the village Rastas and who have been persuaded to sample the occasional spliff. Respectability and ganja smoking are firmly incompatible and no man who has pretensions to *social* position in the village would admit publically in mixed company to having smoked it.(81) Whilst rum drinking becomes more acceptable the older a man is, ganja smoking is rare in those over 40 and is then particularly identified as a vice.

In summary then, the use of alcohol and ganja are linked with respectability as in Fig. 4.

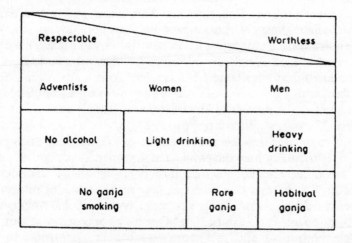

Figure 4

Biomedical and Lay Representations

Alcoholism is regarded by the Ministry of Health as one of Trinidad's major health problems.(82) There is a new unit for its treatment attached to St Ann's and an annual 'Alcoholism Awareness' week is accompanied by radio programmes and street events. Its initiator, Professor Michael Beaubrun, is well known throughout Trinidad and is closely identified with the event. The idea of 'alcoholism' as a sickness rather than a vice is familiar to those more respectable villagers who take a daily newspaper but they take exception to the idea that one has no 'control' over it. Nevertheless the idea of the autonomy of the developing vice as an addiction, eroding free choice is close to the contemporary biomedical notion. In town, identification with the disease concept of alcoholism is associated with the better educated *social* individual, and with Indians rather than with Creoles. (82–84) It is commonly said in Trinidad that alcohol is more of a problem for the Asians. As the villagers put it, Indians lack the flexible *according* strategies of the Creole with their periodic catharsis: Indians do not get tabanka – they kill the offending spouse ...

Ganja is recognised by Trinidadian psychiatrists to lead to short-lived acute psychotic episodes characterised by clouding of consciousness.(85) In Pinnacle little distinction is made between different symptoms in madness as caused by different agents (except studiation). Whilst 'Once mad always mad,' some villagers may suggest that the madness associated particularly with the vice of ganja smoking may be more confused (*bazody*) than other forms and may depart as the immediate effects of ganja wears off: 'You don' always stay mad but go crazy again if you smoke it. It have this boy in Mango Rose take it an' want to fight everybody an' thing. An' they take he to St Ann's an' the doctor give him tablets an' say don' do it a next time.' As we have seen, whilst the theory of madness seems harsh and inflexible, in actual practice the process of identification is flexible and *according*.

Since Carstair's pioneering paper,(86) the choice of ganja as opposed to alcohol has been a question of considerable theoretical interest, particularly how the psychoactive properties of the one rather than the other are incorporated into opposing social institutions. Beaubrun (87) suggests that in the Caribbean, the smoking of ganja as opposed to the drinking of rum is more typical of the Anglophone islands, of poorer communities and Creoles as opposed to Asians. In Pinnacle both rum and ganja are together in opposition to the respectable ideal. They are principally consumed by men as opposed to women, and by the poorer villagers. They stand for the demotic values of *reputation*, the bush as opposed to the house, Creole rather than English, *outside* rather than *inside*, for egalitarian village relationships rather than for the *social* hierarchy of the White world away from Pinnacle. Both are defined as vices, ganja always and rum in excess. As such they form part of a set of values known as *worthlessness* by the *respectable*, placed together with the practice of obeah, Shango and other 'African' traditions. Nevertheless they are not by themselves the occasion for social ostracism, particularly as the consumption of alcohol extends into the privileged '*social*' world. Actual use of these notions in the village articulates subtle personal movements on the respectability–worthlessness dimension, movements compounded of wealth, gender, education, personality and circumstance.

Madness and Vice as Ideological Representations

How independent then are the explicit interpretive Creole schemata of 'naturalistic' (bush and biomedicine) and 'personalistic' (madness, vice)? Particular meanings are certainly common to both: the theoretical hot–cold dichotomy, the ideal of autonomy under external constraints, of balance to be maintained by periodic catharsis, the association of bush, spirits and vices with Creole self-identity; and in experience, a particular pattern of behaviour may be ascribed by different observers to sickness, madness or vice.

This is not syncretism. On the contrary, I have argued that, whether or not we assume a previously unitary Creole system of knowledge of the self and the natural world (and this is particularly unwise for the Caribbean whose history has been a dynamic interpenetration of conflicting systems of domination and resistance), under the influence of colonial Christianity ultra-human concerns have been radically dichotomised into deity and spirits (the latter ascribed to the 'African' tradition), whilst the pragmatic knowledge of bush medicine is both shaped and eroded by biomedicine. As in other systems of medical knowledge the two paradigms leave an ambigious area where the constraints on human agency are debatable and uncertain.

The failure of biomedicine either to treat or offer a convincing understanding of *madness* reaffirms its inexplicable nature, making it a particularly apt representation for Creole identity: a final reassertion of the African past (*spirits*) but increasingly an attribute of contemporary Western life (*pressure*). The ultimate image of the worthless man, of vice carried to its logical and inexorable conclusion, is that of the madman. If the madness of tabanka and studiation can be interpreted as ironic commentaries on pretentious attempts to imitate White and middle-class behaviour when not 'according to circumstance', vices represent the opposite danger – that of abandoning the respectable pole altogether, of abandoning contemporary *social* life for the bush, of being too Creole, too pragmatic and individualistic. Tabanka is the over-valuing of respectability whilst vice is the under-valuing of it.(88) Both lead to madness, a caricature of the impoverished and *worthless* Black. Neither are 'indigenous' theories of disease, ethnoscientific understandings independent of external constraints. Both are rooted in the history of the West Indies, in the inescapable irony of being poised between two ascribed sets of values one derided as worthless, the other only precariously attainable.

Acknowledgements

My fieldwork in Trinidad was funded by a Social Science Research Council Post-Doctoral Fellowship 1979–81. I am particularly grateful to Michael Beaubrun for his assistance and advice, and to William Dressler, William Wedonoja and Carole Yawney for their suggestions. Without the time of the staff and patients at St Ann's Hospital and the hospitality and the patience of the Pinnacle Villagers and the Earth People, this study would not have been possible; to them, particularly Carmen Salvary and Mother Earth, my grateful thanks.

References

1   Foster G. M. Disease etiologies in non-western medical systems. *Am. Anthrop.* **78**, 773–782, 1976.
2   Horwitz A. V. *The Social Control of Mental Illness*, Chap. 2. Academic Press, New York, 1982 examines the literature on popular perception of analogues of 'mad behaviour' in a variety of societies and concludes that its major characteristic is unintelligibility – it is impossible to perceive mad behaviour as any intelligible personal or cultural pattern for which affected individuals have a plausible explanation; and thus one cannot empathise with mad experiences.
3   I am following the current medical anthropological convention of employing *disease* to refer to any professional systematisation of illness experience rather than in its other sense of 'underlying biological process'. Eisenberg L. Disease and illness: distinctions between professional and popular ideas of sickness. *Cult. Med. Psychiat.* **1**, 9–23, 1977; Kleinman A. Editor's Note. *Cult. Med. Psychiat.* **7**, 97–99, 1983.
4   I have suggested that the neuroses can be interpreted as a subtle interplay between naturalistic and personalistic explanations: on the surface they are diseases independent of human agency and thus a proper matter of concern for medicine, whilst there is also an implicit understanding that the pattern

is motivated. (Littlewood R. and Lipsedge M. The butterfly and the serpent: culture, psychopathology and biomedicine. *Cult. Med. Psychiat.* See Chapter 13) The ambiguities may be resolved through psychiatry, that aspect of biomedicine which negotiates between the two types of interpretation and which thus has provided an area of particular interest to sociologists and historians. The history of Western psychiatry demonstrates a variety of conceptual shifts: the developing profession of mad-doctors moved beyond an immediate concern with the layman's madness to develop an interest in alcohol use, criminality and masturbation, culminating in the biomedical folk panic of the 19th century – the theory of degeneration through which a broad selection of Victorian ills were brought together in a pessimistic notion of 'race suicide'. Porter R. *Mind Forg'd Manacles: A History of Madness in England from the Restoration to the Regency.* Athlone, London, 1987; Dowbiggin I. Degeneration and hereditarianism in French mental medicine. In *The Anatomy of Madness* (Edited by Bynum W F., Porter R. and Shepherd M.). Tavistock, London, 1985. The sociology of 'neurotic' disorders is now extensive: on pseudo-disease and factitious disease, see Helman C. Disease and pseudodisease. In *Physicians of Western Medicine* (Edited by Hahn R. A. and Gaines A. D.). Reidel, Dordrecht, 1985; Littlewood R. Gender, role and sickness: the ritual psychopathologies of the nurse. In *Anthropology and Nursing* (Edited by Holden P. and Littlewood J.). In press. Whether psychodynamic theories can properly be called 'personalistic' is debatable; their attraction is of course in Freud's attempt to cut through the distinction between 'naturalistic' and 'personalistic' and the assessment of his success is beyond the scope of this paper, whether we term his method positivist or hermeneutic. In any event psychodynamics have failed to produce any type of 'personalistic' understanding which is generally acceptable either to the layman or the physician as an understanding of 'madness'. (As White G. M. has noted, such broad typologies as naturalistic versus personalistic are overly abstract and independent of the contexts in which local ideas are elaborated. The ethnographic study of cultural knowledge of 'mental disorder'. In *Cultural Conceptions of mental Health and Therapy* (Edited by Marsella A. J. and White G. M.). Reidel, Dordrecht, 1982.) Foster's classificatory dichotomy is one which, under a variety of names, has been used extensively by social scientists. As my Trinidadian evidence suggests, it is a schema which may closely fit actors' own accounts; as such it provides an immediately heuristic model for further analytical consideration, through which the radical differences between the two sets can be seen to be temporary, even illusory. Nor is it eurocentric for, as I have argued both sets of understanding are present in all societies, nor is there at the interpretative level an inevitable association of an increasingly 'naturalistic' emphasis with industrialisation.

5   Fisher L. E. *Colonial Madness: Mental Health in the Barbadian Social Order.* Rutgers University Press, New Brunswick, N.J., 1985.
6   Young A. The creation of medical knowledge: some problems of interpretation. *Soc. Sci. Med.* **15**, 379–386, 1981.
7   Good B. J. and Good M-J. D. V. The semantics of medical discourse. In *Sciences and Cultures* (*Sociol. Sciences. 5*) (Edited by Mendelsohn E. and Elkana Y.), pp. 177–212. Reidel, Dordrecht, 1981.
8   Kiev A. Folk psychiatry in Haiti. *J. nerv. ment. Dis.* **132**, 260–265, 1961.
9   Kiev A. Beliefs and delusions of West Indian immigrants to London. *Br. J. Psychiat.* **109**, 356–363, 1963.

10 Barrett L. E. Healing in a balmyard: the practice of folk psychiatry in Jamaica. In *Case Studies in Human Rights and Fundamental Freedoms*: 2 (Edited by Voenhoven W. A.). Nijhoff, The Hague, 1976.

11 Simpson G. E. *Religious Cults of the Caribbean*. Institute of Caribbean Studies, Puerto Rico, 1980.

12 Ward C. Spirit possession and mental health: a psychoanthrological perspective. *Hum. Relat.* **33**, 149–163. 1980.

13 Beckwith M. *Black Roadways*. Negro Universities Press. New York. 1969.

14 Collis R Attitude research in Jamaica. *Newsletter*. Jamaican Association of Mental Health, Kingston, 1972.

15 The only interpretative accounts are Ref. (5) and Wilson P. J. *Oscar: An Inquiry Into the Nature of Sanity*. Random House. New York, 1974.

16 Herskovits M. J and Herskovits F. S. *Trinidad Village*. Knopf, New York, 1947. For a detailed discussion of this argument see Littlewood R. Pathology and identity: the genesis of a millennial community in north-east Trinidad, D.Phil. thesis, Oxford University, 1987: I suggest there that under the influence of contemporary Christianity a partial separation between human society, nature and the ultra-human world has been effected, the latter radically dichotomised between good and evil. Cutting across the distinctions a dualistic ideology consigns men to a locally recognised 'African' sphere, identified polythetically with Nature and with non-Christian powers (see Ref. (34) below). On the spirits as 'incorporating a conception of history' see Larose S. The meaning of Africa in Haitian Vodu. In *Symbols and Sentiments* (Edited by Lewis I. M.). Academic Press, London, 1977. Michael Taussig makes a similar plea for the privileged status of the shamanic vision over Western scholarship in *Colonialism, Shamanism and the Wild Man*. Chicago University Press, Chicago, Ill., 1987.

17 I am certainly not suggesting any simple historical materialism; as Kleinman has recently reminded us in the case of the Chinese Cultural Revolution, a simple ideological shift can rapidly alter the social construction of personal distress from a 'personalistic' to a 'naturalistic' mode *(Social Origins of Distress and Disease: Depression, Neurasthenia and Pain in Modern China*. Yale University Press, New Haven, Conn., 1986). And by and large, the growth of 'therapy' in the West over the last 20 years has shifted distress in a personalistic direction. Even in the Third World, conceptualisations of madness may be highly naturalistic (Edgerton R. Conceptions of psychosis in four East African societies. *Am. Anthrop.* **68**, 408–425, 1966).

18 Evans-Pritchard E. E. *Witchcraft, Oracles and Magic Among the Azande*. Clarendon Press, Oxford. 1937. Restated in current medical anthropology by (amongst others) Horacio Fabrega (Culture and psychiatric illness: biomedical and ethnomedical aspects. In *Cultural Conceptions of Mental Health and Therapy*, (Edited by Marsella and White), Dordrecht, Reidel, 1981).

19 It will also be apparent that my 'structural' approach is not monothetic nor a frozen rejection of social solidity independent of ideology and social conflicts but one polysemously constituted by them.

20 Roberts G. W. and Braithwaite L. Mating among East Indian and non-East Indian women in Trinidad, *Soc. Econ. Stud.* **13**, 148–162, 1962.

21 Rodman H. *Lower-Class Families: The Culture of Poverty in Negro Trinidad*. Oxford University Press, 1971.

22 Harrison D. Social relations in a Trinidadian village. Ph.D. thesis, London University, 1975.

23 Lists of Trinidadian medicinal bushes are provided in Refs (11, 16); Wong W. The folk medicine of Blanchiseuse, Trinidad. Brandeis University MSc. thesis, 1967; Some folk medicinal plants from Trinidad. *Ecol. Bot.* **30**, 103–142, 1976; Seaforth C. E., Adams C. D. and Silvester Y. *A Guide to the Medicinal Plants of Trinidad and Tobago.* Commonwealth Secretariat, London, 1983. None describe the associated medical knowledge in any detail but Aho W. R. and Minott K. (Creole and doctor medicine: folk beliefs, practices and orientation to modern medicine in a rural and industrial suburban setting in Trinidad and Tobago. *Soc. Sci. Med.* **11**, 349–353, 1977) provide a short list with a hot–cold classification. Pedersen D. and Baruffati V. review the different approaches to local ethnomedicines (Health and traditional medical cultures in Latin America and the Caribbean. *Soc. Sci. Med.* **21**, 5–12, 1985).

24 For example St Lucia (Dressier W. W. Ethnomedical beliefs. In *Hypertension and Culture Change: Acculturation and Disease in the West Indies.* Redgrave, New York, 1982) or Jamaica (Long J. K., Jamaican medicine: Choices between folk healing and modern medicine. Ph.D. thesis, University of North Carolina, 1973).

25 Messer E. Hot–cold classification: theoretical and practical implications of a Mexican Study. *Soc. Sci. Med.* **15**, 133–145, 1981.

26 Similarly in the islands further North (see Ref. (24)). By contrast Latin American and Asian nosologies are more abstracted from personal experience: in the subjectively neutral elements may be variously classified. In Unani (Graeco-Arabic) medicine, coffee is cold and tea hot; the opposite in Trinidad. See Harwood A. The hot–cold theory of disease. *J. Am. Med. Ass.* **216**, 1153, 1971, Foster G. M., Relationships between Spanish and Spanish-American folk medicine. *J. Am. Folklore* **66**, 203–221, 1953.

27 Colson A. B. and Armellado C. D. An Amerindian derivation for Latin American Creole illnesses and their treatment. *Soc. Sci. Med.* **17**, 1229–1248, 1983. This may have influenced Afro-Caribbean societies (Staiano K. V. Alternative therapeutic systems in Belize: a semiotic framework. *Soc. Sci. Med.* **15**, 317–332, 1981; Staiano. *Interpreting Signs of Illness: A Case Study in Medical Semiotics.* Mouton de Gruyter, New York, 1966). But direct Carib influences on Trinidad are hard to trace beyond place names. (The Shouter Baptist *mourning* however does resemble Amerindian 'vision quests' and contrasts strongly with the 'possession states' of other Afro-American religions). As Aho and Minott point out, Trinidadian Creole medicine resembles other Afro-American ethnomedicines (see Ref. (23, p.350)), and Snow L. (Folk medical beliefs and their implications. *Ann. intern. Med.* **83**, 249, 1974) has noted common features in all New World ethnomedicines, whatever the original Amerindian society.

28 Creole *menay* (probably from Fr. path, trace, strategy).

29 Many remedies are simply oppositional: 'nutmeg (hot) cuts cold'; *zabopik* a bitter bush 'cuts' sugar (diabetes). Some villagers describe a state of ideal bodily balance in which red corpuscles must balance the white corpuscles, a theory they say they were taught at school or read in the papers.

30 It is not constructed through texts although the popular British and American 'farmers' almanacs' are purchased locally and felt to be

generally in accordance with bush with their emphasis on homologies between the phases of the moon and growth of plants and animals.

31 Cf. Zande 'first spear' ('how') and 'second' spear ('why'). Evans-Pritchard E. E. Zande therapeutics. In *Essays Presented to C. G. Seligman*. Kegan Paul, London, 1934.

32 Whilst admitting the distinction is analytical and arbitrary (Dressler W. Ethnomedical beliefs and patient adherence to a treatment regimen: a St Lucian example. *Hum. Org.* **39**, 89–91, 1980). Using questionnaire responses to elucidate the relations between questions which emphasise the local naturalistic system (bush), the local personalistic system (obeah) and Western biomedicine. Dressler finds statistical associations between bush and obeah (the two local systems) and bush and biomedicine (the two naturalistic systems), suggesting there may be independent and cross-cutting complexes of 'naturalistic' and 'modern' conceptualisations.

33 Herskovits too considers obeah, shango and bush as a unitary system (see Ref (34)). Whatever the distant origins of the schemata (Refs (26, 27)), the distinction between theories of bush and madness described in this paper are emergent, not syncretic differences (cf. Greenwood B. Cold or spirits? Choice and ambiguity in Morocco's pluralistic system. *Soc. Sci. Med.* **15**, 219–235, 1981). Maljo (evil eye) however may be a recently introduced idiom from Venezuela although it is found in other French Creole societies (see Ref (26)) and is recorded by Herskovits. In Jamaica balm, the equivalent of bush, which has professional practitioners, is employed for inter-personal and 'psychosocial' difficulties (see Ref. (24)).

34 Whilst only 4 men in Pinnacle told me they had practiced science, almost all adults agreed they had used *tricks* but none admitted to attempting malevolent obeah. Obeah is regarded as the 'African' system in Trinidad and is sometimes called *negromancy* (cf. necromancy); it involves in particular the use of *grave dirt*, charms and other *tricks* to persuade or harm others and the sending of spirits (*lespwee, jumbies*) onto enemies. High Science is based on the interpretation of texts in the European 'Hermetic' tradition as found in the illegal DeLawrence Company books, principally concerned with becoming wealthy or attaining secret knowledge. Both are said to be in opposition to normative Christianity although the mourning (vision quests) of the Shouter Baptists involves communication with spirits who may be regarded as demonic by other Christians. Public communication with explicitly African powers is only found in Port of Spain, in the now rapidly disappearing Shango cult (Refs (11, 16)) (Carr A. T., A Rada community in Trinidad. *Caribb. Qt.* **3**, 35–54, 1954). In Shango the identity in a single power of Christian saint, African deity, ancestor and natural force and its relation to the human personality during possession makes for a less sharp distinction between naturalistic and personalistic. Obeah is the practical application of the Shango powers though few Shango cultists would admit it, for obeah, whatever it once may have been, is now publically perceived as solely malevolent.

35 *Maljo*, probably from Fr. *Mal oeuil*, possibly Sp. *mal ocho*. cf. Roberts J. M. Belief in the evil eye in world perspective. In *The Evil Eye* (Edited by Maloney C.). Columbia University Press, New York, 1976. *Maljo* closely recalls Evans-Pritchard's Zande 'witchcraft'.

36 *Malkadi:* Sp. *mal caida*. 'falling sickness' also called *pzasm* ('spasm'). *Doltishness* has a variety of alternative names (*moumou, heavy tongue, mamapoule, stupidy et al.*) all of which also connote everyday 'stupidity'.

37 A government questionnaire of public attitudes to 'mental health' elicited more sympathetic attitudes, perhaps because it started by listing psychological difficulties rather than the notion of the madman (Rambachan S. *Community Mental Health Services Attitude Survey.* Ministry of Health, Trinidad and Tobago, 1981, mimeo).

38 A broadly similar description is offered in Barbados and Jamaica (see Refs (5, 14)).

39 Wilson P. J. *Crab Antics: The Social Anthropology of English Speaking Negro Societies of the Caribbean.* Yale University Press, New Haven, Conn., 1973. The bipolar opposition of values has been previously related to the psychiatry of West Indian communities (Littlewood R. Anthropology and psychiatry: an alternative approach. *Br. J. Med. Psychol.* **53**, 213–225. 1980; see Ref. (51). Such a duality is both manifest in local perception and in theoretical interpretations (Greenfield S. M. *English Rustics in Black Skin.* College and University Press, New Haven, 1966; Austin D. J. History and symbols in ideology: a Jamaican example. *Man* **14**, 497–514, 1979). Austin is concerned, correctly, with criticising Maurice Bloch's distinction between everyday knowledge and ideological ritual. I follow her here in interpreting local knowledge as ideological, directly reflecting and representing class conflicts.

40 Kochman T. Rapping in the Black Ghetto. *Transaction* **6**, 56–71, 1969.

41 *Picong* is cognate with Creole *pica* (thorn) and also connotes heat. Elsewhere in the Caribbean it is known as *broad talk* or *nigger talk* (Abrahams R. D. *The Man of Words in the West Indies: Performance and the Emergence of Creole Culture.* Johns Hopkins University Press, Baltimore, Md, 1983). Patterson O. In *The Sociology Of Slavery* (MacGibbon & Kee, London, 1967) has called attention to the levelling effect of humour in Afro-American slave societies. On calypso, see Warner K. *The Trinidad Calypso.* Heinemann, London, 1982.

42 Wilson (see Ref. (15)) offers a similar idea in his portrayal of a West Indian *madman.*

43 Nettleford R. *Mirror Mirror: Identity, Race and Protest in Jamaica*, pp. 56–57. Collins, Kingston, 1970. Ras Tafari in the West Indies and elsewhere has been described in many publications. Perhaps the best is Owens J. *Dread*, Heinemann, London, 1976.

44 See the interview with the leader of the Earth People in *Ras Tafari Speaks*, Port of Spain, November 1980. To an extent this argues against William Dressler's model (Psychosomatic symptoms, stress and modernisation. *Cult. Med. Psychiat.* **9**, 257–286, 1986) in which he suggests that in a post-colonial society, individuals who fail to achieve upward social mobility conceptualise psychosomatic symptoms as stress/pressure unlike Rastas who have opted out altogether. However Trinidad Rastas have not opted out to the extent of establishing separate communities, and their emphasis on *pressure* is only in the area of madness, not everyday somatic complaints. I have argued elsewhere (see Ref. (16)) that Rastafari is not only a reaffirmation of Creole identity but may be taken in some particulars as a move to universalism and thus to 'modernisation'.

45 Or all simultaneously. In St Lucia these 3 usages seem more clearly differentiated (see Ref. (24)). In Trinidad there is a blood related disorder *dirty blood* which is treated by cooling and is associated with a heated body; similarly in Belize (27, pp. 253–256).

46 *Mauvay lang* (Fr mauvaise langue) is also known as *bad talking*, being a

maco. Comess or *confusion* are sometimes called by the same term as for obeah: *nastiness*. Another term for *lighting a candle* on someone is *washing you mouth* on them which is also used to mean gossip or insult. An old Creole word for obeah is *wanga*, the name of a maize porridge which required much 'stirring' (cf. British Eng.). Obeah and gossip both spread confusion, undervaluing social ties, too individualistic and egalitarian. A modicum of respectability is required.

47 Common terms include *vex, turn beas', fachay, bite up* (all 'angry'); *harrars, geegeeree* (tense); *cosquel* (humiliated); *conta* (glad); *mauvay quality* ('difficult'); *boncretien* (virtuous); *outstandish* (proud); *mauvay labitude* (insolent); *malprop* (ill at ease, awkward); *troconfidence* (candid); *sotte* or *couyant* (silly); *chacal* or *mingy* (mean and stingy); *bruck up* or *cargo* (tired); *bwave* (brave); *guff up, bravo danjay* (put on a brave front); *tenon* (lazy); *beton* (annoying); *touchou* or *tuchous* (touchy); *avar* (greedy); *long eye* (envious); *jalou* (jealous); *bramble* (deceive); *melay* (meddlesome); *congossay* (quarrelsome); *saf* or *lickerish* (greedy, 'like he got a jumbie in he'); *bebe, mamon, mingy, pilling, duncy head* (stupid); *cocksure* (convinced): *doncarcish* (worthless); *bisquankay, discaltay* or *obzocky* (unbalanced, usually but not always physically malformed); *vieux negre, dreevay* or *salop* (worthless); *selfish* (solitary, proud); *caway* (self-indulgent rage); *fedupsy* (bored); *ready made* (alert); *bazody, tie up* (giddy, confused), *ashame* (shamed by others); *feel a how* or *feel bad* (guilty, shamed by self); *ignorant* or *hasty* (ill mannered, quarrelsome); *with I trouble, noah, primprim, social* (pretentious, conceited); *gambage, queff, matador, loud, exantee* (extravagant, showy); *hot up* (restless); *fufuya* (fussy); *bad, pissintail, ordinary, loacho* (vulgar, lazy); *razzy, moxy* (untidy, feckless); *sandymanitee* (without compassion); *lahay* (temporise); *paytay* (hide anger and wait). With the exception of 'candid', all my standard English glosses are used by villagers although a conversation in English rather than Creole is likely to use a number of Creole expressions of this type; many are socially contextual, moral and behavioural as well as 'internalised' personality traits or mental states (to use our etic assumptions) and this appears to be implicit in the continued preference for Creole psychological terms, such as *tabanka*, which are specific to social relations. See Ottley C. R. Creole talk of Trinidad and Tobago, publisher not stated, 1966; Mendes J. *Cote Ce Cote la*. Syncreator, Trinidad, 1985.

48 Taking the usual psychiatric descriptions of neuroses such as anxiety states, phobias or obsessions, many villagers described equivalent but unnamed experiences: (a) 'I have a fear something going to happen. It stupid but I keep going back to the house: someone go and thief ... I don't know who. I nervous for true! Everything make me jump. They say (my) goitre get me worse or maybe my age.' (b) 'It odd you ask that! I was like that. Some years ago I never leave the house. I stay in house with 1 child, with 9 children. I suppose it get like a habit 'cepting I nervous. I got so I too anxious to go to the shop (50 yards away). If anyone strange come I don't know how to behave.' During this period her husband was away from home and consistently unfaithful, and she herself received sexual invitations which she did not accept, although she was tempted. Most instances of nerves mashup in the village involve respectable women, usually in a conflict about personal autonomy.

Horwitz (see Ref. (2)) notes that psychiatric hospital admissions in

Jamaica are associated with previous violence in the working class, with 'depression' in the middle class.

49 'Books', like *science* and *study*, may connote sorcery. The Indian Trinidadian novelist Naipul V. S. has mocked the notion of studiation madness with its implied hopelessness in competing with Europeans (e.g. *The Overcrowded Barraccon*. Deutsch, London. 1972). (Studiation madness recalls the *brain-fag syndrome* described in West African students.) The late Prime Minister of Trinidad, Eric Williams, an ex-Oxford scholar, was frequently cited as an instance of studiation madness (Ramdeen B. Somebody must be mad. *Trinidadian Express* 3 July, 1981; The Enemy, Was Dr Williams Mental? *The Bomb* 1 May, 1981). So sensitive was the Cabinet on this issue that my work permit to go to Trinidad was delayed for 7 months (or so I was informed by an official in the Ministry of Health). The former political rival of 'The Doc' was known as the Mad Scientist.

50 Which also denotes, with conscious irony, the opposite of tabanka, sexual intercourse.

51 Littlewood R. An indigenous conceptualisation of reactive depression in Trinidad. *Psychol. Med.* 15, 278–281, 1985. See Chapter 7.

52 Some villagers suggest intermediate stages *toutoubay* and *foufourou* but others maintain these merely mean doltish in love (*amour fou*).

53 *Bacchanal* – a term for fêting and also general mayhem and confusion. I have previously outlined associations between individual and social 'symbolic inversion' (Littlewood R. The individual articulation of shared symbols. See Chapter 3). See also Scheff T. *Catharsis in Healing, Ritual and Drama*. California University Press, Berkeley, Calif., 1979.

54 Douglas M. *Natural Symbols: Explorations in Cosmology*. Harmondsworth, Penguin, 1973.

55 Nunez P. We do have a Carnival Mentality. *Sunday Guardian*, Port of Spain, 3 July 1981; Therapy à la Beaubrun. *Sunday Guardian*, 1 March 1981; not to mention visiting European psychologists (Gillan P. Carnal Carnival. *Forum* 55–62, June 1984). For an account of Carnival as a national institution see Hill E. *The Trinidad Carnival: Mandate for a National Theatre*. University of Texas Press, Austin, Tex., 1972.

56 Naipul, as one might have expected is less enthusiastic. He compares Trinidadian society as a whole to Carnival, a masquerade directed against 'phantom enemies', metaphor rather than catharsis. He points out that Carnival in 1805 and 1970 was followed by anti-White political activity: 'after the masquerade and the music, anger and terror' (49, p. 267). Naipul traces a continuity from the slaves' Kingdoms of the Night with their secret regiments, uniforms, ranks and titles though Carnival to Black power, 'the carnival lunacy of a lively well-informed society which feels itself part of the world, but understands at the same time that it is cut off from this world by reasons of geography, history and race ... Black power in these black islands is protest. But there is no enemy. The enemy is the past of slavery and colonial neglect and a society uneducated from top to bottom' (p. 271). Offering a less jaundiced perspective (and one which illustrates the use of *mad* and *bad* (= Creole)) Mighty Sparrow sang in the calypso *Trinidad Carnival:*

The biggest bacchanal
Is in Trinidad Carnival

All you got to do when the music play
Take you' man an' break away
Regardless of colour creed or race
Jump up and shake you' waist
This is the spirit of Carnival
It is a Creole bacchanal
So jump as you mad this is Trinidad
We don' care who say we bad.

57 Or *vees* (Creole, as Fr).

58 *Mamapoule* (= mother hen) is also used to refer to the *doltish*, the weak
    or non-assertive. *Zamis* is locally derived from 'friends' (*des amies*) but it
    may be cognate with Haitian *zemi* ('twins', 'two of a kind') itself cognate
    with *jumbie* or *duppy* (spirit). Zamis are also known as *cocks* because
    their *pims* stand up during intercourse like a cock's comb.

59 Between ego and parent, child, sibling, grandparent, grandchild (or cousin,
    uncle or aunt to a lesser extent). Incest has no particular local name and
    was reported for only 1 family (Suzanne, see text).

60 What I have called 'witch-like transformations' (*lagahoos, soucouyants*)
    and forest spirits (*dwens*, the *jabless* (who does seduce), *papabois*) are
    regarded by most villagers as pure 'folk-lore', not real entities, in contrast
    to a universal belief in obeah. I was inclined to put gumboglissays (*glisser*,
    slide; *gumbo*, slippery vegetable stew) into the same category until the
    story of Picklocket (see Ref. (63)).

61 It is felt that villagers with homosexual inclinations would go to Port of
    Spain where mamapoules are accepted, and indeed some there do dress as
    women. Both mamapoules and zamis are distinct from the mythical
    maphrodite, the woman whom a man takes to bed after marriage without
    having had sex with her, only to discover she is really a man. The 'model'
    of a homosexual is however 'inter-sexual' – he or she may be called *shim*
    ('she–him'). A related one is the weak use of *doltish* (or the synonyms
    moumou, mamapoule, half-rise, cunamunou) to mean stupid, weak and
    thus by extension a male homosexual – a *manicou man*.

62 Recalling the 19th century psychiatric theory of 'degeneration'. A blight
    can also be caused by brushing under the branches of a pigeon peas tree;
    but both this sort of blight, that from maljo and, to a lesser extent, blight
    from others, obeah, can be treated with a *bush bath*.

63 See the cases of Samuel and Augustin (pages 90–92). The tale which may
    be called the 'mythic charter' (Malinowski) for the current state of the
    Village contains a similar theme of nemesis. Forty years ago a White
    Creole family of French origin, settled for some time in Pinnacle, were the
    owners of the principal shop. The uncle of the shopkeeper was the
    Catholic priest, Father Bastian, who, using *science* induced the villagers
    to shop with his nephew. By *trusting* on credit the nephew involved the
    community in such debts as to force them to sell land to him or to leave it
    to the Church. The last member of the family died childless and no
    Whites have lived along the coast since then. The Bastian graves, fenced
    off and ornate with wrought iron, remain uniquely neglected on All
    Saints' Day when the Villagers carry candles up to the graves in the
    cemetery which overlooks Pinnacle river. The Bastian land and shop
    passed onto the hands of a Chinese from Sangre Grande (the nearest
    town), whose daughter fell in love with a local villager who served in the
    shop. This assistant, visited the Bastian graves, learned science and

became a gomboglissay, a type of dematerialised Peeping Tom who, as his nickname Picklocket suggests, was able to squeeze through key holes. In a failed conjuration, an enraged spirit he had summoned set fire to the store which burnt down. The Chinese family and Picklocket escaped, although badly burnt, and they left the village. He is now rumoured to be mad. The shell of the store, incinerated some 20 years, remains in the centre of the village, overgrown with bush and avoided even by the more worthless marauding children. The agricultural land near the houses stayed in the hands of the Church and another Chinese who seldom comes to visit. The villagers' own remaining land is so far distant that it is no longer economically viable to work and ambitious young men must leave their families to seek work elsewhere.

64 As in Jamaica (2, p. 45) or elsewhere, family members are less prepared to perceive madness than are others.

65 *Ron* (rum) has been distilled in Trinidad from molasses since the Spanish occupation (Barty-King H. and Massel A. *Rum*. Heinemann, London, 1983). The English word 'rum' is of uncertain 16th century origin, possibly from *rumbullion* (cognate with 'rumbustuous'). For the history of rum in Trinidad see Yawney C. Drinking patterns and alcoholism among East Indians and Negroes in Trinidad. MA thesis, McGill University, 1968; Angrosino M. V. Outside is death: alcoholism, ideology and community organisation among the East Indians of Trinidad. Ph.D. thesis, University of North Carolina, 1972.

66 In the course of general *liming* (gossiping and sitting about) around the village and assisting in fishing and agricultural work I was drinking about a third of a bottle a day.

67 A respectable woman 'have she man train'; she stops him spending too much time in the rum shop. An older woman who is outgoing and confident may have a quick shot of rum whilst engaging in bantering picong with the liming men around the rum shop but she has to be invited. The outrage occasioned by female emigrants returning for a holiday in Pinnacle from the United States is partly due to their 'loud ways', make-up and pants but principally to their going to the rum shop and airily purchasing a round of drinks.

68 Have another drink doudou. Have another drink you go feel all right. And remember we go home tonight. (Calypso cited in Warner K. *The Trinidad Calypso*, p. 96. Heinemann, London, 1982.)

69 cf. Helman C. Tonic, fuel and food: social and symbolic aspects of the long-term use of psychotropic drugs. *Soc. Sci. Med.* **15**, 521–533, 1981.

70 Thus the calypso *Rum and Coco Cola* (Lord Invader) was a symbol of North American influence (68, p. 22). In Pinnacle rum is sometimes drunk with coconut water 'because it ai' a sweet thing' but the theories about alcohol do not obviously relate to those about *sugar* (diabetes) Another locally recognised dangerous drink is *bay rum*, usually used for hairdressing or as an external *heating* embrocation; to drink it is equivalent to drinking methylated spirits in Britain.

71 By the 17th century rum was recognized as *hot* by the Europeans, necessary for cold-blooded English who 'find a debility' when in the tropics (Ligan *A True and Exact History of the Island of Barbados 1641–1650*, cited in Barty-King H. and Massel A. (65, p. 18)). In local terms, as with the classification of madness as hot, to say Africans are hot and Europeans are cold, is not to slot ethnicity simply into the hot–cold

system (see pages 84, 96). I myself, as a white, was constantly warned of the dangers of taking a cold dip in the early morning when heated with sleep, or of too much studiation.

72 But see Ref. (71) above.

73 The taxonomy of cannabis is variable but the plants in Trinidad correspond to the *sativa* rather than the *indica* type (Schuttles R. E., Klein W. M., Plowman T. and Lockwood T. E. Cannabis: an example of taxonomic neglect. In *Cannabis and Culture* (Edited by Rubin V.), Mouton, The Hague, 1975).

74 Also called *reefer*. Herskovits (16) working near Pinnacle in the 1930s does not mention it, whilst Simpson (11) quotes Williams R. O. *The Useful and Ornamental Plants in Trinidad and Tobago* (Port of Spain, 1951, p. 104) to suggest its 'intoxicating, narcotic effect' was generally well known and that cultivation was made illegal in the twenties. Rubin V. and Comitas L. (*Ganja in Jamaica*. Chaps 1 and 2. Mouton, The Hague, 1975) review the evidence and conclude that, whilst cannabis had been grown for hemp in the Americas since the 16th century, its psychoactive use could be dated in Jamaica to the 19th century Asian indentured labourers: '*ganja*' is a Hindi word. Its history in Trinidad is likely to be similar, but the smoking of ganja rather than its use as bush tea by Trinidadian Africans may be as recent as the immediate prewar period. The spread of Ras Tafari into Trinidad in the 1970s probably hastened its appeal to young working class men. The 5 village 'Rastas' perhaps identify less with the Jamaican (and hence despised) ideology than with everyday working-class male life. They cut their locks to get a job, attend the church, go fishing with the others and are not so very distinctive from other young men. Like Rastas in Jamaica they cite Biblical (and hence 'African') texts for its consumption in antiquity (Comitas L. The social nexus of ganja in Jamaica. In Rubin V. (Ed.)).

75 Jamaica where ganja is more institutionalised (Rubin V. The 'ganja' vision in Jamaica. In *Cannabis and Culture*, Ed. Rubin. Mouton, The Hague, 1975) and where ganja and rum may be used simultaneously in certain sects (Ref. (11, p. 185)).

76 Jamaica (see Ref. (75)).

77 *Kickapoo* (from the American cartoon Lil'Abner which is syndicated to a Trinidad newspaper). Datura is recognised by villagers as particularly likely to send you mad. As *jimson weed* it has been used periodically as a hallucinogen in the United States and its use was probably imported to Trinidad in the 1950s (Nehaul B. B. G. Datura poisoning in British Guiana. *West Ind. med. J.* 4, 57–67, 1955: Irvine R. A. and Tang K. Datura poisoning. *West Ind. med. J.* 6, 126–128, 1957). In Port of Spain the St Ann's patients sometimes sell their tranquillisers to optimists hoping to *build a head*.

78 Yawney C. Strictly Ital: Rastafari livity and holistic health. Manuscript in press; Schaeffer J. The significance of marihuana in a small agricultural community in Jamaica. In *Cannabis and Culture* (Edited by Rubin V.). Mouton. The Hague, 1975.

79 In practice they worked less than other villagers but, given their social position at the bottom of the respectability scale, and their relative lack of family resources, this cannot be taken as evidence of the 'amotivational syndrome'.

80 Littlewood R. The imitation of madness: the influence of psychopathology upon culture *Soc Sci. Med*. See Chapter 8.

81 The use and sale of ganja in Pinnacle is more complex and widespread than I have outlined here but it is illegal and it would be inappropriate to discuss its ramifications in greater detail.

82 Beaubrun M. H. Treatment of alcoholism in Trinidad and Tobago. *Br. J. Psychiat.* **113**, 643–658, 1967.

83 Lloyd A. J. *Alcoholism and Its Treatment in Trinidad.* Clark Institute of Psychiatry, Toronto, 1967.

84 As reflected in participants in Alcoholics Anonymous, many of whom are upwardly socially mobile Asians as contrasted to middle-class Creoles. Asians are more likely to be total abstainers, especially those who belong to the Presbyterian Church. Creoles are usually Catholics or Anglicans.

85 Beaubrun M. The diagnosis and management of acute psychotic reactions due to alcohol and drugs. *West Ind. Med. J.* **36**, 1–11, 1975; Spencer D. J. Cannabis induced psychosis. *West Ind. med. J.* **19**, 228–230, 1970. Beaubrun and Knight (Psychiatric assessment of 30 chronic users of cannabis. *Am. J. Psychiat.* **130**, 309–311, 1973) find little evidence of the amotivational syndrome in Jamaica, nor do Rubin and Comitas. Compare Gerard de Nerval's account in *Voyage en Orient* (Translated as *Journey to the Orient*), p. 103. Haag, London, 1984.

86 Carstairs G. M. Daru and Bhang: cultural factors in the choice of intoxicant. *Q. J. Stud. Alc.* **15**, 220–237, 1954.

87 Beaubrun M. Cannabis or alcohol: the Jamaican experience. In *Cannabis and Culture* (Edited by Rubin V.). Mouton, The Hague, 1975. Asian attitudes to alcohol have been described by Yawney (65) as 'ambivalent'. By contrast nearly all Creoles drink at some time and their use of alcohol is, as we have seen, not individualistic but firmly rooted in social action. It is commonly said in Trinidad that the higher rates of domestic homicide in Indians are due to their 'uncontrolled' drinking pattern.

88 If the Trinidadian survives as 'circumstance-orientated', pragmatic, flexible and *according*, then *tabanka* and *vice* each represent a fixed and rigid dependence on one or other pole of the *respectability* (White) reputation (Black) dichotomy. Whilst I would follow Austin in understanding such local everyday knowledge as a legitimation of class inequalities, it is evident that I agree with Wilson that they contain a potential for an active reassertion of Creole identity: they are not simply ascribed understandings but represent correctly the experiential and historical context.

7 An Indigenous Conceptualization of Reactive Depression in Trinidad*

Indigenous Conceptualizations of Depression

Although a variety of studies have now demonstrated that the depressive symptoms described in the West are found throughout the world (Singer, 1975), the universality of 'depression' remains a controversial issue (Kleinman, 1977). The term refers us simultaneously to certain symptoms recognized as depressive, a discrete syndrome, and to a putative psychological state. In developing countries 'depression' is seldom described locally, either as a syndrome or as a mental state. This may be because depressive states lack the exotic salience so characteristic of the 'culture-bound syndromes' which have monopolized the interest of psychiatrists, and thus have not appeared to justify psychiatric concern (Littlewood & Lipsedge, 1985). In addition, international comparisons have tended to be based on the symptoms characteristic of the industrialized West (supposedly 'culture-free') and may therefore have missed both patterns of behaviour and beliefs which are more firmly embedded in cultural values than are the symptomatic psychoses. If, as Kleinman (1977) suggests, the dominant explanatory model of comparative psychiatry has been that of a 'real' biological disease surrounded by a series of cultural encrustations, its theorists will find it inappropriate to emphasize indigenous folk models of psychopathology.

At the same time, it does appear likely that the small-scale tribal communities traditionally studied under the rubric of 'transcultural psychiatry' have seldom chosen to select out, label and amplify depressive reactions for social purposes (Fabrega, 1974). While depressive reactions locally identified (*hiwa-itck*,** *wacinko*, *tawatl* and *ye sni*) have occasionally been described among North American Indian communities (Lewis, 1975; Shore & Manson, 1983), the presence of a discrete state of 'anomic depression' has also been noted which is only

---

* First published in *Psychological Medicine* (1985); there is some overlap with chapter 6.
**Local idiom is italicized to distinguish it from international English. I have retained the rather objectionable orthography of published calypsos.

partly glossed by the local term *syn 'wan* [spirit intrusion] (Jilek, 1982; Klausner & Foulks, 1982). A similar pattern among Australian Aborigines (Eastwell, 1982) is also not locally remarked. As Waxler (1977) has suggested, depressive experiences in the Third World receive little local attention or specific treatment.

Why should this be? Earlier notions of 'primitive mentality' can now be discounted: social anthropologists have rejected the idea that cultures differ by their psychological *abilities* in favour of one in which they differ through their *vehicles* of thought – conceptual systems and classifications of space and time, the sexes and the natural world, which are encoded in systems of symbols, notably language, and which 'lie outside the boundaries of the individual organism as such, in that intersubjective world of common understandings into which all human individuals are born, in which they pursue their separate careers, and which they leave persisting behind them after they die' (Geertz, 1966).

The recognition of depression as a separate entity probably entails an indigenous popular psychology with the postulation and differentiation of mental states (Leff, 1981) and particular notions of personhood and personal attribution (Marsella & White, 1983). Murphy (1978) suggests that during the seventeenth century in Britain, the first industrialized country, the predominantly somatic notion of melancholia was replaced by the psychological one of depression. He associates the change with the development of Protestant concepts of guilt, new child-rearing practices, increased geographical mobility and elective economic individualism (Murphy, 1982). The continuing primacy given to introspective psychology is exemplified by the clinical tendency to talk of individual patients' *somarization* of a pattern of depressive illness which is 'really' psychological, a tendency which curiously coexists with assumptions that depression has a biological aetiology. Psychological descriptions are regarded as more mature, and failure to employ them by the patient results in a clinical failure to diagnose depression (Littlewood & Lipsedge, 1982; Katon *et al.* 1982). To generalize, there seems to be a tendency for industrialized societies with social mobility and a pluralistic ideology to develop more individualized notions, including the postulation of internal mental states (Harré, 1983). A psychological rather than a somatic lexicon is not essential, and the culturally homogeneous small-scale societies typically studied by anthropologists may articulate quite complex interpersonal relations through shared moral imperatives (Howell, 1981).

Local psychologies and nosologies are ideologies, not facts of nature. 'Culture does considerably more than shape illness as an experience; it shapes the very way we conceive of illness' (Kleinman, 1974). Local conceptualizations are not more or less accurate stabs at empirical reality, but are patterns of belief embedded in society which serve to explain and thus legitimate that society (Good & Good, 1983). To an extent, that is true of Western biomedicine, and we now know that many of the classic culture-bound syndromes are less discrete entities, located 'out there' independent of the professional observer, than the products of Western political influence or artefacts of the psychiatric approach (Littlewood & Lipsedge, 1985). Thus, rather than examining direct psychological and social influences on the individual *per se* in an attempt to explain differential patterns of depression, we should start with the context of indigenous conceptualizations of psychopathology (Kleinman, 1977).

We may expect to find locally identified psychological descriptions of depression in the Third World in those societies whose history and social relations are 'Western' – individualistic, flexible and in which personal identity is orientated to circumstances rather than to shared and relatively collective notions of group values or to kinship.

Trinidad

The Caribbean island of Trinidad lies in the Orinoco delta a few miles from Venezuela. Colonized by the Spanish until its capture by the British in 1797, it was largely ignored by Spain but a few French planters settled with their slaves to grow sugar in the lower areas to the west along the Caroni River. Apart from some sense of French cultural identity, Trinidad's history is typical of the English-speaking Caribbean: the development of sugar plantations; the emancipation of the slaves followed by indentured immigration from India in the latter part of the nineteenth century; the collapse of the price of cane sugar, economic stagnation and Imperial neglect; increasing local participation in government and the establishment of trade unions, culminating in internal self-government. The governing party is pro-Western and social democratic, and has maintained power through parliamentary elections since independence in 1962. Approximately half the population are of Asian descent, while those of African ancestry include a substantial minority of Venezuelan origin. Virtually the whole population speaks English, but older villagers may also speak Spanish or French Creole, and the local English is peppered with Creole idiom.

Tabanka

Tabanka occurs 'when you wife left and you take it on, keep study it'. It particularly affects a working-class man when his wife deserts him and goes to live with another man. It is said to be most common among those formally married in church and among the *tibourgs* (petits bourgeoisie), nurses and teachers, and *békés negres* [black whites] who aspire to white and middle-class values and life-style. While symptoms include a 'heavy heart' (lassitude, anorexia, stomach contractions, insomnia and a loss of interest in work or social life), the *tabanked* male is characterized by wandering about or remaining alone at home, feeling worthless and continually turning over in his mind angry thoughts of the faithless one; this behaviour is known locally as *grinding*.

'They don' do anything to pass off studiation, they drink, they smoke, they ain' eat, often they ain' coming home. They concentrate on how they was before. You broken down; it does take an effect on you' body also; from brain to body; according as the brain function the body deteriorate to an extent; you not eating, you not drinking, you not sleeping, everywhere you turn your thinking.' Tabanka is caused not just by the act of leaving, but by the victim's mental state: 'Once you take it on you get Tabanka. If you don' take it on you ain' get Tabanka.'

The vegetative symptoms of Tabanka are recognized in a lesser degree as part of the fluctuation of everyday mood (sometimes, but not often, called *depression*), unlike Tabanka which is a discrete state with specific consequences. *Tabanka* is sometimes used to refer to bereavement or other losses, but it is then regarded as less severe and is only used with the primary sense – sexual desertion – in mind: 'Love is the first thing. It must damage your love. If someone rob your house you don' take it on so much.'

The consequences of Tabanka can include death from accidents while drunk and the loss of work: 'You drink to keep off studies. It act on the brain: you drink it out, you cast it out, you taking away thoughts.' If unresolved it can lead to murder or suicide: 'It happen to nearly every man in Trinidad. You hear man poison self? It Tabanka. A man hang on tree? It Tabanka.'

While not regarded as an illness itself, Tabanka can progress to chronic insanity [*folie*] and country people believe that there is a special ward for victims in the psychiatric hospital in the capital. 'It have this boy die through grief. He die in mental. He quiet, you take food into the house an' he throw it away.' Another villager, a chronic schizophrenic, had been 'mad once but that wear out from him, then the girl leave him an' he get crazy again'.

Tabanka only occurs when a sexual and economic relationship has been established between a man and a woman. It is thus distinct from *lovestruckness* [*amour fou*], the pursuit of a hopeless and unconsummated attachment. It is particularly severe if the couple have been church married rather than just living together, because of the economic as well as the emotional investment involved. 'If it you' girlfriend you shrug it off – in three days you halfway to a next! ... He love his wife, he have all his trust in she, he give she all his money and she go an' leave him an' he remain blank; you love you' love and you love you' money. It come double degrees!' Another male informant said 'It ain' the loss of her, but what you've given her.' The majority of the male population over the age of forty admit to having been *tabanked* at some time, but few women say they have experienced it and less than 10% of them are considered locally to have been *tabanked*.

Women are rather contemptuous of men with Tabanka: 'Men take it on so! They tell you leave but, if you does, they craziness itself!' Even men admit that Tabanka is a sign of personal weakness. 'Some don' get it because they have a strong heart. It all depends on personal feelings. You shouldn't get Tabanka. However you take it, someday you and that person got to part, so why the harass?' Women pride themselves on being less likely to experience Tabanka, for both sexes regard women as being made of sterner stuff. Men suggest that, as breadwinners, they are more vulnerable: 'You studying your two ends meet an' your wife not studying ... Women more on a side. They can take a love here and take another tomorrow. Men find it more difficult. If women get Tabanka they recover themselves faster.'

The expression of Tabanka is necessarily private, for its public recognition is the opportunity for barbed jests and humiliation. The very mention of the concept is greeted by men and women alike with mirth, if not derision. Unless Tabanka leads to other difficulties, treatment consists in the victim being encouraged by other men, usually a few close friends, to turn his mind to other interests. They counsel self-control, to forget the faithless one, and not to attempt to retrieve the situation or seek revenge, but to make fresh attachments. The power of Tabanka lies not in its contravention of acceptable normal behaviour (indeed, it is almost regarded as inevitable) but in the infatuation of the deserted man. All men appear equally vulnerable and the reaction is situation specific.

The symptoms of Tabanka are those of reactive depression and it appears to be an example of what is probably the universal sadness and anger which follows the loss of a spouse. Why is it selected out and perhaps amplified by working-class Trinidadians for remark compared with their relative lack of interest in other possible depressive reactions? My interpretation emphasizes two issues: male/female relations, and the amusement which the notion of Tabanka provokes.

Relations Between Men and Women

Trinidadian working-class life is characterised by widespread movement about the country for work. While land provides food, cash wages are required for clothes, building materials and luxuries, but paid employment is variable. Traditionally, there was only plantation, estate and government road work; recently, the exploitation of oil has allowed the development of heavy industry and most 'local' foodstuffs are now imported from other islands. Working-class values have been described as 'circumstance-orientated': flexible and individualistic, not bound by close kin ties but by a web of bilateral individual relationships (Rodman, 1971). Individuals do not find their primary identity through kin roles, which are fluid and elastic. Local ideology is fiercely egalitarian, and upward social mobility is scorned by men. Wilson (1973) describes these values by a local expression – 'crab antics'; as crabs try to climb out of a crab barrel they are pulled down by others. This, particularly male, ideology is articulated by an extensive local repertoire of *picong* [satire], represented nationally in the calypso (Warner, 1982; Abrahams, 1983).

Women have little opportunity for employment, apart from selling crops locally or performing domestic work in the town. Access to money is primarily through sexual relations with men. *Church marriage* is regarded as the seal to a successful period of cohabitation or *living* which develops from *friending* (a sexual relationship with the partners living separately). *Marriage* or *living* involve the husband in providing for the woman, while in *friending* 'You is not responsible for her, you only jus'' come and frequent her and what you have you give her.' To set up a household, even *living*, is a measure of economic success and potential danger among the poor. House and land are typically owned by one party and each keeps a separate income; spouses regularly lend money to each other, often with interest. Marital relationships are mutually respectful but guarded; as the Creole proverb says, '*Mari teni dents*' [Marriage has teeth]. Both sexes accept that by church marriage a woman gains more than the man; typically, she gains the title of 'Mistress' and stops any paid work outside the home.

Wilson (1973) and Austin (1979) have described West Indian society as orientated to two opposed ideals: the working-class male-orientated egalitarian *reputation* is contrasted with *respectability*, associated with church marriage, middle-class white values, education, hierarchy and chastity, which is represented most typically in women. *Reputation* is represented by the footloose 'circumstance-orientated' man theoretically pursuing comparatively indiscriminate sexual adventures. As the calypsonian Sparrow sings (Warner, 1982):

Because a woman is a woman for me
Ah don't care how she ugly and obzocky
I'm a busy man wid no time to lose
Ah don't pass my hand, ah don't pick and choose
So any kind o' woman, one foot or one hand
Dey cannot escape from me, Mr. Rake-and-Scrape.

Wilson and Austin suggest that respectability is the principle of social stratification reflecting the colonial and post-colonial society with its close relationship of class and colour, while reputation is the response to this, an affirmation of ascribed working-class and black values. Both sexes move towards respectability as they get older, as they get richer, or as they marry lighter-skinned mates. Respectability is precarious, always dependent on income: 'The higher a monkey climb the more he expose himself.' To adopt the outward signs of respectability (frequent church attendance, 'good English', or an affection of social superiority) too soon, or without possessing a reliable income, is to be considered pretentious. Marriage for the man is to move away from 'circumstance-orientated' reputation towards *tibourg* respectability, and its economic obligations are assumed half-reluctantly: 'why must I buy a cow when I know how to get milk free?'

Moving around the country for work may result in the man with a reasonable income establishing a second household of an *outside wife* and her children. If he manages it discreetly, avoiding *comess* [scandal], and adequately supports all his children, a man's reputation can be enhanced with little cost to his respectability. Men are expected to provide for their children, even if the mother is *friending* or *living* with another man. An unmarried man who supports another man's children is ridiculed, and a child's physiognomy is carefully scrutinized, assisted by a complex local classification of 'colour':

An Indian couple up Belmont
Make a white baby I'm sure you heard the stunt
What a loving father
He said his wife was drinking milk of magnesia
(Mighty Dictator quoted in Rodman, 1971).

A woman is expected to be sexually faithful to the man who is giving her money if they are *living* or *married*. The possibility that she is not is a constant preoccupation of men: 'There's more in the mortar beside the pestle.' It is not acceptable for a *married* or *living* woman to have other partners, and a man is not recognized as becoming truly tabanked in a *friending* relationship, unlike marriage. In all cases, then, sexual access is exchanged for cash. From the man's point of view:

Not another cent you wouldn't get until you hand up
I'm a big big man and dis thing must stop
(Mighty Sparrow quoted in Warner, 1982).

So, in Tabanka, a man has no reputation and no respectability, having failed to recognize his own ultimate interests and to control his life. An older man who accepts the infidelity of his wife is despised as irreversibly *doltish* (mentally handicapped or senile). In contrast, Tabanka is a mistake which can be successfully transcended by a reaffirmation of the individualistic ideal. A woman is less likely to be tabanked for she has not sacrificed her reputation to attain a precarious respectability and, by common consent, she can only expect to be provided for: only the most worthless of males fails to support his children and she is regarded as well rid of such a man.

The Humour of Tabanka

The very mention of Tabanka is greeted with laughter in a wide variety of social settings: personal and private, between the sexes, among men, and among women themselves. Although unsuitable for jokes between sexual partners or between adults and children, it is not context dependent. Its humour lies in its theme.

Douglas (1968) has extended Freud's notion of wit as an arbitrary order that allows a freeing of otherwise restrained motives to suggest that jokes 'attack classification and hierarchy'. Like *picong* and calypso, Tabanka express the ideals of an egalitarian community with non-hierarchical and 'circumstance-orientated' social relationships. The notion of Tabanka, the inappropriate psychological response to desertion, is working-class, while the notion of *adultery*, the moral conceptualization of the act of desertion itself, is restricted to respectable settings such as the church. The humour of Tabanka lies, not in a criticism of white middle-class notions of church marriage and fidelity, but in surface adherence to their forms when they are not economically justified. Tabanka mocks the masquerade of respectable ideals and reaffirms the tyranny of individual physiology and accident in the face of unsuccessful attempts at rigid social structures which are no longer according to circumstances.

CONCLUSION

Tabanka thus reinforces communal values but it is also functional for the individual in diverting his attention from an irreversible loss to fresh attachments: 'Everyday is fishing day, not every day is catching day.' While a violent attempt at redressing the situation is regarded as understandable, it is not sanctioned. The higher rate of domestic homicide among Trinidadian Asians is probably related to a less developed notion of the absurdity of Tabanka than among Afro-Caribbeans.

Similarly, among the Spanish-speaking peasantry of the north coast with close-knit family groups based on small cocoa and coffee estates, and who have early church marriage, marital infidelity is believed to result in frequent homicide. The absurdity of Tabanka is clearly distinct from Hispanic notions of 'honour and shame', and is more congenial to Anglo-Saxon and Afro-Caribbean values, to an ethos of psychological pragmatism rather than an absolute one of morality.

The vegetative symptoms of Tabanka, although context-specific, are identical with those of classic depression and, as in other psychological theories, are regarded as secondary to an internal mental state. If Tabanka offers Afro-Caribbeans a psychological model for depression which the Asian Trinidadian community has developed less, we might expect that Afro-Caribbean Trinidadians are more likely to be hospitalized with endogenous depression and more likely to demonstrate personal guilt, as Burke (1974) and Rubin (1959) have shown.

8   The Imitation of Madness:
The Influence of Psychopathology
Upon Culture*

We have, I think, reason to believe that the person who has
attained perfection of balance in the control of his instinctive
tendencies, in whom the processes of suppression and sublimation
have become wholly effective, may thereby become completely
adapted to his environment and attain a highly peaceful and stable
existence. Such existence is not, however, the condition of excep-
tional accomplishment, for which there would seem to be necessary a certain degree of instability. I believe that we may look to
this instability as the source of energy from which we may expect
great accomplishments in art and science. It may be also that,
through this instability, new strength will be given to those
movements which under the most varied guise express the deep
craving for religion which seems to be universal among Mankind.
W. H. R. Rivers, *Instinct and the Unconscious*, p. 158. Cambridge
University Press, Cambridge, 1920.

Introduction

Innovators and leaders of new political and religious movements are
frequently dismissed as mad, particularly when their innovations are
unacceptable or based on premises at odds with those of their critics.
To denigrate them as mad is to deny them rationality. It is to mock
their followers, for only the credulous and simple-minded could take
madmen seriously.

The use of 'mad' or 'crazy' or their equivalents to imply unre-
strained or unreasonable actions is of course common to most,
perhaps all, societies. For a journalist to describe a community torn
between two options as 'schizophrenic' may be a metaphor more
currently fashionable than 'the horns of a dilemma'. The journalist

* First published in *Social Science and Medicine* (1984)

may permit himself further licence: for the Caribbean to seek identity with the Third World is 'madness', whilst the former Prime Minister of Grenada (who was famed for his speeches to the United Nations on the subject of flying saucers) may be characterised as 'a street-corner eccentric, a mystical maniac'.(1) To explain the origins of war as the conspiracy of a mad dictator may be a commonplace conceit but how seriously are we to take the ethnographer who suggests that Hitler had a 'hysterical phobia, conversion symptoms and classical paranoia' and that St Paul, 'another vatic with inchoate ego boundaries' was epileptic, or the psychologist who confidently asserts that Tiberius and Calvin were schizophrenics, and Stalin 'a paranoic'? (2)

The idiom of disease is a powerful political metaphor (3) and we take it as such when the journalist tells us that doctrine of the Peoples' Temple in Guyana (Jonestown) was 'infected with disease'.(4) It is perhaps a metaphor when Kroeber calls magic 'the pathology of culture' or La Barre dismisses snake-handling sects as 'zany' or 'crazy'. (5) But when ethnographers explain shamanism as the very specific consequence of 'epilepsy, hysteria, fear neurosis (and) veritable idiocy' (6) or the psychoanalyst characterises the shaman as psychotic and his religion as 'organised schizophrenia',(7) one may be permitted to wonder as to the explanatory value of such designifications. The Hebrews attempted to discredit their more embarrassing prophets by suggesting they were insane (8) and the anthropologist who talks of the 'authentic schizoid component' of the members of the cult he is studying is clearly not a potential recruit.(9)

Since the aftermath of the French Revolution (which was regarded by some doctors as a veritable epidemic whilst others dwelt on the psychopathology of the hereditary monarchs (10)), the medical profession has not scrupled to use diagnosis to interpret history. The Professor of Medicine at Makarere University, fleeing Idi Amin, offered this diagnosis of his former President: 'grandiose paranoia, hypomania, probably schizophrenia, hypomanic paranoia, possibly GPI and the Jekyll and Hyde syndrome'.(11) American psychiatrists in a well-publicised report suggested that Senator Barry Goldwater, then a candidate for the Presidency, was mentally unstable, and as a consequence were very nearly sued.(12) In their attempt to understand society and social change, psychiatry and psychoanalysis have formulated interpretations couched primarily in psychopathology: Freud suggested that religion is essentially a codification of individual neuroses, particularly when it took the form of innovation.(13) Whilst sociologists following Durkheim's dictum have (at times) been able to dispense with purely psychological or psychopathological interpretations of existing institutions, they appear to have near universal recourse to them when describing social change, particularly when it takes a dramatic or chiliastic form. It may be that functionalist steady-state theorists of society always have difficulty with the problem of innovation and rely on a psychological idiom which lies outside the social domain and which can initiate the necessary changes.(14) Certainly, when faced with millennial movements, particularly those Linton has characterised as 'nativist',(15) not merely do social scientists frequently describe them in psychological terms, but they appear to regard them as somehow *more psychological* in nature than the social institutions of quieter times: millenial movement are more 'affectively laden' and they operate at 'high intensity'.(1 6) Bryan Wilson, conceptually far removed from the psychoanalytic anthropologists of the United States, nevertheless describes 'affected members ... uttering gibberish (in) outbursts of frenzy' and suggests the social organisation of millenial groups is hampered by their 'affectivity'.(17) Similarly, the 'dancing mania' of Madagascar and the 'Vaihala madness' of Papua are described as 'spontaneous and stimulated frenzy' (18): i.e. they are either pathology or passive manipulation, in either case outside normal psychological and social functioning. The contemporary use of 'charisma' unites the two – the disordered prophet with his suggestible flock.

The visions of millennial leaders have been described by scholars as schizophrenic even when normative for their contemporaries: Hung Hsiu-Chu'an, the leader of the Taiping rebellion; Te Ua, the founder of the Maori Hau Hau.(19) Theory aside, colonial and national authorities have frequently interned chiliastic sectarians in psychiatric hospitals: Ne Loiag, the leader of the 1943 Jonfrum movement in the New Hebrides; Rice Kamanga, founder of the Barotse Twelve Society; Alexander Bedward, the Jamaican revivalist; Leonard Howell, the Rastafarian.(20) In Canada participants in a Doukhobor nude protest were put in the local asylum, as were Jehovah's Witnesses in Germany in the 1930s and Baptists and Pentecostalists in contemporary Russia.(21)

Popular perception of madness leads to official denigration: 'The wider (Jamaican) society associated Rastafarianism with madness' and leaders were 'taken to gaol on sedition or to the asylum for lunacy ... The process of becoming a Rastafarian is still regarded by the wider society as one of mental deterioration and the more modern embrace of the creed by young educated high school and university graduates is seen as an urgent matter for the psychiatrist'.(22)

To employ the idiom of insanity in order to discredit implies the prior recognition of a distinct sphere of psychopathology, one that is characterised by a defect, either a disorder of the individual mind analogous to physical disease or a physical disturbance of the brain itself. The small-scale non-industrialised societies with whom anthropologists have been largely concerned may have such a separate domain of psychopathology, or they may regard what the psychiatrist terms mental illness as the secondary and unnamed consequence of unsuccessful interaction with mystical forces.(23)

The Legitimacy of Madness

There has, of course, been an alternative tradition in the West which, while accepting the existence of a separate domain of psychopathology, nevertheless refuses to denigrate it or divorce it from the possibility of active meaning. This tradition asserts that psychopathology can be both creative and innovative. In any period it seems likely that both positions – the denial of meaning in madness and the affirmation of meaning – are held by some individuals. The first attempt to assert meaning in psychopathology appears to be that of Plato. Whilst he agrees that madness is a 'disease of the body caused by bodily conditions', he is concerned with meaning, not aetiology, and meaning can only be ascribed by reason, coming after the illness or from others: 'We only achieve (prophecy) when the power of our understanding is inhibited by sleep or when we are in an abnormal condition owing to disease or divine inspiration ... It is not the business of any man so long as he is in an irrational state to interpret his own visions and say what good or ill they portend'.(24) In medieval Europe insanity was perceived as a punishment or test, sent by God or the Devil; although in itself it was meaningless as a communication, by rational meditation on it by the healthy part of the mind it could become 'a healing agent of penitence'.(25) At the same time there existed a Christian tradition which placed a positive value on the state of 'folly' itself (including foolishness and insanity) for its intimations of child-like innocence: if the world was rational and thus compromised, then the Incarnation could only have been an act of folly.(26)

The shift in authority from clergy to medicine in the early modern period deprived psychopathology (now totally shorn from its supernatural origins), of any possibility of conventional meaning: it was merely symptomatic of bodily disease. Scot and Bright daringly asserted that the practice of witchcraft was the consequence of *brain disease*. In the eighteenth century Swift and Pope used the presumed physical origin of mental states as the basis for satire: in *The Mechanical Operation of the Spirit* Swift says eloquence is no more than an orgasm without stimulation, and that when the vapours in Louis XIV's head went up he engaged in war, whilst if they descended

Europe was at peace. Like Plato, the Romantics accepted the separate existence of psychopathology but divorced its origin from its potential values as a communication: it was natural and elementary and hence a source of creativity. Madness was akin to genius as it was to the thought of the child or primitive. 'The greater the genius the greater the unsoundness'.(27) So far from the biological aetiology of madness devaluing its products, abnormal mental states, and hence genius, were artificially cultivated; the mentally ill were regarded as additionally advantaged through being placed outside social constraints, and thus resistant to cultural indoctrination.(28) Whilst a few writers like Lamb (in *The Sanity of True Genius*) deplored the necessary equation of madness and genius, the thesis was to grip the poetic and popular imagination into the twentieth century. Nietzsche wrote that 'it seems impossible to be an artist without being diseased' and suggested that in ecstatic madness man gave reign to underlying emotions and participated 'in a higher community ... a collective release of all the symbolic powers'.(29)

In *The Varieties of Religious Experience* William James suggested that the essence of religion lay in the 'pattern setters ... for whom religion exists not as a dull habit but as an acute fever ... (They) frequently have nervous instability'.(30) He quoted with approval the English psychiatrist Henry Maudsley: 'What right have we to believe Nature under any obligation to do her work by means of complete minds only? She may find an incomplete mind a more suitable instrument for a particular purpose'.(31) Whilst James says that religious experience should be measured 'by its fruits' rather than its origin, he clearly prefers pathological religion as more authentic. It is probably Lombroso who is still most closely associated with the equation of madness and genius – 'a system of hereditary degeneration of the epileptoid variety'.(32) If human nature was naturally conservative then change could only be initiated through abnormality, and he distinguished between 'true genius' (of the epileptoid type) aligned with 'the general course of evolutions', and 'pseudogenius' associated with unsuccessful rebellions (33): Francis Galton too, postulated a link between madness and eminence but Havelock Ellis' subsequent report that there was little evidence for the hypothesis has been confirmed generally. A recent suggestion is that it is the relatives of schizophrenics who are more creative than the general population (34) and the common contemporary conclusion by writers on creativity is that whilst creative people may have more 'psychological conflicts' they are unlikely to be insane because they possess 'greater ego strength'.(35)

The two Romantic axioms, the equation of mad, child-like, primitive and archaic, and the idea of the artist-genius as an

unbalanced prophet without honour, formed the European avant-
garde's image of itself: Van Gogh, who experienced epileptic fits and
periodic depression regarded himself as insane: 'For a madman is also
a man to whom society did not want to listen and whom it wanted to
prevent from uttering unbearable truths ... It is a man who has
preferred to go mad in the sense in which society understands the
term, rather than be false to a certain idea of human behaviour'.(36)
What George Lukács has called 'modernism's obsession with pathological and extreme states' was most clearly seen in Surrealism:
Breton's dictum that the surrealist endeavour was 'Dictée de la pensée
en l'absence de toute controle' (37) returned the artist or poet to the
untrammelled primitive core of creativity; the models were the mad,
the eccentric, the mediums, the cranks, inventors and self-publishers.
Antonin Artaud observed that 'Delirium is as legitimate, as logical, as
any other succession of human ideas or acts'.(38)

The 'anti-psychiatry' movement in Europe and the United States in
the nineteen-sixties and seventies similarly decided that 'the boundary
between sanity and madness is a false one'.(39) In the writing of R. D.
Laing we can note a movement from victimology (the psychotic is
formed by a process of social labelling) to one in which he is a hero, the
artist who can offer a privileged critique of social reason. The
counter-culture however failed to establish a situation in which
psychopathology could be perceived as a meaningful everyday communication. Mark Vonnegut's autobiography 'The Eden Express' describes how the hippie commune in which he lived proved unable to
cope with his episode of schizophrenia.(40) After a good deal of debate
they took him to the local mental hospital for treatment.

The main anthropological contribution to the question of whether
psychopathology can offer a meaningful communication has come
from those anthropologists who were influenced by psychoanalysis.
For Freud culture was a product of instinctual strivings and social
demands, a dynamic conflict whose resolution could include social
integration in the form of instinctual sublimation or individual
psychopathology. Health was a balance between instinctual strivings
and social restraints; if culture was a product of individual conflicts
writ large, cultural innovation was only possible through such an
individual conflict. As Roheim, the ethnographer who most closely
adhered to an unmodified Freudian position, put it '(Social) change is
only the discharge of suppressed emotion'.(41) It is not my intention
to review here the vast literature, principally American, which seeks to
demonstrate the social role of psychopathology by employing psychodynamic theories. Suffice to say that when Devereux and La Barre (42)
suggest that culture may originate in individual psychopathology, their

use of terms like 'schizophrenia' are unrecognisable to descriptive psychiatrists who would find little to add to Ackernecht's critique in 1943: 'The custom of covering moral judgements with a pseudoscientific psychopathological nomenclature is no advance at all and is equally bad for both morals and science ... When religion is but "organised schizophrenia" (Devereux's expression) then there is no room or necessity for history, sociology, etc. God's earth was, and is, but a gigantic state hospital and pathography becomes the unique and universal science'.(43) Ackernecht suggested that the only possible instances for religious roles being *routinely* proceeded by mental disturbance were the classical Siberian Shamans described by Sieroszerski and Bogoras.

The social institution of Shamanism thus *might* include the mentally ill, those recovered from mental illness and those incipiently ill.(44) Where medical anthropology has been concerned with the major psychoses it has regarded them as 'natural symbols' upon which social meanings are imposed, not as a potentially active social forces in their own right. Is there anything which can be salvaged from a debate now confined to studies of 'the history of ethnographic theory?

The Influence of Psychopathology Upon Culture

If we accept the existence of an autonomous domain of psychopathology, closely allied to the popular Western concept of 'insanity', can it influence society? If it does, under what conditions may the statements of the madman be taken by his contemporaries as valid? As there is no biological marker of psychopathology independent of social action, and observers (as we have seen) ascribe psychopathology to normative situations on rather slender grounds, it would be appropriate initially to restrict our search to situations where we find evidence of a biological component in psychopathology, or least to psychopathology defined on descriptive rather than dynamic grounds. There appear to be five situations under which such as 'imitation of madness' is possible.

(a) An individual who is already influential becomes psychotic but is validated for a time by the inertia of the political structure. A limited example of this is *folie à deux* where, in a close but socially isolated family, a dominant member develops delusions which dependent family members then accept: the 'passive' delusions of the dependents rapidly disappear when they are isolated from the dominant originator. (45) Something like this is the idea behind the popular perception of Hitler or Amin as charismatic madmen. Whilst it is probably rare for an influential individual to maintain his influence if actually insane, there are frequent instances of absolute rulers becoming increasingly isolated and suspicious as a result of their situation. If leaders become seriously psychotic they are probably soon eliminated as Suetonius suggested in the case of Caligula. Mad rulers are unlikely in the general run of things, for their predisposition is likely to have manifested itself earlier and to have eliminated them from the power struggle: Idi Amin for instance, had been Head of the Ugandan Armed Forces for some years before he sought absolute power.

(b) Alternatively the individual may be only periodically insane and in between episodes lives in the shared social reality where he can validate his delusions as acceptable communications by explaining them in conventional terms. He may find his previous psychopathological ideas strange and the quest for their meaning may then be identical with external validation. In his *Journals* George Fox describes an episode when passing near Lichfield, he felt impelled to take off his shoes in a field and run through the town shouting 'Woe unto the bloody city of Litchfield'; returning later to his shoes he was puzzled as to the meaning of his act and appears relieved on discovering later that the town had been the site of Christian martyrdom under Diocletian. (46) Psychopathology, like schizophrenia, which includes widespread personality changes and a lowering of social competence, is unlikely to be subsequently integrated in this way. Early psychosis, isolated psychotic episodes or phasic reactions like manic-depressive psychosis, are more amenable to reentry into the shared world, and thus to imitation – what Devos has termed 'pathomimesis' (47); the episode itself may be less a spontaneous transformation of existing themes than the signal that legitimates a change which is previously or subsequently conceived of in a normative state. If epileptic fits are believed to be of divine origin then the presence of divinity will be ushered in by fits whether spontaneous, sought or simulated.

The isolated psychotic episode, whether truly innovative or merely a signal for mystical imputation, may resemble the shamanic employment of altered states of consciousness where the visions are culturally standardised and their import agreed by consensual validation. Among the Trinidadian Shouters, fasting and sensory deprivation are used to attain vision but the pattern and authenticity of these are validated by the church as a whole. In fact, members of the group I am going to describe were expelled from the Shouters for their idiosyncratic visions. The psychopathology of the psychotic is likely to be more idiosyncratic than everyday shared beliefs. However, as in the case of Sabbatai Svi, the innovation involved may be merely tapping certain generally available but latent beliefs, or reversing the everyday themes. The innovative power in these cases comes from the conviction with which psychosis imbues the novelty, or the performance of it in action, as opposed to the more casual mention others may make of its possibility.

(c) Nietzsche, Strindberg and Artaud are not automatically discredited by the Western intellectual because they developed, respectively, general paralysis of the insane, paranoia and schizophrenia, even though it is impossible to separate the later work of each from their psychopathology. Delusions may be isolated from the recognition of pathology: 'He's mad but ...'. There is a recognition that there is something valid in psychotic statements without denying the primary illness. In early eighteenth century North America it was quite acceptable for all whites, including members of the Society of Friends, to own slaves. Two insane inmates of a Friends' asylum independently declared that slave-owning was no longer acceptable for Quakers; the idea spread beyond the asylum walls and within a few years the practice of slavery was incompatible with membership of the Society. The two innovators, however, appeared to have remained within their asylum.(48)

(d) It is the meaning for the community which determines whether psychotic delusions result in the originator becoming a prophet. In his study of 'charisma' (49) Bryan Wilson points out that 'If a man runs naked down the street proclaiming that he alone can save others from impending doom, and if he immediately wins a following, then he is a charismatic leader: a social relationship has come into being. If he does not win a following, then he is simply a lunatic ... The very content of "plausability" is culturally determined. It may be a more than average endowment of energy, determination, fanaticism, and perhaps intelligence. Or it may be an altogether different set of attributes, epilepsy, strangeness, what we should regard as mental disorder, or particularly when children are regarded as prophets, even sheer innocence.' If innovation is meaningful it has to respond to certain themes in the audience. At times of crisis, solutions are likely to be accepted or sought from those who at other times would be stigmatised as mad: 'desperate times need desperate remedies'. In the 1660s, Solomon Eccles wandered about London with a brazier of fire on his head, naked apart from a loincloth, proclaiming the imminent destruction of the city: he was largely ignored until the Plague, and then the Fire, made him a fashionable prophet. London was rebuilt whilst Solomon continued to preach the identical doctrine, and he lapsed back into his former obscurity.(50) If we accept with Laing, that the girl who says she is dangerous because she has an atomic bomb inside her is 'less crazy' than a government prepared to use nuclear weapons, this is because we are so concerned about the possibility of atomic war that we are prepared to modify our conceptions of reason.

(51) Murphy has taken this further: 'Delusions may occur in times of increased stress as if, in reaction to changing conditions, the culture does call on individual members to sacrifice their mental health by the development of individual delusions which relieve communal anxieties'.(52) Like La Barre (but without La Barre's pessimism) he offers an active innovative role for psychopathology.

(e) To say a mad individual would have been 'accepted' at another time or in another place is a biographical commonplace: the audience has failed the author. Artaud's biographer suggests that 'in other epochs he might have been a shaman, a prophet, an alchemist, an oracle, a saint, a gnostic teacher or indeed the founder of a new religion'.(53) If we accept that both the individual and psychopathology are located in a particular society then this is meaningless, but it is likely that some societies, particularly small-scale preliterate ones, are always open to a greater variety of idiosyncratic communications that is our own. In other words there may be societies which do not share our rigorous exclusion of all psychopathology from the possibility of meaning. This is true of the Quakers and the 1960s 'counter-culture', both open to 'the workings of the spirit'. It may occur when societies have a more restricted concept of psychopathology than our own. While a majority of tribal societies appear to recognise a state akin to 'insanity', this may be restricted to *chronic* mental illness; the early stages of what psychiatrists regard as schizophrenia may be conceived of as a potentially meaningful experience. As Kroeber pointed out, 'In general the psychopathologies that are rewarded among primitives are only the mild or transient ones. A markedly deteriorated psychosis ... would be rated and deplored by them as much as by us.' Murphy suggests that there is a cost: 'Societies which encourage greater contact with unconscious feelings can freely accept the idiosyncratic behaviour and delusions of the mentally ill but they pay a price in economic and social inferiority'.(54) We do not have to accept Murphy's idea of the unconscious to agree that societies which take madness seriously are probably not the most appropriate ones for developing and operating advanced technology. I shall now examine two specific instances and attempt to see how psychopathology may provide a model for the experiences of others and provide a charter for a common set of beliefs.

Sabbatai Svi (55)

The exile of the Jews from Palestine at the beginning of the Christian era dispersed a single self-contained community from its own land into a series of complementary relationships with Christian and, later

Islamic communities. The rabbinical tradition preserved the original culture, elaborated into the Law which defined the boundaries between Jew and non-Jew and explained the separation from the historic land as a temporary interlude until the messianic redemption. The traditional Messiah was a conquering king who would re-establish the historical kingdom. Alternatively he was pictured as the suffering and rejected servant who held a message for the gentiles. For others the exile was a metaphor for personal alienation from God and the promised redemption was purely spiritual. One tradition suggested that the Messiah would come when the existence of the community was threatened by internal disharmony and external violence, and another, only when Man had deliberately entered into the sinful world to release the divine sparks hidden there.

Within the development of the modern nation state, the traditional Jewish accommodation in Eastern Europe began to fail. The physical identity of East European Jewry was threatened by assimilation and attrition: massacre and forced conversion accounted for perhaps half a million Polish Jews in the 1640s. Sabbatai Svi, a devout young rabbi in the Ottoman Empire, began to engage in frequent fasts, ritual purifications and all-night prayer. After two successive marriages were annulled for non-consummation, he commenced increasingly antinomian behaviour – breaking the Law for the value inherent in this act. A Kabbalistic tradition had asserted that as the Messiah had to redeem evil he was in some measure evil himself and Sabbatai offered a new prayer: 'Praised be Thee O Lord who permits the forbidden'.

Expelled by the local rabbis, Sabbatai was proclaimed Messiah by a follower and the movement spread rapidly. Sabbatianism was characterised by miracles, prophecies, mass visions, states of possession and ecstatic confession and penance, fasts to death and self-burials. Sabbatai invented new ceremonies and fantastic titles: days of ritual mourning became days of rejoicing. He married a prostitute and encouraged free love, nudity and incest: if the messianic age could only be ushered in by sin the people must sin. Within a year Sabbatai was arrested by the Sultan for sedition, had converted to Islam under pain of death and was pensioned off under house arrest. Most followers abandoned him in this ultimate rejection of Judaism and returned to traditional rabbinical teachings, but for others his apostasy was the ultimate messianic sacrifice: 'The Lord was but veiled and waiting'. A few followed him to Islam and some converted to Christianity. Many continued as apparently orthodox Jews but conducted Sabbatian rites in secret. As an organised body of belief the movement soon died away, but in the 18th century a Sabbatian, Jacob Frank, proclaimed himself Messiah. The relation of Sabbation messianism to the subsequent Hassidic movement remains controversial. It has been described as a 'neutralisation of messianic elements into mainstream Judaism' and as a 'dialectical synthesis of the two'.(56)

There is a certain amount of evidence that Sabbatai Svi was manic-depressive. He was constantly depressed 'without his being able to say what is the nature of this pain'. Extreme apathy and withdrawal, known to his followers as 'The Hiding of the Face' alternated with periods of 'illumination': infectious elation and enthusiasm, restlessness and a refusal to eat or sleep, practical jokes and flights of apparent nonsense. Jewish mystics already used high/low (aliyah/yorinda) to refer to nearness to / absence from God, and Sabbatai employed this spatial metaphor to explain his moods as religious experience: 'high' was associated with religious ecstasy, 'low' with self-doubt. His followers accepted his explanation of his mood swings and followed them, themselves experiencing episodes of religious exultation and despair which became normative experiences for many. His psychosis thus provided a natural symbol of the Kabbalistic doctrine, together with a firm conviction on Sabbatai's part (when 'high') of his messiahship and also a model for explaining the fluctuating relations between God and Man, and thus the waxing and waning of the movement. It is likely that the jokes and tricks and inversions of normal behaviour make an individual with periodic manic-depressive psychosis a particularly well-placed person to modify traditional modes of belief and behaviour through antinomian acts.

To what extent does Sabbatianism meet our five possible conditions? Sabbatai was certainly respected as a promising scholar before his antinomian actions and it is not easy to see how he could have been taken seriously otherwise: he was not, however, so influential that his community would accept any ideas immediately (situation a). His reputation did establish his acts as antinomian – controlled and motivated contraventions of the Law rather than a simple failure to follow it. His episodes of madness were periodic, enabling him to explain their meaning within the common shared assumptions (b). The audience did not have a restricted concept of psychopathology and they did not recognise Sabbatai as 'mad but ...' (57) (c, e). Certainly Eastern European Jews were living in desperate times (d) but the movement was most significant under Ottoman rule, where Jews were more secure than in Christian countries. Sabbatian adherents were as likely to come from the affluent and assimilated sections of the Jewish community as from the pauperised and insecure peasantry. Our example is limited by the usual problem of conjectural psychohistory: 'diagnosis' across time based on secondary sources. Our assumption of Sabbatai Svi's manic-depression is based on sources compiled by his followers. The fact that his 'highs' and 'lows' were so neatly coded in Kabbalistic terms may lead us to wonder whether the 'coding' was not prior to the experiences, and merely shaped everyday mood changes.

Mother Earth

Trinidad, the most southerly of the Caribbean islands, lies in the Orinoco delta, eight miles away from the South American mainland. A Spanish possession until its capture by the British in 1797, it was largely ignored after the extermination of the Amerindians although a few French planters from other West Indian islands settled with their slaves who grew sugar in the lower areas in the west. Trinidad's history has been typical of the British Caribbean: the development of sugar plantations; the emancipation of the slaves in 1838 followed by indentured immigration from India in the latter part of the nineteenth century; the collapse of the price of cane sugar, economic stagnation and imperial neglect; increasing local political participation progressing to internal self-government in the 1950s and independence in 1962. The governing party since 1956, is pro-Western and social democratic, committed to a mixed economy and a welfare state, derives it support predominantly from the African (58) population, and has comfortably maintained power through patronage and regular elections, apart from a brief hiccup in 1971 when an army mutiny sparked a short-lived Black Power rebellion.

The oil industry has been exploited since independence and the standard of living is high, reputedly the third highest in the Americas after the United States and Canada; certain rural areas excepted, concrete houses, electricity, piped water and metalled roads are standard. Secondary education is compulsory and the oil revenues have allowed the establishment of a steel works and large construction and other industries. The labour intensive agricultural cultivation of sugar, coffee, cocoa and *ground provisions* has been effectively abandoned and the bulk of 'local' food is brought in from the smaller and poorer islands to the north.

In the north-east the mountains of the Northern range, the geographical continuation of the South America Cordillera, rise from the sea to 3000 feet. They were only occupied in the late nineteenth century by isolated families who established a peasantry of small *estates* of coffee and cocoa in the lower reaches, growing coconuts and provision in the narrow littoral.

Few Trinidadian people have not heard of the Earth People, a small community established on this coast. In a country familiar with the millennial religious response of the Shouter Baptists, and with the Rastafari movement, a recent import from Jamaica, the Earth People remain an enigma. Their appearance, from the villages to the capital Port of Spain, causes public outrage to all, for their most outstanding characteristic is that they are naked. Public opinion favours the view that these young men, carrying cutlasses, and with the long matted dreadlocks of the Rastas, are probably crazy: if not the whole group, then Mother Earth, whose visions gave birth to the movement and who leads their marches to 'Town'. Every year the group comes from the coast to Port of Spain to pass on their message and gather new recruits from the poorer working-class areas around the capital, areas which appear to have missed out on Trinidad's oil wealth. Communication is hampered by the Earth Peoples' characteristic language, their deliberate and frequent use of obscenities and Mother Earth's striking doctrines. She announces to Trinidadians, a largely devout if not church-going population, that God does not exist but that she is the Biblical Devil, the Mother of Africa and India, Nature Herself.

In 1973 when she was 39 she left Port of Spain together with her children and husband, to settle in one of the deserted hamlets overlooking a rocky bay and a long curving beach bisected by a river which, laden with mangroves, slowly enters the sea as a modest delta between the overgrown coconut groves.

The family had been Shouter Baptists (59) and they continued to 'pick along in the Bible', fasting in Lent and interpreting the visionary import of their dreams. After the birth of twins in their wooden hut in 1975, Jeanette experienced a series of revelations. She became aware that the Christian doctrine of God the Father as Creator was untrue and that the world was the work of a primordial Mother which she identified with Nature and the Earth. The Mother had created a race of black people, originally hermaphrodite, the Race of Africa and India, but her rebellious Son re-entered His Mother's womb to gain the power of creation and succeeded in modifying part of her creation to produce the white people, the Race of the Son who are the Race of Death. The Whites, acting as the Son's agents, enslaved the blacks and have continued to exploit them. The Way of the Son is the Way of technology, cities, clothes, schools, factories and wage labour. The Way of the Mother is the Way of Nature: a return to the simplicity of the Beginning, a simplicity of nakedness, cultivation of the land by hand and with respect, of gentle and non-exploiting human relationships.

The Son, in his continued quest for the power of generation has recently entered into a new phase. He has succeeded in establishing himself in black people and is also on the point of creating non-human people, robots and computers. The Mother, who has borne all His behaviour out of Her Love for Him, has finally lost patience. She is about to end the current order of the Son in a catastrophic drought and famine, a destruction of the Son's work, after which the original state of Nature will once again prevail.

Jeanette herself is a partial incarnation of the Mother who will only fully enter into her at the End. Her role is to facilitate the return to Nature by organising a community on the coast, called Hell Valley, the Valley of Decision, to prepare for the return to the Beginning and to 'put out' the truth to her people, the black nation, the Mother's Children. She has to combat the false doctrines of existing religions which place the Son over the Mother and to correct the distorted teaching of the Bible. For She is the Devil and represents Life and Nature, in opposition to the Christian God who is her Son, the principle of Death and Science. As the Devil she is opposed to churches and prisons, education and money, contemporary morals and fashionable opinions.

As God is 'right' she teaches the Left and the Earth People interchange various common oppositions: 'left' for 'right'; 'evil' or 'bad' for 'good'. Conventional obscenities are Natural words and should be used, for She Herself is The Cunt, the source of all life. The exact timing of the End is uncertain but it will come in Jeanette's physical lifetime. Then Time will cease, disease will be healed and the Nation will speak one language. The Son will return to His Planet, The Planet Sun, which is currently hidden by Fire placed there by the Mother.

Since her revelations which mark the Beginning of the End in 1975 Mother Earth's family have been joined by numbers of black Trinidadians, usually young men who sometimes bring their girlfriends and children to come and 'Plant for the Nation'. The community has a high turnover and, whilst over 50 people have been associated with the Earth People, when I stayed with them (60) there were 23 living in the Valley of Decision with perhaps 20 close sympathisers in town.

Some of the younger village men in the villages along the coast demonstrate an allegiance to Rastafari and say they remain in the country to pursue a 'natural' life. They express sympathy for the Earth People and would actually join the group if it were not for the nudity, Mother Earth's repudiation of Haile Selassie, and her reputation for making everyone in Hell Valley work so hard. Some of them meet the Earth people in the bush, smoke a little ganja and exchange fish for *provision*. Through them and other friends in the village who knew Mother Earth before she went naked, the Earth People are kept well informed of village activities and any gossip about them. The older Creole-speaking villagers regret the passing of traditional rural life and the depopulation of the coast. Whilst valuing the benefits of piped water, state pensions and a higher standard of living, they criticise the young men's expectations of an easy life: 'It come so all they want is fêting. They can't take hard work again.' They accord grudging respect to the return to the old life in the Valley, all the more so as the Earth people themselves come from the town. Their own opinions about Trinidad's future parallel those of the Earth People: the oil is a natural part of the earth, the blood of the soil; and its removal is slowly turning the land into a 'cripsy', an unproductive arid desert; they too are suspicious of the newer farming techniques advocated by the government agricultural officers and, refusing pesticides or fertilisers, they continue to plant and harvest according to the phases of the moon; the oil wealth is transitory and will eventually cease, to leave Trinidadians starving in a once fertile land.

Their disagreement is less with Mother Earth's eschatological doctrines than with her practice of nudity, for no Trinidadian has gone naked since slavery. Trinidadians who have met her when 'putting out', regarded her less as insane than as eccentric: "she come half-way mad then". She has, however, twice been taken by the police to the mental hospital in Port of Spain; there she was diagnosed as psychotic and given psychotropic drugs. Interviewing her with the Present State Examination suggested that she had periodic episodes of hypomania associated with the puerperium: she is also clinically thyrotoxic. In between episodes she is frequently despondent if not depressed. The explanation accepted by the group is that the Mother is only partially incarnated in her and withdraws at intervals (this *withdrawal* corresponds to depression, a different physical metaphor to Sabattai's). The practical organisation of the group at these times is left to her husband.

With regard to our five conditions. Mother Earth was not initially an important person (a), but her episodes of psychopathology, like those of Sabbatai, have been temporary (b). The local concept of *folie* (madness) is more restricted (e) than the popular British one and emphasises chronic mental deterioration, although it is also used in a consciously figurative sense as in *tabanka* (love sickness). Sympathisers who are not members may accept that she is mentally ill whilst accepting the validity of her ideas (c), although her followers say 'If she mad, then we mad.' Trinidad can hardly be described as living in desperate times (d) but for the rural migrants to the towns and the remaining country people, the disappearance of an agricultural economy and its associated way of life, has certainly been traumatic, particularly for the young male proletariat of the slums, unemployed and non-unionised.

A Universal Dispensation?

To conclude, I shall say a little about the mode of intellectual innovation we can expect in situations such as those as Sabbatai Svi and Mother Earth. Firstly it is *dramatic* – when we have a tradition of linear intellectual development and open dialogue with the dominant culture it is perhaps unnecessary. It seems particularly relevant to those small scale conservative societies which principally interest ethnographers. It is not limited to them – indeed neither Sabbatai nor Mother Earth come from a tribal society. They are, however, members of a group dominated by another culture. It is dramatic then – often an overturning of the accepted patterns – an *inversion* of them.(61) As Scholem says 'Sabbatai took over items of Jewish tradition and stood them on their heads'.

Whatever may be the merits of the current anthropological debate on systems of dual classification,(62) there appear to be particular situations where two opposed sets of binary oppositions play an important social role: those societies which have been politically dominated for a considerable period of time by outsiders. We may include here colonies and ex-colonies, including much of the Third World, blacks and whites in the Americas, and Jewish communities in Europe. Caribbean society, like Jewish society, has been described as dualistic – 'Us' and 'Them' – in this case Black and White (for Jews – Jew and Gentile). For the black person there are two contrasted modes of social behaviour, exemplified by 'black' and 'white' and usually glossed as 'respectability' (the white mode) and 'reputation' (the black mode).(63) The black mode is characterised by sexual prowess, cohabitation, seduction, the rumshop, home produce and egalitarian society, and is typically represented in men. The white mode is characterised by chastity, legal marriage, education, the church, imported goods and hierarchy, and is represented most typically in women.

The individual has to attain an identity by personally articulating the various elements of the two contrasted sets of values: the minority culture itself is defined by its difference to the dominant set of values (Fig. 1). Some groups in society, particularly women, are already in an 'inverted' symbolic position relative to men. If West Indian 'respectability/reputation' are articulated by 'white/ black' values, then the black middle-class man is, in some sense, white. If the relation Jew/non-Jew parallels that of observance of the Law to Ignorance of it, it thus parallels that of male/female so that the Jewish woman, to a certain extent, takes on Gentile qualities

(64) and the black woman is in the same way 'white'.(65) Trinidadian Rastas accept this dichotomy bur change its value: in contradistinction to the majority who (as Fanon showed) are trying to become 'white', they take the black mode as the ideal. The symbolic position of Whites is either as evil or they are somehow supposed to exist in harmony with Blacks – both Black and White accepting each other's values. In other words, there is no major symbolic change. Mother Earth's teaching transcends this dualistic position by asserting that blacks have become corrupted by the Son and their mind is white: only the Flesh, itself part of the Earth, is truly the Mother's.

SHEYN/PROST

$$\frac{\text{Jew}}{\text{Gentile}} = \frac{\text{Observance of Law}}{\text{Violation of Law}} = \frac{\text{Aesthetic}}{\text{Desire}} = \frac{\text{Adult}}{\text{Child}} = \frac{\text{Male}}{\text{Female}} = \frac{\text{Sacred}}{\text{Profane}} =$$

$$\frac{\text{Sin for its own sake}}{\text{Observance of Law}}$$

SABBATAI SVI

REPUTATION/RESPECTABILITY

$$\frac{\text{Black}}{\text{White}} = \frac{\text{Democracy}}{\text{Hierarchy}} = \frac{\text{Home Produce}}{\text{Imported Goods}} = \frac{\text{Cohabitation}}{\text{Marriage}} = \frac{\text{Rum Shop}}{\text{Church}} =$$

$$\frac{\text{Sex}}{\text{Chastity}} = \frac{\text{Seduction}}{\text{Education}} = \frac{\text{Male}}{\text{Female}} = \frac{\text{Devilish}}{\text{Godly}} = \frac{\text{Good}}{\text{Bad}}$$

MOTHER EARTH

Figure 1 Antinomianism and symbolic inversion

I am suggesting that certain patterns of psychopathology can, as it were, hot up these latent contradictions, by overt statements and actions, inverting the normal schema in certain areas (represented by a chiasmus in the polythetic classifications of Fig. 1). Symbolic inversions can be regarded as intellectual tools which have the potential to enlarge the conceptual repertoire.(66) Although oppositions may be a dominant mode of symbolic ordering, their inversion provides the basis for change. The apparent paradox is resolved at a 'higher' implicit level: simple oppositions thus may become the means by which a more sophisticated, radical and universal conceptualisation may be attained.(67) As the original symbolic schema was closely related to the social order, the weakening of this schema in some particular is likely to lead to a greater autonomy of ideology from specific environmental and political determinants and thus perhaps to more 'internalised' values. Thus, when Jesus denied that plucking corn on the Sabbath was *work*, he implied a new dispensation in which 'the Law was broken in Form to be fulfilled in Spirit'. Scholem suggests that the Judaism always contained a 'dialectic' between the rabbinical and apocalyptic traditions, what I have termed the Law and its inversion. Sabbatai Svi confused the dual classification, calling women to read the Torah, ridiculing the learned, encouraging Gentiles to join the movement and maintaining evil could be transformed into good. To follow the traditional Law in the Last Days was, he said, like working on the Sabbath. It has been suggested that the attack on the traditional Law by the Sabbatians both reflected and precipitated the development of modern secular Judaism (68); freed from traditional constraints, the method of criticism and argument perfected in the ghetto was harnessed to the development of modern rationalism.

It is perhaps too early to characterise any universalist influence for Mother Earth. Certainly her overturning of the dual classification in certain areas allows the Earth People, like the Rastas, to escape from an externally imposed system of values. Her rejection of binarism, her interpenetration of black and white, and of male and female, appear to offer us all a more universal dispensation than the limited 'ethnic redefinition' of Rastafari.

References

1   Naipul S. *Black and White*, Sphere Edition, p. 17. Hamish Hamilton, London, 1980.
2   La Barre W. *The Ghost Dance*, pp. 348, 603, 607. Allen & Unwin, London, 1970: Wolman B. (Ed.) Sense and nonsense in history. In *The Psychoanalytic Interpretation of History*, p. 95. Harper, London 1973.

3 Susan Sontag in *Illness as Metaphor* (Allen Lane, London, 1979) discusses the political use of the medical metaphor at length but restricts it to the metaphors of physical disease – 'infection' and 'cancer'.

4 Naipul S. *op cit.*, p. 134.

5 Kroeber cited in Lifton R. J. *Exploration in Psychohistory.* Simon & Schuster, New York, 1974: La Barre W. *They Shall Take Up Serpents,* pp. viii, 109. Schocken, New York, 1969.

6 Cited by Ackenecht E. Psychopathology, primitive medicine and primitive culture. *Bull Hist. Med.* **14**, 30–68, 1943.

7 Devereux G. Normal and abnormal: the key problem in psychiatric anthropology. In *Some Uses of Psychopathology, Theoretical and Applied* (Edited by Gladwin J. and Gladwin T). Anthropological Society of Washington, 1956.

8 Rosen G. *Madness in Society,* pp. 21–70. Routledge & Kegan Paul, London, 1968.

9 La Barre W. *op. cit.*, 1960.

10 Rosen G. *op. cit.*, 1968; Ackernecht E. *op. cit.*, 1943.

11 Association of Psychiatrists in Training. *Newsletter* p. 1, September, 1977.

12 Ballard R. An Interview with Thomas Szasz. *Penthouse* pp. 69–71, October, 1973. The poll was published in *Fact* magazine, September, 1964.

13 Freud S. *The Future of an Illusion.* Hogarth, London, 1928.

14 Kenniston K. Psychological development and historical change. In *Exploration in Psychohistory* (Edited by Lifton R. J.). Simon & Schuster, New York, 1974; Bourdieu P. *Outline of a Theory of Practice,* Chap. 1. Cambridge University Press, Cambridge, 1977.

15 Linton R. Nativist movements. *Am. Anthrop.* **45**, 230–240, 1943.

16 Beckford J. A. *The Trumpet of Prophecy: A Sociological Study of Jehovah's Witnesses.* Blackwell, Oxford, 1975.

17 Wilson B. *Magic and the Millenium.* pp. 317–319. Heinemann, London, 1973.

18 Williams F. M. The Vaihala Madness in Retrospect. In *Essays Presented to G. C. Seligman* (Edited by Evans-Pritchard E. E.). Kegan Paul, London, 1934. He describes the movement as 'an epidemic', 'antics' which 'originated in delusions'.

19 La Barre W. *op. cit.*, pp. 233, 294, 197; Wilson B. *op. cit.*, p. 135, 1973; Yap P. M. The mental illness of Hung Hsiu Chu'an, Leader of the Taiping Rebellion. *Far East. Q.* **13**, 287–304, 1954: Williams F. M. *op. cit.*, p. 372, 1934.

20 Armytage W. H. G. *Heavens Below: Utopian Experiments in England 1560–1960,* p. 282. Routledge & Kegan Paul, London, 1961; Worsley P. *The Trumpet Shall Sound,* pp. 168–169. Paladin, London, 1970; Wilson B. *op. cit.*, p. 42, 1973; Simpson G. Jamaican Revivalist Cults. *Soc. Econ. Stud.* December, 1956: Nettleford R. *Mirror, Mirror: Identity, Race and Protest in Jamaica.* Chap. 2. Collins, Kingston, 1970.

21 Woodcock G. and Avakumaic I. *The Doukhobors,* p. 59. Faber, London, 1968; Beckford J. A. *op. cit.*, p. 34, 1975; Bloch S. and Reddaway P. *Russia's Political Hospitals.* Gollancz, London, 1977, *passim.*

22 Nettleford R. *op. cit.*, pp. 56–57, 1970.

23 Compare the Yoruba and Temba (Littlewood R. and Lipsedge M. *Aliens and Alienists,* Chap. 9. Penguin, Harmondsworth, 1982).

24 Plato, *Timaeus*, Penguin, Harmondsworth, 1965.
25 Feder L. *Madness and Literature*, pp. 106–107. University Press. Princeton, 1980.
26 For instance in Erasmus' *In Praise of Folly* or Savanarola's iconoclastic Feast of the Higher Folly.
27 Cited by James W. *The Varieties of Religious Experience.* Mentor, New York, 1958.
28 Hayter A. *Opium and the Romantic Imagination.* Faber, London, 1968, *passim*.
29 Nietzsche F. *The Will to Power*, cited by Harrison M. Mental instability as a factor in progress. *The Monist*, **32**, 19, 1922.
30 James W. *op. cit.*, p. 24, 1958.
31 James W. *op. cit.*, p. 36, 1958.
32 Cited by Kurella H. In *Cesare Lombroso.* Rebman, London, 1911.
33 Ibid., p. 72.
34 Karlsson L. Schizophrenia and creativity. *Acta psychiat. Scand.* **247**, Suppl., 76, 1974.
35 Storr A. *The Dynamics of Creation.* Secker & Warburg, London, 1972.
36 Translated from Cabanne P. *Van Gogh.* Aimery Somogy, Paris, 1961.
37 Breton A. *Manifestes de Surrealism*, p. 37. Gallimard, Paris, 1969.
38 Esslin M. *Artaud*, p. 52. Fontana, London, 1976.
39 Feder L. *op. cit.*, p. 242, 1980.
40 Vonnegut M. *The Eden Express.* Cape, London, 1976.
41 Roheim G. *Psychoanalysis and Anthropology.* International Universities Press, New York, 1950.
42 Devereux G. *op. cit.*, 1956; La Barre W. *op. cit.* 1969, 1970.
43 Ackernecht E. *op. cit.*, pp. 31, 35, 1943. This criticism is not taken to include the 'new psychohistorians' (Lifton, Erikson, Kenniston) for they have largely restricted themselves to a consideration of normative psychodynamics and have developed a considerably more sophisticated conceptualisation of the relationship between individual personality and the social order. Erikson's 'great man of history' is not the charismatic psychotic of Devereux and La Barre but one who articulates the 'dirty work of his age' (Erikson E. *Young Man Luther*, Norton, New York, 1958).
44 Following Eliade, no contemporary students of shamanism have claimed that the shaman is invariably psychopathological. What Eliade (*Shamanism: Archaic Techniques of Ecstasy.* University Press, Princeton, 1964) terms 'signs of election' have been recognised as including acute psychosis, along with physical disease or misfortune, but the pattern of shamanism is a conventional pattern superimposed on the psychotic individual and not derived from him. With acculturation however, increasingly deviant individuals may come to occupy the shamanic role (Murphy J. Psychotherapeutic aspects of Shamanism on St Lawrence Island. In *Magic, Faith and Healing* (Edited by Kiev A.). Free Press, New York, 1964).
45 Gruenberg E. Socially shared psychopathology. In *Explorations in Social Psychiatry* (Edited by Leighton A. H.). Basic Books, New York, 1957.
46 Fox G. *Journals.* pp. 71–72. Cambridge University Press, Cambridge, 1952.
47 Devos G. A. The inter-relationship of social and psychological structures in transcultural psychiatry. In *Transcultural Research in Mental Health* (Edited by Lebra W. P.). University Press, Hawaii (1972) derives the term

from an unpublished paper by T. Schwartz and restricts himself to the mimesis of epilepsy, which, if believed to be of mystical origin, authenticates religious experience. The imitation of epilepsy is cited by Eliade, 1964, in numerous cases and Williams, 1934, describes a Melanesian millenial leader who spread a stylised epilepsy in his group modelled on his own pre-existing illness (pp. 371–72). 'Psychotomimesis' would perhaps be more appropriate in our context.

48 Davis B. D. *The Problem of Slavery in Western Culture.* Cornell, University Press, 1966.

49 Wilson B. *Noble Savages: The Primitive Origins of Charisma.* California University Press, Berkeley, 1975.

50 Hunter A. *The Last Days.* Blond, London, 1959.

51 Laing R. D. *The Divided Self.* p. 12. Tavistock, London, 1959, Penguin edition, 1965.

52 Murphy, H. B. M. Cultural aspects of the delusion. *Studium Generale* 2, 684–692, 1967. How radical we take this to be depends on our interpretation of 'as if'.

53 Esslin M. *op. cit.*, p. 116, 1976.

54 Murphy H. B. M. *op. cit.*, 1967.

55 My argument in this section is derived from a previous paper on contemporary Hasidism. The Antinomian Hasid. *Br. J. med. Psychol.* (see Chapter 2) which contains more detailed citations. For the history of Sabbartianism I am completely indebted to the work of Gershom Scholem, particularly his *Sabbatai Sevi*, Routledge, London, 1973.

56 Scholem G. *Major Trends in Jewish Mysticism.* Schocken, New York, 1954: Bakan D. *Sigmund Freud and the Jewish Mystical Tradition.* University Press, Princeton, 1958.

57 Gradik M. Le concept de fou et ses implications dans la littérature Talmudique. *Annal. méd-Psychol.* 134, 17–36, 1976; Scholem G. *op. cit.*, p. 54, 1973.

58 The customary term for the Trinidadian population of African origin.

59 A loosely organised evangelical church of largely working-class origin whose members practice glossolalia and spirit possession. Akin to the Southern African 'Zionist' churches, it is regarded by some commentators as containing distinctive African elements (Simpson G. E. (Ed.) The Shouters' Church. In *Religious Cults of the Caribbean.* University of Puerto Rico, 1980). It does not, however, contain any doctrines incompatible with other Christian denominations.

60 In 1981–1982 on a Social Science Research Council Post-Doctoral Conversion Fellowship.

61 See Littlewood. R. The individual articulation of shared symbols *J. Op. Psychiat.* In press. I am not suggesting that inversion is the only, or indeed the major, mode of the imitation of madness, but it is the one which appears relevant for our two examples, both characterised by 'gratuitous' obscenities and contravention of norms. It appears the more likely mode in bipolar affective psychosis. I have continued to use the term inversion in spite of recent suggestions (Needham R. *Reversals.* Henry Myers Lecture, Royal Anthropological Institute, 1980) that *opposition* might be more appropriate; inversion does not describe the latent possibilities of the system so much as convey the physical sense of overturning institutions so characteristic of the participants' experience. In brief, explanations of symbolic inversion have been offered by observers

and participants from diverse perspectives which we can gloss according to three broad Western modes of characterisation:

(a) Psychological: the return of the repressed, as elaborated in psychoanalytical and literary theory (Scheff T. *Catharsis in Healing, Ritual and Drama*. California University Press, Berkeley, 1979). The inversion may be regarded alternatively as a 'reaction formation' of the socialised individual to the recognition of his physiological drives (Freud A. *The Ego and the Mechanisms of Defence*. Hogarth, London, 1937). There may be a conscious cultural elaboration of some type of catharsis or discharge of tension to restore equilibrium, usually associated with a quantifiable conception of sin or emotion which can penetrate boundaries: we find it in the Jewish rituals of the scapegoat, excretion before prayer, the treatment of illness by enema or the 'purging' of the house at Passover. Theories of catharsis in drama, following Aristotle, stress the resonance (Mimesis) of the dramatic role with the personal experiences of actor and audience: in extreme situations both may run amok together in the deviant role (Geertz C. Religion as a cultural system. In *Anthropological Approaches to the Study of Religion* (Edited by Banton M.). Tavistock, London, 1966). A tentative psychophysiological basis for this type of experience has been elaborated in Smith and Apter's Reversal theory (Apter M. J. *The Experience of Motivation: The Theory of Psychological Reversals*. Academic Press, London, 1982).

(b) *Sociological:* inversion is presented by a culture as the only alternative to the established order and as it is both temporary and allowed only in certain specific ritual contexts (or limited to a powerless minority) it reaffirms the boundaries of control and thus cements the existing system (Gluckman, M. *Rituals of Rebellion in South-East Africa*, University Press, Manchester, 1962). While orthodox Jews are usually forbidden to play cards or get drunk, these two activities are tolerated and even encouraged on two specific days in the year; similarly the blood of humans or animals is scrupulously avoided at all times except at circumcisions when it may actually be sucked. In communities where the idea of cannibalism is totally repugnant the homicide may be purified by ritual ingestion of the deceased's liver (Goody J. *Cooking, Cuisine and Class*, University Press, Cambridge, 1982). Inversion thus marks a principle by constrained contravention of it.

(c) *Cognitive*. Both the 'psychological' and 'sociological' approaches are functional and static: they emphasise the homeostasis of a given system; inversion is either the catharsis of undesirable elements or the passage between the equivalent and co-existing systems. Similarly the antinomian individual who contravenes the norm gives unity to a simple bipolar system (Peacock J. *Rites and Modernisation: Symbolic Aspects of Indonesian Proletarian Drama*. University Press, Chicago, 1968). Inversion may however be innovative – see text below.

62 Particularly the structuralist debate on the universality of dual systems of thought (see Littlewood R. *op. cit.*, In press).

63 Fanon F. *Peau Noir, Masques Blancs*, Seuil, Paris, 1952; Wilson P. J. *Crab Antics*. Yale University Press, New Haven, 1973.

64 e.g. Zborowski M. and Herzog E. *Life is with People: The Culture of the Stetl*. Schocken, New York, 1962; for an analysis of the dual classification of diaspora Judaism see Littlewood R. *op. cit.*, 1983.

65 Fanon F. *op. cit.*, 1952.

66 Turner V. *Dramas, Fields and Metaphors*, Cornell University Press, Ithaca, 1974.
67 Babcock B. (Ed.) *The Reversible World: Symbolic Inversion in Art and Society*. Cornell University Press, Ithaca, 1978.
68 Scholem G. *op. cit.*, 1954.

9 Putting Out the Life
From Biography to Ideology
Among the Earth People*

> I know Science has to search me out
> to fight me, to check me out. I have
> to love them. You got to put it down
> as it come to you' own senses.
>
> Mother Earth

The Pinnacle villagers had warned me about the Earth People. Dangerous and unpredictable strangers to the coast, they were no friends to a White. Immediately I arrived in this fishing village to look at local understandings of health and sickness, I had been told about the community established nine miles away, which its members knew as the Valley of Decision or Hell Valley. A few weeks afterwards I happened to see three of them exchanging sacks of coconuts for a cutlass in one of the village stores; they looked at me with surprised disdain (I was the only White along the coast except for the two Irish Dominicans at Toco), but otherwise ignored me. A few months later I took the opportunity to join some of the villagers on a Government forestry expedition into the bush near the Earth People, both to see the forest and mountains but also, it was evident, to visit the Valley.

One of the foresters had met Mother Earth on her march to town to in a previous year and offered to take me. Leaving the abandoned *ajoupa* (forest hut) which had served now as our base camp for two days, we passed along a disused track, waded through a turbid stream, occasionally recognising among the scrub and forest debris the relics of the wooden houses which, twenty years before, had comprised small hamlets along the shore, to climb to a small plateau facing the sea, backed by the mountains which descended to behind the settlement and then on either side dropped down to a rocky bay thirty feet below. The Valley of Decision is hardly a physical valley, a declivity really.

* First published in *Anthropology and Autobiography* edited by Okely and Callaway (Routledge, 1992). There is some overlap with Chapters 8 and 11.

The most outstanding characteristic of the settlement is surely its neatness and precision. The lower slopes of the mountains are cleanly cut into well-tended terraces, planted with banana, plantain, tobacco and *ground provision* – yam, tannia, dasheen, cassava. Between piles of slowly burning scrub remain breadfruit and papaya, orange and avocado trees, coffee and cocoa. Nearer the house, pumpkins and coconut palms frame the first lawn I have seen since leaving Port of Spain, the grass cropped short by a couple of goats.

The lawn stretches down from the house to the track along the edge of the cliff, down which a slippery path twists along the rock face, down to an elaborately carved canoe and two rafts resting up on the shingle. A shallow ravine can be seen passing along the side of the house and then across the lawn while the area near the house is neatly paved with rocky stones. The house itself is the only building remaining of a once thriving village: a large wooden hut with an attic, boards unpainted apart from the words 'HELL VALLEY, THE DEVIL LIVE HERE' facing the sea; window and door spaces open, fronted on one side by a small silk-cotton tree and on the other joined to an open-sided and rudely fashioned extension, the bottom of which comprises basket-work receptacles woven into the supporting posts and containing extraordinary quantities of harvested fruit and provision. Unlike other isolated country huts, there was no rubbish, no rusting tins or discarded tools lying about, no fragments of clothing, old papers or fading copies of the farmers' almanacs. Everything here was wooden, simply carved, polished through use, giving a strong sense of permanence, of place. Tall, aged, dignified, the house existed for itself, nor as the outpost of some society located elsewhere, in town, in Britain or in the United States.

The sound of axes could be heard from behind the house. Chickens picked underneath: like all those in rural Trinidad, it is raised up on short stilts. In the space where a door had once hung stood a middle-aged woman of African ancestry, medium stature, naked, her hair in short dreadlocks. Two small children played around her on the threshold. She greeted us with polite reserve, discreetly avoided shaking hands and acerbically admonished my companion who had, as usual, thrust our cutlasses into the earth when we neared the hut: 'The Earth is the Mother'. He seemed ill at ease, refused an invitation to stay and wandered off, saying he would return to pick me up later. I entered, accepted some coconut water in a calabash together with a Valley-rolled cigar, and was told that my visit had been anticipated in a dream the previous night. Indeed I was late. I stayed in the Valley of Decision on and off for over a year.

The Beginning of the End

Few people in the West Indian island of Trinidad have not heard of the Earth People, a small community established on the north-east coast above the rough seas where the Atlantic meets the Caribbean, not far from where Columbus obtained his landing in the New World on his voyage of 1498, and whose local Caribs he identified as living in the Earthly paradise; not far, either, from the rocky point where, within a hundred years, the remnant of one Carib group were to leap to their deaths rather than face slavery, and where, another three hundred years later, Melville and Frances Herskovits conducted among their African successors fieldwork for the first ethnography of the English-speaking Caribbean.

In a country long familiar with the millennial religious response of the Shouter Baptists, frequently gathered by the roadside in their coloured robes, intoning lugubrious 'Sankey and Moody' hymns and ringing their handbells, and also with the newer Rastafari movement, taciturn and reserved, recently introduced from Jamaica, the Earth people remain an enigma. Their appearance in the villages or in the capital, Port of Spain, causes public outrage, for their most obvious characteristic is that they are naked. Public opinion favours the view that these young men, carrying cutlasses and with the long matted dreadlocks of the Rastas, are probably crazy: if not the whole group then certainly their leader Mother Earth whose visions gave birth to the movement and who leads their annual marches to town. Every year they come from the coast to Port of Spain to pass on their message and gather new recruits from the poorer working-class areas around the capital, Belmont and Laventille, Pitch Road; areas which appear to have missed out on Trinidad's new-found oil wealth. Communication is hampered by the Earth People's characteristic language, their studied and frequent use of obscenities, and Mother Earth's striking teachings. She informs Trinidadians, a largely devout if not exactly church-going population, that she is the Biblical Devil, the Mother of Africa and India, Nature herself.

The community of the Earth People, Hell Valley, straddles a coastal track, some nine miles from the nearest village. The local smallholdings of coffee and cocoa have long since returned to forest; their owners either left the area for good or moved back to the village. The mountains behind the Valley, never settled and seldom crossed, remain part of the island's extensive forest reserves, exploited for wood only on their southern side where they meet the central plateau. The track follows the coast, occasionally passing over headlands and allowing a glimpse of the sea, but usually winding along the mountains through the dense bush of secondary forest, hidden from the sun, occasionally dipping down to ford small rivers and mangrove swamps. Through the tangled foliage of overgrown coffee and cocoa and the tall, spreading *immortelle* trees planted eighty years ago to give them shade, the occasional traveller can glimpse the remains of abandoned *cocoa boxes* (1) and rotten wooden huts. This coast is regarded by Trinidadians as the most desolate part of the island, 'behind God's back', a fitting retreat for the handful of Black Power activists who established themselves there briefly in 1972 after blowing up the village police station. They were tracked down and shot by the Regiment, Trinidad's modest armed forces.

A year after the 'guerrillas' were killed, Jeanette Baptiste, a thirty-nine year old woman from Port of Spain came to the coast, together with six of her twelve children and her partner. The family settled in the remains of one of the deserted hamlets midway along the track, where it overlooks on one side a small rocky bay, and on the other a long, curving beach bisected by a river which, laden with mangroves, slowly enters the sea as a gentle delta. Initially, they were paid by an overseer to collect copra but after an argument they continued to squat on the land by tacit agreement, growing their own food.

Two years after they arrived, when Jeanette was eight months pregnant, she had a dream in which the moon told her she should have her child on top of a hill. Not understanding why, she followed the dream nevertheless and gave birth to twins under the roof of the broken-down house. When they were five months old, Jeanette, in a period of inspiration, sang a song to Yemanja, the Yoruba mother deity of the *shango* cult, and started burning all her possessions: neither she nor her family understood at this time what was happening, but her husband, a Shouter Baptist, presumed some hidden meaning in it and did not interfere. When questioned by her family, Jeanette gave answers that flashed into her head: her actions were those of a Natural Spirit in her. The burned objects she now relates to her life back in town, to religion (the Bible), science (her spectacles) and to her domestic tasks (bedding, kitchen utensils and the sewing machine with which she made the children's shirts). Together with the destruction of all their clothes, the Burning resulted in the family remaining naked, cooking in the embers of an open fire, sheltering together at night against the cold Atlantic winds.

Pondering over these extraordinary actions, Jeanette realised that the Christian doctrine of God the Father as creator was false and that the world was really the work of a primordial Mother, to be identified as Nature, as the Earth. Nature had originally created a race of Black people, but her rebellious Son/Sun re-entered his Mother's womb/ moon to gain her power of generation and had succeeded by producing White people. The Whites, the Race of the Son, enslaved the Blacks and have continued to exploit them. The Way of the Son is that of Science, of Society, of cities, clothes, schools, factories and wage labour. The Way of the Mother is that of Nature: a return to the simplicity of the Beginning, a simplicity of nakedness, cultivation of the land by hand and with respect, and of gentle and non-exploiting human relationships.

The Son, Science, in his continued quest for the power of generation has now succeeded in establishing himself in *Africans* and *Indians* (2) and is also on the point of creating mechanical non-human beings. The Mother, who has borne all his behaviour out of her love for him, has finally lost patience. The current order of Science will end in nuclear war or in a catastrophic drought and famine, a destruction wrought through the Son's own power, after which the original state of Nature will once again prevail.

Jeanette herself is a partial aspect of the Mother who will only enter into her fully at the End. Her task now is to facilitate the return to Nature by organising a community on the coast, Hell Valley, the Valley of Decision, to prepare for the return to the Beginning and to Put Out The Life, her life, to her people, the Black Nation, the Mother's Children. She has to combat the false doctrine of *religion* which places the Son over the Mother, and to correct the distorted teaching of the Bible in which she is represented as the Devil. She stands for Nature and Life, in opposition to the Christian God who is only her Son, the principle of Science and Death. As the Devil she is opposed to churches and prisons, education and money, contemporary morals and fashionable opinions.

As God is 'right' Mother Earth teaches the Left, and the Earth People interchange various common oppositions: 'left' for 'right'; 'evil' or 'bad' for good'. Conventional obscenities are Natural words and should be used for She Herself is the Cunt, the source of all Life. The exact timing of the End is uncertain bur it will come in Jeanette's physical lifetime. Then Time will cease, disease will be healed and the Nation will speak one language. The Son will return to his Planet, the Planet Sun, the Planet of ice, which is currently hidden by Fire placed there by the Mother–Fire which will eventually return where it belongs, back to the heart of a nurturant Earth.

Since her visions in 1975 which marked the Beginning of the End, Jeanette's immediate family have been joined by numbers of Black Trinidadians, usually young men, sometimes with their partners and children. The community has a high turnover and, while over fifty people have been associated with the Earth People, when I stayed with them in 1981–2 (3) there were twenty-three living in the Valley of Decision, with perhaps twenty close sympathisers in town. About once a year the group march into town to Free Up The Nation and present their message in the central streets and parks, in particular Woodford Square, the popular site for political demonstrations next to the Parliament building. After a few weeks of Putting Out The Life, and visits to friends and relatives, they return to the Valley to continue to Plant For The Nation. In Putting Out The Life Jeanette harangues the crowd; she poignantly retells her personal struggles, identifying them with those of Nature. The men of the group chorus agreement, and explain and argue with the bystanders.

Putting Out the Life: The Mother

The idiom of childbirth is fundamental both to Mother Earth's formal cosmogony and to her understanding of current relations between women and men. The experience of motherhood has played the single most salient role in her life, as it does for the women in the nearby villages who recounted their lives to me. It is through her own motherhood that Mother Earth represents herself as all Black women.

She was the eldest of ten children born to the domestic servant of a White family in Port of Spain. She only met her father 'once or twice' as she recalls; he died when she was about thirty: 'He call me then. I was not very interested but I go.' At sixteen she left home to live with a boy. This relationship broke up and she returned to stay with her grandmother, a follower of the *orishas* of *shango*, and then lived with one of her mother's previous *friends* by whom she herself had three children. As for most working-class Trinidadian women, emancipation from parents and emergence into adulthood came, not with chronological age, education, employment away from the household or even sexual relations, but with childbearing. She *scuffled* – borrowing, bartering and getting by through help from relatives, and boyfriends: 'a little job here, a next one there. I often plan to get marry but something happen, I ai' fuss.' Her life was similar to that of many poorer women in the town and she recalls she was not aware at the time of any particular anger, any wish for change, just facing the endless round of bearing children and caring for them. Only one aspect of her life in town produced any immediate resentment:

Something happen to me in hospital once which I didn't like at all. Was with one of my babies, I don't really like the labour room because I find the bed is too high, it is too cold, the plastic they put on it is too cold. You have to lie down this wet cold plastic and in my pain I like to be walking.

Whenever a pain take me I jump off the bed and I gone, up and down, up and down, until it ease again, I go back and lie. But in the labour room you cannot do that: you have to bear the pain on the bed there. To me, I get more pain by being lying down there twist up. So I never like the labour room. So what I do is ease my pain on the outside, in the yard, and I remain there whenever it take me and walk: walk until it get very hot and I know when it is time to deliver, I just jump up on the bed and my baby will come. When the baby come I call the nurse. The nurse did just pass and see me comfortable so, when she come back now, she say 'What happen! 'I say 'the baby, the baby'... When she look she say 'Look what you making a mess, you making a mess in the place, look what you doing on the bed! You making a mess! Get up and go in the labour room! I bet you I push it back'. And she hold it, [part] of the baby, and push it. I fire a kick because I feel a pain! An' when I fire the kick my foot pass near her face. When I start to cry one time I say 'Sorry, I didn't really mean to do that but you push it and you hurt me' ... You know and I cry and thing and I make it look [right].

Not until the Burning did Jeanette realise this was a prefiguring, a purely individual representation of the universal striving by which the Mother's Son, indeed all men, tried to return to the mother's womb, to destroy this root of natural fertility and to gain its power, later to attempt to transcend it altogether through science in a purely mechanical creation.

Putting Out the Life: Her Children

The Earth People as a community may be seen as a generalisation and a reinterpretation of personal experiences, Mother Earth's certainly, but also those of their own which resonate with hers. They are not a passive mimesis but a transformation, commentaries, 'experiences put into circulation' (Turner 1986). As Shiro-kogoroff (1915) noted, 'imitative mania' alone cannot become social rebellion. Nor a community. The Earth People do not take Mother Earth's experiences and interpretations as 'metaphor', as merely emblematic. They are Life for them as for her, to be realised through action in the everyday world.

Do the lives and experiences of each member of the Earth People replicate those of Mother Earth's life – generating a *homologous* structure of social organisation and values – or does each member *reciprocally* relate to Mother Earth in the community (cf. Jakobson 1960)? We find both: homology in those aspects which relate to the historical and political situation shared by Black people in relation to Whites (for all the members are Black); and reciprocity in those aspects which concern the relations between Black mothers and their children, and between women and men (for the majority of the permanent members are young men).

The Earth People consider themselves a family arranged around Mother Earth, a family that corresponds to the original Mother Nature with her Black Children. Indeed the Mother is somehow the same person in both. The primordial family of Black Children is already recreated in the typical Afro-Caribbean family, and parallels between it and the group in the Valley are continually stressed. In theory there are no other distinctions beyond that of Mother herself and that of Earth Person (or *fruits*, for each new member takes a fruit or vegetable name); there are no recognised sub-groups, no hierarchy. Mother Earth is regarded with warm, affectionate feelings by everybody as their Mother. Nor is there a sacred text for the Valley of Decision: its origin and continuation lie solely in her past life and in her personality. It is Mother who relates everyday incidents to their central purpose. It is in her that the awesome powers of Mother Nature will finally be manifest. Her mood both follows the events of the day and is itself quickly reflected in the feeling of the others. If she feels unwell, the Earth People are subdued; if lively, they are filled with new energy and confidence. Her usual station is by the central cooking area: shouts of 'Mother want you' are quickly relayed to those working away from the house, and as immediately obeyed. Her critical comments on the progress of the cooking, the tidiness of the men's house or on general morale are listened to with quiet attention and her wishes anticipated. At the same time this is done with much playful abuse. On one occasion, soon after my arrival, she helped herself to Coconut's calabash of *fig* (plantain). He protested 'That my own fig.' Breadfruit immediately reproved him: 'That Mother Earth own. All food come from Mother Earth', but added, to general laughter, 'And she ai' got no fucking manners!'

Until the End comes she does not see herself as having ultrahuman powers in any physical sense; this would anyway be unnecessary for all is Nature:

I is the Mother, the Beginning. But I ai' play chief. You think I want to sit on high throne! ... Imagine you self Ruler of the Earth! It real dread you know ... Not to take it as a kingship. I don't want a crown. The Children are my crown.

How did the Earth People come to join Mother Earth? They themselves told me of their poverty compared with other, particularly White Creole, Trinidadians. Like all working-class men in the shanty areas of Port of Spain, they accept that *tibourg* (middle-class) *society* is not interested in them. They maintain that they had never really dedicated themselves to the material pursuits of the *respectable* (4) classes: by contrast they had experienced a need they described as 'spiritual'. Some of them joined the Shouter Baptists until they realised that these were only 'partial' and had not come to terms with the historical and political relationship with Whites. They had then grown their *natty* (dreadlocks) and adopted Rasta idiom and some Rasta ideas but, again, felt that this was not enough, that Rastas were not living the natural life they proclaimed.

Breadfruit had grown up near Mother Earth who had been a neighbour of his mother and tried to combine Shouter Baptism with the *natural* parts of Rastafari:

And then I let natty grow again and one day minister take me in church and he say 'Why do you don't go and comb it!' I say 'Why!' He say 'For society'. So I think I don't want it; I for meself. So I didn't go to church again ... And at night I go out naked and lie on the ground and say 'Why not pray to a Mother for a few days!' So I do! [Soon he saw Mother Earth again on a visit to town] Me mother always go by she. I see her a next time in '79 when she go up to Laventille. I use to talk about Selassie and thing but she show me my senses. The next day I had a vision and see me self natural, run about with little children. Next day I just put on bag [sack] and start go about with she. What made me see me self was that I see self and see this Black woman naked and walk about with school girls in uniform and I fly by her side. And I move and kiss earth and I burn Bible. And when Mother come up I free to talk it again.

Potato was seventeen when he came to the Valley:

What Mother Earth say it all 'bout, my mother did and so [preparing local food] but Rastas didn't like it. I hardly go off on it [Rastafari], hat and so, and I start going 'bout with bare foot. I didn't like the city, fighting with pollution. This world too crucial to the flesh. Old time people more natural: my old grandmother used to tell us to gather round when she cock up her leg an' pee. Now you run home hold your legs together! ... We live here natural. When we go to town I ai' shit for a week. We come back in bush and take deer bush and pow! Free up yourself! When we little they talk of God the Father. And me say 'Who he' And they talk of Mary, Mother of God and me say 'What!' and I get brain tie up. And now Mother gives me senses. Like we all come from down here [the Earth].

To what extent can we argue that the members who joined the group were in some sense consciously 'looking for a mother', attempting themselves to return to an earlier and harmonious life as a child, some frozen replication of one phase in the family cycle? They themselves argue the reverse – that the human family provides a replication of the original family of the Mother and Her Black children. As a community they feel that they are part of this family, and the Valley as a whole appears to reflect the working-class Afro-Caribbean family. The two possible 'structural imbalances' of the group, which I thought threatened its continued existence, derive from its rooting in the original Mother–Child cosmogony and from the rarity of women members.

Mother Earth is the Mother of every member and yet she has a consort, her partner Jakatan, but the only person resembling a consort of the parthenogenic Mother is her incestuous Son, the God of the Whites: in the group there can be no ultimately grounded status for Jakatan, except as one of the Mother's Children. Although he is much younger than Mother, it was he who had first suggested that the couple and their children should move to the bush and, although he loyally supports her in public, on occasions he leaves the community to visit his family. At other times he takes a select group of Earth People to the *high woods* where he has built a small hut. In his absence Mother Earth decries this 'high woods group' and complains that 'he plays at boss man there'. At times of bitter argument she harangues the group about the role of fathers in general, how they desert women and leave them to look after the children. She retells the story of her life. She is the West Indian mother complaining to her children about the vagaries of their father. While there is much genuine affection between Mother Earth and Jakatan there are times when I thought he resents the role he has in the group as a sort of elder son, particularly when he is berated by Mother for not taking a more active role in encouraging the less experienced members, a role which is in any case restricted in that there is no position for a 'father' in the group. Again the situation recalls the self-perception of the Black

Creole family in Trinidad, constantly measured against their idea of
the *respectable* White family.

The other 'unbalanced' feature, the absence of *mothers* (women),
recalls the problems of sexuality between the siblings of any family.
While Mother Earth is certainly correct in saying that it is Black
women who have particular difficulties in abandoning town to come to
the Valley because of their more *respectable* aspirations, she herself
finds it difficult to accept women members, particularly if they are
likely to form liaisons with her male Children. Whilst celibacy is no
explicit part of her teaching, Mother Earth strongly hints that the time
is not yet ready for sex:

> Roland, they could go off for a woman but it ai' in them. They work
> to preparation for having children. I show them how to live to love
> the mothers. Their outside life ai' no preparation.

Putting Out the Life: The Whites

> The attentive reader will have grasped no doubt from what has
> been said so far that in what I am about to relate I was a witness
> and not an actor. I am not the hero of my tale. Nor am I exactly its
> bard. Though the events I saw convulsed my previously insignifi-
> cant existence, though their full weight still bears upon my
> conduct, upon my way of seeing, in recounting them I wish to
> adopt the cold impassive tone of the ethnologist: I visited this
> sunken world and this is what I saw there. (Perec, *W or The
> Memory of Childhood*, p. 4)

I realised that my own stay with the Earth People would involve two
particular difficulties, for them and for myself. Fieldwork with new
religious groups is rare because uncommitted outsiders are not easily
welcome, particularly when initial enthusiasm is palling and conflicts
develop about the extent of accommodation with the outside world,
and splits in the group are common. The Valley awaited recruits not
students. Conversely, departure can only be a betrayal.

The very specific beliefs of the Earth People were the other
problem. Whites are the Children of Science, the historical oppressors
of Black people. Given its history of genocide, slavery and colonialism,
no White in the Caribbean can anyway conceive of themselves as any
sort of 'neutral' observer. The European is already an integral part of
the local classification (see note 4); the White ethnographer is already
an element in the society (s)he comes to observe. My invitation to stay

in the Valley, the sheer improbability of the situation – the arrival of a White male psychiatrist – an inversion of the earlier situation when, after Putting Out The Life, Mother Earth had been sent by a magistrate to the Port of Spain psychiatric hospital (until rescued by the group in a night raid). The parodic absurdity of my arrival confirmed some sort of implicit Natural meaning. For a world already upside-down, reconciliation could only be absurd.

It was after a few daytime visits, for which I was dropped off by boat from the village or stayed nearby in an abandoned cocoa box, that I was told to remain for a night and then for longer stays. At about this time, after going swimming in the river with Pumpkin and Cocorite, I emerged from the water and walked back to the house naked, to general derision, acclaim and amusement. From then onwards I lived in the Valley for a few weeks at a time over a period of a year. I did not sleep in the men's hut but occupied a space near the central fire, in between Mother Earth and her family, together with the new members. The possibility of my joining fully, cutting my ties with the outside world, was raised occasionally but discreetly. There seemed no great pressure on me to do this and I assumed it was generally recognised that I would eventually return to Britain. Towards the end of my stay, the group persuaded me, over my objections, to bring a camera and tape recorder. I photographed them. They photographed me. My wife and our daughter came to stay also on a few occasions. My daughter's name is Letice and this resulted in our all being given *fruit names*; we were jokingly known as the *short-crops*, the Trinidadian term for 'European' crops newly introduced. At this point, at the suggestion of Mother Earth, I gave an interview in Port of Spain to a magazine (*The People* 1981) and a lecture about them at St Ann's Hospital, and wrote with the group an article for publication in the *Trinidad Guardian*. I recognised I was an immediate bulwark against any action by the police or the hospital, someone who could help gain public support when the Valley faced any concerted campaign in the press for government action against it, as it frequently did (*Trinidad Guardian* 1982).

My stay inevitably led to changing notions of Black and White, leading to a general transformation that Whites could be Black 'inside', and Blacks White, an idea that Mother Earth herself already held in parallel with the more dichotomised schema favoured by the Rastas. I resisted this but settled into working together with Mother Earth on such diversions as determining which culture heroes were already representations of the Son. Prometheus and Jesus? Of course. Odysseus? Probably. I offered suggestions derived from structural group therapy on resolving communal 'tensions', but I became confused as to what was a structural model of what. Could I have a model of a transformation of which my model was itself an element? I still sought distance, innocence, Perec's 'cold impassive tone'. 'How very White you are', sighed Mother Earth, 'still Science'.

For the more Rasta-orientated members my stay was difficult (see *The Bomb* 1982). Their problem was the same as mine: a need for an unadulterated community, a synthesis shorn of its dialectical power. We had frequent discussions as to my implications for the immediate practical concerns of the group, let alone its eschatological aspect: would I too live at the End? Would the police come and rescue me? On many occasions I told everybody that I felt I was making needless difficulties for them but was always told to be quiet and to stay: 'Don't get you' mind tie up now.' In spite of these public demands to stop worrying I remained uneasy about 'universalising' the teaching and my effect on the existing daily conflicts. While I am not now, ten years later, convinced that I 'should' have stayed, at the time I allowed myself to be persuaded by Mother Earth, who as the founder and leader of the group instructed me firmly to remain, saying that my arrival was both predicted and a necessary development of the End. An all too easy persuasion? Perhaps, but for the anthropologist to claim total responsibility is to deny power to the people whose lives we reconstruct for our own purposes, and who at times reconstruct ours. On my final visit to the Valley I recorded her Message to the World, a message of communal singing and Mother retelling once again the story of her Life and her people, and of the coming End.

Myself?

A biography is the intersection of two lives. Myself? (as the personal ads at the back of *The New York Review of Books* put it). A White male. Middle-class British childhood, father of Yorkshire radical Nonconformist stock, a Swiss mother whose uncle was associated with the Zimmerwald movement. Provincial ennui and the worthy *Manchester Guardian*, then, but also Bunyan, Robin Hood, *The Wind in the Willows*, Richmal Crompton's *William*, *Captain Blood* and *Westward Ho!* Grammar school, Rider Haggard, 'backwoods cooking' in the Scouts, Conrad, *The Golden Bough*, Kropotkin's *Conquest of Bread*, Meister Eckhart, Schrödinger's *What is Life?*, *Là Bas*, *The Divided Self*. On leaving school, six months at Shivanandra's ashram in Rishikesh, then St Bartholomew's Hospital Medical School, the Dialectics of Liberation at the Roundhouse, casual work on the periodical *Black Dwarf*, medical support to the LSE occupation, the

Revolutionary Socialist Students' Federation, failed and retook surgery finals, the quasi-hippie Electric Garden and Indica, art school in Whitechapel, house jobs at Barts, psychiatry in Hackney, Jaspers and Dubuffet, psychotherapy training, Rastafarian patients, research on statistical phenomenology, lectureship, first book on racism and psychiatry, anthropology at Oxford (my Jude's Syndrome resolved(5)), last paintings, parenthood, Trinidad.

Plotting some points for my biographical trajectory like that (and we have a variety of selectable trajectories with or without the psychological realism which constructs them as plausible narratives for others) to the moment at which it intersected with that of Mother Earth, the question is hardly 'Why did I choose the Earth People?', rather 'How might I have failed to choose them?' After some months in the village I was getting a little complacent. Everything was reasonably easy, too easy as I was later to understand. I'd finally finished reading Proust and was on course for yet another routine ethnomedical monograph on a small village community (but one totally bereft of any apparent theory, the astounding pragmatism of the villagers' bush medicine seemed to put paid to any neat structural Marxism), when an argument with a *long eyed* fisherman who wanted thirty dollars to disclose the prayers for curing *maljo* (evil eye: they wouldn't work after they'd been sold, I knew that much, and he knew more about fieldwork than I did), turned my thoughts again to the Earth People. A long-standing interest in radical Puritanism, some sort of Romantic yearning for a primitive *Zwischenmenschliche*, the rumours that Mother Earth had been in the psychiatric hospital in Port of Spain? Of course. 'The Pinnacle villagers had warned me ...,' 'the most desolate part of the island ...' indeed: classic appeals to the reader to consider the intrepid ethnographer's narrative as colonial adventure, the Victorian valley utopia which both presents and opposes the Other as 'other'.

Of course. But not just that. I'd often wondered how religions got themselves started: not the routinisation and elaborations, the consolidation of dogmas and hierarchies, but the earlier bit, where the mundane and the fortuitous somehow became central, where personal contingencies and experiences become universal truths, where the nocturnal traveller on his way to Emmaus is recognised as the recently executed prophet, where Mother Ann Lee's endless pregnancies transform the Christian God into the Shakers' bisexual divinity, where transient dysphorias become the very foundations of Hell. (As the Digger Gerrard Winstanley put it, offending against seventeenth-century Calvinism, 'if the passion of sorrow predominate, then he's heavy and mad, crying out he's damned'.(6)

The passage of personal lives, with all their routine accidents, into the stuff of established culture and hagiography had always seemed a little mysterious. Does Christianity demonstrate the personal experiences of Jesus, or of St Paul? Who knows? The biographical fallacy, arbitrary and unprofitable speculation. And yet.

If the random sources of my own religious systems continued to fascinate me, I was contemptuous of the half-baked psychoanalytical speculations of Devereux and La Barre, even Erikson, and bored which the typologies of the sociologists of religion who, too, used the idiom of 'pathology' to qualify any millennial movement of which they disapproved (most of them, it seemed). The Earth People offered me a return to the problem of the interactions between individual experience and social representation, between a psychopathology closer to biology (my first degree had been in biochemistry, and I knew that Mother Earth had thyrocoxicosis) and the procedures of social anthropology: questions that remained vital to me, not to be dispersed in some Foucauldian elision. I still found biological knowledge interesting – biological potentialism, the constraints on our social choice of natural symbols.

If I had chosen the Earth People, they had chosen me. As I learned, Mother Earth herself was concerned with revising the opposition between Nature and Science. More than that, it was perhaps an opposition that could only be resolved through my arrival as their 'Other': male, White and a scientist, my periphery to their centre. A re-enactment by us both. She stipulated that I would live with her community only on the condition that I wrote my D.Phil. thesis about them, as some sort of near final squaring off (or reconciliation?) with Science, the procedure left up to me.

I had been twenty-four when my country relinquished its colonial power over Trinidad. And yet its measure of values remained inescapably European. The models for education, economy, political process and the texture of everyday life are those of Britain and the United States. The marginality which this engenders has been said to present the West Indian with 'no target to aim at, no ideal vision, that is not ultimately self-defeating' (Lowenthal 1972). In the European perception of the West Indies the countries have never been identified with any civil society but rather with nature, raw material awaiting exploitation through heavy capital investment and cheap labour. Disappearing from the European gaze when sugar ceased to contribute significantly to the metropolitan economy, the West Indies have recently re-emerged, but now as a tourist paradise of unsullied nature whose inhabitants exist to provide refreshment and entertainment, and to seduce visitors into discarding temporarily their metropolitan responsibilities – 'Islands in the Sun'. Such a prelapsarian state of nature, what Aimé Césaire has called a mock paradise, compromises:

> environmental delectability, effortless subsistence, carefree disposi-
> tion, devotion to sensual pleasures (music, dance, sex) and easy
> racial intermingling ... When nature is so agreeable, houses are
> seen more as luxuries than necessities. (Lowenthal 1972: 16)

If the Valley of Decision was an appropriation (yet an affirmation) of such a vision, it was also one which contained an explanation of our fall from grace. If in its apparent autonomy, Mother Earth and I collaborated in a renactment of what Pratt (1986) has called 'the first contact scene', we nevertheless fought for an unattainable reconcilia-tion, a starting over again. And one which was not just personal but a reconciliation whose success or failure carried a heavy burden. My transcribed tapes and photographs are less indexical fragments, snapshots *en route*, than set pieces, posed, self-presentations by Mother Earth and myself, not bits of 'as it was' but declarations of 'how it should be', 'how it couldn't be'.

'My' chapter then is less 'about' Mother Earth than it is part of Mother Earth, not in some modish deconstruction but as an explicit element of her cosmogony, explicitly predicted, demanded by her, an intersubjectivity. As is your reading of it. A conventional 'Russian Doll' display of the structures of her biographies (see Figure 1) fails to show my, your, interaction with her, our engagement, our role in the historical oppression of Black people and our potential liberation from history. If the Son, the parodic God of White Science, has produced us through our commodification of Black people, through male domina-tion of women, through our rape of Nature,(7) then the Beginning of the End entails a transformation of us all, subject and object, personal experience and academic discourse alike.

The Meaning of a Life

I do not claim to have achieved that, but I would not have wished to live with the Earth People had I not resonated with much of their world. (And still do:(8) it was only on my return to Britain that I realised the parallels with what was to become ecofeminism.) I'm not sure that they solved any particular personal dilemmas for me (the reverse), merely that they offered a reassertion of the sort of values in which I was brought up (which raises its own questions as to how reciprocal or homologous my values are to those of my parents), values

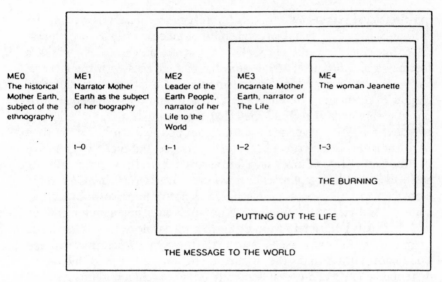

ME0	ME1	ME2	ME3	ME4
The historical Mother Earth, subject of the ethnography	Narrator Mother Earth as the subject of her biography	Leader of the Earth People, narrator of her Life to the World	Incarnate Mother Earth, narrator of The Life	The woman Jeanette
	t–0	t–1	t–2	t–3

THE BURNING

PUTTING OUT THE LIFE

THE MESSAGE TO THE WORLD

THE ETHNOGRAPHY

NB I have adapted the schema of Umberto Eco in *The Role of the Reader* (1979) and *A Portrait of the Elder as a Young Pliny* (1985). It is a considerable over-simplification which ignores the effects of my presence in t–0 on the recitation of the events of t–1 ... t–3

Figure 1 Putting out the life: the structures of the narratives

which I still respect and whose absence in contemporary Britain I profoundly regret: some notion of Dissent, a sense that any authority is inevitably compromised, that the moral life is an individual one to be defined against all institutional power. Adolescent if you will. If the millennium is about anything it is about the suspension of time. Primitivist? An assumption that institutions can be most truly understood through a reconstruction of their origins? It would be naive to imagine that, at one level, ethnography is not motivated by some personal quest for the fundamental, for ourselves (else we would be as tiresome as sociology). So yes, but at an explicit intellectual level I do not think so.

For what questions, then, may I claim Mother Earth as our answer? Her cosmogony condenses down into a single coherent schema a whole series of fragmented or sub-dominant identities which are refracted through her life – those of Black people, of women, the mad, the dispossessed – through an appropriation and reassertion of the existing local 'strategies of everyday resistance'9 *bad talking, obeah, picong* (satire), Calypso, Carnival, *masquerade*, word play, *worthlessness*. But she is not merely seeking the heart of a heartless world, a lost pastoral innocence. More radically, she engages with their White ascription, with complementary parent–child relations, our differentiation from nature, the challenge to traditional ideas of personhood posed by biomedical technologies (10) and by nuclear war, the loss of personal relations in an increasingly commodified world: in short, a multitude of contradictions between experience and meaning.

And yet. Her valuing of Nature over human society and its scientific procedures approaches a hylotheism in which the Creatrix is identified with Her creation. Nature is an active force, form as well as content, and Her representation, Woman is both organising principle and material. Ultimately Mother Earth's eschatology is quietist for it seems that All may well return to the One, recalling perhaps Buddhism rather than the Judaeo-Christian moral and biological dynamic which continues in Rastafari and in psychiatry. The return of the Son to his Mother, of Science to Nature, although implicit, is never clearly enunciated. Perhaps it could never have been, given my own departure. An ultimate *coincidentia oppositorum* between us remained elusive. As she put it, eloquently if eliptically:

If all trees are one tree, that is the Mother.
If all men are one man, that is the Son saying he is the Father.

Notes

1   Sheds with sliding roofs for drying cocoa.
2   Approximately half of Trinidad's population trace their descent to Indians recruited as indentured labourers in the later nineteenth and early twentieth centuries. The remainder, the Creoles, are *Africans* or *Negro* (the sociologists' 'Afro-Caribbeans') together with some *French Creoles* ('Whites'). *Society* already refers in Trinidad English to urban life, while *Science* is the term for European (Hermetic) sorcery (Littlewood 1988).
3   On a Social Science Research Council Post-Doctoral Fellowship 1979–81. I returned again in 1988 for three months, and again in 1991.
4   On the dualism of Afro-Caribbean society and values in Trinidad, see Littlewood (1988). Briefly, an egalitarian working-class and male-orientated notion of *worthlessness* (or *nigger ways*) is contrasted with *respectability* which is associated with church marriage, middle-class and White values, formal education, social hierarchy and chastity, and which is represented typically in women (cf. Wilson 1973).
5   Hardy (1896/1974).
6   Winstanley (1973) p. 351.
7   Science led Man to 'Nature with all her children to bind her to your service

and make her your slave', to a 'truly masculine birth of time (in which Man) would conquer and subdue Nature, to shake her to her foundations.' Mother Nature was to be penetrated by Man after he had 'broken her Seale and exposed her naked to the World' (Francis Bacon and Thomas Vaughan, cited by Easlea 1980, pp. 129, 133, 247–8).

8 Our trajectories continue. For the Earth People: the death of Mother Earth in 1983, mutual recriminations and splits, a visit by me in 1988. For myself: an uneasy accommodation with academic status, clinical power and responsibility, phone calls from the Earth People, rejection by a Port of Spain publisher of our joint pamphlet *The Teachings of Mother Earth* (a transcription of the Message to the World).

9 What Schwimmer (1972) terms an 'oppositional ideology': 'inversions or reversals of putative scale values on which the members of the disadvantaged group suppose themselves to be consigned to the pole of marginality or peripherality by those in the "centre" ... One of the potent ways in which they appear to give meaning symbolically to their communality is by reversing the polarities of the scale to make their values central' (cf. Taussig 1987). Gates (1988) takes Bakhtin's term 'double-voiced' to characterise such ludic tropes as irony, parody and antanaclasis in Afro-American English, Abrahams' (1970) 'direction by indirection' (as Hamlet put it).

10 If Mother Earth's apocalypse seems to reinvent science fiction, read the forty-year programme for transfer of human personality on to computers and our final dissolution as biological organisms as urged by Hans Moravec (1989), director of the Carnagie Mellon University's robotics centre.

10 Verticality as the Idiom for Mood and Disorder: A Note on an Eighteenth-Century Representation*

Reflecting on our immediate engagement with the physical world provides us with a language for elaborating less tangible notions. Thus 'height' is frequently used as an attribute of divinity, supernatural power and shamanic visions.[1] 'Up' is 'more', it is 'better', an attribute of 'superior' secular authority; those of 'higher' status supervise the 'lower' orders, and so on.[2] Ascent is arduous, descent precipitous; moral or social achievement difficult, Adam's Fall all too easy.

Everyday changes of mood recalling those we now refer to in English as 'elation' and 'depression' have not always been articulated as verticality. The word 'depression' by itself (Lat. *de-pressum*, pressed down) seems to have become a common English term for an emotional rather than a spatial state only in the 1700s,[3] gradually replacing acedia, tristitia and melancholy, although the expression 'depression of spirit' is found a hundred years earlier. A more common embodied schema (as Mark Johnson [4] terms it) for despairing or miserable affects may employ an idiom of containment and emptying, in which some vital part of our self is cut-off, lost or stolen.[5] In contrast to depression, 'elation' (Lat. *elario*, lifted up) had a psychological significance in English before any spatial sense, presumably reflecting its earlier Latin meaning of enraptured or transfigured as well as elevated.[6] Linking the two in a single dimension of depression-elation is now common: in the medical category of manic-depression where states of being are expressed by and communicated between doctor and patient as the latter being 'low' or 'high'; in the advertisements in medical journals which represent the action of antidepressant drugs as the vigorous upward movement of rockets and aeroplanes; and of course in our everyday language – 'things are looking up', 'high as a kite', or 'down in the dumps'.

* First published in the *British Medical Anthropology Review* (1994)

Verticality as a representation of one's spirits, mood, affect, vitality, energy or whatever seems an apt and accessible cross-cultural representation.(7) When miserable our bodies seem heavier, more rooted downwards, less amenable to our agency, sluggish, tired, retarded, gravid, dragging. When cheerful or ecstatic we are less encumbered by our physicality, floating, soaring, bouncing, our intentions readily translated into acts.(8) And gravity makes this rather dualistic: if we don't go up we go down or at least stay 'level'. Such a coupling of depression and elation as the opposing poles of a single dimension seems to have appeared in the mid-eighteenth century.(9) Its first visual representation is perhaps William Hogarth's engraving of *Enthusiasms Delineated* (1761) which satirises the religious enthusiasm of the Methodists. In the bottom right-hand corner of a scene of a lustful and lunatic congregation, a sort of thermometer emerges from a brain, calibrated upwards from Despair, through Low Spirits, Luke Warm, Lust Hot, and Extacy, to Revelation. In the revised and marginally less blasphemous plate (1762, illustrated here), the bottom of the scale is now labelled Suicide.

The single scale allows us to objectify the opposing qualities as a single entity, just as our experiences of 'hot' and 'cold' become simply varying degrees of something we call 'temperature'.

How did a verticality continuum representing a bipolarity of mood become salient in the mid-eighteenth century? Hogarth's intentions are of course comic, not just to satirise popular credulity and the occasional evangelical enthusiasms of the Anglican church,(10) but also to mock an excessively objective reading of everyday life – as in his collections of urine-tasting doctors (*The Company of Undertakers*) or his structural analysis of wigs which conflates phrenology with the architectural orders (*The Five Orders of Periwigs*). Yet his work often shows fairly serious concern with elaborating new classificatory dimensions (*Characters and Caricatures*). Subsidiary scales and guides to linear perspective, comic or otherwise, crop up everywhere in his prints, as the scale of vociferation in *Enthusiasms* complements the affective thermometer below. Hogarth wrote a treatise on aesthetics, *The Analysis of Beauty*, and devised a technique he called 'technical memory' by which one could memorise the contents of a visual field serially through an underlying grammar of forms. Advocating a new linear world of analysis or satirising it? As with the current debate as to whether Hogarth was representing or assailing popular urban values (11), we may conclude he was doing both.

A number of commentators have remarked on how the science of the Enlightenment privileged the optical paradigm, what Foucault (12) terms medicine's 'clinical gaze'. Both Howes and Heelan (13) argue

that this was a deployment of Alberti's fixed-position visual perspective, which then became available for generalisation into a correspondence theory of unmediated knowledge to be delineated by the context-independent observer.(14) Such an objective perspective was not natural and had to be learned, just as earlier Durer had needed a wire grid to render the artist's untutored perspective.

Our current phenomenological criticisms of anthropological theory note that the visual modality is less 'embodied' than our other senses, apparently the least mediated by our physical state and thus the most available schema for the objectification of other experiences.(15) And a common critique of contemporary psychiatry is of course that it misses the complex embodied experience of unusual patterns of mood, sensation, kinaesthesia, comportment and gesture, rereading these through rating scales of one sort or another. In Hogarth's engraving we can perhaps find one of the moments in which psychological co-options of gravitational experience became objectified as a master image in a mathematical scale, the flux of everyday moods now concretised as a quantifiable entity.(16)

Notes

1   Eliade, M. *Patterns in Comparative Religion.* London: Sheed and Ward, 1958; ch. 2,3.
2   Cohen, PS. Psychoanalysis and cultural symbolisation. In: ML Foster and SH Brandes (eds). *Symbol as Sense: New Approaches to the Study of Meaning.* London: Academic Press, 1980.
3   'Hope refresheth as much as misery depresseth' (1621, Richard Burton, Anatomy of Melancholy), ' ... in great depression of spirit' (1665), 'he observed their depression' (1752, Samuel Johnson); cf. 'depreced provinces' (1340), 'depressioun of the pol antarktik' (1391). [All OED]
4   Johnson M. *The Body in the Mind: The Bodily Basis of Meaning, Imagination and Reason.* Chicago: University of Chicago Press, 1987.
5   Shweder R. Menstrual pollution, soul loss and the comparative study of emotions. In: A. Kleinman and B. Good (eds). *Culture and Depression.* Berkeley: University of California Press, 1985.
6   'Elacion is when he ne may neither suffre to have maister ne felawe' (1386, Chaucer), 'a foolish Elation of Heart' (1772, Addison). [Both OED]
7   Osgood CE, May WH and Miron MS. *Cross-Cultural Universals of Affective Meaning.* Urbana: University of Illinois Press, 1975. 'Height' may also retain a more purely spatial sense in ethnomedicines: such as 'high blood' in Trinidad – simultaneously thick and rich blood, congealed blood, blood going to your head causing a stroke, high blood pressure, a high reading on the doctor's instrument, European blood (Littlewood, R. *Pathology and Identity.* Cambridge: Cambridge University Press, 1993).
8   Can a verticality schema be the opposite way round? Excitement as lowered vitality? In Fiji an experience akin to the psychiatric idea of manic

elation is termed *matikuru*, 'low tide' (Price, J and Karim, I, Matikuru: a Fijian madness, *British Journal of Psychiatry*, 133, 228–230, 1978) but the authors' translation 'low' is perhaps an inappropriate vertical rendering, and something like 'out to sea' may be more apposite.

9 'Their time is past between elation and despondency' (Johnson, 1750) [OED]. There are certainly earlier pairings which have not made it into the OED, such as that of the Digger Gerrard Winstanley in 1652: 'And if the passion of joy predominate, then he is merry and sings and laughs, and is ripe in the expression of his words ... But if the passion of sorrow predominate, then he is heavy and mad, crying out, He is dammed ... . And in that distemper many times a man doth hang, kill or drown himself' (*The Law of Freedom and Other Writings*, 1973, Harmondsworth: Penguin, 1973).

10 An astonished Turk peers through the window at a woman giving birth to rabbits; clues to the Cock Lane ghost (investigated by Johnson and Boswell) appear above the affective thermometer.

11 Dorment R. The genius of Gin Lane. *New York Review of Books*, May 27, 1993, 17–20.

12 Foucault M. *The Birth of the Clinic: An Archaeology of Medical Perception.* (Trans.) London: Tavistock, 1973.

13 Howes D. Introduction. In Howes (ed). *The Varieties of Sensory Experience.* Toronto: University of Toronto Press, 1991; Heelan P. *Space-Perception and the Philosophy of Science.* Berkeley: University of California Press, 1983.

14 Rorty R. *Philosophy and the Mirror of Nature.* Oxford: Blackwell, 1980.

15 Leder D. *The Absent Body.* Chicago: Chicago University Press, 1990.

16 On which see George Lakoff (*Women, Fire and Dangerous Things: What Categories Reveal About the Mind*, Chicago: Chicago University Press, 1987): reification is fundamental to social categorisation, giving ontological status to the experienced world. Early in life we are encouraged to perceive our experienced world as nominalised, as composed of entities of recurrent invariance (Laughlin, CD., McManus, J. and D'Aquili, A. *Brain, Symbol and Experience: Towards a Neurophenomonology of Human Consciousness.* New York: Columbia University Press, 1993).

11 'Moments of Creation':
Pregnancy and Parturition
as Cosmological Idiom*

Some Generalities in the Religious Embodiment of Women Prophets and Divine Innovators

Religious language clothes itself in such poor symbols as our life affords. (James 1907: 11)

An explicit parallel between human body and cosmos is commonplace in comparative sociology. Whilst Mauss' lecture on 'body techniques' and his earlier essay with Durkheim on primitive classification both allowed some apparent autonomy to human physiology and anatomy as the source for wider figurings,[1] recent sociological interest in the human body has emphasised the shared preoccupations which inscribe the body physical as discipline and knowledge: no longer may we assume pre-objective natural symbols such as the biological body to serve, unmediated by social cognitions, as intrinsic templates or sources.[2] Yet, bodily experiences such as dreaming, excreting, moving and pain have long been argued to make possible quite specific local categories as well as more general understandings of causality and influence, space, disease and agency (Tylor 1904, Douglas 1973, Merleau-Ponty 1962, Lakoff 1987, Johnson 1987). Without attributing ontological or epistemological primacy to either biological body or to the social order, to bodily experience or to cultural practice, we can certainly note the individual deployment of *novel* idioms to figure the world which may, for instance, draw on pregnancy and childbirth as (to use Mauss' term) 'biological-sociological' phenomena.

Figuring the relationship between cosmos and human in terms of sexuality or parturition appears virtually ubiquitous in human

*A paper given at the Fyssen Symposium on Culture and the Uses of the Body, 1997

understanding, whether as implicit trope, as conventionalised analogy or as some expressly concrete generation. Indeed it is difficult to conceive of any formal set of cosmological ideas (including male religious expression and counter-intuitive Western science) which do not in some way eventually evoke every-day sensory modes. Without making too extravagant claims, we might consider whether idioms of spiritual flight and of creation *de novo* at a distance (by spirit, breath, dream, speech or gesture) may not appear more congenial to the male imagination; idioms of experienced penetration or of a cosmic unfolding more accessible to women. Compare the encounter with ultrahuman agency for Saints Augustine and Teresa of Avila, male and female shamans, and in the ethnography of central and peripheral possession cults. Nor can we assume any sort of historical progression from one to the other: current instances of a reassertion of a 'female mode' of connectedness and inherent obligation may be instanced in Western theology, jurisprudence, philosophy and science (Corea 1988, Weigle 1989, Eilberg-Swartz 1994, Gilligan 1982, Baier 1994, Haraway 1989, 1991, Diprose 1994). Not altogether surprisingly, novel figurings of self and other, self and cosmos, employ our current preoccupations (such as the Life versus Choice debate in the United States) about our body in a physical world (rape, pregnancy, miscarriage, abortion, childbirth) (Littlewood 1996).(3) Revisions of Christianity by radical women prophets in the English tradition have frequently favoured a repeated unfolding (or disembedding) of an immanent creation rather than divine action at a distance. The prophet herself may be a fairly passive vehicle as bride or womb of divine power (Margery Kempe and Joanna Southcott), but sometimes as the female aspect of a bisexual deity (Ann Lee, the founder of the American Shakers), or most radically as our ultimate source now embodied in human form.(4)

This last possibility is exemplified by the founder of the Earth People, an African-Caribbean religion which developed in the 1970s. Her formal narrative of her pregnancies she intends to be read by us not just as her life as a human personage but as the cosmological order. And, in turn, the understandings of the community she establishes are to be identified as her own biography. As with Southcott and Lee, her multiple and problematic childbirths are figured as a universal order of divine generation, one which is constantly threatened by a redundant and lesser male principle which through an incestuous mimesis seeks her 'power to bring forth' only to produce the mechanical simulacra of European technology.

2

In 1971 Jeanette Baptiste, a thirty-nine-year-old woman, left Port-of-Spain to live on the north coast of Trinidad together with six of her twelve children and her current partner Cyprian.(5) She recalls being reluctant to move; only the promptings of Cyprian, a minor partici-pant in the 1970 Black Power Mutiny, persuade her to leave town. The family settle among the remains of one of the now deserted hamlets; initially paid by an absentee overseer to collect copra, they continue after an argument to squat on the abandoned land by tacit agreement. They grow ground provisions, exchanging the surplus with the nearest village some twelve miles distant through the bush. Both Jeanette and Cyprian have been somewhat half-hearted Spiritual Baptists (6) and they continue to 'pick along in the Bible' as they put it, fasting in Lent and interpreting the visionary import of their dreams. From 1975, after the birth of twins in their wooden hut, until 1976, Jeanette experiences a series of revelations which become the foundation of the Earth People. She comes to understand that Christian teaching is false, and that our world is the work of a primordial Mother whom she identifies with Nature, with the Earth and with her own body. Nature gave birth to a race of Black people, but her rebellious Son (the Christian God) re-entered his Mother's womb to steal her power of generation and succeeded by producing (or forcing her to create) White people. The Whites, the Race of the Son, then enslaved the Blacks and have continued to exploit them. The Way of the Son is that of Science – of cities, clothes, schools, books, factories and wage labour. The Way of The Mother is the Way of Nature – a return to the naked simplicity of the Beginning, cultivation of the land by hand, and of gentle and non-exploiting human relationships.(7)

The Son, in his continued quest for the power of generation, has now succeeded in establishing himself in Black People, and is on the point of replacing humankind altogether through mechanisation, computers and robots. His mother, Nature, who has borne all this out of love for the whole of her creation, has finally lost patience. The current order of the Son will soon end in a catastrophic drought and famine, or a nuclear war, a destruction of the Son's world through his own acts. Jeanette herself as Mother Earth is the primordial Mother in bodily form, but the Mother will only fully become her at the End. Her task now is to facilitate the return to the Beginning by organising the community known as Hell Valley, and to 'put out' The Life to her people, the Black Nation, The Mother's Children. She has to combat the teaching of the churches which place the Son over the Mother, and to correct the distorted teaching of the Bible where she is represented as the Devil. She embodies Life and Nature, in opposition to the Christian God who is her rebellious Son, the principle of Science and Death. As the Devil she is opposed to churches and prisons, education and money, contemporary morals and fashionable opinions. Because God is 'right', Mother Earth teaches the Left, and the Earth People invert various conventional oppositions: 'left' for 'right'; 'evil' or 'bad' for 'good', and so on. What others now take as obscenities are only Natural words for she herself is the Cunt, the source of all life. Her community do not 'force the end' – to use Buber's phrase: the exact timing of the End is uncertain but it will come in Jeanette's physical lifetime. Then Time will end, Sickness will be healed and the Nation will speak its one language. The Son will be exiled to his planet, the Sun, currently hidden by Fire placed there by The Mother – Fire which will eventually return to where it belongs, back to the heart of the nurturant Earth.

Since her revelations which initiated the Beginning of the End in 1975, Mother Earth's immediate family have been joined by numbers of Trinidadians, usually young men who bring their partners and children. The community has a high turnover and, while over fifty people have been associated with the Earth People, when I stayed with them there were twenty-two staying naked in the valley with perhaps a similar number of committed sympathisers in town. Once a year the group march into town and present their teachings in the central streets, particularly in Woodford Square, the popular site for political demonstrations next to the parliament. After a few weeks of 'putting out The Life' and visits to friends and relatives, they return to their valley and 'plant for the Nation'. The authorities have responded with raids on the community by police and nurses, with short prison sentences or incarceration in the psychiatric hospital, and sarcastic leading articles in the press.

In her Message to the World,[8] Mother Earth describes our origins:

In the Beginning was Nothing. Nothing was Life. Nothing formed herself into the elements. The elements resolve itself as Life. So Life formed herself: the Fire, the Water, the Earth, Dirt, Slime and Salt, and revolving herself, with the womb in the middle – the Moon. And there were all the planets for and against the Mother inside her ... A Son she bring forth. The Son was inside the Womb. So then Life and Death together once, not in the form as it is now but, as the people say, 'in the spirit'. Death revolving itself in the womb, in the Earth, Slime and Salt, Fire and Water. Well, she give him his own planet (everything carry its own planet by the name) so the Son carry his planet which is the planet Sun which we have up there, covered over with heat.

He left his planet. The reason for the heat around the planet is by him leaving his planet and enter the Earth. He wanted to have life, to bring forth like The Mother so he enter ... When he entered, pain entered the Earth. So he enter the Earth and the Earth change. It keep changing, changing until she put out flesh. And the first Flesh on the Earth were mothers which we were in a form. Not in this form of flesh: what we call the prick and the cunt was one form of Flesh which were the mothers ... The Flesh keep changing because he keep interfering until I divide myself in half and give him half. So the Son call himself Man but it is still The Mother. So now we carry bones and we become weaker. Bones were formed by The Mother but in his shape and form ... Time is he, Time is bones. Always jealous because he said 'I am jealous God'. Well, that is still jealousy, covetousness, all these things, pain, sickness, disease, shame and pride, age, time, all belongs to him. This is why we have these changes, that is why we have so much corruption on the earth. He have his share: the White people is really the Race of the Son because that was the Flesh that Mother prepared for the Son in the Beginning. And she had hers which is the Black Race. You could say all races come from the Black Race because we are the beginning of all races. And now all Flesh mix up and we are living the Life of the Son, not of the Black Race. You is all half Son.

In the Beginning when Flesh was placed upon the Earth, through the interruption of the Spirit of the Son enter in Earth, Mother had was [sic] to put out Flesh. And when she put out Flesh, she put out her Spirits which they were all mothers on the earth ... So when they say you die, you don't really die. When the Flesh grow old it is weak in all the Spirit – the Spirit comes out – and you come again in a new birth as a baby again. That Spirit come back. So then you always live it. You keep going and coming to meet to this stage here – what I call the Beginning. So when they talk about ancestors and these spirits guard you, I am seeing it as yourself spirit, not really a spirit of ancestors, who are they say depart for so much years. It is you yourself. Your ancestor is you!

The Spirit that is in the Flesh is the Spirit of Death, which is the Spirit of the Son, which we call – even we call it – God ... We become a robot for him, a machine. They can't really push him out completely: that is for when the hour come. The Mother allow him to do it because of her love. It is love she have. And she know all that he can never win. All [the Son] does is to put out material: the wars and the fights. the bombs and the [planes], trying to make human, trying to change them, some a mother to a son, change a son to a mother. All these are his experiment, trying to take over. He know everything about Life but not this – not the power to bring forth. That is what he really wants, the power of love. The onliest thing the Son has is machines and chemical. He has to use Science. He gains Science by interfering with Nature. Must he even have to use the oil of the Earth too, which is the Mother, take the oil out, pulling substance from the Earth. It becomes a cripsy (9): the oil is the blood of the earth.

Many of these figurings are of course common to earlier oppositional movements in Christianity: the communality of all; the Christian deity as interfering demiurge; church and society as immoral and compromised; the return to the Edenic past and the abandonment of mechanised technology along with formal education and clothes; the indwelling of divine power; redemption in the near future on this earth; a divine or semi-divine identity for the prophet and others. Some recall anti-colonial interpretations of European expansion: political defeat as moral betrayal; the colonised as the chosen people; the Whites' appropriation of the Bible as they bring of cosmic disharmony; an apocalyptic destruction followed by the return to an idealised pre-colonial past identified with the earth and women. We might remark two less common themes: the incarnation in the prophet herself of the original processes of the world; and thence an idiom of divine creation as her own human history of childbearing. The Earth People are generally celibate but sexuality pervades their ideas: the Son's act of *interference* (rape) initiated colonial and post-colonial power as science, as well as the European assimilation of African women as slaves, domestics, teachers, midwives and mistresses. Contemporary women, including Jeanette herself, have continued to experience something very like the original interference:

Every mother is The Mother ... You got big house but you dead. You children yet to work and you got to pay for them to learn. You learn work hard and your necessaries ... Half of children is born without love. They grow up with a frustration because their parents didn't come together with a love; so they have all sort of corruption. A man watch you and use you and laugh and he don't give you a dollar. And you get twelve big children ... It is because of the Spirit [the Son] and the teachings that you have cause the men to be taking advantage on the mothers. Now the reason for that is the Spirit which is controlling that Flesh. He thinks he's the boss. So then he always use the mother as just a nothing. She's there to bring forth the children, clean the house, wash the clothes, do everything and because, look, he goes out and brings in a penny he thinks 'Well look I am controlling'. That's the Spirit of the Son, really. Well it shouldn't be like that. It should be a love and understanding between the both Flesh ... Because when you beat the mother – your wife in fact – you come just as if you hit your wife, you hit your mother, you hit your sister there, you hit your daughter there. So then it's the teachings that have us in this condition. We suppose to be living different, to have more love, but it haven't got that love; everybody is each for themselves.

Yet local women are not altogether blameless:

Even [among] the mothers you find the same thing. If she's doing a little job and her husband is doing a job sometimes she gets frustrated because, you know, she's working for her own money. Knowing that you working for your own money you feel too that you is boss too, so you do what you want. So the both of you all doing what you want. That isn't a living. Women thinks more materialise. And men are more natural. This is what I am seeing here in this country ... And that is really the Spirit [of the Son] because the Spirit try to hold the mothers more because, knowing that the mothers is the Spirit of the Earth, well then, he must have them more confused.(10) So then they make more spectacle of themselves than the men, too much of dressing, too much of material (11) ... Even now that the mothers reach to a stage that they don't want to be a mother anymore. Most of them they don't want children; they use the contraceptive so that they can't have children. They don't really want that! They want a house, they want a car, you know they want all the material that they can get hold of instead of bringing forth their children. They find when they bring forth a child they can't go where they want, they can't do what they want: the children are confusing them. Contraceptive! We didn't plan to come here – the Spirit brought you – so how you plan now?

Both in the centrality of the female and in her cosmogony, Mother Earth deploys her life as a young mother. As she recalls her early life in colonial Port-of-Spain:

Well, it was a struggle, a very hard struggle for me, because I just been living.(12) I never had to pay rent. I live with my first children's father for three years. He put me out ... I go by my mother. I remain there. I try to live with somebody else again. It wasn't so easy. I leave, go back home, try again the third time. I leave again, go back home and I decide to stay home. So then I been living and struggling, selling, doing whatever little I could do to make a penny for my children. When I get in with somebody we last until my belly is big – I'm pregnant again. They leave me. I have to fight again to mind my children but somehow or the other the spirit always sends somebody to help me ... My spirit always be with me so that someone would help me, come and help me ... But it usually end up I by myself, working again, selling again and feeding my children as much as I could.

The idiom of childbirth is as fundamental to her account of human origins as it is to her account of current relations between women and men: the physical development of each human child recapitulates the original cosmogony.(13) While I was not offered a detailed account of Jeanette's earlier life, motherhood had clearly been her most salient experience, as it was for the women in the coastal villages and eastern Port-of-Spain who recounted their lives to me. It is through her childbearing that Mother Earth objectifies herself and her life to others as a universal principle, a domestic mode raised to a cosmological order, a central experiential metaphor by which she elaborates other ideas.

Jeanette's parents were not *church married*. She was born in 1934 in Port-of-Spain, the eldest of ten children. Her mother had come to Trinidad from Grenada at the age of thirteen to work as a domestic servant for a White family, and Jeanette was born in her mother's thirties, to be 'raised with' the White children of her employer. She met her own father 'only once or twice' as she can recall; he died when she was about thirty: 'He call me then. I was not very interested but I go'. Her mother later *friended* with a policeman who was frequently critical of the established church but was known for his ability to predict future events through conjuration.(14) From the age of one year, Jeanette saw her mother infrequently and lived with various relatives, in particular her grandmother. She attended school sporadically, reads with difficulty and cannot write. At sixteen she left her grandmother to live with a boyfriend. This relationship broke up and she returned with her child to her grandmother, and then lived with one of her own mother's previous partners by whom she herself had three children. As for most working-class Trinidadian women, emancipation from parents and accession into adulthood came from childbearing. She *scuffled*, borrowing, begging, getting by with help from relatives and boyfriends: 'a little job here, a next one there. I often plan to get marry but something happen. I ai' fuss.'

By the age of thirty-seven, Jeanette had borne ten children. Her views on sexuality and reproduction were then conventional: men and women are fundamentally different with characteristic personalities and interests, both contribute physically to the formation of the child, and a woman will bear her predetermined 'set of children'. For working-class Creole women, childbearing is the point of entry into autonomy in a way that secondary education, employment, chronological age, first menstruation or sexual intercourse, or marriage are not: 'You come a big woman now!' Bigger in belly, bigger in status. Childless women may be abused by others when arguments turn bitter (*mule* is the insult in Jamaica), whilst male preferences in female beauty still emphasise large buttocks and a *grinding* pelvic gait which are explicitly emphasised as both sexual and parturitive. Through childbirth young women obtain publicly accepted obligations from the child's father,(15) for an unmarried father is supposed to assume some financial responsibility for his child's mother and for the child which only then may *carry his title* (surname). To have children when one is married is less the expected choice (and for some it is that) than the seal on mutual trust given the resources necessary for sustaining a marriage. An *illegitimate* child is not one without married parents but one who is not recognised by the father, with resulting shame for the woman whose child must then carry her own title, although this is frequently the occasion of much negotiation and retrospective changes. (Occasionally a *de facto* matrilineage of title may continue for a few generations.) Declarations of a child's father by a woman are frequently couched in ambiguous statements depending on the degree of intimacy with the listener, and later quarrels may lead to denials of earlier statements on paternity or even veiled accusations of *badtalking* (a term that connotes not only gossip and lying but sorcery and a variant of the evil eye). As Trinidadians put it, these matters are always *according* (to circumstances).

A man may talk implausibly of a woman trapping him into giving money through falsely claiming he has fathered a child but generally he accepts this obligation willingly; between themselves men may describe sexual relations in agricultural and culinary terms – women are land not only for planting but for realisation of the produce (16). A man's sexual reputation is determined by his fertility, not his virility. When in a relationship, whether church married or just *living*, a man might thus be simultaneously supporting his current partner and their children but also his earlier and *outside* children. 'Paternity' is more than a recognition of begetting: elsewhere in the West Indies the father's continuing financial support is regarded as a very physical feeding of the child, contributing after birth to its body (Sobo 1993). Among poorer families, the declaration of pregnancy by an unmarried daughter is generally the scene for a formalised public row between her and her mother, in which (depending on the revealed identity of 'the man') the mother proclaims her own *respectability* against her daughter's *worthlessness*: the daughter, less shamed than angry, may then leave to stay with other relatives and only return to her mother after some time. Observation of these episodes in the villages and in town suggests that they range from astonishment and indignation on the part of her mother if the daughter is still at school or entering valued employment, or if the father of the child is already married or 'living', to a fairly nominal but similar performance when the mother already knows about the affair but needs to publicly declare her lack of responsibility now that the girl has so evidently attained accountability. A promise to support the daughter made to her family by the man generally leads to a faster reconciliation, depending on their knowledge of his personality and prospects.

Whilst maternal mortality rates in Trinidad are not dissimilar to those of Western Europe, pregnancy is frequently said to be a period of particular vulnerability to sickness and envious sorcery by other women, particularly any having sexual relations with the father. Attendance at a funeral by pregnant women is described as dangerous, as are attempted abortion, strong emotion or the sight of certain animals from the bush, accidents or sickness, any of which may lead to difficult or even monstrous births.(17) Sexual intercourse is generally continued until late in pregnancy and is encouraged to keep the birth canal open. A common Caribbean image of health is an open and ripe (*fresh*) body: frequent purging with infusions of local bushes and barks enable the body to be cleaned out periodically. And these are used particularly after the birth or for abortion. Induced abortion (*drop baby*) is less common than men suspect and, whilst attempted at some time by most adult women with whom I talked, is publicly regarded as murder. 'Freeness' refers simultaneously to personal autonomy, easy and flexible sexual relations, regular menstruation and childbirth, generosity and physical health; 'closed', like 'tied', is an idiom for virginity and infertility, prolonged labour, physical sickness and some types of madness, for marriage and respectability, for the reserved character of Whites as well as for village suspicions of sorcery, envy or self-centredness, and for excessive worrying without ventilation. If sexual intercourse opens the body for a safe delivery, artificial contraception is argued by men and women of Jeanette's age to close the woman's womb like sorcery, and is thus likely to cause aberrant growths elsewhere. There are no longer any untrained village midwives and women usually give birth in hospital. For Jeanette:

My being pregnant and having to go to the doctor and hospital to make my baby I always see something in the hospital that I didn't like, and it is the young mothers. What I find that was wrong in those days that the young mothers should be taken care of more. Because they are young, in their first pregnancy, they don' know anything about it and they usually act inferior to which they should be acting (you know, they cry a lot, they bawl a lot), so by the time they are ready to bring forth the baby some of them are so weak. Nobody to sit down and talk to them. The nurses have no time, you know. I would usually go round the beds because most of my pregnancies, when I go in there, my water bag burst home and I think I am ready; when I reach there I am not ready; sometimes two weeks I am still there, waiting on the pain to come, to deliver my baby. So then I would be helping the younger mothers by going and sit down with them, rub their hands, pass my hand on their face, talk to them, prepare them, tell them 'Don't cry – you know you are crying too much – you will get too weak – eat something – little thing to eat – they say you mus' eat something.' I did talk to them, pat them, show them. Sometime I get through with them, sometime they are very hard to get through with because they are studying the pain that they getting for days and they keep crying and crying. So I did talk to them. And these things use to make me feel good. It make me feel that I am doing something to help my people. I don't know ... but I like it at the time. But yet I am in there for so long I still help myself by doing something, even self is to help share out some food sometime, until my pain come. Well my pain does be very short; if I start about ten o'clock in the morning, by the time twelve o'clock I am already deliver my baby.

But something happen to me in hospital once which I didn't like at all. Was with one of my babies. I don't really like the labour room because I find the bed is too high, it is too cold, the plastic they put on it is too cold. You have to lie down on this wet cold plastic and in my pain I like to be walking. Whenever a pain take me I jump off the bed, and I gone, up and down, up and down until it ease again, I go back and life. But in the labour room you cannot do that: you have to bear that pain on the bed there. To me, I get more pain by being lying down there twist up. So I never like the labour room. So what I do is ease my pain on the outside, in the yard, and I remain there whenever it take me and walk, walk until it get very hot and I know when it is time to deliver. I jump up on the bed and my baby will come. When the baby come [this time] I call the nurse. The nurse did just pass and see me comfortable so, when she come back now, she say 'What happen?' I say 'the baby, the baby'. When she look she say 'Look what you making a mess, you making a mess in the place, look what you doing on the bed! You making a mess! Get up and go in the labour room! I bet you I push it back.' And she hold it, the baby. and push it! I fire a kick because I feel a pain. And when I fire the kick my foot pass near her face, when I start to cry one time. I say 'Sorry, I didn't really mean to do that but you push it and you hurt me'. You know and I cry and thing and I make it look [right]. That nurse, when she did that to me, I felt it.

3

While, at the time, this temporary return of the son back into his mother had seemed just an unhappy fortuity, not uncharacteristic of what might be expected from the *social* (snobbish, 'correct') midwives, it remained a frightening experience on which Jeanette continually brooded. Not until her troubling visions a decade later for which she could find no rational meaning (cf. Sperber 1980) did she realise that this event had been a prefiguring of a universal truth: that The Mother's Son, indeed all men, try to return into a woman's womb, to destroy her natural fertility and then emulate it as Science. And that respectable local women such as nurses are particularly enlisted in his endeavours. This action of the Son – an 'embodied schema' as Mark Johnson (1987) calls it, in which she employs her bodily experience as a figure to interpret the world – recalls that of the culture hero or mediator in those myths which celebrate a passing from matriarchy to patriarchy, and from divine to human. Ethnographic, feminist and psychological explanations all emphasise the technology-bearing culture hero from the perspective of men as an exemplary account which legitimates their power or resolves their sexual anxieties and jealousies. The hero frequently has a prolonged childhood or an abnormal or delayed birth as he straddles the human and ultrahuman worlds (18). Although Mother Earth's ideas recall a pattern found in a number of cosmogonies elsewhere, we are not concerned here with some shared myth arguably structured by a stable set of existing relationships, but rather with a novel schema, one certainly elaborated out of her available memories and knowledge but now proclaimed by the woman herself against the hero. It is difficult to see this simply as a shared legitimation of male power (though it does offer an explanation for current male dominance) or as the expression of men's personal dilemmas.

Is there a local 'social vehicle', as Geertz calls it, which perhaps structures some existing sentiment of female creation? Or is it just that, as Tylor argued, the postulation of telluric mother deities is 'simple and obvious'?: earth as the maternal womb, sky as seminal rain or as chaos or whatever. (For paternity and maternity are hardly terms of the same order (Delaney 1986) and only recently has biotechnology distinguished mater from genetrix: a practice which of course enrages Mother Earth.) I heard no accounts of actual mother–son sexual relations in Trinidad: the suggestion was met with incredulous laughter rather than the disgust reserved for the rare *vice* of father–daughter incest. Nevertheless, the centrality of the mother–child relationship has been emphasised by Caribbeanists and by local novelists and politicians, as matrifocal, matricentral or even matriarchal; most radically in the notion that the local family – always to be contrasted with its idealised European counterpart – is in some way 'denuded' of the father.(19) Talking together, women may lament the general irresponsibility of their men, joke that they are unnecessary except for sexual pleasure, and downplay (but hardly deny) the male contribution to procreation. Behind this 'matrifocal' family, argue some psychoanalysts, lurks the psychological father – the White male – the historical rapist of the mother and the continuing representation of external power within the Creole family he has created. (20) Alexander (1977) has described the 'ancestral myth' of the West Indian middle-class as one which traces descent back to a planter and his female slave, and Trinidadian family stories may give names to the pair. The mother–child relationship is certainly the only kin tie which is expected to continue throughout adulthood, one which cannot be outweighed by acquired relationships with others. Both sons and daughters may quarrel with their father as they get older or ignore him. But not their mother. 'Mother blood stronger than father blood' in the Jamaican peasant aphorism. She remains available as a mother for the whole of her child's life.

My psychoanalytic colleagues may perhaps argue here – and it is difficult to resist the intoxications of condensing down Jeanette's personal life, physical experiences and cosmogony into a unitary psychosocial closure, her visions as reflecting, or at least emblematic of, some 'deep motivations' (21) – that the resolution of her Oedipal wishes for her biological father was thwarted by his absence; that these were then transferred to the doubly unobtainable White father (available in the psychic reality of imperial domination) to be temporarily resolved through bearing children to her 'step-father'; in reaction against which nearly incestuous relationship she then chose a much younger man from a distant part of the island and in joining the Baptists submitted herself, asexual, to God the (White) Father: a complex of unstable relationships which were only resolved through her later identification with a Black female creatrix, thus apparently displacing the White and male principles onto a peripheral figure who interfered with her own pristine Nature, while at the same time she identifies herself with male as well as female, reenacting but reversing the Son's return in her actions during the events she calls the Miracle.(22) In other words the structuring key lies in a daughter–father rather than in a mother–son relationship, and the Son is only a *son* in that he provides an appropriate model of contingency, subordination and rebellion.(23)

Psychoanalytic interpretations are not necessarily to be dismissed out of hand. But they remain more arbitrary than most: even if Mother Earth had told me more about her childhood experiences we might generate a variety of somewhat different 'deep' narratives.(24) Avoidance of sexual relations however may have a rather more prosaic rationale. Margery Kempe, an illiterate brewer in medieval Norfolk who had nearly died during her fourteenth delivery, interpreted a vision of devils as a call from God to abandon married life. Without claiming a general model of 'compensation' or 'resistance', it is hardly surprising that schemata associated with problematic childbearing are plausible for prophetic women such as Mistress Kempe, particularly those who elaborate a religious cosmogony which refigures childbirth. (She later identified herself with the Mother of Jesus.) Psychoanalytical speculation aside, an aversion to conjugal relations or the loss of children signal some personal departure from a conventionally ascribed identity. Male messianic leaders and prophets are frequently celibate or childless as Weber noted, but this appears even more common among their female counterparts. While the death of young children or other family members may simply leave the woman with freedom to engage in new activities, the experience of losing her children may precipitate the potential prophet into action, perhaps in an attempt to restitute or make sense of her loss. All four children of Ann Lee, the eighteenth century factory-worker who founded the Shakers, died in infancy, and one delivery by forceps was particularly prolonged, the child appearing reluctant to be born: 'She saw the deaths of her children as a series of divine judgements on her "concupiscence" ... but once her health was restored, participation was infused with a sense of mission. What she had undergone as an individual she came to believe was really a universal struggle' (Andrews 1953: 8). Only after her husband left her did Ann Lee assume her title of 'Mother'; like Joanna Southcott and Mother Earth, it was then that she was accused of madness and sexual promiscuity, not unusual aspersions to be cast on the single female prophet.(25) Mother Ann was recognised as a divine Mother and advocated celibacy after a vision showed her a 'full and clear view of the mystery of iniquity, of the root and foundation of human depravity'.(26)

The radical Christian tradition contains a number of men identifying themselves as embodiments of Jesus or God, or of such figures as Daniel, Brother of the Almighty or Younger Brother of Jesus. And similarly prophetic women have argued affinities between themselves and biblical or quasibiblical characters, both male and female.(27) It is difficult to assess a personal and consistent identification with divinity from the refutations written by clerical persecutors, but there appear a variety of personal elisions between woman and divinity: from a heightening of conventional analogy in which a mystic like Julian of Norwich or Margery Kempe is spiritually penetrated (all women are Brides of Christ as members of his Universal Church, nuns like St. Teresa and St. Catherine of Sienna more particularly so), to a closer identification with divine or divine beings (many Ranters and Doukhobors have argued they were in a way divine, particularly their leaders, and Quakers and some Beguines such as Marguerite Porete have come close), to a novel and total incarnation as embodied divinity (Joanna Southcott, Jemima Wilkinson, Ann Lee, Mother Earth). If procreation for a woman involves remarking two experiences with rather different female agency, coitus and childbirth, then the less radical revisions still employ something like the former to mark the entry of male divinity into her as a passive vehicle, whether as a visionary identification or more concretely as destined motherhood of the incarnate divinity. The more radical and total identification as ultimate power seem to be the preserve of those Protestant women whose pregnancies, as self-sufficient and parthenogenic, figure a new world without any male contribution at all.

The extent to which, in a given situation, the prophet takes herself as imitating a mythical figure as exemplar, or as a chosen and unique messenger, or as actually consubstantial with other-worldly power, may fluctuate with self-doubt and the acclamation of others. Joanna Southcott, a well-documented West Country instance, appears to have been pushed by necessary expectations in 1813 from her Methodist and Anglican followers, who were coping with a sudden decline in their number, to an attempt to be 'proved', and eventually proclaimed that at the age of sixty-five she was about to give birth to Shiloh, a figure she somewhat uncertainly identified with the Second Coming of Christ. Earlier, after a number of problematic love affairs, probably not involving pregnancy, she had previously identified herself as The Woman, then as Eve, then as the Bride of Christ; in all cases fighting the Devil who had seduced woman in Eden: 'For as the dispute began with the Devil and the Woman, it must end with the Devil and the Woman', now to redeem humankind (Southcott 1995: 2,99). Declared pregnant by nineteen of a panel of twenty-four doctors who examined her, she died some months after the expected date of delivery (Harrison 1979, Hopkins 1982). Her self-ascription as Eve seems to have fitted with certain Hermetic speculations among local Non-Conformists who took Eve as the redeeming figure who, as Genesis has it, would finally bruise Satan's head. Yet Joanna comes close to pantheism in one of her debates with Satan when she affirms 'we shall be as gods'.(28) Nor is her refusal of his offer of marriage altogether idiosyncratic, given that much of her cosmology depicts a rural farming world: thus Satan had tried to 'ruin' her just as other men had tried, unlettered people like her followers can read the Bible more truly than the learned, and so on. In her pamphlets there is a fluctuating identity between her own objectification as 'the woman' of her personal experiences which she narrates to others and The Woman who will crush Satan. Similarly we are never quite sure when we should assume she is talking of 'the man' as a particular individual who has previously let her down, as Satan, Man as Adam, or even Man as all humankind. Mother Earth offers us a consistent and considerably more radical revision of Christianity, now deprecating God but, drawing similarly on her relations with men, she employs her emergent cosmology to explain their past behaviour to her. Unlike Joanna Southcott but in a similar way to Ann Lee, she takes her pregnancy as the grounds for a grander revision of divinity, yet one that does not tack and turn as did the unfortunate Joanna's but which irrevocably reduces God to a representation of her own jealous son.

4

If we accept that new cosmogonies may be developed through immediate human preoccupations (as well as in more figurative idioms worked from an existing tradition), we might not wonder that female models of world creation may be rather different from those of male innovators; a woman's carrying a new being for nine months is a fundamentally different type of procreation, as experience, memory and project. She alone 'gives birth'. Whatever the local understandings of human generation, she is more intimately involved through her body, and later through her child's post-natal nurturance. Childbearing, particularly when multiple and problematic, seems to make possible a more radical cosmogony leaving the male principal interfering, or at best redundant. Are we to regard this as deriving from an accessible and conventionalised symbolisation in which women's religious identity usually privileges their procreative capacity (Hoch-Smith and Spring 1978) or from some more 'inherent' bodily schema?

Pregnancy may be less a customary trope. however socially compelling, than cognition and motivation. As Rabuzzi (1994) puts it, the pregnant woman recognises herself as multiple: not just as her preexisting self plus another but in a new personal identity which distinguishes yet unites her to others in a 'near visionary' mode. There is an increasing identification with her body's altered sensations and appearance, with implicit obligations through it. The distinction between experiencing self and the world of others becomes diffused even as she retains a pre-pregnancy body schema which does not altogether disappear.(29) Her boundaries, postures and actions alter. She occupies a different space in relation to people and objects, with a different receptivity to not so external events. Relations between her body's organs change with a different weight, massiveness and balance; she may find herself grounded in the earth as essential: 'In pregnancy I literally do not have a firm sense of where my body ends and the world begins' (cited in Young 1984). Agency is challenged and reconfigured as what were once automatic and unrecognised movements and gestures now have to be more evidently willed. Yet the body's inner movements are now those of another even as the sensations remain the woman's sensations. Her location of herself shifts to abdomen, her centre of awareness is now not only eyes but also trunk. A private internal world of life develops which is accessible only to the mother; at the same time she is aware that this aspect of her consubstantial self will disembed, and that a moment is approaching when her subjective world will be differentiated, part of her being objectified as an externalised other: yet an other which will maintain an intrinsic relation to her. Some contemporary feminists have argued that pregnancy and lactation may be said to be non-Cartesian cognitions in that an absolute distinction between self and other becomes lost (30); and certainly, in all of this, men and the earlier sexual act may become fairly redundant.

Pregnancy makes available a powerful body schema for wider cognising of generation and multiplicity, emergent agency and connectedness. Other bodily processes and actions may provide dual or multiple schemata,(31) but none, I would suggest, can be quite so compelling. The preceding paragraph drew on contemporary Western women's accounts, and whilst experience of pregnancy may be intrinsic, it is hardly invariant, dependent on a society's 'body techniques' and the woman's own understandings: pregnancy may be taken as the intrusion of an unwanted other or parasitic incubus, not least in male fantasy. Like childbirth, pregnancy may be cognised as willed or as 'other'. (Rarely, contemporary European women give birth without recognising that they have been pregnant; and sometimes not even then.) While the pregnant woman may herself feel enhanced, for instance as more sensual, her associates may feel differently; a male is likely to claim joint or superior rights in the fruits of her body, and to maintain his own agency and meanings in the whole process; her physical comportment and costume may be constrained to enhance or conceal her pregnancy; other contingencies (material consequences, not being married, prostituting, affinal obligations, age, or previous miscarriages, children and infertility) and the likely survival of the child constrain her own cognitions, and thus their potential for wider meta-representations.

Contemporary feminists in Europe and North America have argued, for instance, an opposition between 'birthing' and medical interventions. Hospital birth and its technologies are typically de-scribed as alienating the woman's subjectivity from her own agency in a process which should otherwise be understood as 'willed' or which as 'inevitable' enhances an association between women and a 'natural' world independent of human (here male) interventions. Mechanical intervention in labour is argued by the ecofeminists as an instance of the male rape of nature (32); the woman's body is not only 'interfered with' (to use Mother Earth's identical expression) but it is appropriated and objectified by men as a site of pathology, the pregnant body becoming vulnerable if not frankly dysfunctional. The use of instru-ments to evaluate the success of the process in the public world leaves her own experience and knowledge as redundant. Childbirth becomes a procedure. Women are expected to remain passive: discouraged from walking about even in the early stages of labour, they deliver in a horizontal position orthogonal to gravity, often in stirrups which reduce their ability to push, their legs held apart for speculum or forceps in a mimicry of copulation. Mother Earth's labour involved a similar perception of hospital delivery and of the officiating nurses. The thwarted birth she describes is not implausible in a context where the West Indian midwife may describe women giving birth as 'animals' and tries 'to get [them] on the bed, where they were expected to lie still and be good patients' (Kitzinger 1980: 93,92). Midwives in Trinidad are precarious *tibourgs* ('respectable working-class' in English terms), themselves especially vulnerable to gossip about their own concealed sexuality, their relations with doctors and their knowledge of abortion.

The process of Mother Earth's and Ann Lee's own 'objectification' – employing the cognised experiences of pregnancy and childbirth to figure wider concerns at times of crisis – may seem somewhat obscure. Without stepping into the language of psychopathology (for remark-ably few women have publicly figured the process of world creation through their own bodies),(33) or simply arguing that all women have some inherent religiosity through their bodies,(34) the most compelling psychological process may be that described by psychoanalysts as projective identification. Aspects of one's experience and agency are recognised as more or less 'other', and normalised within culturally appropriate possibilities as a recognised object or process, and which, like one's child, are identified with oneself (or with another person). This recalls the phenomenologists' interest in how the flux of pre-objective cognition becomes congealed into hypostasised entities: a process surprisingly ignored by cognitive anthropologists and psychologists but which has been variously addressed by Marxists, Kleinians and Buddhists through the idea that as categories are less ambiguous than experiencing, we tend to perceive the world as nominalised – as composed of entities of recurrent invariance (Laughlin *et al.* 1992) whose reification is fundamental to social categorisation, giving ontological status to experience (Lakoff 1987). And in this, there is nothing necessarily pathological for we are talking of an available human faculty, whether it is manifest as 'religion' or 'artistic creation', or indeed the anthropological sciences.

5

Physical motherhood provides a 'base model' (Lakoff 1987) for structuring conceptualisations of birth, inheritance, nurturance, marital relations and kinship. Does motherhood in the West Indies generally provide such embodiment for 'religious' speculations? Hardly. Whilst women are recognised as more likely to attend church, and men are certainly more *carnal*, childbearing itself offers no especial cosmological significance. Sexual restraint or concealment go along with church-going, yet local Catholics generally ridicule the idea of the Virgin Birth. Unlike in neighbouring Venezuela, Mary is not particularly revered. Roman Catholicism, the baptismal religion of most Trinidadians of African descent, has here a strongly Protestant (or at least an Anglican) sensibility: few villagers agree that the Host is the physical Body of Christ, or that Mary was Immaculate or that she was Assumed into heaven. Waist-binding is not uncommon among Baptist women, and in prayer, early pregnancy and sickness, but it is nor locally elaborated, as any marking of the profane lower body as against the spiritual, but simply as both a moral and bodily support. Some commentators have likened the practice of *labouring* in Caribbean religious revivalism (when women practice vigorous hyperventilation with synchronised foot and trunk movements whilst singing) to the mother's panting during the labour of delivery but that is seldom locally noted. Jamaican women pressing down in childbirth, have been described as 'calling down Jesus' into their bodies (Kitzinger 1982), but I found no evidence for that in Trinidad: any equivalence would be regarded as decidedly strange if not unseemly. If sexuality and procreation have any association with Christianity they would seem to be in opposition, as Mother Earth herself observes, yet Spiritual Baptist Mothers are certainly regarded as nurturing their congregation, on occasion healing or feeding them just as a mother does for her child (Littlewood 1993, Wedenoja 1989); and the Earth People's central rite of a communal meal was prefigured in Baptist and Shango periodic ceremonies of Feeding The Children of a local neighbourhood.

As cultural innovations, women's cosmogonies of pregnancy and parturition have to engage the interests of others. We are not concerned with some momentary and empathic mimesis by Mother Earth's followers of an extraordinary experience (35) of thwarted birth, but with an active circulation of the images and transformations it offers, of engagement and reverberation with it at a variety of levels, appropriating it and socialising it, eventually codifying it. Generally young men, unemployed and functionally non literate, her followers could share her concern with the situation of Black women, but they could hardly embody so profoundly the meanings of her own parturition except in a reciprocal relationship: as her Children, for they agreed that their historical paternity was, in a sense, through a European rape of African women. A short paper does not allow me to examine their development of Mother Earth's bodily schema into a new social formation. I will conclude with a brief comparison with some other radical groups which have developed in Christianity: in particular those with similar cosmologies of bisexual or female divinity and which emphasise generation and nurturance, whilst simultaneously deprecating sexual relations. This last is hardly novel given Christianity's residual apocalyptic expectations: to transcend sexuality, particularly incest, legendary Christian heroines had remained virgins or became men socially (Thecla and Margaret of Antioch) or even physically (St. Uncumber grew a beard).(36) The Virgin stands for perfect motherhood but not for fecundity,(37) and Christian representations of sexuality and geneation (Incarnation and Virgin Birth, Immaculate Conception, the Church as the Bride of the Divine Bridegroom, the rapture of female saints by Christ) which, to a critical observer like Edward Gibbon, might derive their power from bodily prototypes, generally strive to maintain a purely figurative relation to the parturient body.(38) In the words of St. Jerome: 'As long as a woman is for birth and children, she is different from man as body is from soul. But when she wishes to serve Christ more than the world, then she will cease to be a woman and will be called a man.'

Although women have provided the majority of its devotees, they have rarely been found in Christianity's higher echelons. As Mother Earth puts it: 'Outside they show a statue of the Mother, inside they is all Father ... Rome is he, they have you under control, Church and State.' Martyrs and mystics aside, women are marginal in ritual and text, occasionally serving as intercessors or mediators between a divine progenitor – represented on earth through a male priesthood – and his human subjects. Women exemplify submission to the Father through their submission to earthly father or husband (Genesis 3: 16, I Corinthians 11:3). By contrast, asserted some radical utopians, God is asexual or bisexual, or even female.(39) Movements initiated by divine mothers like Mother Earth or Ann Lee have identified women's childbearing and nurturance with the natural world (as does the church) but also with the original state of things before some causal interference. Not surprisingly this identification of substance with divine spirit eschews a distanced male creator but, rather than proposing a female equivalent, it either goes for an elision of Creatrix and Created (as with Mother Earth) or for an androgynous or paired Creator/Creatrix (Mother Ann of the Shakers was the second 'Christ Spirit' of the bisexual deity). Both Mother Earth and Mother Ann embody immanent divinity, containers of their own unfolding rather than conjurors of inanimate matter *ex nihilo*. Various radical revisions of Christianity have similarly countered the embodiment of the divine creation in the domestic father, while among the Shakers and Earth People, any sexual activity has been avoided in imminent expectation of the End. Refusal of sex (and thus of repeated pregnancy and the death of children) has gone together with an enhanced status for women among many ecstatic utopians; as a sour cleric has observed, 'from the Montanist movement onwards, the history of enthusiasm is largely a history of female emancipation' (Knox 1950). Many argued sexual equality from the passage in the Apocrypha (I Esdras 4) where Zorobabel lists the powers which by their nature women have over men. Like the earlier Cathars, Albigensians and Old Believers, radical millennialists in the industrial era oscillated between sexual abstinence and promiscuity, between 'rigorism' and 'scandal' (*ibid.*); both repudiated recognised associations between inherited property and the subjugation of women. Some of the American communalist projects of the eighteenth and nineteenth centuries attempted celibacy while others practised polygyny, polyandry, group sex or free love.(40) Others experimented with all simultaneously: in the Spiritual Marriage advocated by Lucina Umphreville (the Public Universal Friend) successive physical pairings with different partners continued until a couple found the perfect (celibate) match. On occasion Fabians and Theosophists too have attempted to transcend masculine sexuality.

Those Western institutions we generally account as 'religions' counterpose our imperfect world of human procreation to a transcendent world whose moral purposes offer us an understanding of our origin and end. Without passing comment on the not uncommon idea that in many particulars the religious is *necessarily* an inversion of the everyday,(41) those movements we generally characterise as 'millennial' or 'apocalyptic' are concerned with a dramatic elision of the two worlds, in prophetic visions but more particularly in an actual end to their separation which will be experienced in this-worldly time (yet in the process ending time as the now unified cosmos returns to something like its perfect state or intention).(42) Differences are reconciled, sins purged, suffering dissolved, disease and death are overcome. As the bodily distinction between woman and man appears inevitable in the temporal order of generation, the apocalyptic imagination may transcend sexual dimorphism. Like some first-century Christians, the American Rappites held that Man was originally androgynous but that the biblical Fall had initiated our separation into two sexes who would once again be united through an androgynous Jesus: 'Just at this juncture the first fall of man took place, by which Adam violated his own inward sanctuary and his own female function by means of which he could have been (as Genesis I: 28 has it) fruitful and multiply without an external helpmate, after the order of a Hermaphrodite then, and after the order now, see Luke 20: 34–6'.(43) This is close to Jeanette's account of the Son's interference with the androgynous but parturient *mothers* and indeed to the 'Orphic myth' of contemporary ecofeminists.(44) The Rappites too construed the human fall from its natural origin by the English word 'interference' (Ardt 1965). Mother Ann taught that the original androgynous Adam, created by a paired male-female deity had been overthrown by the male Devil, the Christian's 'Father Of All': redemption would be through the return of the deity in both male (Jesus) and female (Mother Ann) humanity: 'the Father's high eternal throne was never filled by one alone' (Andrews 1953: 158). Joanna Southcott seems to have argued at times that Christ would return as a woman and redeem us all in our original androgyneity (Southcott 1995: 106–7). Such revisions of the Christian progenitor are not limited to female initiators (45) but I would suggest that for women they become more plausible. Whilst some might be tempted to characterise Western monotheism's postulate of divine creation at a distance as the objectified 'uterus envy' of men,(46) my argument here is not psychoanalytical, nor conventionally psychological, except in as much as we accept Mauss' idea of 'psychological facts as connecting cogs and not as causes, except in moments of creation or reform' (Mauss 1979).(47) Pregnancy and childbearing provide a ground for figurings of origin, agency and theodicy, which for Jeanette dramatically invert the existing cosmology.(48) She not only structures an unfolding cosmology embodied in her own pregnancies but allows some acceptance of this as shared reality for others as her children; for while her understandings of motherhood – the earth as our mother, herself as both Earth and as Mother of her group, creation as childbirth – may be representations of parturition and nurturance, they are hardly those of active sexuality.(49)

If we take schemata of human procreation less as conventional representations or 'deep' motivations than as biologically cognised structurings of our biology,(50) inherent and immediate, which serve at moments of cognitive crisis for such metarepresentations as new cosmological understandings, they can be deployed either figuratively or referentially.(51) Continuing movements (and a variety of elisions) between representation and embodiment are mediated by context and reception as well as by personal intention and affect. *Contra* Durkheim, as a religious symbolisation, pregnancy is inherently 'meaningful' in the sense used by Turner and Obeyesekere. It is hardly arbitrary for its elaboration still evokes its intrinsic cognitions. As Mother Earth puts it, 'your ancestor is you'.

Notes

1   Mauss 1979 (1934): Durkheim and Mauss 1969 (1901–2). Even if, in the course of the embodiment of social interests, the capabilities and limitations of the naturalistic body remained somewhat elusive.
2   I need not trace here the various critiques of an empiricist 'representation' of a natural world which pass under a number of current rubrics – interpretation, Foucauldian historiography, anti-essentialism, anti-objectivism, post-modernism and the like – except to note that the dilemmas of the representation-embodiment dialectic are hardly avoided in the newer deployments of phenomenology (Lyon and Barbalet 1994; cf. the variant meanings of 'representation' and 'embodiment') which in their emphasis on personal subjectivities tend to ethnography rather than social anthropology. Psychological approaches recalling nineteenth century intellectualism appear to be undergoing a resurgence in the form of neuro cognitive 'competences' or 'constraints' on cosmological speculation, necessary but not sufficient for these inferences to be acquired (Lakoff 1987; Johnson 1987; Boyer 1993, 1994) but they have yet to provide a more plausible understanding of any set of data; on the whole they work from individual psychology rather than a more situational biosociality. What remains

problematic is the value of findings from experimental psychology: putting it crudely, how does the 'top down' (culture's embodiment in body technique) encounter the 'bottom up' (neuropsychology's representation of an apprehended physical world)? (And that conventional topology may be considered to beg the question.) In a number of recent papers I have argued that the two domains are rather objectified procedures, radically incommensurate modes of thought, both of which we can identify either (personalistically) in Western cultural history or (naturalistically) in the neuropsychological capacity to attribute agency or non-agency to self and others (Littlewood 1993, 1994, 1996; cf. Johnson 1987). And that our analyses, akin to those of the kabbalist (Littlewood and Dein 1995), must be ironic passages between embodiment and representation, and back again; for attempts to reconcile them in a unitary theory simply end up on one side (sociobiology, computational cognitive science) or the other (psychoanalysis, phenomenology).

3 Compare Sudanese *zar* (Boddy 1989) and American multiple personality disorder. The latter recalls existing practices of female self-help and mediumship, psychiatric idioms of loss of agency in 'stress' and 'trauma', and resurgeant evangelical notions of the final 'rapture', not to mention current enthusiams for extra-terrestrials as ultra-human agencies (eg. Scientology).

4 For instances see: Weigle 1989; Southcott 1995; Hopkins 1987; Holly wood 1995; Holloway 1966; Lovejoy 1985; Andrews 1953; Adler 1986; Albanese 1990; Corea 1988; Nelson 1979.

5 Pseudonyms for reasons I explain in Littlewood 1993. Jeanette died in 1984 after disputes in the group, police raids and the burning of her settlement, but I have retained here the present tense for the account she gave me in 1981–2.

6 An informally organised group of local churches with recognised 'African' themes which developed in Trinidad in the 1840s from St. Vincent, and which recall the Jamaican Native Baptists and South African Zionist churches.

7 Capitalisation of the Earth People's recurrent idioms and cosmology is mine.

8 I stayed with the Earth People, on and off, over a period of eighteen months between 1981–2, and more briefly in 1987 and 1991. When not in their Valley I was in the nearest village twelve miles away studying bush medicines. As with any prolonged stay in a millennial community, my status was ambiguous – neither neophyte, casual passer-by nor reporter. I went naked as they did and, at their request, did not bring notepads, camera or other equipment. When my departure to Britain became imminent however I was requested to bring a tape-recorder for Mother Earth's formal Message To The World (in English not Creole) from which the quotes here are extracts. Her daily addresses in the Valley had frequently anticipated it word for word. In this paper I rely extensively on material published in Littlewood 1993.

9 Crispy. A local metathesis: cf. *flim* (cinema).

10 Mother Earth is explaining the local (and Caribbeanist) description of women as more respectable (or social) than men. As in other areas, she inverts the customary relationship, arguing in an explicit opposition that because women are really more *natural* the Son has made particular efforts to change them to the opposite; and that this is through stealing

their power of generation, once through cosmic and colonial rape, now through commerce and science.

11 One of her characteristic puns eliding the physical and the moral.

12 Cohabiting and thus more economically vulnerable than if church married.

13 Pages 174 and 175 above. There are close parallels with local women's accounts of foetal development as a sedimentation from chaos.

14 Bibliomancy but also *high science* (to use the Trinidad term): popular European magic found in farmers' almanacs and the 'De Lawrence books' published in Chicago; generally concerned with theosophical and kabbalistic speculations on prediction, finding buried treasure and conjuring elementals cf. Brooke 1994 for a similar complex developed as Mormonism in nineteenth century New York State). These *science books* (which she would not have read directly) may occasionally figure the world in human form (the Adamic Body), or explain the European system of 'signatures' between plants, planets, animals, colours, personalities, and so on, but generally they are used as recipe books for divination, love magic and sorcery.

15 As Handwerker (1989) notes, the economic advantages of women's fertility in Trinidad have diminished as women have increasingly obtained employment away from household and family land.

16 Thus infidelity may be glossed as 'Man trespassing on my land' or 'There's more in the mortar beside the pestle.' Yet there is no recognition in the West Indies of male monogenesis or female pollution (except in Rastafari), for the 'earth' is not just an incubator but an essential and equal genetrix (cf. Delaney 1986).

17 Kitzinger 1982; Sobo 1993. This was mentioned to me in Trinidad in malicious gossip about specific people but only rarely as a generalisation when discussing pregnancy.

18 Adelman 1992; Newman 1963. Thus Jackson (1979), comparing two versions of a Mande epic (in one of which the culture hero Sundiata is born extremely slowly while in the other he returns after birth to his mother's womb) has argued that prolonged gestation and prolonged infancy are cosmological equivalents. For psychodynamic explanations see the writings on 'the prophet as hero' by Otto Rank.

19 R.T. Smith (1988) argues reasonably enough that the anthropologist, as elsewhere, should not interpret the Black family by comparison with the White ideal but this is certainly what happens locally (eg. Dann 1987: 14–22).

20 For example Frantz Fanon and Jacques André.

21 As Obeyesekere (1981) termed them to avoid the theoretical baggage of psychoanalytical terminology .

22 Soon after her initial visions Jeanette found herself moving her arms down towards her womb, an event the group calls the Miracle, the moment when as incarnate Mother she recalled the veiling heat around the Sun/Son back into the Earth.

23 The psychoanalytic perspective usually ignores Jocasta in favour of the tragic male hero. Olivier (1989) however offers a feminist rereading which emphasises the powerful desires she has for her son.

24 It is difficult to question a divinity about the intimate details of her early life. Concerning actual physical incest with any of her sons I felt unable to enquire; for the reasons below I think this improbable. Her partner and

her adult sons (including the one who was 'pushed back') found the possibility hilariously unlikely. Mother Earth died in 1984. In 1991 I asked her younger and more respectable sisters and her aunt: both derided the idea but they said that she had been rather naive as a girl, easily 'led astray by men who took advantage on her'. I only met Mother Earth's own mother in 1991 three weeks before she herself died when she was too ill to be asked about her daughter's experiences.

25 Andrews 1953; Hollywood 1995. Sometimes these were deliberately provoked: when prosyletising naked with the group, Mother Earth would open her legs towards a street audience, point and call out 'Here is where you all come from!' Christopher Hill records a seventeenth century Puritan who disrupted a church service at Westminster by lifting her skirts up and inviting Christ to enter; as did some of the Camisards who inspired Ann Lee. Compare Gillroy's 1814 cartoon of Joanna Southcott lifting her skirts up to the doctors' view and the street charivari of her giving birth to Shiloh (Harrison 1979: 105).

26 Ie. human sexuality (Mother Ann quoted in Holloway 1966: 57).

27 To take some English Protestant instances; Jemima Wilkinson, the Messiah; the Cornish Trumpeter (following Revelation 8); Sarah Flaxmer, the Revealer of Satan (Revelation 12); Joanna Southcott, the Woman Clothed with the Sun, the Mother of Shiloh (Revelation 12, Genesis 49); Mary Evans, the Bride of Christ; Friend Mother (Luckie Buchan), the Holy Ghost. I am not familiar with instances of men identifying themselves as female biblical figures. Divine identity is not unknown among men in African-American Christianity: the Rasta Leonard Howell; Alexander Bedward, a Jamaican Native Baptist pastor; and the founders of the Black Muslims to different degrees. The most notable was Father Divine whose International Righteousness Government Convention in New York in 1936 unanimously passed the motion 'Father Divine is God'.

28 Although I recall an Epistle which says something similar.

29 I am relying here on the accounts given by contemporary American women collated by Young 1984.

30 Young 1984. And thus inherently more 'religious' (Jonte-Pace 1987).

31 Eating, vomiting, excreting, digesting, menstruation, sexual relations, masturbation, dreaming, sickness, accidents.

32 Kitzinger 1982; Caldecott and Leland 1983; Young 1984; Corea 1988; Haraway 1989; and less enthusiastically, Calloway 1978.

33 In Littlewood 1993 I do however argue a pathological experience (thyrotoxicosis) for Mother Earth. Madness, like political catastrophe or cosmological speculation, is likely to soon exhaust our everyday rational mode, to produce 'symbolic' explanations (cf. Sperber 1980). As the local villagers put it: 'Religion hell of a thing, it send you mad.'

34 Well described and criticised by Sered (1993); cf. Needham 1980. Jonte-Pace 1987.

35 In Abraham's (1980) sense.

36 Warner 1983: 154. Compare Galatians 3: 78.

37 Preston 1982; Brown 1989. Colliridian mariolatry perhaps excepted (Zapperi 1991).

38 Margery Kempe (modernised, 1994: 126-7) reports God as saying to her in a vision 'Therefore I must be intimate with you, and lie in your bed with you. Daughter, you greatly desire to see me, and you may bodily, when you are in bed, take me to you as your wedded husband, as your dear

darling, and as your sweet son ... Therefore you can bodily take me in the arms of your soul and kiss my mouth, my head, and my feet as sweetly as you want.' Similarly the thirteenth century mystic Hadewijch spoke of Christ penetrating her: 'After that he came himself to me, took me entirely in his arms and pressed me to him and all my members felt his in full felicity' (Bynum 1989: 168). Speculation on exactly how God incarnated himself in Mary is generally avoided in theological speculation or is highly figurative (such as Augustine's suggestion that it was through her 'ear' in the Annunciation), and a clear distinction is preserved between divine impregnation and human birth ('conceived *by* the Holy Ghost, born *of* the Virgin Mary').

39 As Bynum (1982, 1995) notes, symbolic ramifications within Christianity (typically divine:human::spirit:body::male:female, cf. Barnes 1972), particularly in the late medieval period, did allow female spirituality, precisely because it is more bodily and immanent, to develop such novelties as Christ as Mother, His body as a female body, spiritual consumption of the divine foreskin by virgins, mystical pregnancy, holy anorexia, and so on. Hildegard of Bingen justifies the denial of the priesthood to women precisely because they offer this almost physical access to the deity (Bynum 1989).

40 Like Romantic poets: Percy Shelley's *Queen Mab* similarly proposed a female cosmos, in which God and religion are simply man-made devices for legitimating the tyranny of law and government; the Earth is now physically changing to initiate a period when time will cease and love will govern all. Shelley dreamt of anarchist utopias – 'kingless continents sinless as Eden' – and such visions were integral to the American communalist experiments, religious and secular, which involved over a hundred groups and perhaps a tenth of a million people in the eighteenth and nineteenth centuries. Some emphasised rejection of the state, together with opposition to slavery, and to conventional marriage, in favour of pacifism and economic self-sufficiency. Egalitarians, self-styled 'peculiar people', like Mother Earth they fulminated against racism, war, the criminal code and the treatment of the insane. The Doukhubors of Canada still await the fall of temporal government when 'the complete unification of the nations would result'. Communitarians deprecated 'social' titles and given names, called each other Brother or Sister, and took themselves for a family. They adopted distinctive and sometimes deliberately paradoxical modes of dress and speech, the American Shakers transcribing spontaneous glossolalia into their everyday hymnals.

41 As unlikely a pair as Edmund Leach and Simone de Beavoir argued that religion attempts to negate death and suffering: there are of course the usual problems of what count as inversion, and at which level, and whether this is in local exegesis or academic analysis. Mother Earth certainly seems to stand Christianity on its head but her revisions are still reworked under monotheistic assumptions: suffering as transgression against a first cause, a metaphysical semi-dualism, a collective eschatology in historical time, and herself as the incarnation of the first cause.

42 What Mother Earth terms The Beginning of the End.

43 Cited in Ardt 1965: 583. Curiously, like Jeanette's original *mothers*, these hermaphrodites had only one eye. Father Rapp was rumoured to have castrated his son and we might note a heterodox Christian practice of sexual mutilation as male renunciation (Origen, the Skoptsi); in an

interesting paper Cristiano Grotanelli has likened this to early peasant and anti-colonial resistance through self-mutilation. Speculation on frank androgyneity was generally restricted to the human body after it resurrection (Scotus Erigena).

44 Adler 1986: 260–1; Corea 1988; Caldecott and Leland 1983. There are striking parallels between the cosmogony of the Earth People and those elaborated by the 'neopagan' ecofeminists. Mother Earth could hardly have been directly inspired by ecofeminism (which may be formally dated to March 1980 according to Caldecott and Leland 1983) but she was certainly aware by the early 1970s of the antecedent 'counter-culture' as represented in American cinema.

45 Christian Science (where God is sometimes called 'Mother-Father') was founded by Mary Baker Eddy but the Mormons ('Mother in Heaven') by two males; Unitarianism (an asexual or androgynous deity) has no identified founder except perhaps the Younger Socinus and coalesced from a number of radical Protestant and then deist ideas. We might note the widespread attempt to feminise God by women in the major denominations since the 1970s (Weigle 1989, Sered 1994).

46 The psychoanalyst Fromm called it 'pregnancy envy'. Cf. Bettelheim on subincision.

47 Contrast Boas' rather Judaeo-Christian notion of cosmology as 'a projection into objective existence of a world that pre-existed in the mind of a creator'. If Anglo-French anthropology's disdain for psychology may be likened to a scientific control that endeavours to hold part of the data constant (here as the invariate natural facts of psychology and physiology) so as to examine concomittant variation in the rest, it leaves Mauss' 'moments of creation or reform' somewhat mysterious. How 'large' is a social change to necessitate causes rather than cogs? And after the establishment of a new social formation are the causes now to be understood to be continuing as cogs'? If psychoanalysis conflates the psychology of origin with the psychology of recruitment and persistence, Mauss generally remarks no association at all, relinquishing the study of radical social change to Weberian sociology (Jarvie 1964, Littlewood 1993).

48 That is Christianity as she had access to it in Catholicism and Spiritual Baptism, and later Rastafari. The shango cult in Trinidad, of which she had some knowledge, offers little beyond fragments for a cosmogony, but one can trace a culture hero's incest with a primordial mother in some Brasilian and Yoruba sources on its orisha Emanja (Littlewood 1993), not to mention the numerous West and Central African myths of a primitive matriarchy (Tonkin in Holden 1983).

49 For the Earth People, the relevance of sexuality to the End remains vague. Sexual relations are not encouraged but some members joined the Valley together with their existing partners and they did, I think, continue to have sexual intercourse until the women left. Single members, generally young men, frequently complained about the relative absence of women, and Mother Earth placated them by explaining rather vaguely that all would eventually be resolved. Her more alarming proposal that men and women alike were about to return to a hermaphrodite form was possibly confided only to me.

50 Or more lucidly as: grounded but learnable, as cognitive categories, primary representations, conventional metaphors, focal metaphors, pri-

mordial image schemata or intuitive notions of natural kinds (to take various suggestions from Boyer 1993). Compare Leach (1976) on his terms 'physiological basis' and 'biological foundations' where cognition appears simply in the shared culture which from outside the body employs the uniform body as a metaphor: Durkheim's collective representation. (Similarly Douglas 1973.) In the case of pregnancy, we are not however dealing simply with the relationship between an available image and the collective acquisition of this knowledge, for pregnancy is also a cognition, motivation and praxis, an inherent connection and interaction with others. The last is argued in feminist jurisprudence: thus systemic and ethological rather than psychological evidence may be appropriate. We may argue a spectrum of instances from representations so grounded in intrinsic cognitions that they may be said to be psychological processes and most easily understood in neuropsychological terms, to embodiments of shared figurings such as Mauss' 'techniques'. And what we identify as the 'same cognition' may pass from one to the other.

51 Cf. 'shallow' or 'deep' symbolisations (Barrett and Lucas 1993), Turner's 'ideological' or 'sensory' poles, Jakobson's 'metonymic' or 'metaphorical' creativity.

12   The Effectiveness of Words: Religion and Healing Among the Lubavitch of Stamford Hill*

Letters to the Rebbe

And I shall behold God through my flesh
(Job 19:26)

The Lubavitch Hasidim of Stamford Hill in London are members of a worldwide Jewish movement, whose leader, the 7th Lubavitcher Rebbe, lives in New York.(1) Every year he receives hundreds of petitions (*kvitlekh*) about episodes of sickness and misfortune. He responds to many with reassurance and advice, sometimes suggesting that the household's religious objects are impure and should be checked. A 60 year old rabbi living in the community recalls how he became dangerously ill following a heart attack: after discharge from hospital he continued to experience chest pains, so his concerned wife wrote to the Rebbe in Brooklyn asking why this had happened and what could be done. The Rebbe replied simply that 'one should check one's *mezuzot*'. (The mezuzah is a parchment scroll inscribed with the *shema*, the affirmation of faith in God, enclosed in a metal case and placed upon the door frames of an observant Jewish home.) After a thorough examination of the family's mezuzot by a scribe, it was found that in one, in the ordinance 'Thou shalt love thy God with all thy heart' (Deuteronomy 6:5), the word for 'heart' was wrongly spelt. A new, kosher, mezuzah was obtained and subsequently the man experienced no more chest pains. Both husband and wife maintain that the error in transcription was the ultimate cause of the illness, and its correction was essential to his recovery. The Rebbe's knowledge was, in their words, 'truly miraculous'.

* First published in *Culture, Medicine and Psychiatry* (1995), and co-authored with Simon Dein

The 'Double Register': Efficacy and Meaning in the Anthropology of Healing

The incident certainly recalls the conventional understanding of a 'miracle'. Cause and effect are recognised in the material world through our everyday sensory experience, but also on occasion through direct knowledge of (or actual intercession by) a transcendent other-worldly register which ultimately justifies suffering, one which is generally opaque to full human awareness but which we can supplicate if not sometimes actually constrain.

The anthropology of what has been termed 'symbolic' or 'mythic' healing explained such *efficacité symbolique* (Lévi-Strauss 1949) as a close coupling of embodied experience to a society's received cognitions (*ibid*, Rivers 1924, Dow 1986). Since Mauss (1950) and Moerman (1979), few social scientists would now claim any intrinsic association between the body as a biological fact and such language-based representations. Where a formal isomorphism has been recognised between the body and the social order (eg. Durkheim and Mauss 1903, Douglas 1966, 1973), transformations in either are no longer explained as somehow participating in or causally influencing the other. Indeed, when challenged as to the relationship between the body understood natur-alistically and its symbolisations, many – whilst admitting some Kantian antinomy yet discreetly avoiding any apology for 'magic' – evoke the local moral rhetoric of the body to interpret what it is to be healed (Scheper-Hughes and Lock 1987, Good 1994). Phenomenological anthropology argues similarly that the experiencing self must be under-stood without recourse to any objectifications of the material world (Csordas 1994a, 1994b). If any physiological consequences of 'symbolic therapies', systematised or folk, are still recognised by medical anthro-pologists, then these are assumed to be through non-specific mecha-nisms such as alleviating anxiety or somehow promoting the body's immunological response (McGuire 1983, Laderman 1987). With contemporary interest in the political context of biomedicine, the natu-ralistic body has itself become theoretically redundant, as just another social representation of an external reality whose ontological status is no concern of anthropology.

This shift from empirical explanation to cultural interpretation and thence phenomenology parallels certain developments in Western psychotherapy whose nineteenth century origins lay in an explanation of hysteria which presumed a direct homology between the physiologi-cal body and its representation, akin to the homunculus inscribed in figures of the cerebral cortex to illustrate cortical localisation: an

isomorphism generally accessible to awareness but not in the 'dissociated' patient who in treatment was returned to this awareness
(Grunbaum 1984). Similarly 'hypertension' not only stood for but
physically expressed 'emotional tension' (Alexander 1939). Psychotherapy, like anthropology and complementary medicine (Beckford
1985), has only with reluctance abandoned this powerful idea of a
'double-register' with its direct and intrinsic correspondence between
physiology and its social cognition, between two rather different states
of being – or, as we might now say, different maps of reality. Rather,
psychotherapy too is now concerned not with efficacy but with
'meaning', 'self-actualisation' and 'awareness': as Frazer might have
argued, with those problems still resistant to immediate biophysical
intervention.

Western monotheisms, the 'revealed religions', had expressly
distinguished material experience from some type of ultimate, here
divine, meaning (Tambiah 1990). Christianity's explicitly paradoxical
elision of nature and divinity in the Incarnation enhanced a tendency
in the Jewish scriptures to mark a sharp distinction between the two
(with theological problems of then establishing the relations between
them [Brown 1989]),(2) a distinction which was developed later into
the increasingly secular dualism of Renaissance science, thence to the
epistemologies of Sydenham, Locke and Kant, and to contemporary
scientific empiricism (Foucault 1966, Rorty 1980, Tambiah 1990,
Gellner 1992, Littlewood 1993, Good 1994). Whether simply appropriating Jewish and Christian dualism which identified ultimate
reality with the divine meaning, or reversing it to privilege the
material, one level or other was taken as outside human agency and
thus as somehow more 'real' (Berger and Luckman 1966) and
determining of human interests.(3) Such an attempt might be termed
'structuralist' or even 'foundationalist' (Piaget 1968, Ardener 1978,
McMullin 1978, Hage and Harary 1983, Lawson and McCauley
1993): one which is exemplified by the Comptean hierarchy of
explanation which still underpins biomedicine, and by those expressly
'structuralist' approaches in the human sciences which place some
generative power (and thus for the theorist the formal analytical key)
in social relations (Durkheim), practical instrumentality (Marx),
psychology (Tylor, Freud, Malinowski) or neuro-psychology (Chom-
sky, Lévi-Strauss). And these carry with them certain assumptions
about 'representation' and 'symbolisation': less an arbitrary correspondence between fairly autonomous registers than the necessary
enactment of the one 'real' level as individual agency and thus as
historical event. In Lévi-Strauss' words (1970: 10), there is an attempt
'to reduce apparently arbitrary data to some kind of order, and to

attain a level at which a kind of necessity becomes apparent, underlying the illusions of liberty'.

Medical anthropology's shift from an empirical and sociological perspective to the discursive is characteristic of recent tendencies in the social sciences, away from the idea of such privileged analytical access to the 'real' level (whether biological or social) which determines subjective agency and implicit knowledge at another, to a single understanding in which both local experience and our analysis are taken as culturally and historically intended (eg. Clifford 1988, Crapanzano 1992). It is not surprising that one discipline which has been central in the move away from structuralism is anthropology, with its concern with alternative epistemologies in non-Western societies where things may quite variously hang together in local knowledge even if one or another mode of reality was identified by ethnographers as primary. In this sense then, the varieties of post-structuralism all signal an apparent rupture with a Western mode of understanding which goes back to the Jewish scriptures with their privileging of some determining reality. As Hegel predicted, our distinction between form and function has perhaps finally broken down.

Some sort of 'congruence' (Torrey 1971) between bodily illness as experienced and the systematised social representation of it is still recognised (Kleinman and Sung 1979, Dow 1986, Good and Good 1986, Bilu et al. 1990, Kirmayer 1993). Indeed it seems difficult to characterise any social action as 'healing' without assuming some agreement on a shared representation of the immediate problem. And it is this agreement which itself now constitutes what Tambiah (1977) terms 'performative efficacy', successful healing being justified not through some objective criterion of health external to the understanding of healing – as biomedicine still argues – but rather in the acceptance by patient and others that a transformation of bodily state or sensibility has been effected (McGuire 1983, Csordas 1988, Good 1994). 'Ritual' in general is now taken as an action intended in some way by participants to aesthetically evoke or modify their consensual experience, as well as (or indeed instead of) instrumentally effecting events in the material world (Tambiah 1968, 1990, Young 1976, Ahern 1979, Kapferer 1993, Csordas 1994a), together with a more subtle distinction between instrumental and representational models (Caws 1974, Holy and Stuchlik 1981). If for some anthropologists there remain a number of paths from physical experience to representation which are not mediated by agency and language (Sperber 1980), the observer cannot claim to fully elucidate the 'meaning' of healing symbols but merely record what they evoke in a particular situation.

'Symbolic meanings' are now not only naturalistically arbitrary, polysemous and manifest creatively in immediate situations (Good 1994), but are to be demonstrated as the participants' own understandings and intentions, through description rather than explanation (Parkin 1982, cf. Lawson and McCauley 1993). As such they may be quite diverse (Sperber 1985), circumscribed (Caws 1974), of variable 'depth' (Feinberg 1990, Barrett and Lucas 1993), unrelated to actual experience (Jackson 1983), ambiguous (Bourdieu 1977, Hobart 1982) or of little general concern (Sperber 1975, Schieffelin 1985). Healing idioms may be considerably less systematised than anthropologists recognise (Young 1976, Laderman 1987, Kirmayer 1993) and indeed may gain their very efficacy through some meta-communicative unintelligibility (Last 1981, McGuire 1983, Csordas 1988) – Malinowski's 'coefficient of weirdness'.

The so-called 'interpretive turn' in medical anthropology, like its phenomenological successors, claims a greater closeness to individual agency and intention than that achieved through an objective and context-free criterion of efficacy derived from biophysical medicine: for biomedicine is now recognised as a map not a mirror. Whilst we have criticised elsewhere anthropology's complete abandonment of the objectified naturalistic body as one valid commentary on human experience (Littlewood 1991, 1995; pace Csordas 1994c), our concern here is rather different. Does the emphasis on 'meaning' do justice to the explicit concerns of those involved situationally as sick individuals?(4) Medical anthropologists still imply some greater validity to their own 'holistic' methodologies in, typically, suggesting that the flux of experiencing should not be reified into entities, and that a dualist epistemology is in some way misconceived (Lock and Scheper-Hughes 1990, Good 1994, Csordas 1994b). The generality of bodily afflictions are however experienced as real, as immediate and arbitrary (Ellen 1977, Feinberg 1990, Littlewood 1993); neither 'symbolic' nor demanding rhetorical transformation, they have a compelling physical urgency which demands instrumental redress in the same register (Last 1981, Gellner 1992). While we may sometimes, particularly with chronic afflictions (Kleinman and Sung 1979, Good 1994), be driven to a search for significance and justification, we are generally concerned with immediate practical amelioration: with countering the 'first spear' as best we can before worrying about the second, to use Evans-Pritchard's Zande idioms.

The structuralist schema had required what Ardener (1980) terms 'P-structures': paradigms or blueprints which had some primary instrumental or formal relationship to the secondary registrar, whether as base and superstructure, myth and experience, or simply template and artefact. Structuralist models of healing such as that of Lévi-Strauss (1949) seemed to correspond closely with local exegesis in societies where the body and its sickness were indeed already highly 'mythologised': where upper and lower register, mythic reality and bodily experience (and, as in this paper, social group) were understood as already reflecting and recreating each other in a ubiquitous and closed narrative, where psychology was a cosmology, mythic reality being experienced by individuals as in accordance with events and actions which were not seen as situationally specific, nor generally justified as personal agency.(5) In increasingly less 'tight' societies ('low grid, low group' in Douglas' [1973] terminology), such as the pluralistic postmodern world where biomedicine, whilst arguably evoking core notions of self and agency (Lock and Gordon 1988), has considerably less representational coherence and certainly no obvious formal homology with some ultimate reality, we may expect the notion of 'mythic healing' to become more extraordinary both for observer and participants.(6) The greater the gap between divinity and experience, the more miracles are indeed 'miracles'.

The Besht

While Western monotheisms radically distinguished the sensible world from its ultrahuman reality, an explicit image of 'healing' has been common to both the restoration of the body to health and safety and to the deliverance of a 'wounded spirit' or indeed the redemption of a whole community (cf. Gk. soteria, Lat. salvus). Prophets and the founders of new religious dispensations commonly engage in, or are recorded by later hagiographers as having employed, miracles of healing. They assert a double register, usually enhancing the very separation, yet at the same time they show that it may be mediated by certain individuals; indeed their very authority appears to be justified through their tapping higher realities to heal sickness and insanity, as well as to predict or avert other misfortunes, evil forces or disasters to the community. The expectations for a prophet to reconcile the two worlds through healing – and his occasional resistance to these – are well demonstrated for Jesus in the Christian Gospels (Mathew 4:23, 8:16, 9:32, 12:22, Mark 5:25), together with his use of the idiom of 'healing' for an increased turning to the spiritual, through confession and absolution, with conversion of the sick soul to a fundamentally new perspective.

In this paper we are not concerned with whether the conversion of individuals to the new religious perspective can be usefully termed 'therapeutic' (Heelas and Haglund-Heelas 1988, Witztum and Green-berg 1990, Littlewood 1993), so much as with the public apologies for physical illness offered by its members. Such testimonials, and those offered by their Rebbe, are however referred back to the moment of awakening to the moment's ideals, an experience which is frequently couched in a therapeutic idiom.

Hasidism developed as a popular movement in Eastern Europe in the 18th century.(7) Its immediate founder was the Master of the Good Name, the Baal Shem Tov, popularly known by the acronym Besht. Epstein (1959) argues that two events were instrumental in its emergence: the Cossack insurrections of 1648–1649, which killed tens of thousands of Jews in Poland and the Ukraine, and the subsequent Sabbatian crisis. Buber (1948) and Sharot (1982) both emphasise the increasing gap between the urban rabbinate and the rural Jewish population after the death of Sabbatai Svi (1626–1676) whose mes-sianic claims and antinomian acts had swept the Jewish diaspora with promises of immediate redemption and speedy release from all their trials (Scholem 1973). When Sabbatai converted suddenly to Islam, some followers returned to rabbinical Judaism or converted to Islam or Christianity. Others maintained Sabbatian ideas under the guise of orthodoxy, citing the Kabbalah to explain how Sabbatai had commit-ted the ultimate transgression of apostasy: for the Messiah had to descend to the lower levels to redeem the divine sparks exiled there since the beginning of time (Scholem 1971, Littlewood 1995).

The relationship of Hasidism to the Sabbatian movement remains controversial and some scholars deny any direct continuity.(8) The Besht, a clay-digger and itinerant healer of humble origin, taught that every present moment contained the possibility of redemption for each individual and for the community. Every person, whatever his status, wealth or learning, could participate in this cosmic process. Between the scholarly elitism of the rabbis and the apocalyptic messianism of the Sabbatians, the Besht's followers put forward an egalitarian interpretation of the Kabbalistic teachings which we consider below. They taught that God was to be known immediately in all aspects of life, since the physical world existed with Him and within Him, and He could be reached through everyday activities (Jacobs 1973). People were encouraged to 'cleave to God' and experience Him through ecstatic song, prayer and dance, and even, initially, by the use of tobacco and alcohol. Any act – eating, work, sexual relations – was a religious act if the intention was to attach oneself to God.

The Besht was apparently well known in his hometown as a healer, 'a master of practical Kabbalah, a magician' (Scholem 1954). It has been suggested that he employed the existing practices of the miracle worker to persuade people of his ethical teachings (see also Ben-Amos and Mintz 1970). 'There can be little doubt', argues Sharot (1982), 'that the Besht's reputation for miracle making was accepted as an important proof of his charisma and of his teachings'. While he generally employed recognised physical methods such as herbal remedies or bleeding with lancet and leeches, like other local healers and magicians (baalei shem), he would sometimes use a prayer or the secret names of angels to exorcise a dibbuk (earthbound spirit) from the body of a sick person or out of a house (Trachtenberg 1977). Baalei shem protected the individual against sickness, and against such misfortunes as infertility, miscarriages, fire, theft and the evil eye. They reframed non-Jewish folk therapies in a Jewish idiom, and employed the sacred writings of the rabbinical tradition for practical magic, together with the names of God and the angels and prophets, sometimes as anagrams, acronyms, acrostics and inversions derived from them. The mezuzot had originally been amulets of this sort, and they retained their thaumaturgical function despite rabbinical attempts to transform them into simple emblems. When a child was ill or a woman in obstructed labour, the Torah scroll was laid on top of them. Psalm 20 was read over the mother to alleviate the pains of childbirth, for its nine verses corresponded to the nine months of pregnancy, and its seventy words to the seventy pangs of labour. The Besht himself was famous for his blessed coins and psalms or other formulae written on parchment enclosed in a small metal case which contained the names of angels and imprecations against malevolent powers (Ben-Amos and Mintz 1970). Fifty years after his death, the Shivhei ha-Besht, a book compiled by a follower, relates many stories of his ability to heal:

> I heard from the Rabbi of our community that Rabbi Leibush of the holy community of Meserich visited the Besht for the Days of Awe. Before Rosh Hashanah [the New Year] he became sick. The Besht was busy curing him on the eve of Rosh Hashanah and the entire night as well. When he went to the beth hamidrash [study hall] at the time for prayer, Rabbi Leibush became faint and felt very weak. They tried to tell the Besht, but they were afraid to shout and he did not hear them. When Rabbi Isaac of the holy community of Meserich saw that the Besht did not respond, he shouted to him in a loud voice. The Besht answered, 'Why didn't you tell me?' He hurried home and found the Angel of Death standing at the head of the bed. The Besht scolded the Angel of Death severely and he ran away. The Besht then held Rabbi Leibush by the hand and he recovered immediately. (Ben-Amos and Mintz 1970:116)

The Besht's teaching was systematised by this biographer, Dov Ber of

Meserich (1719–1772), known as the Magid (Preacher), who took the existing term zaddik (righteous man) for the local leader of a Hasidic group (Dresner 1974). The founder of Lubavitch, Rabbi Schneur Zalman of Ladi (1745–1812), who studied under Dov Ber, later commented 'we drew up the holy spirit by the bucketful, and miracles lay around under the benches, only no one had time to pick them up' (Wiener 1969). According to Epstein (1959), Hasidism would not have spread with such rapidity nor attained such dimensions but for the 'extraordinary galaxy of saintly mystics' it produced during its first fifty years. Hasidism holds that only the zaddik can attain the highest form of devekut (attachment to God at all times with one's thoughts always on him). Other Jews have to attach themselves to a zaddik through whom in turn they can become attached to God. (The term rebbe is now used virtually synonymously with zaddik.) The zaddik develops the spirituality of his adherents while at the same time, through his mediation with God, he can secure favours for them in both mundane and divine matters.

After Dov Ber's death, groups following various zaddikim developed in the Ukraine and Poland, each known by the name of their centre of activity. Their leaders are now recalled through a particular quality or activity: some were distinguished for their fervent devotions, others for their ecstatic visions, spiritual insight or miraculous healing. Their surviving texts are characterised by an accessible popular style rooted in folk-lore: anecdotes, homilies, marvellous tales, puns, jokes and semantic paradoxes. Despite accusations of antinomianism and even pantheism, Hasidism spread rapidly in Poland and was introduced to Lithuania by Schneur Zalman who developed the variant called Chabad which reintroduced the more intellectual elements of Kabbalah – but now into more general accessibility – through his Tanya (Book of Teaching), the major text of Lubavitch.

Both orthodox Judaism and secular Zionism have maintained an ambivalent relationship to Hasidim, at times critical of their overt emotionalism and dependence on miraculous rebbes (Dresner 1974), on other occasions taking them as the authentic voice of Jewish spirituality and identity. Hasidic folk tales have now become widely accessible through the popularisations of Martin Ruber (1948). By the 19th century, Lubavitch was recognised as the 'rationalist' form of Hassidism which could appeal to the educated. It fought to secure economic and political benefits for all Jews in Eastern Europe, and developed a number of charitable and educational projects. Discouraged from migrating to America because of the dangers of secularism, the majority of Hasidim were to die in the Holocaust, but the 6th Lubavitch Rebbe organised communities outside Eastern Europe from which in 1948 most of the survivors settled in New York (Mintz 1992). Today, the major Lubavitch centres are in New York (Brooklyn), London (Stamford Hill), Israel (Jerusalem and Kefar Chabad), Canada (Montreal) and Belgium (Antwerp). It has been generously estimated that by the 1980s there were perhaps 250,000 adherents and close sympathisers worldwide (Sharot 1991).(9)

The Stamford Hill Lubavitch

Stamford Hill is an inner-city area in north-east London, with a population of around 27,000 people in an area of three square miles. There are now nearly a thousand Hasidic families living here, about two hundred of them Lubavitch. Other local Hasidic groups include Satmar, Belzer and Gur.(10) Although today 'Stamford Hill' is virtually synonymous with Jewish ultra-orthodoxy, this was not always the case. Before the Second World War many local congregations were United Synagogue or Sephardic, who later moved out to the more affluent suburbs (Kupfermann 1976). Today, less than half of the population of Stamford Hill are Jews, mainly lower-middle-class tradesmen, religious teachers and small businessmen.

The number of Lubavitch families increases every year, not only through the encouragement of large families but through conversion.(11) The majority of the adult Stamford Hill community are British converts from non-orthodox Judaism who are more likely to speak English than Yiddish. Some informants have even been adherents of Western-based Buddhist and Hindu sects although they were born Jews. Many had already been familiar with popularised accounts of the Kabbalah (eg. Wiener 1969) or with that continuing counter-culture interest in matters Jungian and Hermetic (eg. Hall 1962). Rarely a Christian may convert to orthodox Judaism to then join Lubavitch. The community conduct mass campaigns to reclaim 'stray' Jews: public meetings where rabbis preach, mezuzot campaigns (checking local Jews have kosher mezuzot on their doors) and perhaps the most striking of all, the 'mitzvah tank', a truck going round the streets inviting male Jews to enter and lay tefillin.(12) Besides encouraging every Jew to be more observant, Lubavitchers attempt to attract into their group educated young single adults, and campaigns are sometimes held on university campuses. 'Conversion' is less a sudden accession of faith than a gradual process in which the individual 'returns', employing more and more Jewish rituals in their daily life. Joining may cause conflict with the families of the converts, especially when a student gives up university studies or career.(13)

Daily activity within a Hasidic group is determined in principle by *Halacha* (the Way), largely derived from the Talmud, the rabbinical compilation of legal, ethical and historical writings. Minimum standards of observance for all the community include strict *kashrut* (food must be ritually pure; milk must neither be cooked nor eaten with meat), together with Sabbath and festival observance. For men there is regular attendance in the prayer house and daily study of the sacred texts, with conservative clothing, beard and covered head. For women, an enthusiastic attitude to child bearing is expected, with modest dress including covered hair (married women cut their hair short and cover their head with a *sheitl* or wig), and in most groups, regular prayer (not always in the synagogue) and some religious learning. Marriage and parenthood are sacred acts, and couples are expected to adhere to the laws governing family purity. Marriage of members is arranged by a *shidduch* maker and agreed by their fathers, and at least nominally by the rebbe; choice of spouse depends on their families' wealth, lineage and learning (*yihus*). Children are educated in single-sex Jewish schools, with secular education valued less than Jewish learning; in their late teens some are sent to residential seminaries. Rarely university education may be considered appropriate. As for other orthodox Jews, the Hasidic injunction to study affirms it as a religious experience which brings the scholar ever nearer to God.

Lubavitch do not have careers, they earn a living. Favoured occupations include small businesses, especially those serving the wider orthodox community such as food stores, or teaching and other religiously-linked occupations, slaughterer (*shohet*), beadle (*shammes*) or circumciser (*mohel*), and the rabbinate. Families tend to be large: one couple has sixteen children living in two adjoining houses. The average number of children per family is seven; parents are expected to trust in God to help them provide, educate and care for large families. During fieldwork it was found that people usually adhered strictly to the orthodox public norms. Occasionally a degree of flexibility is agreed in the interpretation of religious law; one woman from the community went to live in the north of England far from the nearest synagogue so the Rebbe allowed her to travel by vehicle on the Sabbath, or so we were told.

Although there is some association with other local Hasidic groups and occasional intermarriage, there are frequent tensions: the Satmar, who retain the kaftans and hanging sidelocks of the East European *shtetl* (Zborowski and Herzog 1962), argue the Lubavitchers' adaptation to 'modernity' has been too enthusiastic, while some orthodox Jews accuse the current Rebbe of messianic ambitions (Beeston 1992). To an extent, one may take these other Hasidic groups as continuations of small shtetl communities linked by descent and endogamy, now concerned with preserving the group's traditions and boundaries in the modern world, while Lubavitch's use of new communication technologies, its public profile and emphasis on conversion, argue for many similarities with contemporary 'new religious movements'.

In a study of another Hasidic group, derived like the Lubavitch from the pre-war world of the shtetl, we noted that the mundane and the religious remained 'tied together' through the mediating symbolisms of everyday actions (Littlewood 1983). The term *kosher* was applied simultaneously to food, clothes, non-menstruating women, books and ideas. The geography of community prayer house, home, room, clothes and body were carefully ordered, each commenting on and reflecting the others. Prayer books were divided into sections which corresponded with the rooms of a house and the parts of the body. The Torah (Law) gives contemporary Hasidim explicit norms for all daily activities. In addition, through a complex numerology employing the numerical value of words and letters, cardinal numbers (the number of good or bad deeds, gifts, objects, alms) and ordinal numbers (sequence of a text or family birth order), it inscribes the social and physical worlds in a tight network. There is no act or event, good or bad, which is arbitrary or neutral. Indeed it can be said that contemporary Hasidim aspire to have no 'secular' life in that all everyday events and actions are aligned to a divine reality which is always to be held in mind. Members of the community isolate themselves where possible from the non-Jewish world. They argue a practical advantage in their distinctive attire which makes them less likely to go into sinful places. Mixing with non-Jews (*Goyim*) is minimal except for business purposes for they are said by some to be impure and polluting: a not uncommon idea is that their souls are somehow inferior. Douglas (1970; *cf.* Gilman 1992), following Durkheim, has argued that the orthodox Jewish concern with the boundaries of the physical body – with its entrances and exits, with food, purification after excretion and menstruation, and masturbation (whence semen provides embodiment for evil powers) – follows a concern with the boundaries of the body politic faced with the ever-present threats of assimilation and intermarriage. Certainly, for Lubavitch, return to orthodoxy is primarily through ritual actions which inscribe a gradually increasing sanctity onto the individual body marking it off from the world of the Goyim.

Hasidic wives, *akeres habayis*, are the mainstay of the family; their domestic role is praised, particularly in guaranteeing the purity of food and household, and thus their family's health. These tasks are not recognised as 'symbolic' in the vernacular sense – as not instrumental – for failure to perform, for example, the prescribed clearing of the house of bread before Passover allows sickness to intrude (eg. Littlewood 1983). Whilst Lubavitch women argue that household tasks are sacred, many consider themselves more independent than other Hasidic women and to have a higher level of education, and some claim a responsibility equal to that of the men in doing the Rebbe's work. Several women are involved in 'reclaiming' other Jewish women to religious orthodoxy and, compared with women of other Hasidic groups, they are less discouraged from attending the synagogue.

The Rebbe

Every room in a Lubavitch house has several pictures of the current Rebbe on the walls, as a young man and as a nonagenarian. Families take great pride in showing pictures of their visits to him, especially at *Dollars* when he distributes a dollar (signifying charity) to every one of the hundreds who visit him in Brooklyn on Sunday mornings.

Menachem Mendel Schneersohn has led the group since the 1950s. Lubavitchers describe him as 'the most phenomenal Jewish personality of our time' and it is through his direction that Lubavitch has developed its distinctive outward orientation. Born in Russia in 1902, he became a 'Torah prodigy', is said to be fluent in ten languages, and – unusually for Hasidim of his generation – received a secular higher education, a degree in engineering from the Sorbonne. Many miraculous stories are told about him during the fourth meal by which Hasidim seek to prolong the Sabbath: he sleeps for just one hour a day, and fasts for three days in the week; he 'gives Torah' for several hours without needing a break; he meditates weekly at the grave of the 6th Rebbe with whose soul he communicates; he predicted the end of communism in Eastern Europe a year before it occurred. Although he has never visited Israel, nor indeed left Brooklyn for the past 40 years, the Rebbe is widely credited with single-handedly halting at least one set of Middle East peace talks, and with directly influencing the 1988 Israeli elections. Many of these 'miracle tales' (Mintz 1968) have personal resonances.(14) Those told about earlier zaddikim recall European fairy tales – stories of lost children, secret parentage, tribulation and reward, buried treasure, ghosts and dibukkim, miraculous escapes from Cossacks and Nazis (see Mintz 1968 and the stories of Bashevis Singer). A common theme is the fundamental distinction between Jew and Goy, and the near-impossibility of passing from one to the other.

Succession to a rebbe is usually dynastic. Menachem Schneersohn is the son-in-law of the previous Rebbe, and in his father's line, the descendent of the Alter Rebbe (Schneur Zalman). Under his leadership Lubavitcher institutions and activities have been established throughout the world to cater for the educational needs of the alienated Jew and 'late beginners' who would otherwise be unable to attend a *yeshiva* or a girls' school.

The process of joining Lubavitch is characterised not only by the use of ritual objects, but by an increasing attachment (*hitkashrut*) to his person and to his work. Among the most important gatherings of the community are those that commemorate the deaths and key events in the lives of past zaddikim (*yohrstait*). Lubavitch are expected to be familiar with their lives, works and teachings (*hasides*), and the movement's sense of itself is a moral history understood principally through their written works and stories about them. In its shallow chronology, Hasidic rebbes are recognised as the incarnations of previous rebbes or of biblical prophets, and scriptural events have a contemporary action or significance; biological evolution is denied. Children are taught to revere the zaddik, and in everyday conversation Lubavitchers frequently discuss his objectives and his teachings, particularly his extraordinary personal powers and wisdom. Couples engaged in marital intercourse on the Sabbath are enjoined to fix their minds on him. Through him mundane happenstance takes on new, deeper, meanings: what might otherwise be seen as 'coincidences' are to be understood as brought about by the Rebbe's intervention. He is the guide on matters of spiritual and physical health, education, marriage and business:

> Miriam Hirsch had always intended to visit the Rebbe in America for Dollars, but had never had the necessary money. One Sabbath, her American sister in Brooklyn went to see him. Mrs. Hirsch was unaware of this but admitted that on that particular day she had thought a lot about the Rebbe. Her sister didn't mention Miriam to the Rebbe but was unexpectedly given two dollars. She sent one to London. Mrs. Hirsch understood that the Rebbe was aware of the thoughts of every Jew; he knew how she was worrying and therefore gave her sister two dollars. 'Truly a miraculous man.'

Lubavitch are prepared for the arrival of the Messiah. They envisage a time very soon when the world will change fundamentally, for sickness, envy, greed and hatred will disappear. Several rabbis argue that many existing institutions will probably remain, a commonly mentioned instance being capitalism. The appearance of Moshiach is now imminent: 'If he does not come today he will come tomorrow.' When asked why he has not yet come, the following explanation was

often given to us: in each generation there are 36 righteous (but
hidden) men, one of whom is a potential Messiah, but not enough
merit by Jews has been acquired for him to emerge. Many Lubavitchers suggested that perhaps now there is enough merit, and admitted
that they thought Rebbe Schneersohn might be the Messiah, an idea
which he, like other rebbes, has done little to contradict (Beeston
1992). They point out that he is the seventh rebbe, and that Moses
was of the seventh generation after Abraham.

The Mystical Body

Through daily readings of Tanya, Lubavitch makes accessible the once
esoteric knowledge expounded in the texts known as Kabbalah. The
term kabbalah (tradition, 'that which has been received') had been
used since the 11th century CE for that diffuse tradition of Jewish
mystical thought said to be hidden in the religious Law and which was
received from the remote past, from Ezekiel, or even, in some
accounts, through Adam from the angels before the Fall. Gershom
Scholem, the major historian of Jewish mysticism, has argued for a
continuity with Jewish Gnosticism which had sought to reconnect the
immediate and divine worlds which rabbinical Judaism so austerely
divided; 'the Kabbalah was a mythical reaction in realms which
monotheistic thinking had with utmost difficulty wrested from myth',
an 'eruption of subterranean forces' which attempted 'to construct and
describe a mythical world by means of thinking that excluded myth'
(Scholem 1965: 98, 99); a return back across the 'abyss' which had
developed between the registers of the physical and the spiritual
(Scholem 1954) (see note 2). Scholem (like Bulka 1979) suggests that
the rabbinical tradition of established institutions and canonical texts
had provided no help in dealing with disaster and sickness, or indeed
with the spiritual vacuum left by the Sabbatian apostasy. Kabbalists
however have never seen themselves in opposition to rabbinical
orthodoxy but rather as its commentators and developers.

Kabbalah is said to have first been communicated as secret
teaching only to a privileged few, but by the early modern period it had
become a more open pursuit, a trend particularly evident in Hasidism.
It speaks of the ultimate ultrahuman order as now manifest in Man,
and as one which can be directly known through study or ecstatic
experience, and upon which we can call and obtain practical power in
this world. We may argue, as does Scholem, affinities with South
Asian religious systems, Christian and Islamic mysticism, and particularly with the sort of Western theosophico-astrological tradition

currently recognised under the rubric of New Age thinking (Hall 1962, Beckford 1985, Tambiah 1990, Littlewood 1993). The material world of our experience is to be understood as an imperfect reflection of hidden, 'deeper' (or 'higher') underlying principles, knowledge of which serves as a practical key to confer insight and sometimes power over everyday events. Instead of the rigorously dualistic cosmogony in which the inscrutable and austere Hebrew deity suddenly creates the material world out of nothing, and across which gap occasionally pass angels or the souls of the dead, we have here a mythic narrative gradually unfolding in cosmic time through which the progress of individual souls can be mapped, with infinite gradations of being between God and Man. This metaphysical reality is often figured in anthropomorphic, if sometimes explicitly allegorical, terms; as gendered and embodied, emanating in physical space, with impulses and motivations not entirely dissimilar from those of humankind.

The most important of the more than three thousand extant texts is the *Zohar*, the bulk of which was probably written in Spain by Moses de Leon (died 1305); its themes were elaborated by Isaac Luria (1514–1572) in Palestine among the Iberian Jews exiled in 1492, in what is generally known to scholars as the Lurianic Kabbalah. The Zohar, a lengthy collection of tales, anecdotes, homilectics and commentaries, is in late literary Aramaic with occasional Hebrew, Arabic and Spanish expressions, the whole interwoven with paraphrases, neologisms, allegories, oxymorons, verbal paradoxes and invented quotations. There are frequent digressions retelling popular tales (*aggadah*) and on medical and demonological questions (Preis 1928, Trachtenberg 1939). According to Epstein (1959), it is, after the Talmud, the post-scriptural book which has exercised the profoundest influence on Judaism. Its recurrent themes are the nature of the Deity and the way He made Himself manifest in the universe; the mysteries of the divine names; the soul of man, its source and destiny; the nature of evil; the importance of the written and oral Torah; and the promised Messiah and our future redemption.

According to the Zohar, the Infinite (*En-Sof*), who has in Himself neither qualities nor attributes, made His existence perceptible by projecting ten successive channels of light which served as media for His manifestations in the finite. These ten channels are the *Sefiroth* (numbers, elements, spheres), which in the Zohar are understood as the names, indeed the actual qualities and agencies, of God: the intelligible divine attributes which make up all existence. The Sefiroth are figured in different patterns, but may be divided into three triads or dimensions. The first triad represents the immanent intellectual power of the universe, the second triad the moral world, and the third the physical universe. The tenth Sefirah is the female aspect of divinity, the Shekhinah, now manifest in the physical world, and which Adam, the first man, mistook for the whole of divinity. The human individual is to be understood as a microcosm of the whole universe by which each person reproduces what is above in the celestial worlds. The Sefirotic structure of man simultaneously reflects and is reflected onto that of the universe, and the Sefiroth may be represented as concentric circles, as the Tree of Being, or as the Cosmic Man (the lower parts being the outer circles of the first representation).(15) They may be identified with certain numbers, letters and colours, and they are gendered: in the first triad, Wisdom – masculine, the father, the giving element – is counterposed to Understanding – feminine, the mother, the receiver; the offspring of their conjunction is Knowledge.

Later Kabbalists describe four distinct realms corresponding to different orders of Sefiroth: in descending order of divinity, Aziluth (emanation), Briah (creation), Yetzirah (formation), Asiyah (making, the divine archetype of the material world). The four are both simultaneous and successive (Scholem 1965), structured by the Sefiroth in a similar pattern and subject to common influences. Anything which involves one level cannot fail to involve all others for 'from an activity below there is stimulated a corresponding activity on high' (Zohar 1934). There is an intrinsic relationship between what we may gloss as the 'material' and 'spiritual' worlds, each not only influencing but continuously participating in the other as prefigurings and memories (Bloom 1984). And these relationships may be understood through a complex but variable numerology in which the twenty-two letters of the alphabet are exchanged (temurah) or substituted for their numerical value (gematria). The absence of numerals, vowels or punctuation in the written Torah (the first five books of the scriptures) leave it open to a bewildering number of interpretations. Some have argued that there are actually 600,000 possible interpretations of the Torah, corresponding to the 600,000 holy souls each of whom has a letter in the Torah.(16) The scriptures begin with the second letter, beth, to show that God's manifestation is on both levels, for the Hebrew alphabet is itself the direct manifestation of the divine, as are the shape of the letters and even the spaces between, each possible pair of consonants forming a 'gate' for the passage of divine energy. The Torah (and the alphabet) is represented variously in Kabbalistic writings as the individual physical body, the body of the Jews as a whole, or even that of God: some maintained it existed before the creation of the physical world (Scholem 1973).

A rigid distinction between 'material' and 'spiritual' is hardly perceptible given the everyday as an immanent unfolding of the divine language. 'The Torah is to [Jewish mystics] a living organism animated by a secret life which steams and pulsates below the crust of literal meaning; every one of the innumerable strata of the hidden region corresponds to a new and profound meaning of the Torah' (Scholem 1954: 14). Kabbalistic texts embody a variety of complex, sometimes playful, shifts and cross-cuttings between 'depths' of interpreting the Torah, from the referential to the figurative: literal reference (*peshat*), conscious allegory (*remez*), Talmudic commentary (*derasha*) and mystical (*sod*) (*cf.* Feinberg 1990, Barrett and Lucas 1993). These four levels are known by the acronym *pardes* (orchard).

No unfettered speculation, even *sod* remains closely constrained by adherence to the literal interpretation of the Law and the authority of the rebbe, and its sources lie within the religious texts and practices of all Jews. There have been no radical innovations in Jewish mysticism since the seventeenth century but, in Buber's words, Hasidism transformed the once esoteric Kabbalah into a 'folk ethos'. Unlike most other orthodox Jews, the Stamford Hill community have immediate knowledge of Kabbalah for, as part of their education, every Lubavitcher child studies Tanya (Kehot 1981) which is based on Lurianic concepts. Tanya (*Likutei Amarim*) was compiled by Rabbi Zalman, the founder of Lubavitch, and is regarded as 'the written law of Chabad'. Other orthodox groups adhere to the old Talmudic ruling that only married men over forty with a good knowledge of the Talmud may proceed to Kabbalah. (Much of the Zohar employs erotic imagery in figuring the exile and eventual reconciliation of divine and mundane: the human conjunction of husband and wife on the Sabbath night is a realisation of the union between God and His exiled Shekhinah.)

Another name for Lubavitch is *Chabad*: an acronym from the Hebrew words *Hokhmah*, *Binah* and *Da'at* (the first triad: page 16). They refer simultaneously to personal experiences and to the Sefirotic realm where these are reflected. Anything occurring in the mind mirrors that occurring in the universe as a whole. Indeed, like other systems which approach pantheism (eg. Horton 1983, Tambiah 1990), the Sefiroth are as much a psychology as a cosmology. Hokhmah (wisdom) is the intuitive flash by which an idea emerges into the mind. Once it has come into being, the thought becomes actualised through deep reflection as Binah (understanding). When the idea becomes an aspect of the person engaged in contemplation, the third stage of Da'at (knowledge) is attained. The psychological and spiritual body of man 'participates in' (Lévy-Bruhl's term), rather than 'represents', the same principles and structural counterparts as his physical body. 'If we want to know something about the ultimate reality of the world we live in, and how God the creator manifests himself through this reality, we must begin with a study of the human being' (Mindel 1974). In Jewish mysticism, our phenomenological world is far from illusory (as it is in Buddhism) but one end, as it were, of ultimate reality.

Thus Lubavitch speak of the Sefiroth, not only as symbols or allegories (Kehot 1981: 820) or even resonances, but as immanent in bodily experience. 'We were formed after the supernal pattern, each limb corresponding to something in the scheme of wisdom' (Zohar: *ii*, 212; *cf.* Genesis 1:27). One young rabbi describes how the Torah is figured thus in the Zohar as the 'blueprint' (his words) with which God provided Himself for the physical creation: the Torah comprises 248 positive and 365 negative injunctions (*Tanchuma ha Kadum*) and these 'upper roots' have their respective manifestations in the 248 'limbs' and 365 'sinews' (or blood vessels) of the male body. Each limb of the body embodies one of the commandments, and each sinew and each day of the year embodies self-restriction. (The Tanya argues that the spiritual aspects of these 613 parts comprise the individual soul.) In this way every observance (or breach) of the commandments of the Torah directly causes, through its counterparts in the human body, a reaction in the corresponding portion of the world of Sefiroth: in Zoharic terms, each is the 'clothing' of the other. In his Tanya, Schneur Zalman associated specific parts of the body with other psychological and moral attributes: 'the evil spirit is in the left ventricle of the heart, and the love of God flames in the right ventricle'. While there are intrinsic homologies between the two realms, the correspondence is realised practically not only through mystical computation but through such objects as the tallit (see note 12).

Exile and Restitution

Sickness has its place in the divine schema. Luria's development of Zoharic cosmology postulates an initial voluntary contraction (*Zimzum*, self-limitation) of the Infinite to make room for the finite world of phenomena. Into the vacuum thus formed the Infinite projected His light, providing it at the same time with the 'vessels' which were to serve as the media for its manifestations in creation. Some of the vessels, unable to endure the inrush of light, gave way and broke. The breaking of the vessels caused a deterioration in the worlds above, together with chaos and confusion in the worlds below. Instead of uniform distribution throughout the universe, the light emitted by the

Infinite was broken up into sparks illuminating only certain parts of the material world; other parts were left in darkness, their sparks trapped in matter. This confusion was aggravated by the failure of Adam to restore the fragments, and thus human history is born in exile. The universe remains in a state of disharmony, and the mission of every Jew, say Lubavitchers, is to restore (*tikkun*) the scattered divine sparks back to the Godhead through performing *mizvot* (divine commandments and thus ritual and charitable deeds): 'the perfection of the upper worlds waits on the perfection of the lower worlds'.(17) The distinction between the more divine and the more human elements in the cosmic unfolding may be understood as one of dimension, distance, time, quality, procedure, potential, or indeed sometimes identity. Sickness and evil thus refer not to some malevolent power external to the created world of experience, evil in a strong sense (Parkin 1985), but to a lesser state of being of this world which can be redeemed in this life or in another incarnation:

> 'How, Reb Zusya, do you explain evil?' [his] students asked. 'What evil?' said the rabbi with wide wondering eyes. The students pointed out that Reb Zusya was himself suffering from illness, pain and poverty. 'Oh that', replied the rabbi, 'surely that is what my soul needs.' (Wiener 1969)

The Lurianic cosmogony – the 'great myth of exile' as Scholem (1954) calls it – informs the Lubavitchers' explicit concepts of 'health' as knowledge and order obtained through following Talmudic teachings (Weisel 1978). It refers simultaneously to physiological and psychological dysfunction, to failure to perform ritual correctly, to disharmony and conflict within the family, and to the historical exile of the Jews – all as a separation from the divine. The original 600,000 souls have become fragmented and now seek to be restored (Mintz 1968). To recover one's health is, in some small measure, to restore our alienated world. Stamford Hill Lubavitch commonly argue that the 'universe itself is now in need of healing' for which they quote the Lurianic cosmogony. Since the shattering of the vessels God Himself is in exile. If there is a single image, a core symbol (Ortner 1973) which incorporates and subsumes others (Laughlin and Stevens 1980), and which captures the manifold connotations of sickness and misfortune, what Victor Turner termed a 'root paradigm', it is that of exile and restitution.(18) 'The very nature of man ... makes him an admirable intermediary between the material and the spiritual. By means of these religious acts, not only are the material things spiritualised, but the infinite light is, at the same time, diffused in the physical world' (Mindel 1974). While not answerable to the Mosaic Law, the Goyim too are subject to the covenant God made with Noah, and thus have some small role in tikkun. It is the rebbe who is to do most, for he alone can safely descend into our material world among the shattered vessels to redeem the exiled divinity, to mediate evil into good, ignorance into knowledge, sickness into health.

THE REBBE'S HEALING

I do not ask not to suffer. I ask only that there is a reason for my suffering.
(Hasidic rabbi cited in Weiner 1969)

The conventional understanding of a 'myth' is that it is some narrative about ultimate reality to which we have particular recourse when everyday cause-and-effect explanations are inadequate (when 'overloading the rational device triggers a symbolic processing' – Sperber 1980: 39 following Malinowski, but see Toren 1983); and which to the observer exemplifies our society's fundamental values. Social anthropology continues to debate the relationship of normative myth to everyday praxis, the representational to the instrumental (Caws 1974, Sperber 1975, 1985, Sahlins 1976, Bourdieu 1977, Holy and Stuchlik 1981, Godelier 1986, Tambiah 1990). Laughlin and Stephens (1980: 335), like Sperber, argue in Malinowskian terms that myth is 'the quintessential form of a symbol system, operating to organise experience around a society's core symbols. A society's core symbols are invariably orientated upon the zone of uncertainty – that is, the set of events giving rise to significant effects for which there exist no readily perceivable causes for a large number of society's members.' Certainly, the Jewish myth of exile and restitution has served as a 'template' (Ardener 1980) to articulate the destruction of the Temple and the subsequent Diaspora, antisemitic pogroms, the Holocaust and the establishment of Israel. Yet, as a written text it has a continuing existence through time which provides an 'archive' (Foucault 1969) from which individuals take elements to figure their collective history and their personal dilemmas – and as the non-arbitrary and referential exemplified by instrumental Kabbalah (see note 4).

In spite of his earlier Marxism, Scholem takes Jewish mysticism as a major determinant of modern rationalism. Defending it against accusations of superstition, he argues practical Kabbalah and magic (and indeed Hasidism) are degenerate forms: shifts, as we might say, from the figurative to the concrete and the instrumental. Indeed, Hasidism emerges not only from Kabbalistic texts but through the everyday medical practice of early modern shtetl communities. Zoharic passages were used before Hasidism to cure sickness or to serve as protective amulets against the evil eye of envious neighbours and against dibbukim (Trachtenberg 1939). They can be read in multifarious ways: not only as a divine unfolding – a type of contemplative field theory – but as a pluripotent map of direction by which the dualism of everyday life, the material and the divine, can be practically transcended.(19)

In listening to public accounts given by Lubavitch of their healing, they retain a normative 'top-down' textual quality akin to the structuralist accounts of Lévi-Strauss and Dow: individuals suffer apparently arbitrary affliction here below, and then, through some recourse to the transcendent world, are healed. It was initially difficult in fieldwork to look through these narratives to see how individual experiences and social relations might simultaneously embed the mythic structure.(20) The multitude of possible (and conflicting) correspondences between the physical and spiritual worlds which the Zohar theory offers are hardly accessible to every contemporary Hasid; as with other apparently closed nosologies based on correspondences (Foucault 1970, Littlewood 1993), quite variant explanations are volunteered for a particular crisis, from a fairly abstract theodicy to the concrete and immediate efficacy of transactional objects. Among Lubavitch, it is through the person of the Rebbe that Zoharic cosmology is usually operationalised in immediate situations to be used as an exemplary account. Compared with the other Hasidic groups in London (Littlewood 1983), individuals seem less likely to employ practical Kabbalah; our informants are reluctant to talk of possession by dibbukim (a potential consequence of failed conjurations) but this explanation is occasionally volunteered in cases of consistently deviant personal actions. One local rabbi was prepared to tell us he had witnessed it but was reluctant to give details. Another rabbi has elaborated his own treatment of jaundice using a white dove based on Zoharic complementarities.

How then do the Lubavitch of Stamford Hill act when they become ill? Their first thoughts, they say, are always about immediate pain and disability, then they consult their family or friends for a practical remedy to alleviate it, and later perhaps a Jewish physician sympathetic to the community: one of the two orthodox, but non-Hasidic, general practitioners who live locally. According to one of these doctors, their medical treatment is generally accepted but a common practice is to write later to the Rebbe asking why one became ill. Not every illness episode results in a *kvitl* being written. This is done, say some, when the illness is judged to be life-threatening by patient or doctor, or when the patient does not like the treatment given by the doctor: Mrs. Goldstein explained that she wrote to the Rebbe only because her doctor's advice had been 'too simplistic'. The Rebbe is consulted particularly when the patient does not get better despite receiving physical treatment.

The Rebbe does not respond to every letter although it is said that he reads them all. Even when he does not reply, Lubavitchers maintain that he still sends out a *bracha* (blessing) to the person writing to him. Not infrequently he advises against surgical interventions for 'they make their living by cutting, I make my living by not cutting' (Rebbe Schneersohn cited by Wiener [1969]).

Samuel Drazin is a thirty-five year old married man who was interviewed on several occasions in Lubavitch House. He had just written to the Rebbe about a persistent toothache which he had experienced for some months. He had visited two dentists but no obvious physical cause had been found. The first dentist told him that he could not see anything immediately wrong with his teeth – 'in fact, for someone of your age, your teeth are in very good condition'. He could certainly not account for the pain. The second dentist asked if Mr. Drazin was under a lot of stress and he left with the impression that the dentist thought it was in his mind. 'I've never had much faith in dentists', he says 'they cannot do a lot for you.'

The pain became so bad that he could not sleep. It affected his concentration at work. He tried several types of proprietary painkillers without much effect. His wife suggested that he visited a homoeopath which he thought was a good idea although he knew very little about them. Homoeopathic remedies did not alleviate the pain although he felt more relaxed.

Born in East London in 1957, Mr. Drazin had grown up in Stoke Newington on the borders of Stamford Hill. His father, who died three years ago, had worked as a baker for most of his life, a calm gentle man, in contrast to his mother who was 'very anxious' and fussed over his childhood ailments (she died suddenly two years ago). An only child, he recalls his childhood as generally happy; after leaving school with few qualifications, he completed a two-year catering course. Although he had a non-orthodox Jewish upbringing (indeed he rejected religious ritual and only fitfully observed the Sabbath), he had met several Lubavitchers as an adolescent, but had not paid much attention to them. After leaving college at the age of twenty, he was unemployed for two years – 'there was not much work about and I wasn't very interested in doing catering jobs'. Having a lot of free time and 'lacking in direction', he started to visit the Lubavitch centre in Stamford Hill 'in order to learn more about my religion'. Over several months his participation in Jewish ritual increased. Starting with daily laying of tefillin (see note 12), he soon began to attend thrice-daily religious services.

He bought several mezuzot and put them up on his doors of his flat. His nights were now spent at *shiurim* (study sessions) where he learnt Tanya. After a year Samuel Drazin moved in with a Lubavitcher family who introduced him to his future wife Rachel who also came from a non-orthodox background. They now have eight children aged from six months to ten years.

Mr. Drazin now works as an administrator in Lubavitch House, the administrative centre of the community. A friendly and charming man, always immaculately dressed in a white shirt and tie and wearing a Homburg hat, with a long flowing grey beard, he speaks openly about his health, emphasising that he is certainly not one to be preoccupied with minor aches and pains, but that this toothache was very bad. He had never been 'really ill' before. Mr. Drazin had written to the Rebbe on several occasions in the past for in his early days as a Lubavitcher he had some doubts about becoming orthodox. The Rebbe reassured him that this was the right thing to do and encouraged him to perform further mitzvot. He met the Rebbe last year for Dollars and recounts how his 'heart was filled with joy'. Now, quite despondent, he sent a kvitl to the Rebbe asking about his toothache. The Rebbe responded by offering a blessing and emphasising that one should check one's tallit. Mr. Drazin examined his prayer shawl to find that one of the strands was distinctly worn. Here indeed was the explanation of his toothache, for the thirty-two strands on the tallit correspond to the thirty-two teeth. A worn strand may cause pain in a tooth. He triumphantly emphasised again how the physical and spiritual worlds reflected each other, for after replacing his tallit his toothache had disappeared in a few days. For him the episode of illness and the Rebbe's response recalled his original 'spiritual healing' on joining the group.

Our second instance, like that of the misspelt mezuzah, provides a formal homology between the words of a text and the physical body:

Earlier this year Mrs. Halpern, aged forty-one, asked her daughter in Brooklyn to contact the Rebbe about the 'unbearable and unrelenting' back pain she had experienced since the birth of her eleventh child. Although the pain had started late in her pregnancy ('probably due to the baby pressing on my spine'), it got much worse following the delivery. It was so bad that she could not sit still for longer than a few minutes. Lying down did not help either. She consulted the family doctor who 'after a very brief examination' recommended bed rest and analgesics. Mrs. Halpern was not happy with this advice: for one thing, it prevented her giving her son, Isaac, the care and attention a newborn baby required. Over the next couple of weeks the pain got worse: 'my legs felt weak and my feet were tingling'. She recounted that 'although it was the Shabbat, the pain was so bad that I asked my husband to phone for an ambulance'. (It is permitted to use a phone on the Sabbath in the case of an emergency.) She was seen in the local hospital casualty department by an orthopaedic surgeon who told her that she needed to be admitted for absolute bed rest and, if the pain did not settle in a few days, she would need an operation to remove a slipped disc. She reluctantly agreed to go into hospital but was perturbed by the thought of an operation. 'I had heard of someone having a similar operation who was permanently paralysed, I knew that these operations are not always successful.' As soon as the Sabbath had gone, her husband phoned their daughter Sarah and asked her to see the Rebbe's secretary and obtain a blessing for her mother.

Mrs. Halpern is a short plump lady with a large blonde sheitl who looks somewhat older than her forty-one years. Her personality can only be described as 'motherly'. Born locally, her parents were orthodox Jews who had contact with Lubavitch. An only child (unusually for an orthodox family), she attended a Lubavitcher school in Stamford Hill where she did well and at the age of eighteen went to a seminary in France for two years. 'Although I could have gone to "Sem" in Israel or America my parents told me to ask the Rebbe's advice first. Whatever he says, you must do.' Following her return to England she was introduced to her husband Shmuel, himself a Lubavitcher who works as a printer. Mrs. Halpern now works in a local group providing religious activities for children.

The Rebbe responded to her daughter's request by faxing a reply within a few hours (she was particularly keen to impress on us that 'he receives several hundred letters each day, yet he responded to mine so quickly because he knew it was important: surely no ordinary man could do this!'). The Rebbe suggested in his reply that all the household mezuzot were checked. (He had underlined the word 'all'.) This was done by a local scribe who found a crack across the words 'when you sit in your house' (Deuteronomy 6:7). Mrs. Halpern pointed out that she had the worst pain when sitting for any length of time. The scroll was replaced and after a week in hospital she was almost pain free and did not require an operation. How did the Rebbe know about the posul (unkosher) mezuzah? 'The Rebbe has a connection with HaShem [God]. He has a feeling for holiness because his soul is more spiritual than that of other men and the power of his prayer is greater. Because of this he can know these things.'

Sometimes the Rebbe's explanation is not validated so immediately:

Rabbi Nifield is now sixty years old. He recently had a small stroke which left him paralysed in his left arm (although it did not impair his walking or speech). He has suffered from hypertension for some years but admitted that he had not taken it as seriously as he should have although he had been in hospital on several occasions with angina. Following the stroke he spent a week in his local hospital where he was given physiotherapy which only slowly helped his weakness. Being a rather impatient man, as he put it, he wrote to the Rebbe.

Born in Poland, Jacob Nifield came to Britain in 1936 at the age of four, the third of ten children, his parents a rabbi 'a very learned man who spent all his time studying' and an 'ideal Jewish mother, a very quiet woman'. Both parents died several years ago. Jacob grew up in an ultra-orthodox environment and carried out the prescribed rituals from a very young age. He spent a year in a Jewish seminary in northern England and became a rabbi at the age of twenty-six, and has been teaching since in Lubavitcher schools. He is married with ten children ranging from eleven to thirty-two years old. His wife is reputedly a distant relative of the Rebbe, whom they have visited in America on a number of occasions.

He is a rather austere sixty-year-old man, dressed like many older Lubavitch in a long black coat and broad-rimmed Homburg. He has a particularly long beard, is serious in manner and always rather impatient. 'When do you think that I will get better?' he asked repeatedly. Rabbi Nifield has written to the Rebbe in the past about the education of his children, especially as to whether his sons should proceed to rabbinical training. He was impressed by the Rebbe's wisdom in this matter and several of his friends had been helped after writing about health and financial problems. He proudly recalled that he had visited the Rebbe on three occasions for Dollars: 'Every day you hear more stories about his miraculous power.'

The Rebbe now responded to Rabbi Nifield's letter by offering a blessing and suggesting that he check his mezuzot. His wife took the mezuzot to a scribe who thoroughly checked the scrolls and casing, only to find they were ritually pure. He could not understand this. Could the Rebbe be wrong? 'No, the Rebbe is never wrong; if he says the mezuzot are not kosher, they really are not kosher.' He sent a second letter to the Rebbe telling him of the first scribe but the Rebbe responded by suggesting the mezuzot were checked again. A second scribe was found but he too found them to be kosher. A third letter to the Rebbe brought the same reply. The third scribe spent a long day examining the mezuzot, working until the early hours of the following morning. It was only then (21) that, holding up one scroll, he found the problem: a small beam of light shone through a hole in one of the letters. The hole rendered the mezuzah unkosher. Rabbi Nifield had the scroll replaced and immediately regained some movement of his left side. Three months after his stroke he had only some slight weakness in his left arm.

Several people were asked about this healing. How did the Rebbe know that there was a problem with the mezuzah? Rabbi Nifield himself responded immediately: 'the Rebbe's soul represents the soul of the whole Jewish nation. He is aware of the life of every Jew. Every Jew's actions are known to him.' When we asked if it could possibly be a 'coincidence', he objected, 'Of course coincidences occur but I have heard too many accounts of the Rebbe's healing for my healing to be a coincidence.' He likened the mezuzah to 'a suit of armour in the spiritual realm. It protects a person from influences which can cause illness. An unkosher mezuzah simply makes a person more vulnerable.' Again Rabbi Nifield took the opportunity to emphasise that the physical and spiritual realms were interrelated: the woman who fails to take the prescribed monthly bath (mikveh) after her menstruation may bear a defective child.

Mr. Bright wrote to the Rebbe not about himself but about his two-month-old son. Shortly after his birth Daniel had developed 'rattling breathing' about which the parents were very worried. The baby's breathing sounded much worse at night, 'like an old man with bronchitis'. A visit to their family doctor did not prove helpful: 'I cannot find much wrong with the baby, it's just his throat. I'm sure he will grow out of it.' The family were not happy with this reply and they discussed whether or not to take Daniel to a private hospital. Mrs. Bright suggested to her husband that perhaps the Rebbe's advice should first be sought.

Chaim Bright was born in Manchester and moved to Stamford Hill in 1980. He is now in his late forties. Brought up in an orthodox household, he always had close links with Lubavitch for, although his parents were not Hasidim, they attended a Lubavitch synagogue. After doing well at school he went to university to study computing and now works as a computer analyst for an insurance company. He teaches Talmud part-time in the local boys' school where his wife Leah also teaches. In addition to Daniel, the couple have six other children aged from two to nineteen, Mr. Bright proudly adding that Isaac, his eldest son, was in a seminary in Brooklyn, the home of the Rebbe.

The family had experienced much illness in the past. One child had died several years ago in a cot death: 'I suppose that's why we were so concerned about Daniel.' Two children suffered with asthma and were hospitalised on a number of occasions. In 1986 their daughter Hannah, then aged seven, had a mysterious illness and was dangerously ill in hospital. 'First the doctors said it was a virus, then they said a kidney infection. We did not know what to believe. I wrote to the Rebbe on this occasion who suggested I got a second opinion from a well known Jewish paediatrician. He found that she had an abnormal kidney. The Rebbe always gives good advice.'

In reply to the kvitl about Daniel, the Rebbe wrote offering a blessing and suggesting that Mr. Bright check his mezuzot. He did this but all were found to be kosher. He discussed the matter with a rabbi who noticed that the mezuzah in Daniel's room, although kosher, was much older than the others. He suggested it should be replaced. Mr. Bright did this, and after several weeks Mrs. Bright commented on how much better Daniel's breathing had become.

The Rebbe is consulted on a number of health-related issues apart from immediate sickness. A serious concern is infertility which is considered disastrous for Lubavitchers with their emphasis on large families.(22) Whilst the Rebbe himself is childless he is considered to have particular foresight about infertility:

Rabbi Lehrman was very concerned about his wife who had still not become pregnant after five years of marriage. Repeated hospital tests had not demonstrated any physiological abnormality either in himself or his wife so he wrote to the Rebbe. About a week later when (rather unexpectedly on a business trip) he was able to visit the Rebbe in person, the Rebbe told him 'your fears are irrelevant'. He was surprised by this and asked what the Rebbe meant, to be told 'your wife is already pregnant'. He telephoned home to learn that his wife was indeed pregnant.

The Rebbe's replies may indicate that he has talked with the petitioner's deceased parent's soul, and they frequently cite well known texts and aphorisms, employing puns and rhymes in Hebrew or English (such as health/wealth) and logical paradoxes, as well as explicit instructions. Do the Rebbe's words themselves have power or does he just have a better knowledge of divine matters? When questioned by sympathetic observers, the Lubavitch Rebbe has agreed he has personal power to help others unite the seen and unseen realms (23) for he argues 'there is a continuous relationship between the creator and the creation ...' (cited by Wiener 1969). He can cure by physical touch, or through a mezuzah he has blessed (Mintz 1968: 111, 125).(24) The imagery employed by Rabbi Nachman, the founder of the Bratislav Hasidim, was that of a 'banker' who could receive the bad qualities of the supplicant and exchange them for good. Woocher

(1979) prefers the analogy of a 'mirror', whilst one Lubavitcher rabbi who has studied psychology likens the Rebbe to a mediating archetype who lowers himself to the petitioner's level of spirituality; Rebbe and Hasid 'invest' in each other, spiritually as well as financially (Schachter 1979).(25) Strikingly, he argues that for the Rebbe to teach someone who does not absorb the knowledge is like masturbation – indeed the Rebbe may actually experience a nocturnal emission as a consequence. He thus rematerialises what Schachter calls, in the language of psychoanalysis, the 'transference' of therapy (cf. Lutsky 1989): the Lubavitcher Rebbe physically takes on and redeems the transgressions of the Hasid.(26)

Representation and Embodiment Across the 'Double Register': Towards a Zoharic Reading of Medical Anthropology

'The secret world of the Godhead is a world of language, a world of divine names that unfold in accordance with a law of their own ... Letters and names are not only conventional means of communication. They are far more. Each one of them represents a concentration of energy and expresses a wealth of meaning which cannot be translated, or not fully at least, into human language' (Scholem 1965: 36). If the 'efficacy' of the kvitl and its response may be regarded as an illocutionary manipulation of transactional symbols which stand for events in the material world, then it is difficult to find a formal system of healing in which the two can at times be so closely tied together. Our informants say that even our transcriptions of the healing miracles printed in this chapter have some power to heal. We have here an elision of the material and its divine representation so profound that it is not easy to imagine any Hasidic observance which is not a type of physical healing.

Scholem (1965: 124) argues that 'those who carry out the mitsvah always do two things. They represent in a concrete symbol its transcendent essence, through which it is rooted on and partakes of, the ineffable. But at the same time they transmit to this transcendent essence (which the later Kabbalists called the 'upper root' of ritual action) an influx of energy' [emphasis in the original]. If psychiatrists and anthropologists have postulated correspondences between, or actual causal effects across, a 'double register', the Zohar and hence the Tanya are perhaps unique in the extent of mutual influence. Man has two souls, argues the Tanya, the animal and the divine, each dialectically constituting the other (Mindel 1974); the divine spiritualises the material as the material spiritualises the divine (Kehot

Publications 1981: 778). Language is not an obstruction, nor even the path, to ultimate reality, but rather its actual nature (*cf.* Stoller 1984, Wagner 1986). The letters of the Torah are not just God's Law, but the very name of God; indeed they *are* God, the upper roots of our physical world. The ten Sefirot together form that great, unutterable Name of God which is the act and goal of creation; and hence of human history. Representation (upper root) and embodiment in the sensible world (lower root) necessarily participate in complementary causalities.

All 'mystical' ideas developing within Western monotheism are, like miracles, concerned with reconciliations of the two registers. Rather than just representing matters as two qualitatively distinct registers, the divine and the physical, with certain rare passages between them, the concentric spheres of the Zohar allow participation in either the divine or the physical directions – a stereomorphic cosmos but one in which any event or entity is located simultaneously at the centre and the periphery.(27) A 'miracle' in the sense of a radical but temporary resonance across the two registers, a local drama of the structural anthropologist's or psychotherapist's transaction of the bodily through the symbolic, is thus hardly novel – for, in a sense, here everything and nothing is miraculous. In Zoharic theory physical healing and spiritual healing are the same event, even if the contemporary Hasid visiting his family doctor hardly has the latter foremost in mind. If the Zohar, as a theory of representation, anticipates the 'interpretive turn' in medical anthropology in its concern with directions and procedures rather than with entities (albeit with what Bloom [1982] terms its 'wandering meaning'), in reconciling structural order with moral agency (*cf.* Bourdieu 1977), it goes further in retaining the physical as valid as the representation. Representation itself is an aspect of the natural world.(28) Where all is symbolic in that everything both represents and embodies everything else, there are, in a sense, no 'symbols': everything is concrete reality, everything 'works'.

In everyday practice, things are rather different. Scholem (1954), here surprisingly akin to countless guardians of religious orthodoxy, warns us against too deep a Kabbalistic immersion in the Infinite, in which everyday actions become translated as the ineffable and back again. Explaining why he had not written down his ideas, Luria is supposed to have said 'It is impossible, because all things are interrelated. I can hardly open my mouth to speak without feeling that the sea bursts forth its dams and overflows' (Scholem 1971). The rebbes, ever aware of the eruptions of the Kabbalah embodied in the antinomian madness of Sabbatai Svi (Littlewood 1995), set firm rules for the incorporation of Zoharic speculation into the practice of everyday life, always subordinate to the prudent rabbinical ordinances. To attempt to coerce rather than supplicate the upper register (theurgy) was of course sorcery, and if Hasidim still sought access to the strong dangers of ultimate power, it was to be only through the circumscribed intercession of the Rebbe. While scholarly Lubavitch may endlessly argue about the minutiae of the Kabbalah, their founder disdained such miraculous interventions (Sharot 1982), yet it is through the person of their current rebbe that ultimate redress is mediated. Hasidim refer to him as a 'channel' between the physical and the spiritual registers (Sharot 1982), an idiom which recalls the 'passages' of Moerman's (1979) somatosocial anthropology.(29) In his mediations the Rebbe reorders the everyday experiential dualism which the Kabbalah always threatens to banish: in the terminology of this paper, a double-register now reemerges in a distinction between material experience and its ultimate meaning, between the physical world and some determining transcendent reality.

If we are justified in talking of the Kabbalah as a 'folk model', then it is one with a close reflexive engagement with wider Western knowledge including now biomedicine. Contemporary Lubavitch do not live in an eighteenth century enclave, and their emphasis on conversion constantly invokes the individual remaking of secular and sacred worlds. Their exemplary illness narratives do not simply articulate Zoharic cosmology and personal suffering but justify the normative rules of a small community, one always preoccupied with its own continuity and boundaries, and with its vulnerability in the wider political world. Yet for these rules individuals may argue quite various religious justifications; for no single interpretation of sacred texts can ever be taken as completely valid (Scholem 1954). Judaism is characteristically praxis, not doxa.

In conclusion, we would recommend a reading of medical anthropology through the Zohar.(30) Western monotheism's double register of immanent and transcendent has, we have argued, formal and historical continuities with that of material and representational in contemporary science. Both Kabbalah and contemporary anthropology essay an epistemological turn away from such a dichotomised universe in which the meaning of one world was simply to be read as the reality of the other. The complex correspondences and isomorphisms between lower and upper 'roots' in the Zohar certainly allows for Hasidic recourse to an ultimate reality by which immediate suffering occurs and is resolved but only imperfectly as a distinct realm we may recognise as 'otherworldly'. If this healing is itself amenable to the conventional procedures of sociological inquiry, as we have attempted here, the mythic corpus to which it refers is nevertheless one which articulates problems of reconciling embodiment and representation identical with those of anthropology. It thus constitutes an 'interpretive turn' so radical that it is able to encompass our material reality as reality, albeit a reality dialectically constituted through its own representation.

Notes

1 Earlier fieldwork in Stamford Hill (1990–1992) by one of the authors (S.D.) has been briefly described in Dein (1992). The Rebbe died in 1994 and the ethnographic present here refers to 1991–3.The personal names of informants are pseudonyms, and we have generally used here the Hebrew rather than the Yiddish transliteration; interviews were in English. Many informants were rabbis who comprise about a fifth of the male adults.

2 'Dualism' is used variously to refer to distinctions between immanent and transcendent; between corporal and spiritual (and thus temporal and religious authority); or between what we may term evil and good (Parkin 1985). In Pauline Christianity, as in Kabbalah, these three 'slid together' (Brown 1989:48). In this paper we are using the term primarily in the first usage, one which is closely allied to the second whilst not altogether independent of the third. In the second and third senses, Judaism is arguably less dualist than Christianity: 'I form the light and create darkness: I make peace and create evil: I the Lord do all these things' (Isaiah 45:7). For a more extended consideration of how the various scriptural and post-scriptural texts did, or did not, distinguish between *nephesh* ('soul', 'spirit') and *basar* ('body'), and for possible Hellenistic influences, see Preuss (1978), Bottomley (1980), Rubin (1988), Gilman (1992), Eilberg-Schwartz (1992).

3 Lock and Scheper-Hughes (1990) comment that 'a singular premise guiding Western science and clinical medicine is its commitment to a fundamental opposition between spirit and matter, mind and body, and underlying this real and unreal'. This remained true of anthropological structuralisms even if these abandoned direct one to one correspondences between the registers (A::B) in favour of relational patterns (A1:A2::B1:B2).

4 To argue for the primacy of a semantic approach is problematic given that *meaning* itself refers to a multitude of types of understanding (see the papers in Parkin 1982), and *interpretation* is a residual anthropological category (Sperber 1985). If biomedicine is relegated as merely one local interpretation of the physical world, then 'experience-near' anthropology remains an academic interpretation of a (local) interpretation (*ibid*), and one that still offers an intellectualist metanarrative in proposing that humans are essentially driven by their quest for meaning. (The interpretive genre paradoxically enhances dualism through displacing the truth claims of medicine onto that discipline itself.) We do not argue here for a particular sense of 'meaning' or 'symbol', let alone a psychological or linguistic explanation of human signification and representation, except

to say that we favour the observations of many of the authors in Foster and Brandes (1980) that one can locate the same 'symbolisations' on a spectrum between the expressly referential and the figurative, the shallow and the deep (Barrett and Lucas 1993), and that movement between the two modes seems mediated by intention, contextor affect. As we argue below, movement in the referential direction may be such that lexical representations become objectified as entities in themselves, less meanings to be unravelled than themselves directly gaining ontological status in the cognised world (McGuire 1983, Wagner 1986, Lakoff 1987, Tambiah 1990: cf. Foucault 1966): whether in everyday life (Berger and Luckman 1966) or in anthropological theory (Boyer 1986).

5 Not altogether surprisingly, given anthropology's earlier organicist analogies of social structure. This is not to say that individual agency could not be recognised in such tightly ordered schemata (Bourdieu 1977, Godelier 1986), but that some implicit sense of the overdetermined complex was always assumed to be born in mind by – or rather to constitute – individuals; and any innovation by them took place through various combinations of identification and negation (Littlewood 1984, 1993). We would argue that the demise of such tight structuralist isomorphisms is not only an attribute of changing intellectual fashion or the demise of colonial objectification, but that everyday life in the 'timeless small-scale societies' with which anthropologists have been concerned *has* generally become more pluralistic and subjectively instrumental (*cf*: Bourdieu 1977, Featherstone 1990): certain religious groups excepted.

6 Taking 'myth' in its restricted sense as a narrative about personages in a sacred world and time akin to some ultimate reality (*cf*. Kirmayer 1993), it may be argued that Western biomedicine offers no such *narratives* but simply *paradigms* of sickness reality which only implicitly recall the ultimate justification of our world (Lock and Gordon 1988).

7 For accounts see Buber (1948), Dresner (1974), Katz (1961), Mintz (1968), Sharot (1982). The attribute *Hasid* (pious one) had previously referred to the Jewish rebels against Antiochus Epiphanes (2nd century BCE) and to the German followers of Rabbi Yehuda the Hasid (13th century CE).

8 Scholem (1974) argues that the Sabbatian attack on the literal law through an antinomian enactment of Kabbalah both reflected and amplified the development of secular Judaism, opening up the ghetto to more universalised and psychologised ideas as the medieval Jewish accommodation with feudal power collapsed through the growth of local nationalisms (Katz 1961). Like Sharot (1982), he (1954) sees Hasidism as a 'neutralisation of messianic elements into mainstream Judaism,' whilst Bakan (1958) goes so far as to talk of a 'dialectical synthesis' of the two. For a review of the debate see Sharot (1982).

9 On Lubavitch in New York see Mintz (1968); in Montreal, Shaffir (1974); in London, Kupferman (1976), Wallach (1977); on ultra-orthodoxy in Jerusalem, Bilu *et al.* (1990).

10 The Satmar who generally settled in Williamsburg do not recognise the state of Israel, arguing that the Hebrew nation cannot be restored before the advent of the Messiah. The Gur live mainly in Israel, as do the Belzers. The Bratzlav are unusual in having no living rebbe.

11 The idiom of *conversion* is somewhat inappropriate: rather Lubavitch 'reclaim' Jews to orthodoxy (*cf*. Wallace's (1958) term *revitalisation*).

12 For orthodox Jews, relations between the mundane and the ultrahuman are mediated through a number of objects. At one level the whole household may be said to be 'sacred' in opposition to the Gentile world (Littlewood 1983) but additionally there are three more specific 'ritual' (transactional) objects to which this paper refers. *Tefillin* are phylacteries, worn during prayer on the head and on the arm near the heart, which contain scriptural texts written on parchment exhorting the Jew to love God and to subject to Him everyday life, thoughts, feelings and actions (Exodus 3: 1–10, 11–16; Deuteronomy 6: 4–9; 11: 13–21). Similar texts, affixed in a case to the door frame of the main entrance as well as of every living room of the house as the *mezuzah*, summon the Jew to consecrate his home, making it an abode worthy to be blessed by the presence of God. The *tallit*, a prayer shawl donned by adult males during morning and additional prayers, has eight fringes at each of its four corners.

13 Joining involves a gradual detachment from significant others outside the group with increasing interaction with established members, approximating to the general model of conversion proposed by Lofland and Stark (1965). This is not the place to argue why, in a generation after Auschwitz, certain Westerners should seek to 're-enchant' their secular world.

14 Mrs. Lévy visited the Rebbe for Dollars some ten years ago and asked for a blessing for a shidduch. She was carrying several books which she dropped accidentally in front of him. On her second visit last year he looked carefully at her and said "Be careful with your books!" Another informant approached the Rebbe about his son who was physically handicapped and for whom he was unable to arrange a shidduch. The Rebbe gave him two dollars, one for himself and one to take to Israel; not understanding the reason behind this he went nevertheless to Israel taking the second dollar with him. In Jerusalem he happened to speak to a Hasid on a bus sitting opposite him and recounted the story. The other said he himself had a disabled daughter and had written to Rebbe Schneersohn to find her a partner, the Rebbe had given him the identical advice. Subsequent friendship led to the marriage of their two children.

15 A common representation, allied to that of the circles, is that of a nut: sensible experience is the shell which has to be broken to reach the 'real' essence. This is a common figuring in any system in which, as in biomedicine (Littlewood 1991), a distinction is made between 'reality' and 'appearance'; in biomedicine, the physical is the kernel, in Hasidic medicine it is the husk. Other systems of Kabbalah offer either a more personified deity or one more ethereal who, as in Gnosticism, is counterposed to the demiurge mistakenly represented in Genesis as the Creator.

16 This requires further complexities as there are only 340,000 physical letters in the Torah.

17 Scholem (1954) suggests that the scattering of the sparks may be read directly as the historical exile of the Jews, restitution as redemption. Sharot (1982) points out that whilst Luria himself did not expressly relate his schema to the Iberian expulsion of 1492, we, as observers, can note a Weberian (or euhemerist) affinity between historical event and subsequent myth. Certainly there is occasional explicit reference to this by others, together with a shared idiom. In prayer, Hasidic men tie a cord around their waist to separate the spiritual upper part of their body from

the mundane lower half, for *aliyah* is physical height as well as ascent to the divine, and more recently the term for secular migration to Israel (Jacobs 1973). In the arguably manic-depressive illness of Sabbatai Svi, *aliyah* described his periods of elated mood, and thus his messiahship (Littlewood 1995).

18 Sullivan (1987) proposes that the 'most important figure or symbol in any given religious tradition is the source of healing'. Our identification of an overarching representation is of course likely to reflect immediate concerns: in which case his observation is tautologous. Yet the heavy semantic load embedded in 'core symbols' ('enabling symbols' – Lawson and McCauley (1993) is perhaps fully accessed only in particular situations.

19 Whilst we have emphasised here a linear image of exile, this can be figured also as a three-dimensional containment and catharsis, well presented in public and household ritual (Littlewood 1983).

20 Fieldwork with conversionist groups is distinctive in that they continue to offer presentationlist justifications of normative actions (Littlewood 1993). Unlike other illness narratives (Good 1994), these have a fixed and formal (Lawson and McCauley 1993, *cf.* Early 1982) tripartite pattern – appeal to Rebbe about a problem, Rebbe's response, resolution of the problem – which recalls the exemplarly legends Hasidim recount of past zaddikim. They may be taken as standardised and edifying testimonials, emblematic self-presentations for other Hasidim and for the anthropologist as a potential convert: to use Crapanzano's (1992) term they have become 'meta-pragmatic'. Thus the story described here of the misspelt mezuzah has already been recorded among Brooklyn Lubavitch in very similar terms but there about a tefillin (Mintz 1968:334).

21 The early dawn is the best time to study Kabbalah and kindred matters: the Hebrew words of 'mystery' and 'light' are equivalent in gematria.

22 Margolin and Wiztum (1989), in their discussion of Sephardic interpretations of infertility and impotence, suggest that a common explanation is having been 'tied' by jealous sorcery.

23 In the accounts cited here the petitioners argue that they expect, through the Rebbe, to effect some definite change in the natural world: in Ahern's (1979) terminology, following Austin, their petitions were, like spells (Tambiah 1990), performative, 'strong illocutionary acts'. Although offered retrospectively as efficacious, it is likely that at the time many were 'weak', simply performed as immediately appropriate or 'felicitous' (Lloyd 1990) or little more than wishes, Wittgenstein's 'actions of instinct' (Tambiah 1990:56); and they of course have a perlocutionary context which we do not detail in this paper.

24 Although our narratives emphasise the Rebbe's knowledge, collections of exemplarly stories published by Lubavitch emphasise something more like instrumental power over the physical world. The term 'miracle' is commonly used. An eighteen-year-old boy, Rafi, is seriously ill with leukaemia (Lubavitch Publications 1992). The hospital doctor advises an immediate operation but Rafi's tearful brother tells his teacher who contacts the Rebbe only to be advised that the operation must be delayed until he has prayed on the Sabbath. The doctor, an atheist who is furious at this interference, decides to proceed. He arrives late at the hospital after being held up with a burst tyre; the nurses report the instruments have gone missing, and he has to postpone the operation. The boy's condition

suddenly improves and the operation is no longer necessary. Many Lubavitchers offered us the word 'charisma' for their Rebbe's power, the term suggested by Weber (1947) to designate situations where an individual who embodies a group's concerns through 'extrasocial qualities' leads them independently of tradition, physical coercion or role-bound status. Sociologically, charisma is less an explanation of social action than a description, one defining element in a typology; what is significant is not the 'personality' of the leader, but their social function as symbol, catalyst and message bearer (Littlewood 1993). He or she may be relatively unimpressive as a practical leader, serving like Sabbatai Svi as the locus on which current preoccupations are placed. In the popular sense, however, 'charisma' refers to something like 'strength of personality' or even 'ultrahuman power'. The Rebbe approximates better to Weber's 'traditional authority' or even the 'divine king' of Oxford Africanists. In Hasidic stories, he recalls another anthropological figure – the trickster of folk tales, outwitting the powerful official or greedy peasant, on occasion ironically defeated through his own stratagems.

25 Which recalls the prestations of food and money offered by the shtetl Hasid to his Rebbe which the latter then redistributed (Zborowski and Herzog 1962).

26 (Like Christ.) One rabbi reading an earlier draft of this paper argued that the emission was impossible. See also Hoffman (1981). A more appropriate image may be that of a 'condensor' or 'container' (Parkin 1992, Lutzky 1989), an idiom which becomes a little clearer when we consider the converse of a miracle – the 'scandal' of medieval Christian terminology. In February 1992 the Rebbe, then aged 90, had a stroke. The medical details were unclear, although local newspapers such as the Jewish Chronicle reported that it was minor and he was making a good recovery. Lubavitch House requested that all Jews recite psalms once a day. Although apparently not seriously ill, the Rebbe was unable to give out Dollars, nor to respond to petitions. Members of the community were asked why he himself had become sick, and what they thought this sickness meant. Among the explanations given was this one from a young rabbi:

'The soul of the Rebbe represents the group soul of the Jewish people. His suffering represents the suffering of every Jew. It is like a body and head, the Rebbe being the head of the Jewish body. The two cannot exist independently. If the body is sick it can give rise to a headache. If the brain does not work, how can the body function? If every Jew does not perform good deeds the Jewish body will become sick and in turn the Rebbe. If more Jews perform these deeds the Rebbe will recover.'

In order to heal their leader a new Torah was written in New York, and every Jew asked to donate a pound towards a letter in it. Another rabbi explained:

'All Jewish souls are tied to the Rebbe's soul. In the Torah there are 600,000 words (328,000 complete words and 272,000 incomplete words). In the world there are 600,000 general souls which each divide up into many more souls. These general souls are linked to the Rebbe's soul. By writing a perfect Torah the Rebbe's soul becomes perfect again and this will affect his body.'

He described how the Rebbe must first undergo a descent into the shattered vessels before he can ascend to a higher level taking with him some of the hidden sparks. This descent is associated with a decay in the physical body. The rabbi intimated that perhaps this was a prelude to the messianic arrival. He admitted that it was quite possible that the current Rebbe was indeed the Messiah. 'Every descent of the Zaddik means an elevation of divine light' (cited by Scholem 1954). (Before the Rebbe's death in June 1994 Lubavitch intensified a public 'Moshiach campaign' implying he was the Messiah, and expectations of some sort of 'resurrection' have surfaced throughout late 1994.)

27 The Cosmic Man is made up of all men (Ben Shimon Halevi 1974), 'members and parts of various ranks all acting upon each other so as to form one organism' (Zohar). If we need a figuring, the notion of a *fractal* (in which each part replicates the whole – Mandelbrot 1977) is more apposite than of a single spiritual-physical dyad: perhaps Pribram's hologram or Wagner's (1986) holograph, the linguistic trope of synecdoche or the participatory symbols of Lévy-Bruhl's primitive mentality. Compare notes 15, 19.

28 In Bolinger's (1980) words 'the culture inserts a sign and gets back a symbol', as the increasingly referential word itself becomes materialised as an independent entity, Tambiah's (1990) 'objectified charisma'. (See note 4.) Whilst a similar potential exists in Christianity – 'the word made flesh' – we might argue it is more esoteric theology than instrumental practice although there are analogues in the sacraments and in popular healing (Cramer 1993, McGuire 1983), and of course in Islamic medicine (Parkin 1992). Bloom (1984) proposes that the deity of the Kabbalah may be (mis)read as language; for Scholem (1954). He exists as a theory of representation. Foucault (1970) takes the late medieval 'signatures' (in which natural object and name were intrinsically linked, as in Hermetic and Kabbalistic typologies) as not properly a theory of representation at all but rather one of resemblance through sympathy, mimesis, repetition and transformation: representation proper requiring the Renaissance distinction between an object and its name which itself is not of the natural order but arbitrary (and hence the natural world cannot be replicated or coerced through such devices as numerology or alphabetic order). He notes the primacy given in the European systems of signatures to Hebrew, the universal language spoken by Adam which retained something of the material creation. The recovery of this or some other language which directly embodied (or later, represented) reality was a recurring Renaissance preoccupation (Eco 1993). The more figurative numerology of religious texts by Kabbalists proceeded from already existing referential practices: Hebrew lacks numerals, so numbers have always been represented by a letter of the alphabet (on which see Crump 1990), and there had long been a popular tradition that misspelling the paraphrases of the divine name in a Torah was likely to visit serious sickness and misfortune on the community (Trachtenberg 1939). Even a misspelt Torah was too powerful to be safely destroyed and was buried in a vault.

29 Or the 'channels' of structuralism (Laughlin and Stephens 1980). Any dualist epistemology, whether religious or scientific, has difficulties in justifying the nature of the links between the two registers. Again we have to be wary of assuming a uniform local understanding: for the less scholarly or recently 'reclaimed' Hasid, the Rebbe is often not so much a

channel as a thaumaturge. (Contrawise, most people regularly check their mezuzot anyway.) If mediation between the two registers occurs typically through a particular individual, it is difficult not to locate in them some personal 'magical' power (Tambiah 1990, cf. McGuire 1983): what Scholem and Bastide, following Andrew Lang, term a 'degeneration' of religion as a cosmological figuring. Frazerians would argue the converse – for the figurative as the degeneration of the instrumental: as does Robertson-Smith (1927) in his account of the origins of Jewish religion.

30 In Bloom's (1982) terms, a *misprision* or creative misreading, analogous to Freud's physiological reading of Brentano, or Lévi-Strauss' sociological reading of Jakobson. Arguably this is less of a 'misreading' for both Kabbalah and contemporary anthropology offer not dissimilar epistemologies of signification, and Ellen (1977) proposes that 'analytical classifications' such as the Zohar are particularly amenable to the procedures favoured by structural anthropologists.

13 The Butterfly and the Serpent: Culture, Psychopathology and Biomedicine*

Introduction

Psychiatric research is carried out principally in the comparatively homogeneous culture of urban industrialized societies. Psychopathology in the West thus tends to be regarded as if it were culture-free. Murphy (1977) correctly emphasizes that 'the time is overdue when the relationship between cultural background and psychopathology should be more formally examined, and when we should cease thinking that our behavioral expectations are all "neutral", not requiring re-examination'. As Gaines (1982: 167) points out, although 'the conceptual basis of Western psychiatric theory and practice are often assumed a *priori* to be culturally neutral [and] scientific', we can study Western psychiatry in the same way as we study a traditional theory of disease, 'one no less constructed, informed and communicated than another'. We shall argue in this paper that certain contemporary biomedical conceptualizations and their associated patterns of social action are closely tied to implicit cultural and political assumptions, particularly those concerning sex roles and notions of personal identity and attribution: conceptualization, therapy and the illness itself are articulated by a shared set of values. Whilst the notion that biomedicine is fundamentally different from other disease theories is being abandoned, there remains an assumption that Western science is too pluralistic to submit to the type of symbolic analysis which has proved so fruitful in the study of small-scale communities. However, in this paper, in an attempt to minimize the reduction of our subject, which includes biomedical concepts, to such concepts themselves, and to achieve a greater degree of 'universality', we shall employ a model derived from ethnographic interpretation of non-Western patterns of 'psychopathology'.

While biomedical and traditional *therapies* have frequently been compared, the points of similarity have either been predicated upon

* First published in *Culture, Medicine and Psychiatry* (1987) and co-authored with Maurice Lipsedge.

the presumed universality of the physiological or psychodynamic mechanisms of Western therapy or upon 'non-specific' aspects of the therapist client relationship (Janet 1925; Frank 1961; Kiev 1964: Torrey 1972; Sargant 1973; Prince 1976). The direct mapping of Western *categories* onto traditional *systems* has not been attempted because of the highly salient cultural contextuality of the latter as they appear to Western professionals (which has not prevented them from conducting the reverse procedure, mapping traditional categories onto Western systems, still the characteristic operation in 'transcultural psychiatry'). To attempt to identify traditional non-Western patterns in a Western population demands more than claims based on superficial phenomenological similarities that *koro*, or *amok* occur in the West (see the examples cited in Littlewood and Lipsedge 1985; Simons and Hughes 1985); it requires the application to the West of the sociological models developed for small-scale communities. To the extent that such models are derived from within the Western academic tradition they remain culture-bound but at a higher degree of universality than explanations which themselves form part of the clinical construction of the reactions.

This paper examines certain relatively discrete reactions which appear, historically and geographically, to be specific to industrialized cultures, especially to the United States and Britain. While culture-specific reactions may of course have a distinct biological component (*kuru*, amphetamine psychosis), the term 'culture-bound syndrome'[1] as found in small-scale communities has usually been taken to refer to: (i) local patterns of time-limited behavior, specific to a particular culture, which, whilst regarded as undesirable,[2] are recognized as discrete by informants and observers alike; (ii) few instances of which have a biological cause: and (iii) in which the individual is not held to be aware or responsible in the everyday sense; (iv) the behavior usually has a 'dramatic' quality (Littlewood and Lipsedge 1985).

Symbols as Symptoms

Such reactions frequently articulate personal predicament but they also represent public concerns, usually core structural oppositions between age groups or the sexes. They have a shared meaning as public and dramatic representations in an individual whose personal situation demonstrates these oppositions, and they thus occur in certain well-defined situations. At the same time they have a personal expressive meaning for the particular individual and they have been regarded as functional ('instrumental'). 'In situations of deprivation or frustration where recourse to personal jural power is not available, the principle is able to adjust his or her situation by recourse to "mystical pressure"' (Lewis 1971), appeals to values and beliefs which cannot be questioned because they are tied up with the most fundamental concerns and political organization of the community. How 'conscious' the principal is of pragmatically employing the mechanism as a personal stragey is debatable but it may be noted that observers frequently describe the reactions as 'dissociative'; Turner (1969) aptly calls this side-ways recourse to mystical action 'the power of the weak'; the popular psychiatric term is 'manipulation'.(3)

'Wild Man'

To consider in more detail some examples: 'wild man behavior'(4) (for example, negi-negi, nenek) is the term given to certain episodes of aggressive behavior in the New Guinea Highlands (Newman 1964; Salisbury 1966; Koch 1968; Langness 1968; Clarke 1973; Reay 1977). The affected man rushes about erratically, threatening people with weapons, destroying their property, blundering through the village gardens tearing up crops. Episodes last for a few hours, or at most, days; during them the wild man fails to recognize people and, on recovering, claims amnesia for the episode. Behavior is locally attributed to possession by spirits, and treatment may include pouring on of water or exorcism, although observers have felt these measures were applied 'half-heartedly' (Newman 1964). The insipient wild man's initial announcement that he no longer wishes to eat and his rejection of his share of the prepared food, advertise his coming performance (Clarke 1973:209). This is always public. 'It would be possible for a man to run wild in seclusion but no-one does' (Newman 1964:3). The audience participate by feigning terror or attempting to mollify the principal, or alternatively pouring water over him and ostentatiously hiding weapons. To observers he retains a high degree of control. Like the shaman in his trance 'though he flings himself in all directions with his eyes shut [he] nevertheless finds all the objects he wants' (Eliade 1964). In negi-negi and similar reactions there is 'a disproportion between the injury threatened and actually inflicted. It is generally more alarming to the white onlooker than the native' (Seligman 1928). Similar episodes of spear throwing by Western Desert Aborigines remain constrained and relatively safe; only participants with organic brain syndromes are 'out of control' (Jones 1971).(5) If we examine the social context of the pattern, it typically occurs among young men, politically powerless, in situations such as working to pay back an enormous bride price debt raised through a complicated network of kin. Negi-negi exaggerates this social dislocation to the point where the young man dramatically declines membership of his social community altogether. Resolution may include latitude in repayment. The net result is to restore and legitimate the status quo, not to question it.

Tikopian Suicide Swims

Audience participation is essential to *negi-negi* and to certain parasuicidal behaviors. In the Western Pacific island of Tikopia, aggrieved or offended women swim out to sea (Firth 1961). As an islander comments, 'A woman who is reproved or scolded desires to die, yet desires to live. Her thought is that she will go to swim, but be taken up in a canoe by men who will seek her out to find her. A woman desiring death swims to seawards; she acts to go and dies. But a woman who desires life swims inside the reef' (Firth 1961:12). While completed suicide is regarded as a revenge on the community, the pay-off for the survivor of a suicide swim includes enhanced status together with a renegotiation of the original problem. Thus an adolescent girl who is rebuffed or censured by parents reacts by exaggerating this extrusion, detaching herself further from the community, and the resolution restores the equilibrium. For the community, the tension between parental authority and filial independence is presented as dramatically as the account of a lovers' suicide pact in the American popular press.

Saka

Sympathy for the Tikopian suicide swimmer wanes with repetition; like *saka* among the Kenyan Waitata, the reaction can occur 'once too often'. Approximately half of married Waitata women are subject to *saka* ('posssession') after a wish is refused by their husband, typically for an object that is a prerogative of men (Harris 1957). It is locally recognized that *saka* is clearly something to do with male/female relations. While women provide food for the family they are also expected to supply domestic objects which can only be purchased through access to the profits of the sale of land or livestock. Such access is denied to women. 'Women are said to have no head for land or cattle transactions. They do not have the right sort of minds for important community affairs because they have little control over emotions and desires. Indeed femininity is made synonymous with an uncontrolled desire to acquire and consume ... In *saka* attacks, women are caricatured as uncontrollable consumers ... They are shown as contrasting, in every way with men and the contrast is symbolized as a personal malady' (Harris 1957: 1054, 1060). Harris argues that 'women can acquire male prerogatives or the signs thereof through illness', and compares the reaction to a European women's 'sick headache' or 'pregnancy cravings'.(6) While observers feel the reaction can be either 'real' or 'simulated', some local men say the whole reaction is a pretence. *Saka* is regarded by the Waitata simultaneously as an illness, as a possession by spirits, and as consequence of a woman's personal wishes and her social role. Possession ceases when the woman's wish is granted by her husband or when he sponsors a large public ceremony in which she wears male items of dress or new clothes.

Sar

Pastoral Somali women may become possessed by the *sar* spirits who demand gifts and attention (Lewis 1966, 1971); 'therapy really consists in spoiling the patient while ostensibly meeting the demands of the spirit as revealed to the expert therapist'. In such a patriarchal Islamic society, in which women are excluded from the public realm, the outrageous behavior of possession coerces husbands into gestures of reconciliation and consideration while at the same time the formal public ideology of male dominance remains unchallenged. The cost of *sar* ceremonies may be such as to preclude the purchase by the husband of additional wives.(7) The typical situation is a 'hard-pressed wife, struggling to survive and feed her children in the harsh nomadic environment, and liable to some degree of neglect, real or imagined, on the part of her husband. Subject to frequent, sudden and often prolonged absences by her husband as he follows his manly pastoral pursuits, to the jealousies and tensions of polygamy which are not ventilated in accusations of sorcery and witchcraft, and always menaced by the precariousness of marriage in a society where divorce is frequent and easily obtained by men, the Somali women's lot offers little stability or security ... Not surprisingly the *sar* spirits are said to hate men' (Lewis 1971: 75, 76).

Diagnosis of *sar* possession is in the hands of women and the treatment groups provide an organization for women in opposition to the public ritual of Islam dominated by men. The participation of women in such healing groups may be said to 'allow the voice of women to be heard in a male-dominated society, and occasionally enable participants to enjoy benefits to which their status would not normally entitle them' (Corin and Bibeau 1980). Ogrizek (1982) comments that the healing rituals associated with possession trance enable women to explore their female identity. Such self-help groups may partially maintain the stigmatized ('sick') identity in opposition to complete reversion to normative values: thus Janzen (1979) likens them to Western groups like Alcoholics Anonymous. In other societies they may even take on important roles including taxation, redistribution and welfare (Janzen 1978); their organization may then provide, in contrast to a hypothesized 'homeostatic' function, whether individual or communal, a dynamic mechanism for social mobility and even institutional change (Corin 1978: Janzen 1979: Lee 1981).

Hamadsha

In certain situations it may be men who are unable to employ the public system of everyday power and who resort to supernatural manipulation. They may be the young men of the New Guinea Highlands or Moroccan males unable to live up to the ideal values of manhood in a patriarchal society whom a female *jinn* (spirit) may cause to develop certain male illnesses – impotence, functional paralysis or deafness (Crapanzano 1973). Illness is a feminization and the *jinn* herself must be placated to achieve a cure: she is explicitly involved in treatment whose main aim is to establish a mutually acceptable relationship between herself and the man. During *hamadsha* therapy a man must first become a woman completely and then be transformed back into a man. The *jinn* herself is 'transformed, from a force disruptive to the social and moral order into a force to preserve that order. So long as her follower obeys ... his society's moral code, she enables him to live up to the idea of male dominance, superiority and virility' (Crapanzano 1973).

Function and Opposition

To summarize, this pattern of culture-bound reaction appears to occur where major points of political and cultural oppositions are represented in a particular situation and thus, not surprisingly, where the everyday articulation of power relationships are not appropriate as solutions to a perceived problem. Employing our (emic) Western psychological categories, these ambiguous points may be represented as 'tensions'. Turner (1969) says such tensions do not imply that society is about to break up: they 'constitute strong unities ... whose nature as a unit is constituted and bounded by the very forces that contend within it. [The tension becomes] a play of forces instead of a bitter battle. The effect of such a "play" soon wears off, but the sting is removed from certain troubled relationship'. As Harris (1957: 1065) comments about the *saka* attack, it 'allows a round-about acknowledgement of conflict, but in the *saka* dance there is again peace, dignity and festivity'. Indeed individual components of this key institution are included as parts of other rituals of the community. 'The use of symbols in ritual secures some kind of emotional compromise which satisfies the majority of the individuals who comprise a society and which supports its major institutions' (Richards 1982: 169). The reactions appear characteristically to have three stages.(8) In their course, the individual is *extruded* out of normal social relationships in an extension of the usual devalued or marginal social status. This is followed by a prescribed role, deviant but legitimate, which represents further *exaggeration* of this dislocation (frequently suggesting a direct contravention or 'symbolic inversion' of common social values) to unbalance the social equilibrium to such an extent that it is succeeded by *restitution* back into conventional and now unambiguous social relationships.(9) 'The *saka* dance turns the *saka* attack on its head' (Harris 1957: 1060). The suicide voyager's 'attempt at detachment has failed, but he has succeeded in resolving his problem. He is once again absorbed and an effective catharsis has been obtained' (Firth 1961: 15). Taking the 'womens reactions' as occurring in a symbolic field in which women are regarded as more 'natural' and less 'social' than men,(10) we obtain;

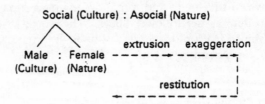

Figure 1

The curved line represents a 'degenerative causal loop' to use the cybernetic terminology, one which returns the relationship to a more complementary form. This may also be represented as a signed diagraph (Figure 2) in which positive lines represent complementary relationships and negative lines represent antithetical relationships. Note that **de** is negative because of the hierarchical nature of the 'Nature/Culture' distinction at different levels; thus the graph is 'unbalanced' and hence is not 'colorable' (Hage and Harary 1983).

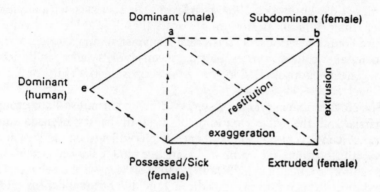

Figure 2

'Direction' represents dominance at the three stages between the principal actors.

A similar three stage model of separation, transition and reintegration has been postulated for those psycho-social transitions usually glossed as 'rites of passage' (Van Gennep 1960), such as shamanic trance possession (Peters and Price-Williams 1983) and women's cults in Africa (Wilson 1967: Turner 1969). While medical convention divides such patterns into 'symptoms' and 'treatment' we should prefer to consider them a single ritual complex. 'Attack and dance are two manifestations of a single situation ... [they] can be translated into one another' (Harris 1957: 1061).(11) Leach (1961: 135–6) suggests that ritual is 'normal social life ... played in reverse' and offers the terms *formality*, *role reversal* and *masquerade* to represent the equivalent of our three stages. The prescribed deviant role amplifies the rejection by the community, frequently taking the form of behavior which contravenes the core values of the society (Littlewood 1984a), female modesty or decorum (Harris 1957; Lewis 1969; Geertz 1968). During this period the principal is regarded as the victim of external mystical forces (which must be placated) and is not accountable:(12) when *negi-negi* 'a man does not have a name' (Langness 1965: 276): he is an animal escaped from everyday social control (Newman 1964). Whilst we are emphasising here the instrumental, rather than the expressive aspect of this behavior, we may gloss the personal experience for the principal (and audience) by the Western term 'catharsis', similar to the collective experience of social inversions found in carnivals, licensed rituals of rebellion and contravention of norms in certain specific and tightly controlled situations (Turner 1969: Littlewood 1984a). In large scale societies (with a linear rather than a cyclical notion of time (Leach 1961)), individual culture-bound reactions of 'hysterical conversion' may succeed the periodic and collective rites of role reversal of smaller and more homogeneous groups; Loudon (1959)) describes such a shift for Zulu women.

Sociological explanations of symbolic inversion stress both group catharsis and the social marking of a norm by its licensed and restricted contravention. The audience is placed between distress and safety, the position of 'optimal distancing' and balanced attention reserved for group catharsis (Scheff 1979).(13) Because the behavior is 'entertainment' is not to say that the 'actors' do not fully identify with their parts (Beattie 1977). Even in the more stylized display of the Balinese theatre, the actor portraying the witch Rangda may disrupt the performance by running *amok* and the audience follow suit (Geertz 1966): some members of the audience remain unentranced and direct the activities of the 'audience'. For the community as a whole, social contradictions are demonstrated but shown to be susceptible of a solution, albeit a temporary and restricted one (for these contradictions are not ultimately resolved). The spectacle of reversal of values in, say, *negi-negi*, articulates the structural imbalance between affines and kin, wife-givers and wife-receivers, and between older and younger men. The performance articulates these social oppositions for all members of the audience but also permits individual identification with the protagonist: that sex-specific performances are appreciated equally by both sexes suggests that individual identification is perhaps less important than psychodynamic writers have suggested: ritual derives its efficacy and power from its performance (Kapferer 1981).

The 'Mystical Pressure' of Medicine

Our model of culture-bound reactions thus involves non-dominant individuals who display in their personal situations the basic structural social contradictions, expressed through the available intellectual tools, with recourse to 'mystical pressure' permitting personal adjustment of their situation by a limited contravention of society's core values. Each reaction involves dislocation, exaggeration/inversion and restitution. An attempt to look for equivalent 'Western' reactions would appear quite straightforward apart from the notion of 'mystical pressure'. What unquestionable 'other-worldly authority', standing outside everyday personal relations might serve to explain and legitimate them?

For small-scale traditional communities, social organization and normative principles and the categorization of the natural world and human relations to it are articulated through an intellectually tight system of cosmology which we usually refer to as 'religion'. Religion is an ideology: it both describes and prescribes, binding the individual into society and into the natural order. Through its other-worldly authority it legitimates personal experience and the social order. By contrast, in the secularized West, Christianity has lost its power of social regulation and competes both with other religions and, more significantly, with a variety of alternative ideologies, moral and political. Where then can we find an equivalent 'mystical' sanction which integrates personal distress into a shared conceptualization of the world?

We would suggest that the legitimation of our present world view lies ultimately in contemporary science which offers core notions of individual identity, responsibility and action. In its everyday context as it relates to our personal experience, science is most salient in the form of medicine.(14) In all societies illness is experienced through an expressive system encoding indigenous notions of social order (Comaroff 1978). Whilst serious illness 'is an event that challenges meaning in this world, ... medical beliefs and practices organize the event into an episode which gives form and meaning' (Young 1976). 'The power of an illness reality is derived from its ability to evoke deeply felt social responses as well as intense personal affects' (Good and Good 1981). This obligation to order abnormality is no less when it is manifest primarily through unusual behavior. As Scott (1973) points out, the person whose behavior is seen as being unpredictable not only becomes an object of fear; she becomes endowed with a potentiality for a perverse sort of power. The patient's power lies in the unstated assumption that it is society who will be ultimately responsible for what she does.

Professional intervention in sickness involves incorporating the patient into an overarching system of explanation, a common structural pattern which manifests itself in the bodily economy of every human being (Willis 1978; Turner 1984). Social accountability is transferred onto an agency beyond the patient's control. Becoming sick is part of a social process leading to communal recognition of an abnormal state and a consequent readjustment of patterns of behavior and expectations, and then to changed roles and altered responsibility. Expectations of the sick person include exemption from discharging some social obligations, exemption from responsibility for the condition itself, together with a shared recognition that it is undesirable and involves an obligation to seek help and cooperate with treatment (Parsons 1951). Withdrawal from everyday social responsibilities is made socially acceptable through some means of exculpation, usually through mechanisms of bio-physical determinism (Young 1976). 'When faced with a diagnosis for which he has equally convincing reasons to believe that either his client is sick or he is not sick, the physician finds that the professional and legal risks are less if he accepts the hypothesis of sickness' (Young 1976). To question the biomedical scheme itself involves questioning some of our most fundamental assumptions about human nature and agency. Because of its linking of personal experience with the social order, its standardized expectations of removing personal responsibility and initiating an institutionalized response, and its rooting in ultimate social values through science, biomedicine offers a powerful and unquestionable legitimate inversion of everyday behavior. It will thus not be surprising to find many of our 'culture-bound syndromes' already included in psychiatric nosologies. Others we may suspect lie hidden in the fringes of general medicine. Lee (1981) shows how the symbolic inversions of Malay amok, latah and possession states continue, although the attribution of responsibility has been transferred from supernatural agencies onto a notion of psychopathology.(15)

Butterflies and Serpents: The Medicalization of Woman

In all societies women are 'excluded from participation in or contact with some realm in which the highest powers of the society are felt to reside' (Ortner 1974). They are excluded by a dominant ideology which reflects men's experiences and interests. 'The facts of female physiology are transformed in almost all societies into a cultural rationale which assigns women to nature and the domestic sphere, and thus ensures their general inferiority to men' (La Fontaine 1981: 347).

Keller (1974) suggests that the core aspects of the female role in Western society is reflected in the ideals still held out to women: concentration on marriage, home and children as the primary focus of concern with reliance on a male provider for sustenance and status. There is an expectation that women will emphasize nurturance and that they live through and for others rather than for themselves. Women are expected to give up their occupation and place of residence when they marry and are banned from the direct assertion and expression of aggression. Their lack of power is attributed to their greater emotionality and their inability to cope with wider social responsibilities, for dependency and passivity are expected of a woman; her psychological image is of a person with a childish incapacity to govern herself and a need for male protection and direction (Broverman et al. 1970). Contemporary Western women are permitted greater freedom than men to 'express feelings' and to recognize emotional difficulties (Phillips and Segal 1969), enabling the woman to define her difficulties within a medical framework and bring them to the attention of her doctor (Gove and Tudor 1973; Horwitz 1977).

Through childbearing every woman in the West becomes a potential patient: as a recent gynecology textbook put it 'Femininity tends to be passive and receptive, masculinity to be more active, restless, anxious for repeated demonstrations of potency' (James 1963). Jordanova (1980) suggests that medicine and science are characterized by the action of men on women; women are regarded as more 'natural', passive, awaiting male ('cultural') organization. In the heraldry of the British Royal College of Psychiatrists, as sported on the neckties of its members, they continue this tradition as the Butterflies of Psyche, awaiting the Serpents of Aesculapius.(16) Serpent and Butterfly are in an opposed but complementary relationship; action by one engenders the opposed complement in the other (Bateson 1958). Ingleby (1982) has argued that there is a close historical relationship between the psychiatric notions of 'woman' and 'patient', and both Chesler (1974) and Jordanova (1981) have noted the similarity between neurotic symptom patterns and normative expectations of female behavior.

Thus we may summarize the Serpent/Butterfly relationship in complementary (Hage and Harary 1983: 116) pairs:

$$\frac{\text{Culture}}{\text{Nature}} = \frac{\text{Male}}{\text{Female}} = \frac{\text{Active}}{\text{Passive}} = \frac{\text{Cognition}}{\text{Affect}} = \frac{\text{Doctor}}{\text{Patient}}$$

(modified from Jordanova 1980) to this Turner adds:

$$= \frac{\text{Public}}{\text{Private}} = \frac{\text{Production}}{\text{Consumption}} = \frac{\text{Desire}}{\text{Need}}$$

A polythetic classification of this type stresses that the *relationship* between paired elements remains constant, not that there is equality between the superordinate or subordinate elements (Littlewood 1984).(17) Clearly not all doctors are men (indeed, medicine has a greater proportion of women than other professions) but the woman doctor's role in relation to her patient replicates the male/female relationship. A male patient may flirt with his nurse but hardly with his doctor.

Perverse Feminity:
Conversion Hysteria in the Nineteenth Century

In the nineteenth century, hysteria was a socially recognized behavior pattern, mainly affecting women. The middle-class woman was taught that aggression, independence, assertion and curiosity were male traits, inappropriate for women whose nature was emotional, powerless, passive and nurturant and who were not expected to make achievements in any public area. Hysteria offered a solution to the onerous task of running a household, and of adjusting husband/wife or father/daughter relations, and one which did not challenge these core values. The hysteric could stay in bed and was allowed to opt out of her traditional duties and be relieved of responsibilities; as sick she enjoyed sympathy and privileges whilst others assumed her tasks as a self-sacrificing wife, mother or daughter. The development from simple conversion symptoms to a recognized discrete role as a 'hysteric' provided a parody of the core social values: women's expected dependency and restricted social role. The reaction represented an exaggeration of the socially extruded (female) status. The hysteric was characteristically female, the hysterical woman being perceived as the very embodiment of perverse feminity, an inversion of dominant male behavior (Smith-Rosenberg 1972). Hysteria was a conventionally available alternative behavior pattern for certain women, which permitted them to express some dissatisfaction. What Freud was to term the 'secondary gain' conferred by the hysterical role allowed a limited adjustment of husband/wife power relations in the family: 'Ill health will be her one weapon for maintaining her position. It will procure for her the care she longs for ... It will compel him to treat her with solicitude if she recovers; otherwise a relapse will threaten' (Freud 1946).

Turner (1984) suggests that hysteria was a solution to the sexuality of unmarried women in a period of delayed marriage. Many of Freud's patients with hysterical symptoms were women who had been forced to sacrifice their public lives in nursing a sick relative (Krohn 1978). Employing this model they might themselves take to their bed because of pain, paralysis or weakness, and remain there for months or years.(18) The role of the 'hysteric' before Freud did not involve acceptance of individual responsibility for the illness. Male physicians and men in general employed biological arguments to rationalize this exaggeration of traditional sex role as immutably rooted in anatomy and pathophysiology (Smith-Rosenberg 1973). Female problems were problems of biology. As Freud's friend the gynecologist Otto Weininger put it: 'Man possesses sexual organs: her sexual organs possess woman.' According to Moebius 'On the Physiological Imbecility of Women' the woman was intermediate between the child and the adult (Ellenberger 1970). Thus the nineteenth century view of women, or at least of middle-class women, was as frail and decorative creatures whose temperamental excesses were the result of a peculiar functioning of their sexual organs whose very physical nature limited their activities to family roles. The fact that the hysterical woman tended to be particularly sexually attractive to men (Ellenberger 1970) was regarded as a clue to the reaction only in that a sexual (rather than a gender or sex role) etiology was implicated, a notion which led Freud to the delineation of the counter-transference as psychological rather than social.(19)

The dominant male/passive female notion which embodied the hysterical reaction was mirrored in the therapy: the rational physician actively treating his patient in the grip of her nature. The pattern of symptoms of Charcot's patients has been described as 'a folie à deux ... a culture-bound syndrome emerging from the interaction between the professor and his clientele', to be replaced later by a less dramatic pattern of diffuse somatic complaints (Eisenberg 1977). Female identity vis à vis men is particularly reinforced in collective and passive settings such as nurses' training schools and boarding schools, and these are the contemporary settings in which doctors continue to encounter hysteria (McEvedy and Beard 1970), 'a picture of women in the words of men' (Chodoff and Lyons 1958).

Overdoses

A contemporary reaction which offers parallels with the doctor/patient relation in hysteria is parasuicide with medically prescribed drugs. As in hysteria, the normative situation of active male (husband, doctor) and passive female (wife, patient) is reflected in the drama of the hospital casualty department. The unease and anger which it evokes in the medical profession reflect its 'perverse' transformation of the clinical paradigm.

Women are closely identified with psychotropic medication (Murray et al. 1981). A study of prescriptions for mood-modifying drugs in a Canadian city showed that 69 per cent of them were for women (Cooperstock and Sims 1971). Whilst more women than men went to physicians and received prescriptions, there was an even greater disproportion in the number of women receiving psychotropic drugs. During the year preceding a national sampling of American adults, 13 per cent of the men and 9 per cent of the women had used prescribed drugs, especially minor tranquillizers and daytime sedatives (Parry et al. 1973). These American rates are consistent with other Western industrialized nations. Physicians expect female patients to require a higher proportion of mood altering drugs than less expressive male patients (Cooperstock 1971). These are perhaps the 'attractive healthy women who thoroughly enjoy being ill' (Daily Express 1984). That we are not dealing simply with a 'real' gender disparity in psychological distress is suggested by the symbolism of medical advertising. Stimson (1975) found that women outnumbered men by 15:1 in advertisements for tranquillizers and anti-depressants. One advertisement depicted a woman with a bowed head holding a dishcloth and standing beside a pile of dirty dishes represented larger than life size; the medical consumer is told that the drug 'restores perspective' for her by 'correcting the disturbed brain chemistry'. Employed women are rare in drug advertisements and women usually shown as dependent housewives and child-rearers: the world acts on them, they do not act on the world. Seidenberg (1974) too found that psychotropic drug advertisements emphasized women as the patients; they were represented as discontented with their role in life, dissatisfied with marriage, with washing dishes or attending parent-teacher association meetings. The treating physician was never depicted as a woman and all the female patients appeared as helpless and anxious. Prather and Fidell (1975) found that advertisements for psychotropic drugs tended to picture women as patients, while those for other medications showed men: within the psychotropic drug category alone, women were shown with diffuse emotional symptoms, while men were pictured with discrete episodes of anxiety because of specific pressures from work or from accompanying organic illness.

'Overdoses' of medical drugs are up to five times more common among women than men, especially in the age group 15–19. Among girls of this age in Edinburgh, Kreitman and Schreiber (1979) found that more than one in every hundred take an overdose each year. Of a sample of patients who attended hospital following a non-fatal act of deliberate self-harm, 95 per cent had taken a drug overdose. Half of the episodes involved interpersonal conflicts as the major precipitating factor (Morgan et al. 1975). Only a minority had made definite plans to prepare for death, to avoid discovery or subsequently regretted not having killed themselves. Suicidal intent and risk to life appear to be low, especially as overdoses are usually taken with somebody close by (Hawton et al. 1982): 59 per cent of attempters committed the act in the presence of or near other people.

Whilst the reasons given by the individual for taking overdoses may be expressive (explaining the overdose as a result of personal predicament and associated feelings at the time of the act), they are frequently pragmatic – that is they are consciously conceived in terms of the desired consequences of the act, usually increased support or understanding (Bancroft et al. 1979). Overdoses can be interpreted as a transaction between the woman and her intimate group (Kreitman et al. 1970); that they are socially learnt patterns of adjusting one's situation is supported by the finding that they are concentrated in socially linked clusters of individuals. A study of fifty adolescent overdosers suggested they viewed their act as a means of gaining relief from a stressful situation or as a way of showing other people how desperate they felt: clinical staff who assessed their motives both regarded them as expressive but also noted that adolescents took overdoses in order to punish other people or change their behavior (Hawton et al. 1982). Typically a teenage girl took tablets after a disappointment, frustration or difference of opinion with an older person (usually a parent): many patients afterwards reported that the induction of guilt in those whom they blamed for their distress was a predominant motive for the act (Bancroft et al. 1979). Thus, while overdoses can be seen as strategies designed to avoid or adjust certain specific situations, the self-perception of the principal is of social dislocation or extrusion: the reaction exaggerates this extrusion, offering a threat of refusing membership in the human community altogether – an inversion of normal life-seeking norms. As in Tikopia (Firth 1961), attempted suicide is, amongst other things, a dangerous adventure.

The conventional resolution of the inversion involves its complement: medical intervention returns the patient into everyday relationships. Not surprisingly, the overdose meets with little professional sympathy, particularly when it is interpreted as an instrumental social mechanism rather than the sign of underlying individual hopelessness or psychiatric illness. 'Expressive' explanations (communicating despair and aiming at withdrawal, escape or death) are more acceptable and evoke more sympathy or readiness to help in both doctors and nurses than pragmatic motives (Ramon and Bancroft 1975). Doctors tend to distinguish acts as either suicidal or 'manipulative', and are more accepting of the 'wish to die' motive. (Mystical sanctions like biomedicine can only continue as such if ritual participants are 'unaware' of any function of the social drama.) Nurses are generally more sympathetic than are doctors to instrumental motives: perhaps, because of their ambiguous position in the Serpent:Butterfly (doctor-:patient::male:female) equation, nurses are more likely to perceive overdoses as legitimate attempts to escape from distress (Ramon et al. 1975). Patients taking overdoses are regarded by doctors as a nuisance, extraneous to the real concerns of medicine and less deserving of medical care than patients with physical illnesses, especially when the self-poisoning episode appears 'histrionic' (Hawton, Marsack and Fag 1981). Doctors 'feel a sense of irritation which they find difficult to conceal' (*British Medical Journal* 1971).

Women who take overdoses still gain access to hospital, despite the physician's antipathy, since the popular conception of suicidal behavior is as a discrete event, 'something that happens to one', rather than something one intentionally brings about (Ginsberg 1971; cf. James and Hawton 1985). Relatives accept that the patient's problems are outside her direct personal control, and responsibility is thereby attributed to some agency beyond the patient's volition. Thus we have the continuing use of the popular (and passive) term 'overdose' as opposed to (active) 'self-poisoning' or 'attempted suicide'. The official translation of the behavior into *symptoms* takes place under socially prescribed conditions by the physician who alone has the power to legitimate exculpating circumstances (Young 1980). As with nineteenth century hysteria, the resolution of the reaction invokes a 'mystical pressure' which replicates the social structure in which the reaction occurs; like other culture-bound syndromes it displays core structural antagonisms but shows they are 'soluble' within the existing political and symbolic framework. The drama of the scene in the casualty department replays the male doctor/female patient theme without questioning it, but it does afford a degree of negotiation for the principal, who induces a mixture of responses, mainly sympathy and guilt, in close relatives and friends (James and Hawton 1985).

The Housewives' Disease: Agoraphobia

Perhaps ten per cent of women develop agoraphobic symptoms (Robin et al. 1984),the inability to go into public places alone or unaccompanied, particularly without a member of the family. Attempts to do so result in anxiety or other unpleasant symptoms, a fear of falling, fainting or otherwise losing control. Agoraphobics fear any situation in which escape to a safe place or dependable companion might be impeded. The majority are married women (Marks 1970), hence the popular term 'housewives' disease'. Physical space replicates social space (Ardener 1981), and Bell and Newby (1976) point out that the home represents core social values: it is 'the framework within which the deference of wife to husband operates. Encouragement of ideologies of the home and home-centredness enables the identification of the wife with her husband's superordinate position to increase by emphasizing a common adherence to territory, a solidarity of place. A woman's "place" is therefore in the home, partly because to seek fulfillment outside the home could threaten to break down the ideological control which confinement within it promotes. The ideology of the "home" ... is therefore a social control mechanism in the sense that escape from the home threatens access to alternative definition of the female role, as Ibsen realized brilliantly in "The Dolls House".' De Swaan (1981) suggests that agoraphobia reproduces such restrictions while denying any other motive except an inexplicable anxiety: he points out that it only became common when the streets became physically safe for middle-class women and thus when husbands became concerned about their wives' independence: agoraphobia acts as an 'internal chaperone' (as anorexia nervosa is an 'internalized corset') and 'recreates ... the semblance of the nineteenth century bourgeois family'. The wife is the 'angel in the home' in opposition to the 'whore in the street'.

Like overdoses, the agoraphobic reaction employs an exaggeration or caricature of the female role with its lack of control or power, mirroring the situation of Western European and American women in many areas of their lives with their extreme dependence on men (Symonds 1971; Al Issa 1980; Hallam 1983). Major decisions within families are usually made by the husband and the very decisions about the nature of the woman's 'place' (such as its location or whether to sell it) are taken by husbands. In one study (Goldstein 1973) 16 out of 20 female agoraphobic patients had felt strong urges to escape from their marriage and home at the time of the onset of the phobia, but were unable to do so because of realistic fears of isolation, and the loss of economic support. Agoraphobia is conceptualized by some behaviorists as avoidance behavior in the insoluble conflict situation posed by the simultaneous desire to escape and the fear of autonomy (Goldstein and Chambless 1978). Goldstein (1970) notes that agoraphobic symptoms develop concurrently with a sense of dislocation: a wish to end the marriage or to 'violate' the marital contract. The agoraphobic is often an unhappily married woman, low in self-sufficiency, in whom the fear evoked by physical isolation accompanies a persistent but unrealistic fantasy of liberation from the marriage – unrealistic because it is seen as leading to a social abyss (Wolpe 1979; Fodor 1974). It is not simply a reflection of an acceptable fear of the dangers of the street. A patient of ours who successfully brought up three children in a ten-year stint of devoted self-sacrificing denial allowed herself a relationship with a man when the children reached adolescence. Dramatically ensuing agoraphobia prevented this relationship from developing and she became housebound within a few weeks, which necessitated the children doing the shopping.(20)

Whilst the agoraphobic woman demonstrates in her situation certain core social values, and expresses her sense of dislocation through them, the reaction has been regarded as instrumental. Symonds (1971) suggests agoraphobia is an alternative to overt marital conflict and 'refusal to go out can draw attention to oneself, it can be used to control or punish others, it can protect from the dangers involved in living an independent social life, from having a social life, from having ... to face the possibility of failure' (Hudson 1974). The agoraphobic woman conforms even more to the stereotypic publicly extruded role, but she gains a strategy, which, without open defiance of the husband (Andrews 1966), requires him to make sacrifices and gives her a veto over proposed joint activities (Buglass et al. 1977). The very nature of a woman's household responsibility makes her illness the most potentially disturbing of all to family equilibrium, and agoraphobia is thus a particularly adaptive strategy (Parsons and Fox 1952; Lazarus 1972). On occasion it is able to severely restrict the husband's activities to the point where he is virtually unable to leave the home (Fry 1962). 'Husband and wife are compelled to live together in mutual distress, consoling themselves for all their differences with the mutual idea that this thing has been imposed upon them, beyond their control, and they can do nothing about it' (Fry 1962).

Agoraphobia articulates early socialization into the typical 'female' behavior of helplessness and dependency; by the age of thirteen, girls have five times as many 'fears' as have boys (Macfarlane et al. 1954). The norms for appropriate male and female behavior are learned and internalized very early in life. Socialization within the family and within the education system teaches children what women are like and what men are like and how they should behave towards each other. Ardener (1978) notes that 'the nature of women affects the shape of the categories assigned for them, which in turn reflect back upon and reinforce and remould perceptions of the nature of women in a continuing process', producing a complex set of shared images and conceptions which denote their general characteristics and appropriate behavior in society. There is ample documentary evidence of the way girls and women are presented in the media, especially children's books, which points to a relationship between fearfulness and dependency in women's social roles, providing the basis for the later development of agoraphobia. In a study of sex roles in school text books, the illustrations portray girls and adult women as if agoraphobic, pictured behind fences or windows, immobilized, helpless and watching (National Organization for Women 1974). As Durkheim

(1951) wrote: 'The two sexes do not share equally in social life. Man is actively involved in it, while woman does little more than look on from a distance.'

Anorexia Nervosa

Anorexia nervosa was first described in France, Britain and Russia in the nineteenth century, and is now increasingly seen in countries undergoing rapid industrialization. It is particularly common in middle-class Western adolescent girls. Although Prince (1983) and Schwartz (1986) suggest it is a culture-bound syndrome, it differs from the reactions we have described in having a more obvious 'biological' contribution; this is however secondary to a socially determined weight loss and its incidence parallels certain culture-bound (and class-bound) notions of female body imagery. Western women achieve a social identity through their bodies in a way men do not. As Turner (1984) notes, women may 'possess' their bodies phenomenologically but they do not 'own' them. Contemporary medicine is particularly concerned with notions of the physical body (Armstrong 1983; Turner 1984) and we should expect to find many of our Serpent/Butterfly themes reflected onto the body. Contemporary dietary management emerged from a medieval theology of the flesh, through moralistic medicine to a science of the 'efficient body', in which with consumerism, desire is promoted rather than controlled: 'the commodification of fantasies and pleasures, (Turner 1984). The 'anatomo-politics' of Foucault 'regards medical science as the crucial link between the discipline of individual bodies by professional groups (of psychiatrists, dieticians, social workers and others) and the regulation of populations by panopticism (in the form of asylums, factories, schools and hospitals)' (Turner 1984).

Dieting is encouraged by an industry that provides an extensive range of low energy food products to facilitate slimming, reinforced by extensive medical publicity (Ritenbaugh 1982b). The top four British slimming magazines have a joint circulation of over 650,000. In a Swedish study (Nylander 1971), 72 per cent of 21 year old women felt that they had been fat at some time compared with 34 per cent of the men; twice as many women as men attributed their excess of weight to 'weak character'. In a similar study of over 6,000 Americans, twice as many girls as boys perceived themselves as overweight; the girls were dissatisfied with their weight because they equated slimness with beauty. Excessive weight is more of a professional handicap to women than men; successful business women (and the wives of successful men!) are rarely overweight (Dwyer, Felman and Mayer 1970), while women's concepts of themselves in general are more closely tied to their appearance than are men's (Stuart and Jackson 1979). Women are more harshly penalized for failure to achieve slenderness as they are more often denied or granted access to social privilege on the basis of physical appearance (Elder 1969): obese schoolgirls are less likely than their slender peers to be accepted for colleges despite comparable qualifications (Cunning and Mayer 1966); British women can lose their jobs for being 'overweight' (*Daily Telegraph* 1984) for 'a woman increases her market value by being slender' (Millman 1980). While thinness is associated with upward social mobility, fatness is often the sign of 'ethnic minority status' (Millman 1980).

Is anorexia an exaggeration or a rejection of the dominant cultural norm? Its exact relation to core social values is unclear. perhaps because it articulates current uncertainty about women's public roles and their sexuality.(21) Whilst the preferred sex object for men is slender (Garner and Garfinkel 1980), a fuller figure implies sexuality through pregnancy; at the same time contemporary men appear to value the state of pregnancy less. Millman (1980) suggests that fat women are seen as unfeminine, in flight from sexuality, or alternatively, as sexual in some perverse forbidden way, incestuous, out of control, dominant. Anorexia nervosa may be an attempt to emulate a valued youthful body form (Ritenbaugh 1982a) rather than an inversion of the dominant mode; the incidence in modelling students has been estimated to be 7 per cent (Garner and Garfinkel 1980).(22) That anorexics frequently come from all girl sibships, that their mothers are described as career-orientated and 'domineering' and that anorexics tend to menstruate earlier suggests the reaction can serve to maintain the sexual and generational structure of the family;(23) the development of the reaction has coincided historically with earlier menstruation (Shorter 1983). Social and sexual maturity are not synchronous; thus we have sexually but not socially 'mature' children. If plumper girls are seen as more sexually mature (Millman 1975), the male choice of sex object has become increasingly passive and infantile – baby-faced and long-legged with shaven armpits (Cranshaw 1983), a doll. Boskind-Lodahl (1976) takes issue with the standard psychoanalytic interpretation of anorexia as simply a rejection of adult feminity, manifesting as fear of oral impregnation. She suggests that far from a rejection of feminity, the determined pursuit of thinness by adolescent girls constitutes an exaggerated striving to achieve this role and that attempts to control her physical appearance demonstrate a concern with pleasing others, particularly men. She points out that anorexics devote their lives to fulfilling the feminine role and that histories of patients indicate that they have been rewarded for physical attractiveness and submissive 'goodness' while characteristics such as independence, self-reliance and assertiveness were generally punished. A drive towards perfection in physical appearance was often matched by an attempt towards academic achievement with the aim of pleasing parents and potential husbands. Anorexics correctly assume that the effect of having a fat body is to bring about male rejection.

Functional aspects of anorexia have been discerned in the context of the family, particularly as a means of avoiding overt parental separation where the adolescent girl is threatened with extrusion as a daughter. Minuchin describes a pattern of family life in which the parental couple appear united, the parents submerging their conflicts in jointly protecting or blaming the anorexic daughter who is identified as the only problem. 'In several such families the parents required that the children reassured them that they were good parents, or join them in worrying about the family. In most cases parental concern absorbed the couple so that all signs of marital strife or even minor differences were suppressed or ignored' (Minuchin et al. 1975). In a third of one series of families, parental separation had been openly threatened: 'the exclusion implied in refusal to eat is a threat to the parents' capacity as nutritional agents, a role which is always an important measure of a parental function and in many of these families, central to their value system'. Crisp (1980) also suggests the reaction involves the patient remaining a child and describes a typical anorexic: 'Within the context of her mounting panic at the prospect of her parents' marriage breaking up, her dieting quickly escalated, seeming suddenly easy and relieving to her and, as anorexia nervosa supervened, her father and mother were reunited in their unwritten contract together to care for her until she "grew up".'

Given the ambiguous relationship between anorexia and core social values, it is perhaps not surprising that Ritenbaugh (1982a) regards *obesity* as a culture-bound syndrome (albeit in an extremely restricted sense as a locally recognized illness). Medical practice has 'officially' defined half the adult population of America as obese (Ritenbaugh 1982a) and it represents both sin (indulgence), crime (the consumption of limited world resources) and ugliness (Ritenbaugh 1982b). Whilst emphasizing that female fatness and fertility have long been associated, she suggests that slimness as representing a youthful idea and the notion of control are important: 'Important themes in American society are individual control and fear of noncontrol.' Whilst obesity may represent an inversion of core values, its functional aspect is less clear. The Women's Movement has recognized the political nature of male pressure on women to slim (Orbach 1978 but see

Mabel-Lois 1974) and it may well be that negotiating male demands for slimness affords wives and daughters a certain degree of instrumental power. (See Millman (1980) who provides a detailed account of the interpersonal relations of fat people).(24) Obesity and anorexia nervosa are perhaps more similar than might appear. Both offer the threat of a desexualized role. (At both extremes of weight, endocrine changes result in a cessation of periods and the development of facial hair.) If male/female relations are articulated through a mutual concern for female morphology, then weight is one aspect which can be easily negotiated. If women are regarded as 'out of control' by men, they know that it is only by control over their body, often involving pain (sleeping in curlers, depilation) that they achieve relationships with men (Millman 1980). Thus, whilst there is some element of 'beating men at their own game', the rules remain those of men. If nineteenth century hysteria was concerned with the suppression of female desire, anorexia nervosa is concerned with its 'manufacture, extension and detail' (Turner 1984).

Other Reactions

One form of *shoplifting* is that by middle-aged women who steal although they can apparently afford to buy what they take. The characteristic principal is a 50 year old woman with non-specific physical and psychological symptoms who is neglected by her husband and children (Gibbens et al. 1971). Shopping is the occupation of women; whilst agoraphobia is a parody of the 'woman's place is in the home' notion, shoplifting is a public parody of the 'woman as consumer' and an affirmation of woman's irresponsible and irrational nature. As with binging, observers frequently recognize an element of revenge through personal assertion in highly constrained circumstances Thus a patient of ours who was unhappily married stole very publicly from a department store on the very day her husband was appointed as its manager. A successful reaction involves psychiatric diagnosis (Bradford and Balmaceda 1983), public recognition of problems and enhanced domestic interest and concern. The woman herself is not held responsible in the usual way, as she would be if she was stealing for monetary gain, for the reaction is 'irrational' and is often attributed by professionals to 'depression' or the 'menopause'.

In the nineteenth century the *menopause* was associated with insanity (Tilt 1862). Recent medical literature presents the menopausal woman as biologically depressed, irritable, tired and asexual, although the only well-documented menopausal experiences are hot flushes and night sweats (McInley and Jeffries 1974). The menopausal syndrome has become organized out of amorphous complaints and malaise which leads to a possibly functional illness role but also to physical (endocrinological) treatment. Townsend and Carbone (1980) have drawn attention to the devalued status of the post-menopausal woman who remains 'female' but deprived of her sexuality and thus the potential for developing such symptoms. In other societies the loss of the role of reproducer (mother, wife) frequently signals access to an enhanced 'male' role: thus Rajput women in North India enjoy a symptom-free menopause, reflecting a valued change of status with access to activities previously forbidden (Flint 1975).

Agoraphobia and anorexia nervosa are characteristic of women and only a minority of parasuicides are men. In certain situations it is men who are socially extruded and who employ adaptive culture-bound mechanisms to adjust their situation. In British *domestic sieges* the typical principal is a divorced or separated man who has lost the custody of his child. Traditionally fathers have readily accepted the common practice of courts awarding custody of children to the mother; enormous value is placed on the powers of maternal instinct which justified denial of custody to fathers. Occasionally the father responds by seizing or abducting the child from the mother or guardian in violation of a custody ruling and threatens homicide, suicide or both. The house is surrounded by armed police and after several hours of negotiation, the crisis is resolved, generally without anybody being hurt. The legal outcome of the domestic siege is variable but at times the father might secure more generous access (Lipsedge and Littlewood 1985). He is treated leniently by the courts, frequently with the aid of medical reports. Such sieges are not common. To a lesser extent than elsewhere is legitimate fatherhood the *sine qua non* of Western masculinity; divorce, however, can still threaten a man's career in certain situations 'for failure in domestic roles can be taken as a deficiency in the moral virtues essential to public roles' (La Fontaine 1981: 343).

Flashing (exhibitionism), like anorexia nervosa, demonstrates core cultural notions of body imagery and sexual identity (see Polhemus 1978). In a society which condemns the overt display of male sexual arousal and which is, at the same time, intensely preoccupied with avoidance of effeminacy, the flasher is frequently a young adult male, 'passive and lacking in self-assertion' and with poor social skills, reflected in his conviction that he has a small penis (Rooth 1971). Like the *hamadsha* principal (page 294) he fails to live up to cultural norms of male activity. As with sieges, *flashing* is a dramatic time-limited public performance with a contravention of normative behavior, but a caricature of rape rather than of paternal authority, with the female element of being an object of observation, for 'men act but women appear' (Berger 1971: 47).(25) 'A common theme is one of dominance and mastery: the exhibitionist, usually timid and unassertive with women, suddenly challenges one with his penis, briefly occupies her full attention and conjures up in her some powerful emotion, such as fear and disgust, or sexual curiosity and arousal. For a fleeting instant he experiences a moment of intense involvement in a situation where he is in control' (Rooth 1971).(26) The principal is frequently not held responsible; Magnan suggested in 1890 that the irresistible urge to exhibit 'annihilated the will' and should therefore carry exemption from legal sanction. If the dislocation is seen purely in terms of physical sex, flashing does not seem immediately adaptive: the performance seldom ends in coitus. Taking the longer view (and exhibitionism as a syndrome has developed in relation to a biomedical ethos), treatment involves encouragement and facilitation of sexual relationships. As with shoplifting, the immediate result of the drama is the ceding of control to others: 'discretion is not always the rule' (Rooth 1971).

Neurosis as Ritual: Psychopolitics, Opposition and Inversion

The reactions we have described cannot necessarily be taken as phenomenologically discrete. Many similar patterns occur in non-Western societies. Thus, variants of male genital display are found elsewhere, although the *flashing* variant is most common in industrialized societies, particularly Anglo-Saxon ones (Rooth 1974). Murphy (1982) notes that Japanese *taijin kyofusho* (interpersonal phobia) and Eskimo '*kayak angst*' bear a close similarity to agoraphobia. Similarly parasuicide in Singapore with caustic soda offers parallels with overdoses: it is carried out by isolated women faced with the threat of complete abandonment by husband or parents (Murphy 1982). Turner (1984) suggests that anorexia nervosa is an 'internalization' of the nineteenth century corset, similarly controlling female sexuality by giving it an increased but restricted salience. The spread of industrialization and its associated tendency to individualize, psychologize and assign pragmatic motives (and hence perceive socially standardized behaviors as 'only' ritual or theatre) might suggest that 'Western' variants will become more universal. Whatever the origins of *pibloktoq* in European/Inuit relations (Murphy 1982), the reaction is being 'replaced' by parasuicide (Harvey et al. 1976). Whilst industrialization might involve certain inevitable relations of sexual power and notions of gender, it would be inappropriate to see it as a unitary cause: exhibitionism is common in Hong Kong but it is rare in Japan (Rooth 1974).

We have emphasized the specific social and symbolic meaning of certain patterns of behavior in Britain and America which show similarities with our model of Third World culture-bound syndromes. Whilst social meanings and behavior may be superimposed on a variety of existing biological patterns – as in *kuru*, premenstrual tension, adolescence, the symptomatic psychoses, drug intoxications (and perhaps autism, Sanua 1984) – we have restricted our discussion to reactions not primarily associated with human pathophysiology which are public and dramatic presentations of core social issues. In a word, *theatre*: but a ritual theatre which offers a specific pragmatic tool for the principal actor and one which may at times end in her death.

Table 1 sets out some reactions in relation to our defining criteria, together with four less likely candidates for comparison – obesity, menopause, transexualism and reactive depression. The paradigms appear to be overdosing, shoplifting, baby-snatching, agoraphobia and domestic sieges. Many of the reactions seem to show inversion of the shared dominant symbolism (Figure 2: **e**). How helpful is the notion of 'inversion'? Certainly normative roles are in a complementary and opposite relationship in the context in which the reactions occur (Figure 2: **ab**). Our application of 'inversion' is not to imply that each gender simply adopts a role more apposite to the other. In the case of the male reactions, sieges and flashing, the pattern is an exaggerated ritual reassertion or parody of dominant (male) norms rather than their obvious inversion. Although they are clearly extraordinary behavior relative to everyday articulation of the same symbolism, it would perhaps extend the notion of 'inversion' too far to include them (unlike *negi-negi* which occurs in young powerless men *vis à vis* the older ones).

In obesity, *amok* or parasuicide it is the ritual threat which provides bargaining power. Sieges certainly take place in situations which the principal is excluded from full participation in dominant values but the consequent performance is an assertion of such values. We have however seen recently a number of husbands who became agoraphobic after a period of compulsory redundancy during which the wife continued as the wage-earner. The female reactions also appear to be an exaggeration or *reductio ad absurdum* of normal sex roles but in certain cases (agoraphobia, overdosing) women are, as we have seen, already in an inverted and socially extruded position and the reaction is an extension of this accessible to the principal and her audience.(27)

Table 1 Defining Criteria

	Overdose	Shoplifting	Baby snatching	Agoraphobia	Domestic sieges	Conversion hysteria	Anorexia	Chronic pain/Briquet's Syndrome	Exhibitionism	Obesity	Reactive Depression	Menopause	Transsexualism
Time limited	+	+	+	?	+	?	0	+	+	0	0	0	0
Culture specific	+	+	+	+	+	0	+	0	0	?	0	?	0
Discrete (locals)	+	+	+	?	+	?	+	0	+	0	+	+	+
Discrete (observer)	+	+	+	+	+	+	+	+	+	+	+	?	+
No major biological aetiology	+	+	+	+	+	+	?	+	+	?	+	+	+
Individual not aware/responsible	+	+	+	+	+	+	+	+	?	+	+	+	+
Dramatic	+	+	+	+	+	+	+	?	+	0	0	0	0
Dislocation	+	+	+	+	+	+	+	+	+	?	+	+	0
'Inversion'/Exaggeration	+	+	+	+	0	+	+	+	0	?	?	?	0
Restitution	+	+	?	+	+	+	+	+	0	?	?	0	?
Symbolises core values	+	+	+	+	+	+	+	+	+	+	0	?	0
Situations of frustration	+	+	+	+	+	+	+	+	+	+	+	?	?
Non-dominant individuals	+	+	+	+	+	+	+	+	+	+	?	+	0
'Mystical pressure'	+	+	+	+	+	+	+	+	?	+	+	+	0

? = doubtful, unknown or variable.

Exaggeration of behavior provokes a reciprocal response (Bateson 1958) in men. The parody of gender-specific behavior in women may be perceived as inversion of those values *which, at another level, men and women hold in common* (Figures 1 and 2: **de**) but they are also an inversion in that women take temporary *control* (**da, de**). Anorexia like obesity (its apparent reverse) has a close subjective relationship to male/female relations; for many participants both are of course phases in the same reaction. The ambiguity and 'overdetermination' of anorexia reflects a current ambiguity over female sexuality and childrearing which is not characteristic of the role of the woman as housekeeper (agoraphobic) or patient (overdoser). Coherence of the matured syndrome is shaped by interaction between the professional and the principal.

Particular elements of various 'Serpent/Butterfly' relationships thus appear to be employed distinctively in different reactions. Doctor/ Patient in overdoses; Public/Private in agoraphobia; Production/Consumption in shoplifting. They are not discretely related however, and each reaction partly articulates the total complex out of which other ritual situation-specific patterns can be generated. Thus a bank manager's widow, faced with insoluble debts, attempted recently to rob a bank where she was a well-known customer, undisguised and using her perfume spray as a gun: after a suspended court sentence facilitated the adjustment of her finances she commented 'I must have had a brain storm' (*The Times* 1984). The popular notion of a brain storm (28) affords exculpation as an overriding and irrational but excusable impulse, clearly aligned with the medico-legal concepts of 'diminished responsibility' and 'disturbed balance of mind'. This coexists with the professional and lay idea that at some unconscious level the reaction is 'understandable'.

The mystical power of biomedicine as 'external' justification for individual action, and the negotiating 'space' it affords seem relevant to those other situations in which patient enacts a *pas de deux* with doctor: Ganser syndrome, compensation neurosis, irritable bowel, Munchausen's syndrome, Munchausen's syndrome by proxy (Meadow 1984) and chronic pain syndromes (29) apart from the many situations (such as non-compliance) where different explanatory models employed by doctor and patient afford the latter some control over the social drama. The mystical sanction of medicine seems less relevant to our two specifically male reactions (or other similar patterns such as the ritual stealing of cars by male adolescents), presumably because of the Serpent/Butterfly relationship (Culture : Nature :: Male : Female :: Active : Passive :: Doctor : Patient). Those 'medical' reactions which are more common among men such as alcoholism are more easily viewed as a 'response to stress' in itself than as a dramatic and functional method of personal negotiation. For medical professionals themselves, whether male or female, the biomedical 'mystical pressure' is difficult to employ personally; whilst student nurses frequently take overdoses, the reaction is rare among qualified nursing staff; the recourse to biomedical sanction has to be more complex and more 'dissociated' than overdosing.(30) A patient of ours is a married nursing sister of strict evangelical background who has achieved a certain negotiating 'space' between the demands of specialized professional responsibilities and her role as an 'ideal mother' by hospital admissions for recurrent episodes of loin pain hematuria: in a state she recollected in psychotherapy as 'dream-like' she would temporarily leave her professional role to venesect herself, injecting the blood into her bladder. To determine the extent to which the reactions are 'conscious' pragmatic attempts at adjustment is difficult; whilst to the theorist there is an element of parody in all of them, the irony is only rarely perceived by principal and audience. Participants certainly experience despair and self-hatred.(31)

All the patterns we have described are likely to be found as part of an endogenous depressive illness; we suggest the mediating factor is the sense of extrusion and isolation which is so characteristic of depression. Our emphasis on semiotic rather than psychological or physiological antecedents should thus not be taken to mean that individual personality or biology are irrelevant in the choice of reaction. It is not surprising that agoraphobic patients are anxious people or have 'phobic personalities' (Klein 1981)(32) or that anorexics were overweight as children. The final path is polysemous and over-determined: 'The efficacy of ritual as a social mechanism depends on this very phenomenon of central and peripheral meanings and on their allusive and evocative powers. ... All symbolic objects make it possible to combine fixity of form with multiple meanings of which some are standardized and some highly individualized' (Richards 1981: 164–5). Our nurse patient's venesection commenced after she had an extramarital affair (with an anesthetist!) and an attempt to lose the subsequent pregnancy by severe dieting coincided with the death of her father. Nevertheless the individual reaction is socially embedded: the male who takes an overdose or who develops anorexia is inevitably 'feminized'. Another patient of ours shoplifted from a London store where her domineering mother was well known, ostensibly to purchase her own birthday present for her mother to give her later in the week; in this setting the mother stood in a relationship to her analogous to that of husband to wife (cf. notes 24, 30). (We would be surprised to find a man engaging in shoplifting in a similar relationship with his wife or even a son with his mother.) Similarly Moroccan men are in a 'feminine' position with regard to their fathers (Crapanzano 1973). Male reactions occur typically when men are younger (*flashing*), displaced (*sieges*), or depressed (following unemployment).(33)

We have previously outlined the interrelations between social, psychological and symbolic inversion (Littlewood 1984). Reversal theory suggests inversions occur in a universal non-rational 'ludic' mode (Apter 1982), whilst Chesler (1974) emphasizes that it is women who are 'conditioned to lose in order to win'. Devereux (1970) characterizes this passive 'appeal of helplessness' (Symonds 1971) as *chantage masochiste* (masochistic blackmail)(34) and illustrates it with an agoraphobic case history and the 'psychology of cargo cults'. Rather than characterize such life-threatening or constricting reactions as simply 'self-punitive' or 'manipulative' with all the psychodynamic baggage that implies, we would prefer to see the powerless individual as enmeshed in a situation which she cannot control, one which neither reflects her interests nor her perspective but which does afford room for manoeuvre by employing the dominant symbolism itself. If it was not a dangerous game it would not work: physiological integrity is temporarily sacrified to semiology. 'The stakes are high: they involve a real gamble with death' (Firth 1961: 15).

The dominant structures are only represented, possibly adjusted, but not challenged; whether self-help groups or women's therapy groups can, like women's groups in the Third World (Lewis 1971; Jansen 1979), actually develop into alternative political structures ('counter-structures', Turner 1969) is unlikely. It is interesting that these reactions are often 'resolved' through psychiatry: the psychiatrist, relative to other doctors, is more passive, more empathic, more 'feminine'.(35) The inversion can, however, be institutionalized, either as an undesirable identity in relation to dominant norms (Open Door phobic groups) or as valued identities in their own right (the American Big Beautiful Woman (BBW) network). The irony of affirming a stigmatized identity is that this identity remains determined by the dominant culture (Millman 1974).

Structure, Function and Action

'Ritual and the sacred ... bridge the contradiction between norm and action' (Murphy 1972: 243). If, as Bateson claims, 'data from a New Guinea tribe and the superficially very different data of psychiatry can be approached in terms of a single epistemology' (Bateson 1958: vii),(36) a variety of epistemological and explanatory problems still remain. Thus, we have argued that many of these reactions can be interpreted as instrumental (function for) as opposed to the medical and semiological perception of them as reflections of 'stress' (functions of). Where is such instrumentality (which retains its symbolic dimension) located? We can ask the actors: in many instances of overdoses there is a clear pragmatic intention to alter personal relations which is verbally expressed by principals; in anorexia nervosa functionality lies in the therapist's explanations in family therapy; in other instances it can be located in our own, more distanced, method of analysis (Wilson 1967). It is difficult to assign a uniform 'meaning'

to any behavior, particularly one which, once established, is available
for fresh situations. 'What is instrumental for some may be expressive
for others; and moreover, the "etic" categories of instrumentality and
pragmatism may be quite different from the categories of the people
concerned' (Cohen 1985: 307–8). In general such reactions can only
continue when they involve a common assumption that participants
are 'not aware' of any immediate goal, thus allowing society to invoke
the 'mystical sanctions' of biomedicine or the spirit world. It is of
course difficult to distinguish pragmatic from 'unconscious' participation (Cohen 1985: 307), even in such clearly iatrogenic reactions as
the late nineteenth century vogue for multiple possession (Kenny
1981). In the case of work disability symptoms ('compensation
neurosis') the symptoms are now believed to continue longer after
financial settlement than was formerly believed. It is more appropriate
in most instances to talk of identification or 'fit' with models than
'intent' but a complete description of the transformations of partici-
pant experience and reflexive self-perception by cultural typification
lies outside the scope of this paper. Whilst the precipitating event
would appear on our model (Figure 1) to be some type of excessive
'stretch' between the oppositions (37) this may be no more representative of the central symbolic relations than a relative loss of self-
determination.

A related issue is that of 'functioning to' preserve social homeostasis, emphasized by many scholars (Gluckman 1963, Lewis 1966,
1971; see Littlewood 1984a): rituals are taken as adjustment reactions
for a society, allowing repressed impulses and potential rebellions to
express themselves in harmless 'rituals'. As Kapferer (1979: 121)
points out. 'rituals [may] function to paper over and to resolve
conflicts and tensions'. This is often the case, but it is not necessarily
so. To arbitrarily isolate individual institutions as 'functional' is often
little more than seeing how the total field of data under the
observation of the fieldworker must somehow make sense (Leach
1970: 120). Indeed it is only a disguised form of description.(38)
Certainly, if our reactions may be glossed by the observer as 'rituals of
rebellion' (Gluckman 1963) or even parodies, this is not the participants' exegesis: nineteenth century hysterics do not seem to have been
conscious of their part in what De Swaan (1961) calls a 'revolt enacted
as mental disease'.

Rituals can always lead to the development of new tensions. Thus
a common experience of family therapists working with neurotic
patients is that therapy leads to marital separation: we cannot assume
that the illness simply 'masked' an inevitable separation, for therapeutic assumptions and techniques carry their own models and implicit

goals. To what extent can the reactions themselves be regarded as the direct representation of communal tensions rather than some relatively discrete and less central adjustment reaction? One of the problems of defining 'culture-bound syndromes' has been that of distinguishing the two (Littlewood and Lipsedge 1985). Functionalist and structuralist models have the advantage of a hierarchy of causality, allowing us to differentiate 'core' from 'adjustment' patterns. Functionalist explanations assume that rituals are occasioned by social tensions and that they are merely occasions when their tensions find expression, with the assumption that the precipitating cause of the discrete episode is identical with the social themes demonstrated in it (Kapferer 1979: 121).

While we believe that the reactions described articulate the opposition we have called Butterfly/Serpent (B/S), the initial precipitating event may be relatively unconnected with these themes (although articulating the Butterfly's inaccessibility to jural power); however, it is professionally shaped in the cause of medical diagnosis, exegesis and treatment along B/S lines; as the B/S relationship is present both between Butterfly and significant others before the reaction and in the biomedical construction of it, Butterfly's response becomes more truly Butterfly-like.(39) Even after 'resolution' of the individual episode this sensitization continues as a potential vulnerability. 'Aspects of the everyday social experience and world of the actors are made to become explanations, or causes, of the illness event with which they have been brought into contact. Whether these explanations are antecedents to the illness event in the strictly logical sense often assumed in the functionalist argument is open to question' (Kapferer 1979: 121). Nevertheless, if the reactions reflect social oppositions and show that they are soluble without being challenged, they can be said to reinforce them.

The same phenomena are susceptible to a variety of theoretical explanations: reflection of social status or of stress; social catharsis; social homeostasis; cultural loophole; individual catharsis; role reversal; theatre; entertainment; ritual reaffirmation of gender relationships; genesis of sorority or sodality; rite of passage; revolutionary prototype; resolution or expression of symbolic ambiguity; manifestation of lay or professional explanatory model of sickness; not to mention the expression of such basic impulses as distress, parody, play, adventure or revenge. We feel that Western neuroses may be represented simultaneously as all these. Claims to the primacy of a particular theory are ultimately arbitrary and are grounded in the particular perspective of the observer.

Notes

1   We are not concerned here with the question of whether 'culture-bound syndromes' constitute a useful category (Littlewood and Lipsedge 1985). The term is employed to stand for a body of ethnographic material familiar to the reader. Clearly neither these characteristics nor our three-stage mechanism are applicable to all the patterns described under its rubric. But see notes 5 and 8.

2   *Des modèles d'inconduite* (Devereux 1970: 54).

3   Such reactions are flexible and adaptive. Although at times the community may suspect personal advantage, this is not publicly expressed unless the reaction occurs 'excessively' or 'inappropriately'. In Samoa, symptoms which are regarded as the result of possession by angry ancestral spirits are treated by healers; if, however, the authenticity of the possession is doubted, the affected individual is regarded as responsible and may be beaten (Clement 1982). Malay contravention of normal behavior invites social or supernatural retribution unless it is caused by supernatural forces, displacing the attribution of responsibility from the individual (Lee 1981). The observer's own assessment or the 'conscious' use of the reaction is problematic but it cannot be neglected: it frequently follows the local informants' own opinion of a particular event. (cf. Langness 1965, 1967; and Salisbury 1966, 1967). As elsewhere in ethnography we have to distinguish observed behavior, informants' own interpretation and our analytical procedures (Turner 1969). Cohen (1985: 307) suggests that the distinction between instrumental and expressive behavior is irresolvable since it rests upon a definition that is redundant given recent interest in the 'implicit' (Douglas), 'tacit' (Sperber), 'unconscious' (Needham) and 'private' (Firth) meanings in symbolism. We return to the notions of pragmatism versus 'imprisonment' in the main text (page 267).

4   Newman (1964) coined the term to gloss the Gururumba 'being a wild pig' – that is a *domesticated* one, escaped from human society.

5   What of 'culture-bound syndromes' which do not appear to be so clearly 'pragmatic' and which, like *amok*, may end in the death of the principal and others? Whilst *amok* is 'an act of social protest by an individual against his immediate social group", there is no restitution of the individual, and both *amoks* and their society regard the reaction as decidedly undesirable and abnormal (Carr and Tan 1976). The reaction to be considered here is perhaps not completed *amok* but threatened *amok* which does offer a negotiating power. To concentrate only on the *amok* which results in death is similar to concentrating on completed suicide alone in Britain and ignoring the considerable instrumental power of parasuicide, or to consider completed rape in independence from the everyday threat of sexual violence to women.

6   Linblom (1920) described similar patterns among the Akamsa as 'deceitful feminine tactics'.

7   Whilst we are emphasizing the personal and pragmatic aspects of such cultural complexes, they have wide and complex referrants. Tikopia suicide swims are closely related to rather foolhardy canoe trips by young men determined to seek adventures alone, and 'wildman' occurs in a variety of different contexts: Clarke (1973) suggests it, too, may be

'adventure'. *Saka* connotes relations with whites and questions of shrine ownership which are articulated by a woman on 'her only property, her body': *saka* does not 'create solidarity' but maintains the 'current system' (Harris 1957: 1064). The physical symptoms for which 'possession' serves as an explanation may not be easily explained in purely sociogenic terms: thus they may be caused by infectious diseases. Indeed, the 'power' of these sociogenic reactions is generated through an identical mystical imputation to reactions *beyond human control.* Young (1975) has criticized the overly homeostatic theme of Lewis' model of *sar* and points out that all explanatory systems and rituals are flexible and negotiable, that the possession is not available to all those in the particular situation ('Most devotees must be taught how to be possessed': 569–570) and that it is not always adaptive and may even when apparently successful, lead to a 'second-class status'. The reactions may, of course, occur as part of a psychotic process. Wilson (1967), by contrast, criticizes Lewis' model for its failure in homeostasis and its assumption of recognized disadvantage by the female principals and notes that the perceived conflict may be between members of the same sex. Wilson replaces Lewis' psychological model by another one of 'identity definition'. We feel that Lewis adequately demonstrates the social context within which women's action is limited by male jural authority. To anticipate our argument, a girl in Britain may take an overdose in situations of perceived disadvantage *vis à vis* other girls but the reaction still exists within and is made available through the patripotestal biomedical ethos. Lewis' model of *sar* is not one of an overall system of social regulation but of a small 'negotiating space' for the principals.

8 To an extent, the three-stage model is amenable to reactions with a rather different pattern, chronic and undramatic; in Costa Rica, *nervios* (nerves) function as a 'symbolic structuring of a need for acceptance when [the individual] can no longer fulfill his culturally appropriate role' (Low 1981). It is a symbolic 'discontinuity of body perception ... reflecting the individual's relations in the social system'. As culture-bound 'syndromes' are often a misreading of indigenous theories of disease (Littlewood and Lipsedge 1985) it would not be appropriate to assume our model is applicable to all the classic reactions. At the same time it is difficult to agree with Langness' (1976) assertion that they cannot be 'institutionalized'. Certainly many do not seem very adaptive for the individual: *tabanka* in Trinidad is merely the cultural marking of love sickness to show the futility of emotional and economic investment in another (Littlewood 1985). A particular term may be only a theory of disease in one community whilst in another related society it describes a functional pattern of behavior. As Logan (1978) points out, the fact that *susto* is found among children does not invalidate the suggestion that in adults it has a pragmatic role in resolving land disputes, whilst its significance in other places may lie in the pattern of accusation of malevolent causation. The symptoms (symbols) of culture-bound syndromes have multiple referrants. The more the 'middle term' (sickness or ritual episode) is discrete, the more the pattern involves a tripartite 'rite of passage' and the more 'dramatic' the reaction.

9 Most rites 'have transformational and transcendental aspects, i.e., subsuming and resolving contradictions and oppositions apparent at lower levels of organization' (Kapferer 1981: 13). For a summary of symbolic

opposition in social anthropology and its related psychological theories see Needham 1979; Hage and Harary 1983; Littlewood 1984a. An opposition may be antithetical (negation) or complementary. In practice symbolic oppositions are temporary ('calendrical' – Saturnalia, carnival; 'installa-tion' – rites of passage; or 'isolated' – healing rituals, antinomian and millennial movements) or permanent (ethnic minorities, women, homo-sexuals, shamans). Psychological theories of opposition both lay and professional, and cognitive and sociological models, frequently come together in the elaboration of some such notion as 'upside-down', 'catharsis', 'purgation', 'liminality', 'negativism', 'irrationality' and the like. The currency of symbolic opposition obtains from the widespread human tendency to binary classification both cognitive and social; intellectual development and historical or personal change require a movement between (or a superseding of) rigid systems of categorization. These are frequently conceived of as 'inversions'. Psychological and sociological theories of inversion are functionalist, emphasizing the homeostasis of a given system, inversion being either the catharsis of undesirable elements or the passage between two equivalent and existing systems. By contrast, historical models suggest a mode of social develop-ment by which the 'antistructure' develops into a 'counter-structure' (Turner 1974) and offer an active historical role for psychopathology (Lee 1981; Littlewood 1984b).

10 See below and note 17.

11 Ritual 'serves to express the individual's status as a social person in the structural system in which he finds himself for the time being' (Leach 1954: 10–11).

12 Whilst the validity of our three-stage model appears independent of indigenous explanations as to a particular 'personalistic' or 'naturalistic' (Foster 1976) etiology, the choice of mystical imputation of power for female protagonists suggests that in many non-Western societies it offers an important alternative to the exercise of everyday male jural authority (Lewis 1971, Needham 1980); in male reactions like *negi-negi* which involve threatened violence, there seems a greater personal responsibility assumed by the protagonist (see also Spencer 1965), and the possession of the Moroccan man by the *jinn* is associated with 'feminizing' symptoms. On the other hand the female Tikopian swimmer seems to be held as responsible as her male counterpart.

13 Firth (1967: 205) observes that 'for the spirit medium performance to be envisaged as drama rather than ritual, what is required is a detachment of the participant, or at least those who watch, from a personal involvement in the issues portrayed. ... Such detachment allows the tension-pattern of what is being performed to be viewed as non-representational, as a general statement about human values and actions.'

14 Medicine has of course frequently been cited as a successor to religion both theoretically (e.g., Turner 1984) and polemically (Raymond 1982). 'Both the sociology of religion and medical sociology [are] inevitably cultural responses to the problem of theodicy' (Turner 1984: 83–4). Raymond demonstrates a formal similarity between the role of doctor *vis à vis* patient and that of the priest in the Western tradition to the laiety: sin becomes sickness. She agrees with the suggestion that witch hunting was the suppression of women healers by male professionals, an intrigu-ing, if as yet unsubstantiated, notion. Turner suggests the term 'sacred

disease' to distinguish those neuroses which continue to represent male control over womens' bodies.

15 Lewis (1966: 20) suggests that the disappearance of the possession style reaction occurs with increasing 'psychologization', particularly popular knowledge of psychoanalysis. We feel, however, that because biomedicine involves certain moral and causal implications, it contains such a psychology implicitly within itself. While De Swaan (1981) offers the idea that neuroses represent psychologization, an 'internalization' of traditional values which occurs when people are free to do things which are too difficult, too dangerous or too lonesome to do, our suggestion in this paper is that the shift from 'social' to 'psychological' in the development of contemporary neuroses lies primarily in the local exegesis.

16 'Or, a Staff of Aesculapius Gules within a bordure Sable charged with four Butterflies of the Field ... And the Supporters are on either side a Serpent or Langued Gules'. 'Butterfly' and 'Serpent' are interpretive not indexical symbols. We are not suggesting that contemporary patients identify themselves with the protagonists of a classical myth. In the case of the doctors, the identification with the Serpents of Aesculapius may be a little more explicit but they are hardly aware of the B/S relationship.

17 The opposition between Serpent and Butterfly is a *complementary* one (Hage and Harary 1983) (Figure 2: **ab**), distinguished from that between the exaggeration and the restitution in our three-stage model (Figure 2: **db**) which is an *anticontraduality* (conversion plus negation). Our schema is derived from structural anthropology; the use of such models in literate and 'historical' societies (in contravention of Lévi-Strauss' dictum that they are only applicable to small-scale 'tribal societies') is common in Women's Anthropology and has been vigorously defended by others (notably Leach 1983). The structural model was principally derived to elucidate the myth, 'a sacred tale about past events which is used to justify social action in the present' (Leach 1983: 8). the Butterfly/Serpent corpus offers us such a myth. (If, as Lévi-Strauss proposes, the purpose of myth is to provide a logical model capable of 'overcoming' a contradiction (1963:229), then our model offers us a solution' to: (a) Men are dominant, but (b) All humans control their destinies.) As we have seen, the legitimating functions of religion have been replaced by those of science. (See Cohen 1985 for a similar consideration of the role of 'symbolism' in industrial societies.) The notion that contrast is inherent in all systems of symbolic classification is not of course one found only in the Lévi-Straussian tradition although it finds there its fullest flowering (Littlewood 1984a). The doctor/patient or husband/wife relationships are not primarily and autonomous. As La Fontaine (1981) points out, notions of paternity or the family 'are not the building blocks of society but products of its overall organization'. The Nature/Culture distinction, although common in a variety of societies is not universal (Jordanova 1980); societies expropriate their own social area from the raw material of their environment which they transform. 'Nature' is itself a far from neutral term.

18 The scope this allowed for considerable, if ultimately limited, power in the household is superbly described by Marcel Proust in the person of Aunt Leonie (Proust 1958). Proust himself, like Florence Nightingale (Strachey 1981), was aware how the same model could offer a non-dominant individual extensive and sophisticated scope for adjusting social relationships.

19 Women's religious experience continues to be equated with individual 'hysteria' and attributed to 'sexual frustration' (e.g. Moller 1971).

20 She improved equally dramatically in the course of four therapy sessions which involved reading to her an earlier draft of this paper! We would not however like to make any claims for the Butterfly/Serpent model offering an immediately accessible form of cognitive therapy.

21 Thus *Working Woman*, a glossy magazine aimed at would-be professional women in Britain, offers the following maxims: 'Forswear sex in the office' and 'Use sex all you can', 'Don't be feminine' and 'Be feminine' (December 1984).

22 It may be relevant that the polite term for a prostitute (a woman who most clearly separately rates passive sexuality from active childbearing) is a 'model'.

23 There are some suggestions that anorexic girls have been subject to paternal incest. Warner (1983: Ch. 7) suggests that 'androgeneity' may serve as an avoidance of incest with the father (as well as offering a challenge to men). It has been suggested that anorexics have previously been tomboys.

24 'By this time I was eating steadily, doggedly, stubbornly, anything I could get. The war between myself and my mother was on in earnest: the disputed territory was my body. ... I swelled visibly, relentlessly before her very eyes. I rose like dough, my body advanced inch by inch towards her across the dining room table, in this at least I was undefeated ... It was a sort of fashion show, in reverse' (Millman 1980). Obesity is often described by Millman's informants as 'unconscious stealing', an 'irrational' loss of control and rebellion.

25 'Men look at women. Women watch themselves being looked at. This determines not only most relations between men and women but also the relation of women to themselves. The surveyor of woman in herself is male' (Berger 1971: 47).

26 Lacan (1977) has of course suggested that the 'phallus' represents not just male sexuality but the induction of every child into the dominant cultural language of male power.

27 See notes 9, 17. There may be some class differences here: the middle-class woman faces a greater ambiguity over sex roles, and inverts the norm more clearly (anorexia nervosa) than the working-class woman (who is more likely to take an overdose, an exaggeration of the female role). Similarly the middle-class male faces a greater ambiguity over sex roles and inverts the norm more clearly (exhibitionism) than the working-class man (who in our opinion seems more likely to engage in siege behavior, an exaggeration of the male role).

28 Cf. French *remue meninges*.

29 Chronic pain syndrome have been described as strategies which adjust family relations similar to systems theory models of agoraphobia and anorexia nervosa (Katon et al. 1983) but they are less 'discrete' patterns (Deighton and Nicol 1985).

30 'Munchausen syndrome by proxy' certainly employs the Butterfly/Serpent model. Out of 47 mothers who produced medical symptoms in their children, 17 were nurses and 4 others were health workers (Meadow 1984); only in this pattern can the principal obtain pragmatic ends by remaining on the Serpent side of the equation:

Doctor – – – – Parent
_____
Patient

31 See note 2. Related patterns of behavior may be more obviously signals of distress but they often employ highly individual symbols: thus when the crime novelist Agatha Christie wandered from home in a dissociative episode, she booked into a hotel in a bourgeois spa town under her husband's mistress' name.

32 Although Buglass found their personalities were essentially the same as controls (Buglass et al. 1977). Whilst Kandel (1983) suggests agoraphobia is 'derived' from a 'biological' panic attack, it cannot be taken as an autonomous 'generalization' of an independent biological event for only a proportion of people with panic attacks develop agoraphobia, and conversely there are more agoraphobics than patients with anxiety neurosis; panic attacks occur in a variety of settings, and in those cases which do progress to agoraphobia, the cultural meanings conduce to codification of the pattern. An agoraphobic who has starved to death through inability to go shopping has yet to be described in literature: if the reaction was solely biogenic we would expect to find some instances.

33 In other words in situations where the Serpent is threatened with becoming a Butterfly. The male homosexual who until recently was inevitably classed in a 'female' position by a rigorously binary system (Littlewood 1984a) thus had a 'feminine attitude' to body imagery (Millman 1974), and probably greater access to the women's culture-bound reactions (Wilson 1967).

34 There is no common English expression to gloss this idea. We might refer to the Melanesian technique of offering gifts or similar self-denial or self-punishment in order to cause shame, sympathy or contrition in those who have wronged one (Epstein 1984). Perhaps 'turning the other cheek' or even *satyagraha*.

35 Whilst there appears in all the reactions, except overdose, a tacit agreement between principal, her immediate social group and the doctor that a 'disease' is involved, doctors may privately invoke a different explanatory model. Earlier drafts of this paper were read to groups of general practitioners in Britain who afterwards 'privately' commented that psychiatrists were too 'soft' and were glad to find one who realized that patients were really 'playing about'. Shifts in the definition of a reaction are facilitated through the changes in the meaning assigned to a behavior by doctors and associates by transformations of context, identities and symbols (Kapferer 1981). Thus the husband of an agoraphobic patient passed from sympathy, through anger and half-hearted threats of separation to 'ignoring' the symptoms: at this point, the previously reluctant wife agreed to see the doctor. The 'frame' (Kapferer 1979) shifts from one of close kin and associates to one including the doctor. Taking our reactions, it appears that the more 'public' it is, the more short-lived and the more it conforms to our small-scale society prototype. To an extent however, all are 'public': agoraphobia is by its very nature relatively private – but it is not an act which goes on in private, but a relationship to the public domain.

36 Whilst Bateson certainly followed his own prescription, the categories he derived from the *naven* ceremony (and which bear a certain thematic

similarity to our three-stage model) were considerably more context-independent than ours. We have attempted 'the reshaping of categories ... so that they reach beyond the contexts in which they originally arose and took their meaning so as to locate affinities and match differences' (Geertz 1984).

37 Bateson's (1972: 109) complementary schismogenesis – an ever increasing role differentiation and social distance. Too wide a split is prevented by the biomedical system which at a superordinate level differentiates between human and nature and thus prevents the Butterfly disappearing out of human society altogether; a degenerative causal loop restores complementarity (cf. Figure 1).

38 This is not the place for a detailed critique of functionalism and its Panglossian distinction of goals from tools. Clearly the models used by functionalists in relation to the 'culture-bound syndromes' are closer to Durkheim ('The function of a social fact ought always to be sought in its relation to some social end' (Durkheim 1938: 19)) than to Malinowski. The pragmatic motives of individual actors when stated are of course more likely to be Malinowskian (individual need-centred) than Durkheimian. If we have a shift from collective calendrical ritual to individual problem-orientated ritual (as Loudon 1959), the very notion of functionality tends to shift from the Durkheimian to the Malinowskian, from social to individual needs, from social theory to psychological theory and perhaps from status to role, from obligation to contract. Thus not for the first time data determines its own theoretical explicandum.

39 What the psychotherapists, reversing the causal link, term 'transference'. Giddens (1985) has extensively criticized the whole development of sociological theory for exaggerating 'the degree to which normative obligations are "internalized" by the members of societies'; who 'do the best they can with the parts prepared for them'; structuralism and functionalism alike discount agents' reasons for acting and look for the origin of the activities in 'phenomena of which these agents are ignorant'. Whilst his own theory of 'structuration' attempts to cut across the distinction between structure (macro) and action (micro), the instances he gives are unconvincing. The literature on patients' accounts of the experience of neurosis is vast; whether this will prove to be useful in determining pragmatic or other motivations is uncertain, for such accounts, whether in the medical or psychodynamic traditions, are part of a constraining professional situation which constructs and authenticates the reaction in terms of available cultural typifications at the same time as it 'resolves' it. Kapferer's employment of G.H. Mead's symbolic interactionism to delineate the construction, negation and reconstruction of the self may provide a useful approach. Whilst data will probably have to be derived in a 'neutral', fieldwork rather than in the clinical context, it is the clinical setting and the academic research it 'inspires' (such as the papers we have extensively used) which together constitute the reactions.

14 From Demonic Possession to Multiple Personality – and Back Again: The Contexts of Consciousness and Pathology*

entia non sunt multiplicanda praeter necessitatem ...

Provost, colleagues, ladies and gentlemen.

To start with, an epigraph from Nietzsche (not I fear an altogether appropriate quotation but the only one immediately coming to mind which relates the question of spiritual experience to that of academic chairs); it is from a rather enigmatic letter written soon after the onset of his paranoid dementia:

> Dear Herr Professor [he writes to a colleague] – When it comes to it, I too would very much prefer a professorial chair in Basle to being God. But I did not dare to claim to go as far in my private egoism as to refrain from the creation of the world ...

Nietzsche was of course offered his first chair before he had finished an undergraduate degree, and his egoism is perhaps justified. Perhaps not. It depends on what we do when we create our worlds.

There are inaugural lectures which evoke a sort of biographical trajectory, emphasising the inevitable accumulation of knowledge, the accomplished solution to a vexing problem, an exemplarly narrative which confirms the University in the wisdom of its promotion. And then there are those perhaps more puzzled about 'whatever next?', tentative, less certain and decidedly less convinced. I am – of course – going to follow this second approach, one which I think makes sense if I am going to demonstrate any adventures to be shared by my two cultures, psychiatry and social anthropology.

---

*Inaugural Lecture delivered at University College, London, 1994.

Our issue, however, is an old one. How is it that certain instances of what psychiatrists term 'psychopathology' seem to be characteristic of a particular society, to somehow represent its dilemmas? And what is it to say that an individual illness 'represents' social patterns? If we avoid the question of biology, then the question is not too illusive: it is simply one of tracing historically a particular cultural institution or *mentalite*. If we do take biology into account, as I propose, then we are in the midst of all sorts of dreadful problems, from out of which a short lecture will hardly rescue us unscathed: problems of reconciling form and content, cause and action, explanation and narrative.

I shall argue that psychiatry and anthropology start, as it were, from different ends of the problem; with rather different assumptions and procedures. And that if they do not exactly meet at some happy point, they nevertheless have some type of ironical relationship. Multiple personality will be my procedure, as well as my subject.

That a particular type of personal suffering is characteristic of a society is often maintained by its own members. In 1734, the physician George Cheyne characterised *melancholy* as 'the English malady'. In the next century *American nervousness* was similarly identified: 'the chief and primary cause of the rapid increase of nervousness is modern civilisation, which is distinguished from the ancient by these five characteristics: steam-power, the periodical press, the telegraph, the sciences and the mental activity of women'.(1) As I shall suggest, these five were identified perhaps not altogether inaccurately: mechanised labour, rapid publicity, new communication technologies, scientific epistemology, and ... the mental activity of women.

Nor are anthropologists themselves altogether immune from pronouncing one or other social drama as the representation of a society's essential dilemmas. To quote a recent example: 'the current popularity of multiple personality is the product of the disorder of our times'.(2)

The diagnosis of *double consciousness* – in which two different personalities coexist in association with a single physical body – became fashionable in France and America at the end of last century. It collected together in a single category a multitude of other phenomena: fugue and trance states, spirit mediumship and demonic possession, dreams and visions, telepathy and somnambulism, crystal-ball gazing and other forms of divination, the automatism of the urban crowd, the conscript and the criminal, religious conversion and folk panics; and, most centrally, hysteria and hypnotism. Hypnotists had discovered that their subjects could be placed in a state akin to sleep and then induced to perform actions of which they had no memory when they later 'awoke'. Under the influence of two French neurologists, Jean-Martin Charcot and Pierre Janet, the hypnotic state was elided with *hysteria*, a protean term dating from the Greeks which by the late nineteenth century described a number of phasic phenomena: the patient, usually young and female, returning at intervals to her normal state, apparently ignorant of the episode. Symptoms included amnesia, blindness, hallucinations, excited and inappropriate behaviour, together with fits and paralyses which did not conform with anatomical knowledge but rather with popular conceptions of what it was to be amnesic or paralysed. As Charcot put it, the patient 'suffered from ideas'.

Was she then to be considered morally responsible for her actions? Charcot called attention to the *aboulia* – the loss of will – which characterised all these patterns; though the symptoms might seem to be purposeful in hiding or forgetting unpleasant experiences, the patient could not be held fully accountable. For her consciousness was somehow 'dissociated', to use Janet's term,(3) and she seemed blandly indifferent or even unaware of the impact of her symptoms upon others.

It was recognised that double consciousness, the most dramatic form of hysteria, could emerge either spontaneously or in the course of hypnotic treatment for nervous complaints. The patients were characteristically young women who seemed to alternate between two states: the first recalling the original personality as recognised by her family, sick, inhibited and quiet, often a prim martyr who complained of being 'possessed by something'. By contrast her second state was flirtatious and irresponsible. Characteristically there was one-way amnesia, the second 'personality' being aware of the first. A third and subsequent personality might then emerge which had variable knowledge of the others. With practice the experienced physician could summon or dismiss these through hypnosis or simply by firmly instructing the patient. In what is perhaps the classic monograph, *The Dissociation of a Personality*, the American neuropsychiatrist Morton Prince pursues 'the real Miss Beauchamp', eliciting the help of one personality against another, intriguing, making and breaking pacts with them, yet constantly deceived by the emergence of new personalities and half personalities or the elision of the existing ones. He attempts to fuse or else 'kill off' some personalities. They protest. In their struggle, both personalities and doctor frequently evoke the idiom of demonic possession, Dr. Prince threatening to send the lesser personalities 'back where they came from'. His gripping reports on the progress of the case in medical conferences become well known, and one of Miss B's personalities herself develops a professional interest in clinical psychology. The personality Prince eventually identifies as 'the real Miss B' reads his final manuscript before publication, marries one of his colleagues, and her published case-history is soon made into a popular play.

To see, as we might now do, a hundred years later, Dr. Prince as blithely avoiding his patient's conflicting aspirations, concretising her possible identities as fascinating serial phenomena, with Miss B herself continually outwitting her male physician, leading him on, fighting under the guise of aboulia with the weapons at her disposal, is tempting, but this is to impose our own commonsense assumptions of a unitary self somewhere 'behind' all the personalities. Psychiatric interpretation of multiple consciousness assumed (as it still does) that in the general run of things each human body has one single, bounded and volitional self, with a characteristic and enduring identity of personal sentiments, abilities and memories, which are experienced and perceived as hanging together.(4) But this hanging together becomes unstuck in dreams and day-dreams, or in the usual processes of forgetting and inattention, such that chunks of past experience cannot necessarily be recalled simultaneously. And indeed under appropriate conditions the split-off fragments might be so extensive as to actually constitute a parallel personality. It was uncertain how much this secondary personality should be seen as simply split off from some integral unitary consciousness, or whether it should be regarded as clusters of already existing subpersonalities which under-lay the single conscious self of everyday life. In either case, the appearance of secondary personalities was generally taken as a diminution in 'nervous energy' occasioned by hereditary vulnerability and various traumata, including railway accidents, unpleasant news, sexual violence and conflicting moral demands.

Did this nervous energy itself have a physical existence in the newly discovered cells of the brain?(5) In the 1890s French neurologists were still attempting to transfer hysterical symptoms and even personalities from one patient to another by means of powerful magnets or telepathy, but it became increasingly accepted that magnetism and nervous energy were just analogies for something rather less concrete.

This neuropsychological model of hysteria owed much to the Catholic notion of the pathogenic secret in which purgation of guilt for secret crimes, incest or infanticide, resulted in physical and spiritual healing. For Protestants, the 'cure of souls', as their pastors termed it, provided an increasingly secular alternative, confession being reframed as a cathartic recall to awareness of the guilty act. Going further in the same direction, the neurologists of the French Second Republic now claimed that they had uncovered the clinical underpinnings of clerical superstition and popular credulity: the guilty secret life of the gambler, criminal and eccentric now being recognised as the hidden secondary personality. Romantic and Symbolist literature too were preoccupied by this notion of a shadow or double (Hoffman, Goethe, Hogg, Poe, Dostoyevsky, Stevenson, Wilde), a shadow now increasingly less some daemonic familiar or changeling than a deeper and amoral persistence in the human mind of an earlier evolutionary epoche.

Between 1900 and 1910 double consciousness suddenly disappeared from the medical literature. The diagnosis had unified what we might now distinguish as biological and psychological interests; the two then diverged, to come close again only in the cognitive science of the 1980s. Charcot's successors concentrated research on those conditions which presumed an underlying biological disease; they hinted that his working-class patients had deliberately faked double consciousness, and that they had seduced his medical students physically and mentally. Leading in the opposite direction, Freud's psychoanalysis continued to emphasise the meaning for the patient of the symptoms: a psychology in which our lower instincts and appetites sought to translate themselves into higher forms. The 'self' which psychoanalysis elaborated was now one less unified and enduring, but rather a dynamic system of psychological processes. That it could compete with other selves of the same order, each bearing proper names and associated with the same body, became increasingly implausible. Psychoanalytical emphasis on therapeutic integration of the moral self seems to have avoided any proliferation of new personalities in the course of treatment.

II

The academic consensus on the psychophysiology of spirit possession and multiple personality still recalls that elaborated in the 1890s: people have the ability to dissociate their mental processes and do so the whole time – through changing moods, selective attention and putting unpleasant issues 'out of mind', through fantasy and dreaming. And that some of these private experiences are not easily remembered, because they are hardly significant enough to remark, because memories of them have faded, or else because they are unpleasant or painful in some way. Immediate awareness fluctuates, a function of what we recognise as intended perception; the quality of our will being variable, dependent on our immediate interests and customary procedures: you can eat an apple whilst riding your bicycle but you are not equally 'in' each activity at any one moment, nor are you generally aware of switching from one to the other deliberately for your stream of awareness appears a seamless web. To be conscious is to focus attention on something, bestowing reality on perception: a neo-cortical disposition selected in evolution which enables the organism to engage flexibly with different situations. And which process we take as the consequence of our willed decisions. Its converse, our ability to dissociate, is adaptive when we need to switch attention, or avoid physical pain or terrifying and conflictual situations. Dissociation is thus the necessary flip side of human consciousness; it allows us a private system of representation and self-monitoring; it allows anticipation, planning, creative imagination, recognition of another's motives and identification with them, acting and deceit: the basis for our engaging in the social world. Under certain conditions such as hypnosis, or particular types of sensory patterning, hyperventilation or the ingestion of psychoactive substances, dissociation can be facilitated, to daydream or meditate, or to enter another world. These dissociative experiences may, like religious conversion or artistic inspiration, be recognised as external to our given cultural schema of a bounded self as the usual locus of our experience and volition.(6) Their products may cease to be recognised as our own processes, to become personified as human-like other entities.

A convergence has often been noted between the psychoanalytical schema (ego, id and super-ego processes) and certain West African psychologies (the individual having 'agencies' derived from a unique soul, from nature, and from their lineage). These elements, psychoanalytic or African, are not generally experienced or identified as separate centres of awareness for, by and large, our everyday 'self' does seem fairly unitary, with the development in early life of an internally consistent awareness as the locus of our biography: a self which is recognised by others as an embodied entity continuing through time, and morally accountable for its past actions: a centre of narrative gravity, as Daniel Dennett puts it. Both psychoanalytic and West African schemata are accounts which reconcile our understanding that we are indeed such unique self-aware and volitional individuals yet we share something of our identity with other animals and with our culture. In circumstances where this everyday identity does not hang together in the expected way, when our taken-for-granted boundary between action and contingency is radically disrupted by dispute, disaster or sickness, we may objectivise such available distinctions, possibly to give the elements a greater degree of *personified* autonomy. And in which the centrality of our will, our directing self, disappears (*aboulia*). To caricature it in the manner of The Numskulls of the *Beano* comic magazine: your affect gets the upper hand of your cognition; your id decides to overwhelm your super-ego; your bad angel gets the better of your good angel. Or the other way round. Whatever.

There are however less verbalised schemata for a multiplex self: not just our formal psychologies then, but experiences such as pregnancy – in particular – and also lactation, menstruation, masturbation, coitus, play, violence, feeding, excretion, sleeping and dreaming. All of which may at times challenge the experience of our self as some bounded and autonomous entity.

Our experience as an enduring 'self' is multifaceted in other ways. We generally 'occupy' a variety of roles, titles, functions, powers, offices and statuses, without these obscuring some continuing personal identity. We are not distinct individuals in each, and usually these identities do not conflict too much with each other, yet we adopt a different comportment and social character in each, context-dependent yet drawn from and representing an enduring individual. Against the nineteenth century neurologists, we might argue that alternative selves (7) are not simply an existing part of our consciousness which is then split off, but rather new potentials, ambitions, strategems, conventionalised images, symbolisations of moral values, perversities and imagined identities, which we try on to see how they fit: whether we aspire to adopt them permanently, or just in game-playing masquerade or private fantasy.

III

In the late 1970s, following public concern about the widespread sexual abuse of female children, cases of multiple personality began to emerge again in the United States. As before, questions of authenticity and medical suggestion were immediately raised. The psychiatrist whose patient had become well known through the film *The Three Faces of Eve* argued that spontaneous multiple personality was rare. After the film made him famous he was besieged by *multiples*, as individuals with multiple personality were now being called: of the thousands of patients he saw in the thirty years after Eve, only one he regarded as genuine, that is spontaneous and prior to medical intervention.

MPD (multiple personality disorder) differed from nineteenth century double consciousness in the sheer number of personalities who now appeared. Sybil, the first publicised case attributed to repressed memories of incestuous abuse, developed sixteen personalities.[8] Eve, who had retired from public view presumed cured, now returned with twenty-two personalities, to chair the recently formed International Society For the Study of Multiple Personality. A group of increasingly vocal activists, Speaking For Our Selves, criticised doubting doctors, but sympathetic psychiatrists provided public legitimation with a supportive new journal called *Dissociation*. Some psychiatrists now maintain that MPD can be identified in ten percent of our patients whilst popular self-help manuals argue that more than half of the female American population has been sexually abused.[9]

Over a hundred different secondary personalities (*alters*) associated with the same physical body have been identified – and here there is a problem for the anthropologist as well as for the biologist – many with consistent differences in handedness, facial expression, cerebral bloodflow and E.E.G., up to 60 points difference in IQ scores, with their own characteristic visual abilities, handwriting, vocabulary, speech patterns and immunological sensitivities. They have different memories, personal and family histories, different ages, genders and ethnicity. Compared with their nineteenth century predecessors, not only do larger numbers of personalities emerge from a single body but these seem generally more aware of each other, coming and going relatively freely outside the clinical sessions.

Medical treatment of the new epidemic initially recalled that of last century: hypnosis and vigorous persuasion to discharge the pathogenic secret and reintegrate the alters with the original self. As before, the secondary personalities objected to being killed off. But now, with the appearance of the multiple activists on television shows, and through well publicised American court defences that the personality in the dock was not the same one who had committed the crime (the defendant when giving evidence being sworn in separately under their different personalities), the alters have gained a public voice and demand their legal entitlement to life. They are now accommodated not exorcised; killing them off is regarded by the multiple movement as murder, as the concealment of one crime by yet another. The preferred therapy is to keep all the personalities in play, to encourage 'mutual awareness and communication' between them in what has increasingly come to resemble family therapy. Hypnotherapists encourage the 'survivor' to meet and comfort their abused earlier self, or to 'come out' only in dreamtime. Drama therapists enable each individual in their group to take on and role-play one of the various personalities elicited from a single member.

In the 1890s a few American doctors sympathetic to Spiritualism had sometimes accepted secondary personalities as visiting benign spirits. This interpretation too has returned but now in a demonic variant. Sexual abuse of children in both Britain and America has been linked with Satanic cannibalism and child sacrifice, an interpretation encouraged among teachers and social workers by charismatic Christian networks which practise exorcism and generally favour a diabolical interpretation of human malevolence.(10) One Harvard University psychiatric clinic argues that the sexual abuse is carried out not by the child's family but by extraterrestrials who abduct and then return the victim. The multiple selves are variously taken as the possessing aliens themselves or their hybrid children, as the psychological representation or psychic reincarnation of the human perpetrator, as living or deceased family members, as new attempts at self-healing, or as the lost self of an abusive childhood. Christian psychiatrists describe them as incubi, as congealed ancestral vices or as the vengeful spirits of aborted foetuses.

The spontaneous occurrence of MPD has been challenged. Legal suits by adults against their parents for having sexually abused them as children have been met by counter-claims against the self-interested doctors for inducing a 'false memory syndrome' in distressed individuals who are persuaded to recall non-existent sexual abuse, backed up by 'survivors' manuals' and the widespread publicity on MPD. Individual damages against the parent for sexual abuse have been of the order of up to $5 million. Plus lawyers' and experts' fees. The question of induction through mass publicity or through the particular therapies used (hypnosis, guided imagery, body massage) is countered with the argument that genuine MPD is the psychological consequence of hidden trauma: its public recognition now simply enables multiples to seek professional support or to recognise the condition in themselves.

IV

Nineteenth century double consciousness and twentieth-century MPD have sufficient resemblance to each other to justify our comparing them under the common rubric of 'multiple personality'. Contemporary activists regard both manifestations as the same pattern, and they cite the Victorian literature. Whether we read the pattern as a fashionable idiom of distress, as a psychological defence, as a creative fantasy, whether we grant it some existence as a distinct psychophysiological state, its local context and meanings are significant. Can either wave be related to a coherent group of professional interests; or else to some more diffuse susceptibility of the times – 'ideas in the air' as Dostoyevsky put it? We can certainly recognise in both epidemics a committed network of experts who accept the phenomenon as a legitimate matter of interest, diagnosing it where others fail, and who are identified with it through newspaper articles, publicised case histories and, in the second wave, cinema dramatisations and television shows.

Expert groups maintain their authority through the necessity of their therapeutic activities, proposing an individual's illness as emblematic of the current preoccupations, 'the national disease', 'the sickness of our age', 'our number one mental health problem': a prototype to which other ills are referred or into which they are subsumed. (Another vexed contemporary instance is post-traumatic stress disorder.) It is not too difficult to devise neat homologies between individual and society, the experiencing self now offering a microcosm of wider shared dilemmas, the dissociation of the individual now standing for the dis-sociation of the collectivity.(11) It is less easy to show how such models plausibly motivate personal experiences. That the self is a mirror of society is itself a particular psychology.

In the United States, in the nineteenth century as much as now, personal failure requires less some sense of bad luck than of competitive disadvantage, with recourse to the sort of 'positive' transformation, eliding religious conversion, self-knowledge and managerial presentation, exemplified by Dale Carnegie or Vincent Pearle. The United States has always taken itself as the site of strategic self-fashioning, by which diverse immigrant groups realise themselves as Americans as they move to higher status jobs, improve their education, as they change residence, neighbourhood, profession, friends, spouses, political affiliation, even their name and religion. Identity is to be achieved in the very process of transformation, in fulfilling some inherent human potential, both as the normative expectation of what it is to be genuinely American and as a practical possibility; articulated (particularly for men) in popular manuals of self-help and entrepreneurial psychology, for women through remodelling their bodies by dieting and plastic surgery: realising one's 'personality' (12) in the marketing of it, articulated through a politico-therapeutic language of communication, growth, realisation and sincerity. Psychology is *the* American cultural idiom, one which argues for individualism and self-sufficiency, for personal choice and instrumental action, for practically attaining self-knowledge. An autonomy which is always threatened by government or others. What might be regarded elsewhere as an extreme response to current dissatisfaction with personal circumstances – voluntarily disappearing from one's neighbourhood and family to emerge elsewhere with a new name and a new identity – is facilitated by a publishing house which has produced over thirty manuals to teach something British psychiatrists would recognise as a hysterical fugue.

I am aware that this is a European image of the United States which, since Trollope and Toqueville, has seen America as anomic and neotenic, its emphasis on personal self-transformation as an avoidance of the recognition of class conflict, its public institutions sustained by periodic moral panics, its citizens unable to agree on what constitutes reality without recourse to legal or medical expertise. Yet America's 'obsession with self-awareness' (as Christopher Lasch calls it) is well recognised by its own cultural critics. Self-realisation through pulling on one's bootstraps has always been central to what it is to be an American – from the frontier regeneration of the Great Awakening and its transformation of self and nature, to Transcendentalism and managerialism: a quest for 'sincerity', for achieved rather than ascribed status, a fundamentally optimistic view that time and space still lie unlimited before us.

Upward social mobility and perfectionism are hardly limited to America, and it is easy to identify in any society a concern with too rapid social transformations, with the breakdown of family life and traditional personal ties (as did the European pessimism of Herder, Gissing, Pater and Musil) but it has seemed integral to the American way of life to regard incompleteness as the appropriate state of affairs.

In any period of perceived change, society and self may each be seen as fragmented or double, estranged from the past to face an uncertain future. If George Gissing bemoaned the nineteenth century as 'decades of sexual anarchy ... with the laws governing human identity, friendships and sexual behaviour breaking down', now our 'radical democratisation of the personal' (Anthony Giddens' expression), our fragmented and commodified performance of alternative selves, may be argued to be especially part of the late modern condition. With the decline of Calvinist moral imperatives, individualism has become, as T.J. Lears puts it, 'weightless and unreal'. In the United States the brief resurgence of Protestant fundamentalism in the 1980s required public figures to declare that they had been 'born again': recalling the earlier fate of double consciousness, this demand for testimonies of spontaneity has collapsed in religious scandals and cynical accusations; we might wonder if the demand for 'born again' experiences should be taken as a response to the perceived fragmentation of identity (as argued by its protagonists) or simply as a manifestation of it.

One might argue a shift in the contemporary self, perhaps less a dissociation so much as a relocation, the external physical frontiers now becoming congested and foreshortened so that our bodies turn in on themselves, self-sufficient through diatetics and 'body consciousness'. We are both lesser than we thought, as simply elements in a natural world which is indifferent to human interests; and greater, in that we now recognise this world is refracted through our own cognitions. Multiple personality was once attributed to the introduction of the photograph, the phonograph, the telephone and the X-ray.(13) Where then did the new telephone conversation take place? In Denver at one end of the line? In New York at the other? At a point on the wire half-way between each city? We might argue that it occurred in emergent *cyberspace* – as we now term it: in the virtual architecture of electrically, now electronically, sustained memory which we enter through our personal computer, in interactive television (and more recently virtual reality), in electronic mail, Internet, multidimensional graphic user interfaces and hyper-text, in 'personality' profiles generated by our credit card purchases, in Minitel and teledildonics: a global technology which questions our customary ideas of individual work, property and ownership, and which radically resituates our taken-for-granted physical experience in a post-industrial and post-corporeal global space. As do the 'transferable' elements of our human body shop – sperm, egg, embryo and organ banks, fertility drugs and multiple births, cerebral implants of foetal tissue, electronic prostheses and gene splicing.(14) For women these are particularly significant in the current debate on foetal personhood – the obvious schema for two beings housed in one body.

Like the medieval mechanical clock, the computer has become our 'defining technology', a model for the self now seen through an idiom of inputs and outputs, the body as hardware, consciousness as software: yet not just a convenient metaphor, for the computer circuit actually embodies rather than merely represents symbolic logic in a virtual space which in each generation of computers seeks to grow ever larger relative to the physical space of its linear circuits and available telephone bandwidth. Cyberpunk literature, like the not dissimilar 'hard AI' and Artificial Life arguments, offers more than a fantasied model of the self: rather a model for a virtual self which now has no inevitable locus in the physiological body. Human minds have become serial virtual machines implemented on parallel hardware, and MPD just a different program run on this same hardware. To quote the American computer scientists: 'Cyberspace becomes another venue for consciousness itself ... To the body in cyberspace we are the mind. By a strange reversal of our cultural expectations, however, it is the body in cyberspace that is immortal, while the animating soul, housed in a body outside cyberspace, faces mortality'.(15)

I do not want to make too much of this: dedicated on-line computers and virtual reality are just the latest reshaping of embodied individual agency in an historical progression that includes our use of tools, speech, clothing, residence, figurative representation, silent reading, autobiography, linear perspective, the novel and pornography, and mechanised transport. The very history of human technology. But if the problem for nineteenth century philosophers lay in the disintegration of the self, current interest lies in the opposite – in the apparent synthesis of our subpersonal elements; now it is not altered states of consciousness that are problematic but our illusive experience of a unitary consciousness itself. The notion of a multiplex self as a flexible network is available not just in theoretical psychology (Martingdale's state-specific memory) and neuro-philosophy (Sperry, Fodor, Gardner, Dennett, Edelman), but in those more accessible 'human potential therapies' which emphasise the realisation of all our 'selves' recognised under an appropriate multiplicity of names: as our internalised parents or children, as our underdogs, types, archetypes, potentials, personalities, sub-personalities, voices, selves, sub-selves, possible selves, ego states, images, imagos, doubles, clusters, roles, parts, scripts, actors, figures, prototypes, polarities, schemas and sub-systems.

Akin to the manuals of self-perfectioning and managerial efficiency, such psychological schemata employ not just a popularised psychoanalytical idiom of untapped levels of consciousness (as in est and Scientology) but a system of potential selves which are to be serially accessed, in which transformations of our identity have fruitful managerial implications; in which alternative selves are not seen as transitory masks nor imaginary fantasies but rather as the realisation of something authentic, of which we rest unfulfilled until therapeutically liberated, purged of our atavistic memories and lower evolutionary stages, liberated from our naive or hypocritical obligations and ineffective self-marketing; less a Puritan struggle towards arduous refashioning than the freedom for a potential which is already there to assume its natural place. The decisive therapeutic step in concretising these potentials into MPD seems to have been in personalising them with a proper name. Multiple personality is a phenomenon produced in certain expert relationships; and now commodified in a medico-legal marketplace which displaces the sources of affliction beyond a unitary self which feels constricted as it seeks to reappropriate and possess its own 'personal space'.(16)

V

What might constitute the medical reality of multiple personality? Presumably that it should be independent of willed intention, and that it can be objectively demonstrated as a distinct psychological and physical state independent of any local meaning or therapeutic intervention. As with certain other contemporary syndromes (post-traumatic stress disorder, myalgic encephalomyelitis, Gulf War syndrome, total allergy syndrome), the medical debate on multiple personality mobilises supporters and opponents who argue for its validity or otherwise.

Both protagonists and critics agree an essential dualism: either it happens to you or else you do it. Each 'it' is a rather different sort of thing: disease process (or intruding spirit) versus duplicitous masquerade. In a number of recent publications I have argued for a rather different dualism, a conventional dualism. On the one hand we can understand ourselves and the world as a consequence of cause and effect processes, generally independent of, but potentially accessible to, human awareness – the naturalistic mode of thought. (The Faculty of Clinical Sciences.) Yet we can understand the same matters personal-istically – as the motivated actions of agents employing such charac-teristically human attributes as intention, anticipation, strategy, representation, identification, imitation and deceit. (The Faculty of Arts.) And whilst we conventionally allocate one or other area of interest to the naturalistic or the personalistic, even objectifying these ways of thinking as separate domains (nature: culture:: body: mind), we can apply either mode to any phenomenon. The self may be a machine, the natural world may be animate. Psychiatric considera-tions of such phenomena as parasuicide (a symptom of depressive illness? or the attempt to die?) or myalgic encephalomyelitis (disease process? malingering?), like medico-legal debates on criminal respon-sibility (mad? bad?), continually slip between one and the other, for only one mode can be correct at any one time (17). Neither can be demonstrated as completely true, nor false; we always live with the two options.

Psychoanalysis attempted to reconcile this antinomy (which in this form derives of course from Kant) through a psychology which tried to show how human agency emerges dynamically from naturalistic sub-personal structures. Its notion of fantasy (not empirically true, yet not exactly fabricated) elided the duality. Psychoanalysis has now abandoned the naturalistic altogether; and it is from its newer idioms of maturity, self-actualisation, growth and so on that the 'human potential' therapies emerge. That the acceptance of psychoanalysis (currently clinically unfashionable) seems inversely related to the recognition of multiple personality argues against reading the current wave of MPD simply as our postmodern consciousness, for its enthusiasts insist on the objective reality of both the syndrome and of its invariant cause, child sexual abuse, a signifier with an all too real signified. And opponents too generally revert to a pre-Freudian positivism in denying its existence: no reality to MPD because no causal trauma.

This goes along with a reshaping of the political balance between our two modes of thought in the last fifteen years, apparently in a generally more personalistic direction – towards an emphasis on individual responsibility for illness, unemployment and poverty, with a diminished place in a now contracted natural world controlled by self-sufficient individuals for 'accidents' – which remain as real events certainly but experienced now as violating traumata occasioned by the mischief or negligence of others: independent agents whom we hold legally accountable. From studies of our experienced 'locus of control', social psychologists have suggested that the more discrete and autonomous our sense of self and agency becomes, the more any perturbations are then attributed to entities external to this self.

The locus of immediate experience and action however remains a generally unitary and internally consistent individual, bounded, autonomous and fairly undifferentiated, coextensive with its physical body and with that body's history: whether we assume that such unity is given in the body's neural make-up, or else that the idiom of a single rather than a multiplex self has generally proved more successful in our biologically-adaptive and cultural history. Such a unitary individual, however, may recognise themself as losing this will, coherence and responsibility, whether through altered brain physiology (naturalistically), or through their perceived situation – at times of personal self-doubt or radical social change, or in situations standardised as dance, violence and sorcery, as glossolalia, spirit mediumship, hypnosis, hysteria and multiple personality – occasions when existing cultural representations of the self provide the necessary models for multiplicity. For example: through such representations as our mind/body distinction, through idioms of psychological faculties, humours, evolutionary or topographical levels of the psyche, notions of spirit familiars and powers, consubstantial deities, of hidden doubles, guardian angels, twins and other products of unnatural fecundity (18), through the differentiation and naming of kin, our personifications of the foetus, the dead and the dreamer, the sub-personalities of West African psychologies and the human potential movement, and now the cyborgs of the computer technovisionaries; through our society's particular understandings of causality, intersubjectivity, memory and suffering. Our loss of volition and control may be recognised as temporary or permanent, as partial or total, as an amnesia or paralysis, as a conflict, penetration, rape or theft; or we may identify our own moral agency with the intruding other, whether aware of seeking such an identification or just finding it happen – either as what anthropologists term sought (ritual) possession or as involuntary (peripheral) possession. (Or, as with MPD, 'this isn't happening to me, this is happening to someone else'.)

We can map such transformations of self and other along a number of dimensions (bearing in mind that different dimensions may be more salient for different societies and for different individuals) (19):

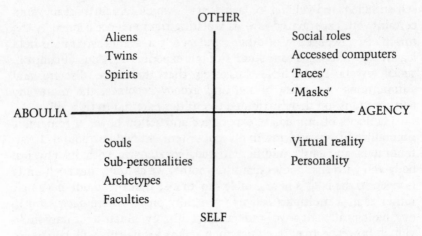

Context, expectation, access to a particular schema, and the example and response of others organise a multitude of possible patterns whether these are standardised rituals or idiosyncratic essays, partial stages or elisions, patterns which in turn confirm the objective reality of our experienced world. Different social positions allow us access to various patterns; thus we might argue that the hysterical fugue, like the shaman's vision quest, is generally more available to men (going with male access to a more extensive geographical and social space), whilst 'static' dissociations, involuntary possession and multiple personality are just more available to women's restricted mobility or with their experience of pregnancy or something like a sick role.

To take these patterns simply as personalistic, as always strategically motivated, as a performance which the participants themselves prefer to recognise as involuntary, assumes that the very articulation of our two modes (naturalistic and personalistic) is voluntary; the currently fashionable notion of role play and performance in anthropology simply recapitulates the public assumptions through which hypnosis and MPD now emerge: the particularly Western idea of the centrality of a directing self. Reading them however in a naturalistic 'bottom-up' way leaves us with the contrary problem – that our loss of volition is necessarily non-volitional, physiological: this medical idiom is limiting, not only because it is in the immediate clinical context that these patterns are legitimated in Western societies, but because of the difficulty in making our customary distinction between aetiology, pathology, symptoms and treatment. Disease and treatment are sometimes less contraries than aspects of the same process.

Why women? At a high level of generality, the pattern identified as the eventual psychopathology by doctors is a reconfiguring of the social identity ascribed to subdominant individuals; if the female is sickly and fearful, vulnerable to demons, controlled by others or lacking in moral will, performing rather than transforming, carrying another being within her, then her illness will embody and make real these characteristics. Usually as an exaggeration of them, sometimes a compromise with them. And MPD is perhaps an extreme variant of those other patterns by which women can negotiate or resist through the characteristics ascribed to them by men. Last century the neuropsychiatrist Moritz Benedikt wondered if women were more prone to hysteria because they had more to hide; and in the sense that women's consciousness argues for a double-voiced tradition, both inside and against the public male way of seeing things, double consciousness seems an apt representation (and practical deployment) of their situation. Like the intruding spirit, a disease is something which limits our moral agency; and society's attribution of an external cause to personal suffering, whether spirit or disease, compels our fellows to legitimation and restitution – what T.S. Eliot called 'the power of the weak'; it is in the slippage between the naturalistic and the personalistic, because of our inability to tolerate contraries, that MPD (or the spirits) emerges. Sexual abuse, like disease, is something that happens to us, against volition; the recognition of the violation of female children, the sense that nothing can ever be enough to recompense that child, powerfully compels acceptance of the reality of the abuse and of its consequences. If illnesses are taken as mirrors of their age, then MPD acknowledges a new and rawer manifestation of male domination, an opening up of Western society's terrible secrets. If the spirits of *shango* and *vodu* still articulate standardised African identities, and the secondary personalities of the nineteenth century's female hysterics were taken by their psychiatrists for earlier levels of evolutionary development, then the fragmented personalities of the current epidemic now offer us an unstable multiplicity of ambiguously welcome children, fantasised selves and wounded healers.

In conclusion. As with certain other illnesses in European societies, women with MPD join together in groups which play down the efficacy of the medical practitioner. They are communities of suffering through which the symptom is accommodated as a testimony to oppression – but at the cost of continued propriation. As in those non-Western analogues known by anthropologists as 'cults of affliction', sufferers in Alcoholics Anonymous or in Speaking For Our Selves come together to affirm their illness, to strike a contract with it and dedicate themselves to its power, often to gain a sense of heightened if limited control. Through this accommodation the group then takes on other, wider, 'non-therapeutic' tasks, in which affected individuals market their experience as emblematic, their suffering as achievement, their recovery as expert knowledge (20).

Some nineteenth century women reframed the existing power of medical hypnotist over suggestible unmarried woman, to reaffirm such female weakness as now privileged access to a higher knowledge, the Spiritualist medium establishing for herself a professional career which offered solutions to the problems of others, and for the social reformers of the period a natural religion. As contemporary multiples affirm the moral legitimacy of their several personalities, they too have aligned themselves with new movements for ethnic and gender redefinition; the stigmata of sexual violence becoming the means of transcending their origin; the ascribed now translated into the achieved; the pathological transformed into a marketable realm of political authenticity.

Notes

1   George Beard in *American Nervousness: Its Causes and Consequences* (1881).
2   Michael Kenny in *The Passion of Ansel Bourne*.
3   The French noun *conscience* denotes psychophysiological state (consciousness) as well as moral identity (conscience). There were a number of similar terms for the more developed instances (*conscience dissociée*) involving idioms of doubling and multiplicity, alternation, narrowing, dissociation, fragmentation, disintegration, decomposition, de-aggregation, splitting-off, or simply variation, depending on the extent of one-way or mutual amnesia.
4   As Clifford Geertz puts it more forcefully in his account of the Western self: a 'bounded, unique, more or less integrated motivational and cognitive universe, a dynamic centre of awareness, emotion, judgement and action organised into a distinctive whole and set contrastively both

against other such wholes and against a social and natural background ...'.
See note 7.

5 'Nervous energy' was a naturalistic reading of an individual's 'will' as a function of the number of their brain cells. Freud's unpublished *Project For a Scientific Psychology* attempted to reconcile the physical passage of energy through neurones with their consequent organisation into structured channels which then facilitated the same mental patterns (an idea that goes back to Descartes' 'canalisation' which also reemerges in Morton Prince's 'nets' or 'neurograms'). His abandonment of the manuscript in 1895 is often taken as Freud's move from the physicalism of Helmholtz and Brücke towards an interpretive and dynamic (purposive) psychology. Edelman's recent 'neural Darwinism' proposes something remarkably similar: rather than simply enacting a genetic program, the connections between cells in the developing post-natal brain are influenced by inputs from their environment and respond correspondingly, actively competing against, and colonising, the organisation of other groups of cells in relation to their outside world. To an extent then their 'design-fixing repertoires' approach what may be termed representation: intentionality in the philosopher's sense. Putting Edelman's theory together with Dennett's and Dawkins' notion of the brain being 'colonised' by memes (the anthropologist's collective representations) argues for one way into my naturalistic-personalistic antinomy.

6 As 'passiones' as Godfrey Lienhardt called them: 'A diviner is a man in whom the division is permanently present; a Power, or Powers, are always latent within him but he has the ability to dissociate them in himself at will, letting them manifest themselves in him. While thus dissociated, the diviner is a Power, for which his body is host.'

7 Marcel Mauss restricted the term *moi*, conventionally translated by anthropologists as *self* (or *person*), to the social and moral representation, not as I have done above to the experiencing and embodied subject: *cf.* William James' 'empirical me', the 'private self' of Lienhardt or the 'biological individual' of Jean La Fontaine. Yet this phenomenological self must be fairly isomorphic, or at least not too disconsonant, with the social conception of the self. In my fieldwork in Creole Trinidad where an individual may describe themselves as comprising a physical body plus various combinations of soul, spirit, mind, shadow and guardian angel, they do not recognise themselves as fragmented except in certain situations where everyday unity is called into question (generally responsibility for otherwise inexplicable or antisocial actions) or during personal cogitations on how to reduce pain or discard undesirable vices. No more does the British Christian generally worry about whether the mind or the soul is in charge except for moments of temptation, guilt, religious doubt or conversion.

8 *Sybil* (1973) was followed by: *The Five Of Me* (1977), *Tell Me Who I Am Before I Die* (1977), *The Flock* (1991), and a male case, *The Minds of Billy Milligan* (1981).

9 MPD (retitled as Dissociative Identity Disorder) is now recognised by the American Psychiatric Association (in DSM-IV) and the World Health Organisation (ICD-10).

10 Why teaching and social work? (And more recently nursing.) I think it is significant that they are low status, poorly paid professions, with a high proportion of women, and a good deal of publicly defined responsibility for

children, much personal commitment yet little independent authority, no consistently accepted intellectual rationale or body of accepted practice, and constantly vulnerable to sudden swings of governmental and professional policy.

11 As in the Durkheimian approach of Mary Douglas, in which loosely organised polities parallel and somehow facilitate individual dissociation and spirit intrusion. Similarly psychologically orientated anthropologists and cultural critics take individual conflicts as the microcosm of wider social fragmentations.

12 By the 1920s 'personality' had become virtually synonymous with 'consciousness' (and later 'identity'), perhaps as a particularly American idea of the self as primarily social performance rather than mechanism or moral character, yet 'personality' has long been associated with individual agency: 'For a time he loses the sense of his own personality, and becomes a mere passive instrument of the deity' (1655: cit. O.E.D.).

13 The phonograph was a common image of the unconscious, as the telegraph was of the medium. In Prince's monograph, clinical engagement with the elusive secondary personalities recalls not only the practice of the medium but of the telephone operator: 'Later in the course of the same interview Chris [another personality] was obtained. The same questions were put to her.'

14 Cf. Warhol's and Oldenberg's multiples, body counts and mass disaster statistics, serial killers and multiple births: the sheer absurdity of industrial multiplication as Walter Benjamin put it.

15 Michael Benedikt and Marcos Novak. The director of the Carnegie Mellon University's robotics centre, Hans Moravec, has recently proposed a forty-year programme for the transfer of human personalities onto computer discs and our eventual dissolution as biological organisms.

16 As if with the 'self as a reflexive project' (Anthony Giddens), late modernity is now unable to sustain the attempt to unify time, place and action, yet cannot cope with flux alone, and retreats to concretised simulacra of an embodied individual.

17 An ironic simultaneity as I have called it elsewhere. Their very distinction may be seen as naturalistic (the distinction in our experience and actions between the involuntary and voluntary nervous system, as Maurice Merleau-Ponty noted) or as personalistic (given by cultural history as, for example, in the dualism of Judaeo-Christianity refined by the mechanical science of the Renaissance, the ultimate truth in the eye of God becoming reframed as that of the context-independent scientific observer).

18 The structuralist will have noted how MPD, perverse multiplicity, is the reciprocal of incest, perverse unity.

19 And here there is the question of how the flux of pre-objective experience becomes congealed into such hypostasised entities – a process relatively ignored or taken for granted by cognitive psychologists and anthropologists but which has been variously addressed by Marxists, Kleinians and Buddhists, generally through the idea that nominalised categories are less ambiguous than experiencing, and under problematic circumstances we shape a fetishised world which may follow our own intense recognition of ourselves as embodied beings. Early in life, the phenomenologists propose, we start to perceive the world as nominalised – as composed of entities of recurrent invariance (Merleau-Ponty); and such reification is fundamental to social categorisation, giving ontological status to the experienced world

(George Lakoff) which is recognised as 'real' in that it both continues independently of our perceptions and is the ultimate ground for our lived experience (Peter Berger and Thomas Luckman).

20 In John Janzen's felicitous term, as 'Drums Anonymous', recalling contemporary groups for survivors of civil disasters and relatives of the victims who transcend their suffering through pragmatically advocating greater safety controls or public accountability. Compare the politics of Survivor Syndrome in Israel, the Russian civil liberties group Memorial, or the significance of 'testimony' in the therapy of people who have been tortured.

15 Thaumaturgy to Human Potential: The King's Evil Revisited*

[The sovereign's] magical virtue is in the strictest sense of the word contagious: his divinity is a fire which under proper restraints, confers endless blessings but if rashly touched or allowed to break bounds, burns and destroys what it touches.(1)

The early modern monarch, an instance of Max Weber's traditional mode of authority, manifests healing power through his body. Particular illnesses may be cured (or induced) by physical touch, for his hands have been anointed in the central act of his coronation – at least in European kingdoms – and thus they partake of the divine.(2) Idioms like *salvus* (Lat.) or *soter* (Gk.) run together connotations of health, safety, protection and welfare in which the state and the individual subject may both be regenerated through kingly power: a power which recalls anthropological conceptions of *tapu* or *mana* (or indeed *baraka*, for regal authority may be ascribed as well as inherited). The classic healing instance was the touching for the King's Evil (or scrofula-tuberculosis of the cervical glands) by English and French kings.(3) And this healing authority could be pragmatically deployed when the claim to the throne was doubtful (England's Henry IV) or its possession shaky (Charles II). With the onset of something presaging 'constitutional' (4) monarchy, William III refused to touch for scrofula, that monarch becoming, at least in theory, simply the first servant of the state rather than the thaumaturge whose own physical body had represented and guaranteed the safety and health of the body politic.

The relationship between the king's two bodies – his physical body and his political or ritual body – has been explored by Marc Bloch (5) and A.M. Hocart,(6) and more recently by E.H. Kantorowicz.(7) The physical body dies, but the political body is immediately manifest in his successor: 'The King is dead, long live the King!' [Yet the distinction between the two was not altogether invariate; with the accession to power of the Tudors as a centralising national monarchy,

*First published in the *British Medical Anthropology Review* (1996)

the physical body could take on increasingly public attributes: the Privy Chamber (later the Privy Council) with its leading political figure the Groom of the Stool (privy closet), body-guards and so on.[8]] Less privy than the Tudors, Louis XIV was washed and dressed by a group of confidants who were simultaneously friends and important nobles, the senior officers of the state and the king's bathing attendants.

With state authority translated into the 'King in Parliament' the personal power of the British monarch declined, at least ostensibly, the ceremonial body shrinking to its moment of installation (the coronation): empowered for the reign through the anointing of hands and breast, the Canopy, the Spurs, Armils (wristlets), Ring, Robes Royal, Glove, Sword of Temporal Justice, Sceptres of Mercy and Justice, the Crown *et al.* The use of talismans is restricted to the fairly impersonal distribution of Maundy Money which is touched only by the gloved hand of the sovereign.[9] But the physical body continued its visits around the realm in what Hayden (10) terms monarchy's minor events: opening factories and schools, visiting barracks and hospitals. Significant amongst these was visiting wounded soldiers during wars, together with sponsoring of royal hospitals and medical charities, acting as their patron (or for the minor royalty, governor), appointing physicians and surgeons to the royal household, visiting survivors of civil disasters, and patronising particular medical thera-pies (in Britain notably homoeopathy).(11) I would suggest that the first of these – ritualised visiting and consoling the nation's wounded – has a particular salience, shared as it is by republican heads of state as their country's nominal commander-in-chief, and indeed by any politically minded general. Yet the touch of the monarch retains a numinous virtue of its own; only with careful security is the British queen saved from the contact of crowds (a common hazard on foreign visits) except in the hospital visit when she herself initiates the physical touching of the moribund: in what the republican Tom Nairn (12) unkindly terms the 'expanding mass delusion of intimacy'. Staff comment that such visits enhance the morale, and thus the healing, of the patients: if not Frazer's contagious magic then certainly some idea of it being 'fitting', or even a psychosomatic healing made significant through the laying on, or just shaking of, the consecrated hand. And in the case of the wounded soldier, this touching partakes of gratitude on the one side, fealty on the other, the occasion of near death or mutilation becoming a social drama reaffirming the mysterious sacrificial contract, now reversed, between subject and sovereign. This pattern seems to have become routinised in the early twentieth century as the monarchy became more evidently British rather than foreign, developing into something like a corporation with private property and tax exemption,[1] (13, 14) whose junior members now shade insensibly into the upper classes.(15)

A recent reconfiguration of all of this may be observed in the hospital visiting and medical patronage of Diana, Princess of Wales, the recently divorced wife of the heir to the throne. She is perhaps the member of the royal household most identified with sickness and healing. In a popular television programme she describes her own post-natal depression, wrist-cutting and bulimia as a protest against her co-option into the Windsor monarchy.(16) Court supporters of her estranged husband in turn accuse her of hysteria and paranoia, and *The Times'* medical correspondent immediately provided a clinical opinion on her broadcast. I am not concerned here with the internecine struggles of the Family nor with their significance for the continuation of Britain's current constitutional arrangements,(17, 18) but rather with the particular quality of her healing acts. When interviewed after her visits, hospitalised patients describe not only their sense of privilege and gratitude, but of some physical power passing from her to them.[2] Kingly healing again? Not quite, because her power comes not from sovereignty – from her now discarded state body – but against it through her physical body's resistance to the Court. Her suffering has conferred the charismatic power to heal and yet she takes back this power from the sick, she is 'inspired' by the sick and dying.(19) Dressed in American jeans and baseball cap, she leaves her palace alone just before midnight to visit selected hospitals 'in disguise' spending up to two hours with a patient dying of AIDS.(20)

Now this recalls less the King's Evil than the human potential movement's identification of healer and healed, in its managerial self-sufficiency and self-actualisation through which individual body and personality are fused with social identity and resulting charismatic authority (Weber again): a secularised version of the radical prophets and national heroes who serve as exemplars in that they take on the dilemmas of their age, and in transcending them as individuals, do so on behalf of their fellows.(21) Their ability to overcome suffering is not through their sovereignty but through their own exemplary suffering. And we might evoke other parallels: with the 'twelve-step' American healing programmes, tele-evangelists, the ascribed charisma of the troubled film- and pop-star: a representative soap opera of pain and outraged domesticity, and of resistance to this through an emblematic illness which is made real to every spectator, Frazer's sacrificial king regenerated not in the succession but in each subject's individual body. And whose imitation (the Duchess of York?) descends from gripping popular tragedy to risible farce.[3]

Meanwhile, in what remains of Britain's National Health Service, new therapeutic idioms gather ideological force: flexibility, creativity, choice, risk management ..., are increasingly divorced from the experience of sickness whose representations must now be sought in the public media.(22)

Notes

1   Only from 1800 was the constitutional monarch allowed to possess property: Hall, P. *Royal Fortune. Tax, Money and the Monarchy*, London: Bloomsbury, 1997.
2   I have mislaid this most significant reference. It was in *The Times* in 1995 or early 1996 describing a visit to North America (thus more charisma than sovereignty).
3   The Duchess frequented a New Age healer (under a blue plastic pyramid somewhere off the Holloway Road) whose forthcoming exposure of her client is expected in 1997.

References

1   Frazer, J.G. *The Golden Bough*, abridged edition, London: Macmillan, 1957 (1922)
2   Starkey, D. Representation through intimacy: a study in the symbolism of monarchy and court office in early modern England. In I.M. Lewis, ed., *Symbols and Sentiments*. London: Academic Press, 1977
3   Bloch. M. *The Royal Touch: Sacred Monarchy and Scrofula in England and France*. Trans., London: Routledge and Kegan Paul, 1973 (1924)
4   Bogdanov, V. *The Monarchy and the Constitution*. Oxford University Press, 1995
5   Bloch, M. *The Royal Touch*, 1973 (1924)
6   Hocart, A.M. *Kings and Councillors: An Essay in the Comparative Anatomy of Human Society*, University of Chicago Press, 1970 (1936)
7   Kantorowicz, E.H. *The King's Two Bodies*. Princeton University Press, 1957
8   Starkey, D. In I.M. Lewis. ed., *Symbols and Sentiments*, London: Academic Press, 1977
9   Hayden, I. *Symbol and Privilege: The Ritual Context of British Royalty*, Tucson: University of Arizona Press, 1987
10   Ibid.
11   Prochaska, F. *Royal Bounty: the Making of a Welfare Monarchy*, New Haven: Yale University Press, 1995
12   Nairn, T. *The Enchanted Glass: Britain and its Monarchy*, London: Century Hutchinson, 1988
13   Ibid.
14   Prochaska, F. The Head that Wears a Crown, *Times Literary Supplement*, July 26, pages 14–15, 1996
15   Hayden, I. *Symbol and Privilege*, 1987

16 *The Times*, Princess will not go quietly, London, 21 November, pages 1–3, 1995
17 Prochaska, F. The Head that Wears a Crown, *Times Literary Supplement*, July 26, pages 14–15, 1996
18 Quigley, D. The paradoxes of monarchy, *Anthropology Today*, vol 11, no 5, pages 1–3, 1995
19 *The Times*, Princess says she is inspired by visits to sick and dying, London, 4 December, page 3, 1995
20 Ibid.
21 Erikson, E. *Young Man Luther*, New York: Norton, 1958
22 *The Times*, Any good diseases on telly tonight? London, 16 November, page 21, 1996

Bibliography

Abrahams, R.D. (1970) *Deep Down in the Jungle: Negro Narrative Folklore from the Streets of Philadelphia*. Chicago: Aldine

Abrahams, R.D. (1983) *The Man of Words in the West Indies: Performance and the Emergence of Creole Culture*. Johns Hopkins University Press: Baltimore

Abrahams, R.G. (1986) Ordinary and extraordinary experience. In V. Turner and E. Bruner (eds.), *The Anthropology of Experience*. Urbana: Illinois University Press

Adebimpe, V.R. (1984) American blacks and psychiatry. *Transcultural Psychiatric Research Review*, 21, 83–111

Adelman, J. (1992) *Suffocating Mothers: Fantasies of Maternal Origin in Shakespeare's Plays*. London: Routledge

Adler, M. (1986) *Drawing Down the Moon*. (2nd edn, revised) Boston: Beacon

Ahern, E.M. (1979) *The Problem of Efficacy: Strong and Weak Illocutionary Acts*. Man (n.s.), 14, 1–17

Albanese, C.L. (1990) *Nature Religion in America: From the Algonkian Indians to the New Age*. Chicago: Chicago University Press

Alexander, F. (1939) Psychoanalytic Study of a Case of Essential Hypertension. *Psychosomatic Medicine*, 1, 139–152

Alexander, J. (1977) The culture of race in middle-class Kingston. *American Ethnologist*, 4, 413–435

Al-Issa, L. (1980) *The Psychopathology of Women*. New Jersey: Prentice Hall

Alloway, R. and Bebbington, P. (1987) The buffer theory of social support: A review of the literature. *Psychological Medicine*, 17, 91–108

Andrews, E.D. (1953) *The People Called Shakers*. Oxford: Oxford University Press

Andrews, J.D.W. (1966) Psychotherapy of phobias. *Psychological Bulletin*, 66, 455–480

Ansel, A. (1982) *Judaism and Psychology*. (Third Edition). New York: Felshelm

Apter, M.J. (1982) *The Experience of Motivation The Theory of Psychological Reversals*. London: Academic Press

Ardener, E. (1971) Introductory essay. In Ardener, *Social Anthropology and Language*. London: Tavistock

Ardener, E. (1972) Belief and the problem of women. In J.S. La Fontaine (ed.), *The Interpretation of Ritual*. London: Tavistock

Ardener, E. (1980). Some Outstanding Problems in the Analysis of Events. In Foster and Brandes, *op. cit.*

Ardener, S. (1975) Introduction. In S. Ardener (ed.), *Perceiving Women*. London: Dent

Ardener, S. (1981) The nature of women in society. In S. Ardener (ed.), *Defining Females*. London: Croom Helm

Ardener, S. (ed.) (1981) *Women and Space: Ground Rules and Social Maps*. London: Croom Helm

Ardt, K.J.R. (1965) *George Rapp's Harmony Society*. Philadelphia: University of Pennsylvania Press

Armstrong, D. (1983) *Political Anatomy of the Body: Medical Knowledge in Britain in the Twentieth Century*. Cambridge University Press

Asad, T. (ed.) (1973) *Anthropology and the Colonial Encounter*. London: Ithaca

Austin, D.J. (1979) History and symbols in ideology: a Jamaican example. *Man* (new series) 14, 497–514

Baier, A. (1994) *Moral Prejudice: Essays on Ethics*. Cambridge: Cambridge University Press

Bakan, D. (1958) *Sigmund Freud and the Jewish Mystical Tradition*. Princeton: Princeton University Press

Bakhtin, M. (1971) Discourse typology in prose. In L. Matejka and K. Pomorska (eds.), *Readings in Russian Poetics: Formalist and Structuralist Views*. Cambridge, Mass.: MIT Press

Bancroft, J., Hawton, K., Simpkins, S., Kingston, B., Cumming, C. and Whitwell, D. (1979) The reasons people give for taking overdoses: A further enquiry. *British Journal of Medical Psychology*, 52, 353–365

Barnes, J.A. (1972) Genetrix:genitor::nature:culture? In J. Goody (ed.), *The Character of Kinship*. Cambridge: Cambridge University Press

Barrett, M. and Roberts, H. (1978) Doctors and their patients: the social control of women in general practice. In C. Smart and B. Smart (eds.), *Women, Sexuality and Social Control*. London: Routledge and Kegan Paul

Barrett, R.J.J. and Lucas, R.H. (1993) The skulls are cold, the house is hot: interpreting depths of meaning in Iban therapy. *Man* (n.s.), 28, 573–596

Barthes, R. (1967) *Elements of Semiology*. London: Cape

Bateson, G. (1958) *Naven*. 2nd Edition. Stanford: Stanford University Press

Bateson, G. (1972) *Steps to an Ecology of Mind*. New York: Ballantine

Beattie, J. (1977) Spirit mediumship as theatre. *Royal Anthropological Institute News* No.20, 1–6

Beckford, J. (1985) The world images of new religious and healing movements. In R.K. Jones (ed.), *Sickness and Sectarianism: Exploratory Studies in Medical and Religious Sectarianism.* Aldershot: Gower

Beeston, R. (1992) 'Messiah' Arouses Rival Rabbi's Wrath. London: *The Times,* 29 February

Bell, C. and Newby, H. (1976) Husbands and wives: the dynamics of the differential dialect. In D.L. Barker and S. Allen (eds.), *Dependence and Exploitation in Work and Marriage.* London: Longman

Ben-Amos, D. and J.R. Mintz (trans. and eds.) (1970) *In Praise of the Ba'al Shem Tov (Shivhei ha-Besht).* Bloomington: Indiana University Press

Benedict, R. (1935) *Patterns of Culture.* London: Routledge

Ben Shimon Halevi, Z. (1974) *Adam and the Kabbalistic Tree.* London: Rider

Berger, J. (1971) *Ways of Seeing.* Harmondsworth: Penguin

Berger, P.L. and T. Luckman (1966) *The Social Construction of Reality.* New York: Doubleday

Berlin, B. & Ray, P. (1969) *Basic Color Terms, their Universality and Evolution.* Berkeley: University of California Press

Bilu, Y., Witztum, E. and O. Van Der Hart (1990) Paradise Regained: 'Miraculous healing' in an Israeli psychiatric clinic. *Culture, Medicine and Psychiatry,* 14, 105–127

Birnbaum, K. (1923) The making of a psychosis: The principles of structural analysis in psychiatry. In S.H. Hirsch & M. Shepherd (eds.), *Themes and Variations in European Psychiatry.* Bristol: Wright, 1974

Blacking, J. (ed.) (1977) *The Anthropology of the Body.* London: Academic Press

Bleuler, E. (1924) *Textbook of Psychiatry.* (Translated by A.A. Brill). London: George Alien & Unwin

Bloch, M. (1977) The past and the present in the present. *Man,* 12, 279–292

Bloom, H. (1984) *Kabbalah and Criticism.* New York: Continuum

Boddy, J. (1989) *Wombs and Alien Spirits: Women, Men and the Zar Cult in Northern Sudan.* Madison: University of Wisconsin Press

Bolinger, D. (1980) Intonation and 'nature'. In Foster and Brandes, *op. cit.*

Boskind-Lodahl, M. (1976) Cinderella's stepsisters: feminist perspective on anorexia nervosa and bulimia. *Signs (Journal of Women, Culture and Society),* 2, 343–356

Bottomley, F. (1980) Ideas of the Body in the Old Testament. In

Bottomley, *Attitudes to the Body in Western Christendom*. London: Lepus

Bourdieu, P. (1977) *Outline of a Theory of Practice*. Cambridge University Press, 1972

Boyer, P. (1986) The 'empty' concepts of traditional thinking: a semantic and pragmatic description *Man* (n.s.), 21, 50–64

Boyer, P. (ed.) (1993) *Cognitive Aspects of Religious Symbolism*. Cambridge: Cambridge University Press

Boyer, P. (1994) *The Naturalness of Religious Ideas: A Cognitive Theory of Religion*. Berkeley: University of California Press

Bradford, J. and Balmaceda, K. (1983) Shoplifting; is there a specific psychiatric syndrome? *Canadian Journal of Psychiatry*, 28, 248–253

British Medical Journal Editorial (1971) Suicide Attempts, 11, 483

Brooke, J.L. (1994) *The Refiner's Fire: The Making of Mormon Cosmology 1644–1844*. Cambridge: Cambridge University Press

Broverman, I.D., Broverman, D.M., Clarkson, F.E., Rosenkrantz, P.S. and Vogel, S.R. (1970) Sex role stereotypes and clinical judgements of mental health. *Journal of Consulting and Clinical Psychology*, 34, 1–7

Brown, G. and Harris, T. (1978) *The Social Origins of Depression*. London: Tavistock

Brown, P. (1989) *The Body and Society: Men, Women and Sexual Renunciation in Early Christianity*. London: Faber and Faber

Buber, M. (1948) *Tales of the Hasidim* (2 vols). New York: Schocken

Buglass, D.D., Clarke, J., Henderson, A.S., Kreitman, N. and Priestly, A.S. (1977) A study of agoraphobic housewives. *Psychological Medicine*, 7, 73–86

Bulka, R.P. (ed.) (1979) Mystics and Medics: A Comparison of Mystical and Psychotherapeutic Encounters. *Journal of Psychology and Judaism, special issue*. New York: Human Sciences Press

Burke, A.W. (1974) Socio-cultural determinants of psychiatric disorder among women in Trinidad and Tobago. *West Indian Medical Journal*, 23, 75–79

Bynum, C.W. (1982) *Jesus as Mother: Studies in the Spirituality of the High Middle Ages* Berkeley: University of California Press

Bynum, C.W. (1989) The female body and religious practice in the later Middle Ages. In M. Feher (ed.), *Fragments For a History of the Human Body: 1*, New York: Zone

Bynum, C.W. (1995) *The Resurrection of the Body in Western Christianity 200–1336*. New York: Columbia University Press

Bynum, W.F. (1985) The nervous patient in eighteenth and nineteenth-century Britain: the psychiatric origins of British neurology.

In *The Anatomy of Madness: Essays in the History of Psychiatry*, vol. 1. (eds. W.F. Bynum, R. Porter & M. Shepherd). London: Tavistock

Caldecott, L. and Leland, S. (1983) *Reclaim the Earth: Women Speak Out for Life on Earth*. London: Women's Press

Calley, M.J.C. (1965) *God's People: West Indian Pentecostal Sects in England*. Oxford: Oxford University Press

Calloway, H. (1978) 'The most essentially female function of all': giving birth. In S. Ardener (ed.), *Defining Females: The Nature of Women in Society*. New York: Wiley

Canguilhem, G. (1989) *The Normal and the Pathological*. New York: Zone Books

Canning, H. and Myer, J. (1966) Obesity – its possible effect on college acceptance. *New England Journal of Medicine*, 257, 1172–1174

Carr, J.E. and Tann, E.K. (1976) In search of the true Amok: amok as viewed within Malay culture. *Culture, Medicine and Psychiatry*, 2, 269–293

Carstairs, M. (1957) *The Twice-Born: A Study of a Community of High-Caste Hindus*. London: Hogarth

Caws, P. (1974) Operational, representational and explanatory models. *American Anthropologist* 76, 1–10

Chesler, P. (1974) *Women and Madness*. London: Allen Lane

Chodoff, P. (1975) Psychiatric aspects of Nazi persecution. In S. Arieti (ed.), *Handbook of Psychiatry*, New York: Basic Books

Chodoff, P. and Lyons, H. (1955) Hysteria, the hysterical personality and hysterical conversion. *American Journal of Psychiatry*, 114, 734–740.

Chrisman, N.J. & Maretzki, T.W. (eds.) (1982) *Clinically Applied Anthropology*. Dordrecht: Reidel

Clarke, W.C. (1973) Temporary madness as theatre: Wild-man behaviour in New Guinea. *Oceania*, 43, 198–214

Clement, D.C. (1982) Samoan folk knowledge of mental disorders. In Marsella and White, op. cit.

Clifford, J. (1988) *The Predicament of Culture: Twentieth Century Ethnography, Literature and Art*. Cambridge, MA: Harvard University Press

Cohen, A.P. (1985) Symbolism and social change: matters of life and death in Whalsay, Shetland. *Man*, 20, 307–324

Cochrane, R. (1977) Mental illness in immigrants to England and Wales: an analysis of mental hospital admissions. *Social Psychiatry*, 12, 25–35

Comaroff, J. (1978) Medicine and culture: some anthropological perspectives. *Social Science and Medicine*, 12, 247–254

Cooper, D. (1967) *Psychiatry and Anti-Psychiatry*. London: Tavistock

Cooperstock, R. (1971) Sex differences in the use of mood-modifying drugs. *Health and Social Behaviour*, 12, 238–244

Cooperstock, R. and Sims, M. (1971) Mood-modifying drugs prescribed in a Canadian City, *American Journal of Public Health*, 61, 1007–1016

Corin, E. (1978) La Possession comme langage dans un contexte de changement socio-culturel. *Anthropologie et Société*, 2, 53–74

Corin, E. and Bibeau, G. (1980) Psychiatric Perspectives in Africa: 2. *Transcultural Psychiatric Research Review*, 16, 147–178

Cramer, P. (1993) *Baptism and Change in the Early Middle Ages c.200–c.1150*. Cambridge: Cambridge University Press

Cranshaw, R. (1983) The object of the centrefold. *Block*, No.9, 26–33 Middlesex

Crapanzano, V. (1973) *The Hadmadsha: A Study in Moroccan Ethnopsychiatry*. Berkeley: University of California Press

Crapanzano, V. (1992) *Hermes' Dilemma and Hamlet's Desire: On the Epistemology of Interpretation*. Cambridge MA: Harvard University Press

Crisp, A.H. (1980) *Anorexia Nervosa: Let Me Be*. London: Academic Press

Crump, T. (1990) *The Anthropology of Numbers*. Cambridge: Cambridge University Press

Csordas, T.J. (1988) Elements of Charismatic Persuasion and Healing. *Medical Anthropology Quarterly*, 2, 445–69

Csordas, T.J. (1994a) *The Sacred Self: A Cultural Phenomenology of Charismatic Healing*. Berkeley: University of California Press

Csordas, T.J. (1994b) Introduction. In Csordas (ed.), *Embodiment and Experience: The Existential Ground of Culture and Self*. Cambridge: Cambridge University Press

Csordas, T.J. (1994c) Words from the Holy People: a Case Study in Cultural Phenomenology. In Csordas (ed.), *Embodiment and Experience, op. cit.*

Daily Express (1984) Wives hooked on illness are giving GPs a headache. 27 March. London

Daily Telegraph (1984) Waitresses told: 'Slim or lose jobs'. 13 August. London

Dann, G. (1987) *The Barbadian Male: Sexual Attitudes and Practice*. London: Macmillan

Davis, D.B. (1966) *The Problem of Slavery in Western Culture*. New York: Cornell University Press

Deighton, C.N. and Nicol, A.R. (1985) Abnormal women's behaviour in young women in the primary care setting: Is Briquet's Syndrome a useful category? *Psychological Medicine*, 15, 15–520

Dein, S. (1992) Millennialism, Messianism and Medicine. *International Journal of Social Psychiatry*, 18, 262–267

Delaney, C. (1986) The meaning of paternity and the virgin birth debate. *Man* (n.s.), 21, 494–513

Deleuze, G. and Guattari, F. (1984) *Anti-Oedipus: Capitalism and Schizophrenia*. London: Athlone

Devereux, G. (1937) Institutionalised homosexuality of the Mohave Indians. *Human Biology*, 9, 498–527

Devereux, G. (1970) *Essais d'Ethnopsychiatrie Générale*. Paris: Gallimard

Devereux, G. (1978) *Ethnopsychoanalysis*. Berkeley: University of California Press

Diprose, R. (1994) *The Bodies of Women: Ethics, Embodiment and Sexual Difference*. London: Routledge

Douglas, M. (1966) *Purity and Danger*. London: Routledge

Douglas, M. (1968) The social control of cognition: some factors in joke perception. *Man* (new series), 3, 361–375

Douglas, M. (1970) *Purity and Danger: An Analysis of Concepts of Pollution and Taboo*. Harmondsworth: Penguin

Douglas, M. (1970) *Natural Symbols: Explorations in Cosmology*. London: Barrie and Rockliff

Douglas, M. (ed.) (1973) *Rules and Meanings*. Harmondsworth: Penguin

Dow, J. (1986). Universal Aspects of Symbolic Healing: A Theoretical Synthesis. *American Anthropologist*, 88, 56–69

Dresner, S.H. (1974) *The Zaddick*. New York: Schocken

Durkheim, E. (1901) *Les Règles de la Méthode sociologique: Revue et augmentée d'une Préface nouvelle*. Paris: Alcan

Durkheim, E. (1938) *The Rules of Sociological Method*. 8th English edition, trans. New York: Free Press

Durkheim. E. (1951) *Suicide*. New York: Free Press

Durkheim, E. and Mauss, M. (1963) *Primitive Classification* (orig. pub. 1901–2), trans. R. Needham. London: Cohen and West

Early, E.A. (1982) The logic of well-being: therapeutic narratives in Cairo, Egypt. *Social Science and Medicine*, 16, 1491–1497

Easlea, B. (1980) *Witch-Hunting, Magic and the New Philosophy: An Introduction to the Debates of the Scientific Revolution 1450–1750*. Sussex: Harvester

Eastwell, H.D. (1982) Australian Aborigines. *Transcultural Psychiatric Research Review* 19, 221–247

Eco, U. (1979) *The Role of the Reader*. Bloomington, Indiana: Indiana University Press

Eco, U. (1985) A Portrait of the Elder as a Young Pliny: How to Build Fame. In M. Blonsky (ed.), *On Signs*. Oxford: Blackwell

Eco, U. (1993) *La Ricerca Della Lingua Perfetta*. Rome: Laterza

Ehrenwald, J. (1979) Precognition and the Prophetic Tradition: from ESP to the Effective Myth. In *Bulka, op. cit.*

Eiberg-Swartz, H. (ed.) (1992) *People of the Body: Jews and Judaism From an Embodied Perspective*. State University of New York Press

Eiberg-Swartz, H. (1994) *God's Phallus and Other Problems for Men and Monotheism*. Boston: Beacon Press

Eisenberg, L. (1977) Disease and illness: distinctions between professional and popular ideas of sickness. *Culture, Medicine and Psychiatry*, 1, 9–23

Eliade, M. (1964) *Shamanism: Archaic Techniques of Ecstasy*. New York: Plenum

Ellen, R. (1977) Anatomical Classification and the Semiotics of the Body. In *Blacking, op. cit.*

Ellenberger, H.F. (1970) *The Discovery of the Unconscious: the History and Evolution of Dynamic Psychiatry*. London: Allen Lane

Epstein, A.L. (1984) *The Experience of Shame in Melanesia: An essay in the anthropology of affect*. London: Royal Anthropological Institute Occasional Paper 40

Evans-Pritchard, E.E. (1937) *Witchcraft, Oracles and Magic among the Azande*. Oxford: Clarendon Press

Fabrega, H. (1974) Problems implicit in the cultural and social study of depression. *Psychosomatic Medicine*, 36, 377–393

Fanon, F. (1952) *Peau Noire, Masques Blancs*. Paris: Editions de Seuil

Fanon, F. (1965) *The Wretched of the Earth*. London: MacGibbon and Kee

Featherstone, M. (ed.) (1990) *Global Culture: Nationalism, Globalisation and Modernity*. London: Sage

Federn, P. (1952) *Ego Psychology and the Psychoses*. London: Image

Feinberg, R. (1990) Spiritual and Natural Etiologies on a Polynesian Outlier in Papua New Guinea. *Social Science and Medicine*, 30, 311–323

Field, M. (1960) *Search for Security: An Ethno-Psychiatric Study of Rural Ghana*. London: Faber and Faber

Firth, R. (ed.) (1957) *Man and Culture: An Evaluation of the Work of Bronislaw Malinowski*. London: Routledge and Kegan Paul

Firth, R. (1961) Suicide and risk-taking in Tikopian society. *Psychiatry*, 2, 1–17

Firth, R. (1967) Ritual and drama in Malay spirit mediumship. *Comparative Studies in Society and History*, 9, 190–207

Fish, F.J. (1962) *Schizophrenia*. Bristol: Wright

Fisher, L.E. (1985) *Colonial Madness: Mental Health in the Barbadian Social Order*. New Brunswick: Rutgers University Press

Flint, M. (1975) The menopause: reward or punishment? *Psychosomatics*, 16, 161–163

Fodor, I. (1976) The phobic syndrome in women. In V. Franks and V. Burtle (eds.), *Women in Therapy*. New York: Bruner/Mazel

Fortes, M. (1959) *Oedipus and Job in West African religion*. Cambridge: Cambridge University Press

Foster, G.M. (1976) Disease entities in non-Western medical systems. *American Anthropologist*, 178, 773–782

Foster, M.L. and Brandes, S.H. (eds.) (1980) *Symbol as Sense: New Approaches to the Analysis of Meaning*. New York: Academic Press

Foucault, M. (1970) *The Order of Things: An Archaeology of the Human Sciences*. London: Tavistock

Foucault, M. (1973) *The Birth of the Clinic: An Archaeology of Medical Perception*. London: Tavistock

Frank, J. (1961) *Persuasion and Healing*. Baltimore: Johns Hopkins

Frasure-Smith, N. and Prince, R. (1989) Long-term follow-up of the ischemic heart disease monitoring program. *Psychosomatic Medicine*, 51, 485–513

Freeman, D. (1965) Anthropology, psychiatry and the doctrine of cultural relativism. *Man*, May–June, No.59, 65–67

Freud, S. (1911) *Psychoanalytic Notes on an Autobiographical Account of a Case of Paranoia*. London: Penguin 1979

Freud, S. (1914) *Interpretation of Dreams*. London: Penguin 1976

Freud, S. (1938) *Moses and monotheism*. Standard Edition XXIII London: Hogarth

Freud, S. (1946) *Fragment of an analysis of a case of hysteria*. Standard Edition LV, London: Hogarth

Fry, W.F. (1982) The marital context of an anxiety syndrome. *Family Process*, 14, 245–252

Gaines, A.D. (1982) Cultural definitions, behaviour and the person in American psychiatry. In A.J. Marsella and G.M. White, *Cultural Conceptions of Mental Health and Therapy*. Dordrecht: Reidel

Garner, D.M. and Garfinkel, P.E. (1980) Socio-cultural factors in the development of anorexia nervosa. *Psychology and Medicine*, 10, 747–56

Gates, H.L. (1988) *The Signifying Monkey: A Theory of Afro-American Literary Criticism*. New York: Oxford University Press

Geertz, C. (1966) Religion as a cultural system. In M. Banton (ed.), *Anthropological Approaches to Religion*. London: Tavistock

Geertz, C. (1984) *Local Knowledge: Further Essays in Interpretative Anthropology*. New York: Basic Books

Geertz, C. (1984) Anti anti-relativism, *American Anthropologist*, 86, 263–278

Gellner, E. (1978) Towards a theory of ideology. *L'Homme*, 18, 69–83

Gellner, E. (1992) *Postmodernism, Reason and Religion*. London: Routledge

Gibbens, T.C.N. and Prince, J. (1962) *Shoplifting*. London: Institute for Study and Treatment of Delinquency

Giddings, A. (1985) *The Constitution of Society: Outline of the Theory of Structuration*. Cambridge: Polity Press

Gilligan, C. (1982) *In A Different Voice*. Cambridge MA: Harvard University Press

Gilman, S.L. (1985) *Difference and Pathology: Stereotypes of Sexuality, Race and Madness*. Ithaca: Cornell University Press

Gilman, S.L. (1992) *The Jew's Body*. New York: Routledge

Ginsberg, G.P. (1971) Public conceptions and attitudes about suicide. *Journal of Health and Social Behaviour*, 12, 200–201

Gluckman, M. (1963) *Order and Rebellion in Tribal Africa*. London: Cohen and West

Godelier, M. (1986) *The Mental and the Material: Thought, Economy and Society*. London: Verso (1984)

Goffman, E. (1971) *Relations in Public: Microstudies of the Public Order*. New York: Basic Books

Goldstein, A.J. (1970) Case conference: Some aspects of agoraphobia. *Journal of Behaviour Therapy and Experimental Psychiatry*, 1, 305–313

Goldstein, A.J. (1973) Learning theory insufficiency in understand agoraphobia – A plea for empiricism. *Proceedings of the European Association for Behaviour Therapy and Modification Meeting 1971*. Munich: Urban and Schwarzenberg

Goldstein, A.J. and Chambless, D.L. (1978) A reanalysis of agoraphobia. *Behaviour Therapy*, 9, 47–59

Good, B. (1994) *Medicine, Rationality and Experience: An Anthropological Perspective*. Cambridge: Cambridge University Press

Good, B.J. and Good, M.-J.D. (1981) The meaning of symptoms: a cultural hermeneutic model for clinical practitioners. In L. Eisenberg and A. Kleinman (eds.), *The Relevance of Social Science for Medicine*. Dordrecht: Reidel

Good, B.J. and Good, M.-J.D. (1982) Toward a meaning-centered analysis of popular illness categories. In A.J. Marsella and G.M. White (eds.), *Cultural Conceptions of Mental Health and Therapy*, 141–166, Dordrecht: Reidel

Good, B.J. and Good, M.-J.D. (1986) The Cultural Context of Diagnosis and Therapy: A View from Medical Anthropology. In M.

Miranda and H. Kitano (eds.), *Mental Health Research Practice in Minority Communities: Development of Culturally Sensitive Training Programmes*, pp. 1–27. Washington: Department of Health and Human Services

Goody, J. (1977) *The Domestication of the Savage Mind*. Cambridge: Cambridge University Press

Gove, W.R. and Tudor, J.F. (1973) Adult sex roles and mental illness. *American Journal of Sociology*, 78, 812–835

Gradek, M. (1976) Le concept de fou et ses implications dans la littérature talmudique et ses exigeses. *Annales Médico-Psychologiques*, 134, 17–36

Grunbaum, A. (1984) *The Foundations of Psychoanalysis: A Philosophical Critique*. Berkeley: University of California Press

Hage, P. and Harary, F. (1983) *Structural Models in Anthropology*. Cambridge: Cambridge University Press

Hall, M.P. (1962) *An Encyclopedic Outline of Masonic, Hermetic, Qabbalistic and Rosicrucian Symbolic Philosophy: Being an Interpretation of the Secret Teachings Concealed within the Rituals, Allegories and Mysteries of All Ages*. Los Angeles: Philosophical Research Society

Hallam, R. (1984) Agoraphobia: Deconstructing a clinical syndrome. *Bulletin of the British Psychological Society*, 3, 337–340

Handwerker, W.P. (1989) *Women's Power and Social Revolution: Fertility Transition in the West Indies*. California: Sage

Haraway, D. (1989) *Primate Visions: Gender, Race and Nature in the World of Modern Science*. New York: Routledge

Haraway, D. (1991) *Simians, Cyborgs and Women: The Reinvention of Nature*. London: Free Association Books

Hardy, T. (1896) *Jude the Obscure*. London: Macmillan, 1974 edn.

Harner. M.J. (ed.) (1973) *Hallucinogens and Shamanism*. Oxford: Oxford University Press

Harré, R. (1983) *Personal Being: a Theory for Individual Psychology*. Blackwell: Oxford

Harris, C. (1957) Possession 'hysteria' in a Kenyan tribe. *American Anthropologist*, 59, 1046–1066

Harrison, J.F.C. (1979) *The Second Coming: Popular Millenarianism 1780–1850*. London: Routledge and Kegan Paul.

Harvey, E.B., Gazy, L. and Samuels, B. (1976) Utilisation of a psychiatric social work team in an Alaskan boarding school. *Journal of the American Academy of Clinical Psychiatry*, 15, 558–74

Hawton, K., Marsack, P. and Fagg, J. (1981) The attitudes of psychiatrists to deliberate self-poisoning: comparison with physicians and nurses. *British Journal of Medical Psychology*, 54, 341–348

Hawton, K., Osborne, M. and Cole, D. (1982) Adolescents who take overdoses. *British Journal of Psychiatry*, 140, 118–123

Heelas, P. and Haglund-Heelas, A.M. (1988) The Inadequacy of 'Deprivation' as a Theory of Conversion. In W. James and D.H. Johnson (eds.), *Vernacular Christianity: Essays in the Social Anthropology of Religion Presented to Godfrey Lienhardt*. Oxford: JASO

Henriques, F. (1953) *Family and Colour in Jamaica*. London: Eyre & Spottiswoode

Hill, D. (1964) The bridge between neurology and psychiatry. *Lancet*, i, 509–514

Ho, M.-W. & Fox, S.W. (1982) The epigenetic approach to the evolution of organisms: with notes on its relevance to social and cultural evolution. In H.C. Plotkin (ed.), *Learning, Development and Culture: Essays in Evolutionary Epistemology*. Chichester: Wiley

Hobart, M. (1982) Meaning or Moaning? An Ethnographic Note on a Little Understood Tribe. In D. Parkin (ed.), *Semantic Anthropology*. London: Academic Press

Hoffman, E. (1981) *The Way of Splendor: Jewish Mysticism and Modern Psychology*. New York: Shambala Press

Hollis, M. and Lukes, S. (Eds.) (1982) *Rationality and Relativism*. Cambridge: MIT Press

Holloway, M. (1966) *Heavens on Earth: Utopian Communities in America 1680–1880*. New York: Dover

Hollywood, A. (1995) *The Soul as Virgin Wife: Mechthild of Magdeburg, Marguerite Porete, and Meister Eckhart*. New York: University of Notre Dame Press

Holy, L. and M. Stuchlik (eds.) (1981) *The Structure of Folk Models*. London: Academic Press

Hopkins, J.K. (1982) *A Woman to Deliver Her People: Joanna Southcott and English Millenarianism in an Era of Revolution*. Austin: University of Texas Press

Horwitz, A. (1977) The pathways into psychiatric treatment: some differences between men and women. *Journal of Health and Social Behaviour*, 18, 169–178

Horwitz, A.V. (1982) *The Social Control of Mental Illness*. New York: Academic Press

Howell, E. and Bayes, M. (eds.) (1981) *Women and Mental Health*. New York: Basic Books

Howell, S. (1981) Rules not words. In P. Heelas and A. Lock (eds.), *Indigenous Psychologies*. Academic Press: London

Hudson, B. (1974) The families of agoraphobics treated by behaviour therapy. *British Journal of Sociology*, 4, 51–59

Huizer, G. and Mannheim, B. (eds.) (1979) *The Politics of Anthropology: Towards a View from Below*. The Hague: Mouton

Hundert, E.M. (1989) *Philosophy, Psychiatry and Neuroscience: Three Approaches to the Mind*. Oxford: Clarendon Press

Ingleby, D. (1981) Understanding 'mental illness'. In D. Ingleby (ed.), *Critical Psychiatry: The Politics of Mental Health*. Harmondsworth: Penguin

Ingleby, D. (1982) The social construction of mental illness. In P. Wright and A. Treacher (eds), *The Problem of Medical Knowledge*. Edinburgh: Edinburgh University Press

Ingold. T. (1986) *The Appropriation of Nature: Essays on Human Ecology and Social Relations*. Manchester: Manchester University Press

Ingold, T. (1989) Culture and the perception of the environment. 6th EIDOS Workshop on Cultural Understandings of the Environment. Unpublished manuscript, revised 1990. School of Oriental and African Studies, London

Jackson, M. (1979) Prevented succession: a commentary upon a Kuranko narrative. In R.H. Hook (ed.), *Fantasy and Symbol: Essays in Anthropological Interpretation*. London: Academic Press

Jackson, M. (1983) Knowledge of the Body. *Man* (n.s.), 18, 327–45

Jacobs, L. (1973) *Hasidic Prayer*. New York: Schocken

Jakobson, R. (1960) Linguistics and Poetics. In T. Sebeok (ed.), *Style in Language*. New York: Wiley

James, C.W.B. (1963) Psychology and gynaecology. In A. Cloge and A. Bourne (eds.), *British Gynaecological Practice*. London: Heinemann

James, D. and Hawton, K. (1985) (1985) Overdoses: explanations and attitudes in self-poisoners and significant others *British Journal of Psychiatry*, 146, 481–485

Janet, P. (1925) *Psychological Healing*. London: Allen and Unwin

Jansen, J.M. (1978) *The Quest for Therapy: Medical Pluralism in Lower Zaire*. Berkeley: University of California Press

Jansen, J.M. (1979) Drums Anonymous: Towards an understanding of structures of therapeutic maintenance. In M. De Vries et al. (eds.), *The Use and Abuse of Medicine*. New York: Praeger Scientific

Jarvie, I.C. (1964) *The Revolution in Anthropology*. London: Routledge and Kegan Paul

Jaspers, K. (1962) *General Psychopathology*. Manchester: Manchester University Press

Jilek, W.G. (1982) *Indian Healing: Shamanic Ceremonialism in the Pacific Northwest Today*. Surrey, BC: Hancock: Washington

Johnson, M. (1987) *The Body in the Mind: The Bodily Basis of Meaning, Imagination and Reason*. Chicago: Chicago University Press

Johnson, M. (1993) *The Moral Imagination: Implications of Cognitive Science For Ethics*. Chicago: Chicago University Press

Jones, E. (1916) The theory of symbolism. In *Papers on Psycho-Analysis*. London: Baillière

Jones, I.H. (1971) Stereotyped aggression in a group of Australian Western Desert Aborigines. *British Journal of Medical Psychology*, 44, 259–265

Jonte-Pace, D. (1987) Object relations theory, mothering and religion. *Horizons*, 14, 310–327

Jordan, W.D. (1968) *White over Black*. North Carolina: North Carolina University Press

Jordanovna, L.J. (1980) Natural facts: a historical perspective on science and sexuality. In MacCormack, C. and Strathern, M. (eds.), *Nature, Culture and Gender*. Cambridge: Cambridge University Press

Jordanovna, L.J. (1981) Mental illness, mental health. In Cambridge Women's Studies Collective (eds.), *Women in Society*. London: Virago

Julian of Norwich (1978) *Showings*. Trans. E. Colledge and J. Walsh. New York: Paulist Press

Kalucy, R.S., Crisp, A.H. and Harding, B. (1977) The study of 56 families with anorexia nervosa. *British Journal of Medical Psychology*, 50, 381–395

Kapferer, B. (1979) Mind, self and other in demonic illness. *American Ethnologist*, 6, 110–133

Kapferer, B. (1981) Ritual process and the transformation of context in the power of ritual. *Social Analysis*, 1, 3–19

Kapferer, B. (1983) *A Celebration of Demons: Exorcism and the Aesthetics of Healing in Sri Lanka*. Oxford: Berg

Katon, W., Kleinman, A. and Rosen, G. (1983) Depression and somatization – II. *American Journal of Medicine*, 72, 241–7

Katz, J. (1961) *Tradition and Crisis: Jewish Society at the End of the Middle Ages*. New York: Free Press

Kehot Publication Society (1981) *Tanya* (Likutei Amarim-Tanya, bilingual edition). Stamford Hill: London

Kempe, M. (1994) *The Book of Margery Kempe*. Harmondsworth: Penguin

Kendell, R.E. (1975) The concept of disease and its implications for psychiatry. *British Journal of Psychiatry*, 127, 305–315

Kenny, M.G. (1981) Multiple personality and spirit possession. *Psychiatry*, 44, 337–358

Kerns, V. (1983) *Women and the Ancestors: Black Carib Kinship and Ritual*. Urbana: University of Illinois Press

Kiev, A. (1964) The study of folk psychiatry. In A. Kiev (ed.), *Magic, Faith and Healing*. New York: Free Press

Kirmayer, L. (1993) Healing and the Invention of Metaphor: The Effectiveness of Symbols Revisited. *Culture, Medicine and Psychiatry*, 17, 161–195

Kitzinger, S. (1978) *Women As Mothers*. London: Fontana

Kitzinger, S. (1982) The social context of birth: some comparisons between childbirth in Jamaica and Britain. In C.P. MacCormack (ed.), *Ethnography of Fertility and Birth*. London: Academic Press

Klausner, S.Z. and Foulks, E.F. (1982) *Eskimo Capitalists: Oil, Politics and Alcohol*. New Jersey Allanheld and Osmun

Kleinman, A. (1974) The cognitive structure of traditional medical systems. *Ethnomedicine*, 3, 27–38

Kleinman, A. (1977) Depression, somatisation and the 'new cross-cultural psychiatry'. *Social Science and Medicine*, 11, 3–10

Kleinman, A. (1987) Anthropology and psychiatry: The role of culture in cross-cultural research on illness. *British Journal of Psychiatry*, 151, 447–454

Kleinman, A. (1988) *The Illness Narratives: Suffering, Healing and the Human Condition*. New York: Basic Books

Kleinman, A. (1988) *Rethinking Psychiatry: From Cultural Category to Personal Experience*. New York: Free Press

Kleinman, A. and L.H. Sung (1979) Why do indigenous practitioners successfully heal? *Social Science and Medicine*, 13, 7–26

Kluckhohn, C. (1944) *Navaho Witchcraft*. Cambridge, Mass.: Peabody Museum

Knox, R.A. (1950) *Enthusiasm: A Chapter in the History of Religion*. Oxford: Clarendon Press

Koch, F. (1968) On 'possession' behaviour in New Guinea. *Journal of the Polynesian Society*, 77, 135–146

Kreitman, N. and Schreiber, M. (1979) Parasuicide in young Edinburgh women. *Psychological Medicine*, 9, 469–479

Kreitman, N., Smith, P. and Tan, E. (1970) Attempted suicide as language. *British Journal of Psychiatry*, 116, 465–473

Krohn, A. (1978) *Hysteria: The Elusive Neurosis*. New York: International University Press

Kroll, O. and De Gank, O. (1986) The Adolescence of a Thirteenth Century Visionary Nun. *Psychological Medicine*, 16, 745–756

Kupferman, A.J. (1976) The Lubavitch Hasidim of Stamford Hill. M.Phil. thesis, University of London

Kurtz, P.D. (1988) Mary of Oignies, Christine the Marvellous and medieval heresy. *Mystics Quarterly*, 14, 186–196

La Barre, W. (1970) *The Ghost Dance.* New York: Doubleday

Lacan, J. (1977) The significance of the phallus. In *Ecrits: A Selection.* London: Tavistock

Laderman, C. (1987) The Ambiguity of Symbols in the Structure of Healing. *Social Science and Medicine*, 24, 293–301

La Fontaine, J. (1981) The domestication of the savage male. *Man* (n.s.), 16, 333–349

Laing, R.D. (1959) *The Divided Self.* London: Tavistock

Lakoff, G. (1987) *Women, Fire and Dangerous Things: What Categories Reveal About the Mind.* Chicago: Chicago University Press

Lane, H. (1988) *When the Mind Hears: A History of the Deaf.* Harmondsworth: Penguin

Langness, L.L. (1967) Rejoinder to R. Salisbury. *Transcultural Psychiatric Research Review*, 4, 125–130

Langness, L.L. (1968) Hysterical psychosis in the New Guinea Highlands: a Bena Bena example. *Psychiatry*, 28, 258–277

Last, M. (1981) The importance of knowing about not knowing. *Social Science and Medicine*, 15, 387–392

Laughlin, C.D., McManus, J. and D'Aquili (1993) *Brain, Symbol and Experience: Towards a Neurophenomenology of Human Consciousness.* New York: Columbia University Press

Laughlin, C.D. and C.D. Stephens (1980) Symbolisation, Canalisation and P-Structure. In Foster and Brandes, *op. cit.*

Law, J.M. (ed.) (1995) *Religious Reflections on the Human Body.* Bloomington: Indiana University Press

Lawson, E.T. and R.N. McCauley (1993) *Rethinking Religion: Connecting Cognition and Culture.* Cambridge: Cambridge University Press

Lazarus, A. (1972) Phobias: broad spectrum behavioural views. *Seminars in Psychiatry*, 4, 85–90

Leach, E.R. (1954) *Political Systems of Highland Burma.* London: Bell

Leach, E.R. (1958) Magical Hair. *Journal of the Royal Anthropological Institute*, 88, 147–164

Leach, E.R. (1961) *Rethinking Anthropology.* London: Athlone

Leach, E.R. (1970) The epistemological background to Malinowski's empiricism. In R. Firth (ed.), *Man and Culture: An Evaluation of the Work of Bronislaw Malinowski.* London: Routledge and Kegan Paul

Leach, E.R. (1973) Structuralism in social anthropology. In D. Robey (ed.), *Structuralism.* Oxford: Clarendon Press

Leach, E.R. (1976) *Culture and Communication*. Cambridge: Cambridge University Press

Leach, E.R. (1978) Culture and reality. *Psychological Medicine*, 8, 555–564

Leach, E.R. and Aycock, D.A. (1983) *Structuralist Interpretations of Biblical Myth*. Cambridge: Cambridge University Press

Leary, D. (1990) *Metaphors in the History of Psychology*. Cambridge: Cambridge University Press

Lee, R.L.M. (1981) Structure and anti-structure in the culture-bound syndromes: the Malay case. *Culture, Medicine and Psychiatry*, 5, 233–248

Leff, J.P. (1973) Culture and the differentiation of emotional states. *British Journal of Psychiatry*, 123, 299–306

Leff, J. (1981) *Psychiatry Around the Globe*. Kecker: New York

Leff, J. (1990a) (Editorial) The 'new cross-cultural psychiatry': A case of the baby and the bathwater. *British Journal of Psychiatry*, 156, 305–307

Leff, J. (1990b) Correspondence. *British Journal of Psychiatry*, 157, 296

Lévi-Strauss, C. (1949) L'Efficacité Symbolique, trans. as The Effectiveness of Symbols. In Lévi-Strauss (1968), *op. cit.* Harmondsworth: Penguin

Lévi-Strauss, C. (1966) *The Savage Mind*. London: Weidenfeld & Nicolson

Lévi-Strauss, C. (1968) *Structural Anthropology*. London: Allen Lane

Lévi-Strauss, C. (1970) *The Raw and the Cooked: Introduction to a Science of Mythology – 1*. London: Cape (1964)

Lévi-Strauss, C. (1977) *Structural Anthropology*, vol.2. London: Allen Lane

Lewis, G. (1975) *Knowledge of Illness in a Sepik Society*. London: Athlone

Lewis, I.M. (1966) Spirit possession and deprivation cults. *Man* (n.s.), 1, 307–329

Lewis, I.M. (1969) Spirit possession in Northern Somaliland. In J. Beattie and J. Middletone (eds.), *Spirit mediumship and society in Africa*. London: Routledge and Kegan Paul

Lewis, I.M. (1971) *Ecstatic Religion*. Harmondsworth: Penguin

Lewis, I.M. (ed.) (1977) *Symbols and Sentiments*. London: Academic Press

Lewis, T.H. (1975) A syndrome of depression and mutism in the Ogala Sioux. *American Journal of Psychiatry*, 132, 753–755

Lewontin, R.C. (1983) Gene, organism and environment. In *Evolution from Molecules to Men* (ed. D.S. Bendall), Cambridge: Cambridge University Press

Lindblom, G. (1920) *The Akamba in British East Africa.* Upsala

Lipsedge, M. and Littlewood, R. (1985) Domestic sieges (unpublished ms)

Littlewood, R. (1980) Anthropology and psychiatry: an alternative approach. *British Journal of Medical Psychology* (reprinted here)

Littlewood, R. (1982) Correspondence. *Royal Anthropological Institute News*, November

Littlewood, R. (1983) The Antinomian Hasid. *British Journal of Medical Psychology* (reprinted here)

Littlewood, R. (1984a) The individual articulation of shared symbols. *Journal of Operational Psychiatry* (reprinted here)

Littlewood, R. (1984b) The imitation of madness: The influence of psychopathology upon culture. *Social Science and Medicine* (reprinted here)

Littlewood, R. (1985) An indigenous conceptualisation of depression in Trinidad. *Psychological Medicine* (reprinted here)

Littlewood, R. (1986) Russian dolls and Chinese boxes: An anthropological approach to the implicit models of comparative psychiatry. In J. Cox (ed.), *Transcultural psychiatry.* London: Croom Helm

Littlewood, R. (1987) Pathology and Identity: The Genesis of a Millennial Movement in North-East Trinidad. DPhil Thesis, University of Oxford

Littlewood, R. (1988) From vice to madness: The semantics of naturalistic and personalistic understandings in Trinidadian local medicine. *Social Science and Medicine* (reprinted here)

Littlewood, R. (1990a) From categories to contexts: A decade of the 'new cross-cultural psychiatry', *British Journal of Psychiatry*, 156, 308–327

Littlewood, R. (1990b) How universal is something we can call 'therapy'? *Holistic Medicine*, 5, 49–65

Littlewood, R. (1991) Artichokes and Entities: Or, How New is 'The New Cross-Cultural Psychiatry?', *Transcultural Psychiatric Research Review*

Littlewood, R. (1991a) From disease to illness and back again. *Lancet*, 337, 1013–1016

Littlewood, R. (1991b) Against pathology: The 'new cross-cultural psychiatry' and its critics. *British Journal of Psychiatry* (reprinted here)

Littlewood, R. (1993) *Pathology and Identity: The Work of Mother Earth in Trinidad.* Cambridge: Cambridge University Press

Littlewood, R. (1994) Verticality as the idiom for mood and disorder: a note on an eighteenth century representation *British Medical Anthropology Review* (reprinted here)

Littlewood, R. (1995) Psychopathology and religious innovation: an historical instance. In D. Bhugra (ed.), *Psychiatry and Religion.* London: Routledge

Littlewood, R. (1996) *Reason and Necessity In the Specification of the Multiple Self.* Royal Anthropological Institute Occasional Paper 42. London: R.A.I.

Littlewood, R. and Dein, S. (1995) The effectiveness of words: religion and healing among the Lubavitch. *Culture, Medicine and Psychiatry* (reprinted here)

Littlewood, R. and Lipsedge, M. (1982) *Aliens and Alienists: Ethnic Minorities and Psychiatry.* Harmondsworth: Penguin

Littlewood, R. and Lipsedge, M. (1985) Culture-bound syndromes. In K. Granville-Grossman (ed.), *Recent Advances in Psychiatry* – 5. Edinburgh: Churchill Livingstone

Littlewood, R. and Lipsedge, M. (1987) The butterfly and the serpent. *Culture, Medicine and Psychiatry* (reprinted here)

Lloyd, G.E.R. (1990) *Demystifying Mentalities.* Cambridge: Cambridge University Press

Lock, M. and D.R. Gordon (1988) Relationships between society, culture and biomedicine. In Lock and Gordon (eds.), *Biomedicine Examined.* Dordrecht: Kluwer

Lock, M. and N. Scheper-Hughes (1990) A critical interpretative approach in medical anthropology: rituals and routines of discipline and dissent, In T. Johnson and C. Sargent (eds.), *Medical Anthropology: A Handbook of Theory and Practice.* Westport: Greenwood Press

Lofland, J. and R. Stark (1965) Becoming a World Saver: A Theory of Conversion to a Deviant Perspective. *American Sociological Review*, 30, 862–75

Logan, M.H. (1979) Variations regarding susto causality among the Cakchinquel of Guatemala. *Culture, Medicine and Psychiatry*, 3, 153–66

Long, E.R. (1965) *A History of Pathology.* New York: Dover

Loudon, J.R. (1959) Psychogenic disorders and social conflict among the Zulu. In M.K. Opler (ed.), *Culture and Mental Health.* New York: Macmillan

Lovejoy, D. (1985) *Religious Enthusiasm in the New World: Heresy to Revolution.* Cambridge MA: Harvard University Press

Low, S.N. (1981) The meaning of nervios: A sociocultural analysis of spirit possession in San Jose, Costa Rica. *Culture, Medicine and Psychiatry*, 5, 25–47

Lowenthal, D. (1972) *West Indian Societies.* Oxford: Oxford University Press

Lubavitch Publications (1992) *A Collection of Stories on the Lubavitcher Rebbe*. New York: Lubavitch Printing House

Lutzky, H. (1989) Reparation and tikkun: a comparison of the Kleinian and Kabbalistic concepts. *International Review of Psycho-Analysis*, 16, 449–458

Lyon, M.L. and Barbalet, J.B. (1994) Society's body: emotion and the 'somatisation' of social theory. In T.J. Csordas (ed.), *Embodiment and Experience*. Cambridge: Cambridge University Press

Mabel-Lois, L. (1974) Fat Dykes Don't Make It. *Lesbian Tide*, October, 11–12

MacCormack, C.P. (1982) Biological, cultural and social adaptation in human fertility and birth. In MacCormack (ed.), *Ethnography of Fertility and Birth*. London: Academic Press

Macfarlane, J., Alien, L. and Honzik, M. (1954) *A Developmental Study of the Problems of Normal Children*. Berkeley: University of California Press

Magolin, J. and E. Witztum (1980) Supernatural impotence: historical review with anthropological and clinical implications. *British Journal of Medical Psychology*, 62, 333–342

Mandelbrot, B.B. (1977) *Fractals: Form, Chance and Dimension*. New York

Marks, I.M. (1970) Agoraphobic syndrome (phobic anxiety state). *Archives of General Psychiatry*, 23: 538–553

Marsella, A.J. and White, G.M. (eds.) (1983) *Cultural Conceptions of Mental Health and Therapy*. D. Reidel: Dordrecht

Martin, E. (1987) *The Woman in the Body: A Cultural Analysis of Reproduction*. Boston: Beacon Press

Mauss, M. (1979) Body techniques (orig. pub. 1934). In Mauss, *Sociology and Psychology*, trans. B. Brewster. London: Routledge and Kegan Paul

Mayr, E. (1982) *The Growth of Biological Thought*. Cambridge, MA.: Harvard University Press

McDougall, L. (1977) Symbols and somatic structures. In Blacking *op. cit.*

McEvedy, C.P. and Beard, A.W. (1970) The Royal Free epidemic. *British Medical Journal*, 3 January, 7–11

McGuire, M.B. (1983) Words of power: personal empowerment and healing. *Culture, Medicine and Psychiatry*, 7, 221–240

McKinlay, S. and Jeffreys, M. (1974) The menopausal syndrome. *British Journal of Preventative and Social Medicine*, 28, 108–115

McMullin, E. (1978) Structurel Explanation. *American Philosophical Quarterly*, 15, 139–147

Mead, M. (1949) *Male and Female*. New York: Morrow

Meadow, R. (1984) Factitious illness: the hinterland of child abuse. In *Recent Advances in Paediatrics*. Edinburgh: Churchill Livingstone

Merleau-Ponty, M. (1962) *The Phenomenology of Perception*, trans. C. Smith. New York: Humanities Press

Miller, P. & Rose, N. (eds.) (1986) *The Power of Psychiatry*. London: Polity

Millman, M. (1974) *Such a Pretty Face: Being Fat in America*. New York: Norton

Mindel, N. (1974) *Philosophy of Chabad*. New York: Kehot Publication Society

Mintz, J.R. (1968) *Legends of the Hasidim*. Chicago: Chicago University Press

Mintz, J.R. (1992) *Hasidic People: A Place in the New World*. Cambridge MA: Harvard University Press

Minuchin, S., Baker, L., Rosman, B., Liebman, R., Milman, L. and Todd, T. (1975) A conceptual model of psychosomatic illness in children, family organisation and family therapy. *Arch.Gen.Psychiat*. 32: 1031–1038

Moller, H. (1971) The social causation of affective mysticism. *Journal Social History*, 4, 305–38

Moerman, N. (1979) Anthropology of symbolic healing. *Current Anthropology*, 20, 59–80

Moravec, H. (1989) *Mind Children: The Future of Robot and Human Intelligence*. Cambridge, Mass.: Harvard University Press

Morgan, H.G., Burns-Cox, C.J., Pocock, H. and Pottle, S. (1975) Deliberate self-harm: clinical and socio-demographic characteristics of 368 patients. *British Journal of Psychiatry*, 127, 574–579

Morris, A. (1985) Sanctified madness: the god-intoxicated saints of Bengal. *Social Science and Medicine*, 21, 221–235

Muller-Hill, B. (1988) *Murderous Science: Elimination by Scientific Selection of Jews, Gypsies and Others, Germany 1933–1945*. Oxford: Oxford University Press

Munn, N. (1973) Symbolism in a ritual context: aspects of symbolic action. In J. Honigmann (ed.), *Handbook of Social and Cultural Anthropology*. Chicago: Rand

Murphy, H.B.M. (1967) Cultural aspects of the delusion. *Studium Generale*, 2, 684–692

Murphy, H.B.M. (1977) Transcultural psychiatry should begin at home. *Psychological Medicine* 7: 369–71

Murphy, H.B.M. (1978) The advent of guilt feelings as a common depressive symptom: a historical comparison. *Psychiatry*, 41, 229–242

Murphy, H.B.M. (1979) Depression, witchcraft beliefs and superego development in preliterate societies. *Canadian Journal of Psychiatry* 24, 437–449

Murphy, H.B.M. (1982) *Comparative Psychiatry*. Berlin: Springer

Murphy, R.F. (1972) *The Dialectics of Social Life*. London: Allen and Unwin

Murray, J., Dunn, G., Williams, P. and Tarnopolsky, A. (1981) Factors affecting the consumption of psychotropic drugs. *Psychological Medicine*, 11, 551–560

Myers, W.A. (1977) The significance of the colours black and white in dreams of black and white patients. *Journal of the American Psychoanalytic Association*, 25, 160–181

National Organisation for Women Task Force (1974) *Dick and Jane as Victims: A survey of 134 Elementary School Readers*. London: Blackstock

Needham, R. (1962) *Structure and Sentiment*. Chicago: Chicago University Press

Needham, R. (1963) *Introduction to Durkheim and Mauss* (1963)

Needham, R. (1975) Polythetic classification. *Man*, 10, 349–369

Needham, R. (ed.) (1977) *Right and Left*. Chicago: Chicago University Press

Needham, R. (1979) *Symbolic Classification*. Santa Monica: Goodyear

Needham, R. (1980) *Reconnaissances*. Toronto: University of Toronto Press

Nelson, K. (1979) *The Origin: An Investigation into Primitive Matriarchal Societies, the Patriarchal Takeover and Its Effect on Society Today, And the Building of a Just and Egalitarian Post-Patriarchal Society*. San Francisco: Venusian Propaganda

Neumann, E. (1963) *The Great Mother: An Analysis of the Archetype*. Princeton: Princeton University Press

Newman, P.L. (1964) 'Wild man' behaviour in a New Guinea Highlands community. *American Anthropologist*, 66, 1–19

Ngui, P.G. (1969) The koro epidemic in Singapore. *Australian and New Zealand Journal of Psychiatry*, 3, 263–266

Nordoff, C. (1875) *The Communistic Societies of the United States From Personal Observations*. New York: Harper and Brothers

Nylander, I. (1971) The feeling of being fat and dieting in the school population. *Acta Sociomedica Scandinavia*, 3, 17–26

Obeyesekere, G. (1981) *Medusa's Hair: An Essay on Personal Symbols and Religious Experience*. Chicago: Chicago University Press

Ogrizek, M. (1982) Mama wata: de l'hystérie à la feminité en Afrique. *Confrontations Psychiatriques*, 21, 213–237

Okley, J. (1975) Gypsy women: models in conflict. In S. Ardener (ed.), *Perceiving Women*. London: Dent

Olivier, C. (1989) *Jocasta's Children: The Imprint of the Mother.* (orig. pub. 1980) London: Routledge

Orbach, S. (1978) *Fat is a Feminist Issue.* London: Paddington

Ortner, S. (1973) On Key Symbols. *American Anthropologist* 75: 1338–1346

Ortner, S. (1974) Is female to male as nature is to culture? In M.A. Rosaldo and L. Lamphere (eds.), *Women, Culture and Society.* Stanford: Stanford University Press

Pagels, E. (1982) *The Gnostic Gospels.* Harmondsworth: Penguin

Parkin, D. (ed.) (1982) *Semantic Anthropology.* London: Academic Press

Parkin, D. (ed.) (1985) *The Anthropology of Evil.* Oxford: Blackwell

Parkin, D. (1992) Dispersing Problems: Muslim Medical Practitioners on the Kenya Coast. (unpub. ms.)

Parry, H.J., Balter, M.D., Mellinger, G.D., Cisin, I.H. and Manheimer, D.I. (1973) National patterns of psychotherapeutic drug use. *Archives of General Psychiatry,* 28, 769–783

Parsons, T. (1951) Illness and the role of the physician: a sociological perspective. *American Journal of Orthopsychiatry,* 21, 452–460

Parsons, T. (1952) *The Social System.* London: Routledge & Kegan Paul

Parsons, T. and Fox, R. (1952) Illness, therapy and the modern urban American family. *Journal of Social Issues,* 8, 31–44

Perec, G. (1989) *W or The Memory of Childhood.* London: Collins Harvill

Perkins, P. (1995) Creation of the body in Gnosticism. In Law, *op. cit.*

Peters, L.G. and Price-Williams, D. (1983) A phenomenological overview of trance. *Transcultural Psychiatric Research Review,* 20, 5–39

Phillips, D.L. and Segal, B. (1969) Sexual status and psychiatric symptoms. *American Sociological Review,* 29, 678–687

Piaget, J. (1968) *Le Structuralisme.* Paris: Presses Universitaires de France

Podrabinek, A. (1980) *Punitive Medicine.* Ann Arbor: Karoma

Polhemus, T. (1978) *Social Aspects of the Human Body.* Harmondsworth: Penguin

Poll, S. (1962) *The Hasidic Community of Williamsburgh.* New York: Free Press

Prather, J. and Fidell, L. (1975) Sex differences in the content and style of medical advertisements. *Social Science and Medicine,* 9, 23–26

Pratt, M.L. (1986) Fieldwork in common places. In J. Clifford and G.E. Marcus (eds.), *Writing Culture: The Poetics and Politics of Ethnography.* Berkeley: University of California Press

Preis, K. (1928) Die Medizin im Zohar. *Monattschrift Für Geschichte und Wissenschaft Des Judentums* 72: 241

Preston, J.L. (1982) Introduction. In Preston (ed.), *Mother Worship: Theme and Variation*. Chapel Hill: University of North Carolina Press

Preuss, J. (1978) *Biblical and Talmudic Medicine*. New York: Hebrew Publishing (1957)

Prince, R. (1976) Psychotherapy as the manipulation of endogenous healing mechanisms. *Transcultural Psychiatric Research Review*, 13, 115–133

Prince, R. (1983) Is anorexia nervosa a culture-bound syndrome? *Transcultural Psychiatric Research Review*, 20, 299–300

Prince, R. (1991) Review of Littlewood 1990a, 1990b. *Transcultural Psychiatric Research Review*, 28, 41–55

Prince, R. and Tcheng-Laroche, F. (1987) Culture-bound syndromes and international disease classification. *Culture, Medicine and Psychiatry*, 11, 3–19

Proust, M. (1958) *A la Recherche du Temps Perdu*. Paris: Gallimard

Rabuzzi, K.A. (1994) *Mother With Child: Transformations Through Childbirth*. Bloomington: Indiana University Press

Radcliffe-Brown, A.R. (1952) *Structure and Function in Primitive Society*. London: Routledge

Ramon, S., Bancroft, J.H.J. and Skrimshire, A.M. (1975) Attitudes towards self-poisoning among physicians and nurses in a general hospital. *British Journal of Psychiatry*, 127, 257–264

Rawnsley, K. & Loudon, J. (1964) Epidemiology of mental disorder in a closed community. *British Journal of Psychiatry*, 110, 830–839

Raymond, J.C. (1982) Medicine as a patriarchal religion. *Journal of Medical Philosophy*, 7, 197–216

Reay, M. (1977) Ritual madness observed: a discarded pattern of faith in Papua New Guinea. *Journal of Pacific History*, 12, 55–79

Reynolds, E.H. (1990) Structure and function in neurology and psychiatry. *British Journal of Psychiatry*, 157, 481–490

Richards, A.I. (1956) *Chisungu: A Girl's Initiation Ceremony among the Bemba of Northern Rhodesia*. London: Faber & Faber (1982).

Rip, C.M. (1973) *Contemporary Social Pathology* (3rd edn.), Pretoria: Academica

Ritenbaugh, C. (1982a) Obesity as a culture-bound syndrome. *Culture, Medicine and Psychiatry*, 6, 347–364

Ritenbaugh, C. (1982b) New Approaches to old problems: interactions of culture and nutrition. In N.J. Chrisman and T.W. Maretzki, *Clinically Applied Anthropology*. Dordrecht: Reidel

Rivers, W.H.R. (1920) *Instinct and the Unconscious*. Cambridge: Cambridge University Press

Rivers, W.H.R. (1924) *Medicine, Magic and Religion*. London: Kegan Paul, Trench and Trubner

Robert, M. (1974) *D'Oedipe à Moise: Freud et la Conscience Juive*. Paris: Calman-Levy

Robertson-Smith, J.S.R. (1927) *Lectures on The Religion of the Semites: The Fundamental Institutions*. Third Edition. London: A. and C. Black

Robins, J. (1986) *Fools and Mad: A History of the Insane in Ireland*. Dublin: Institute of Public Administration

Robins, L.N., Meizer, G.E. and Weissman, M.M. (1984) Lifetime prevalence of specific psychiatric disorders. *Archives of General Psychiatry* 41: 949–958

Rodman, H. (1971) *Lower-Class Families: the Culture of Poverty in Negro Trinidad*. Oxford University Press: New York

Rooth, F.G. (1971) Indecent exposure and exhibitionism. *British Journal of Hospital Medicine*, April, 521–533

Rooth, F.G. (1974) Exhibitionism outside Europe and America. *Archives of Sexual Behaviour*, 2, 351–62

Rorty, R. (1980) *Philosophy and The Mirror of Nature*. Oxford: Blackwell

Rosen, G. (1968) *Madness in Society*. London: Routledge and Kegan Paul

Rubens, B. (1974) *The Elected Member*. London: Penguin

Rubin, N. (1988) Body and soul in Talmudic and Mishnaic sources. *Koroth*, 9, 151–164

Rubin, V. (1959) Approaches to the study of national characteristics in a multicultural society. *International Journal of Social Psychiatry*, 5, 20–35

Sachdev, P.S. (1990) *Studies in Maori Ethnopsychiatry*. PhD Thesis, University of New South Wales

Sachs, O. (1989) *Seeing Voices: A Journey into the World of the Deaf*. Berkeley: University of California Press

Sahlins, M. (1976) *Culture and Practical Reason*. Chicago: University of Chicago Press

Salisbury, R. (1966) Possession in the New Guinea Highlands. *Transcultural Psychiatric Research Review*, 3, 103–108

Salisbury, R. (1967) Reply to Langness. *Transcultural Psychiatric Research Review*, 4, 130–4

Samuel, G. (1990) *Mind, Body and Culture: Anthropology and the Biological Interface*. Cambridge: Cambridge University Press

Sanua, V.D. (1984) Is infantile autism a universal phenomenon? An open question. *International Journal of Social Psychiatry*, 30, 163–77

Sargant, W. (1973) *The Mind Possessed: From Ecstasy to Exorcism.*
London: Heinemann

Sartre, J.-P. (1948) *Anti-Semite and Jew.* (Translated by G.J. Becker).
New York: Schocken

Saussure, F. de (1961) *Cours de Linguistique Générale.* Paris: Payot

Schechter, S. (1970) The Chassidim. In Schechter, *Studies in Judaism.*
New York: Atheneum

Scheff, T.J. (1979) *Catharsis in Healing, Ritual and Drama.* Berkeley:
University of California Press

Scheper-Hughes, N. (1979) *Saints, Scholars and Schizophrenics:
Mental Illness in Rural Ireland.* Berkeley: University of California
Press

Scheper-Hughes, N. and M. Lock (1987) The Mindful Body: A
Prolegomenon to Future Work in Medical Anthropology. *Medical
Anthropology Quarterly,* 1, 6–39

Schieffelin, E.L. (1985) Performance and the cultural construction of
reality. *American Ethnologist,* 12, 707–724

Schneider, K. (1959) *Clinical Psychopathology* (5th edn.) (trans. M.W.
Hamilton). New York: Grune and Stratton

Schochet, J. (1979) *Mystical Concepts in Hasidism.* New York: Kehot

Scholem, G.C. (1954) *Major Trends in Jewish Mysticism.* Third
Edition. New York: Schocken

Scholem, G.C. (1965) *On the Kabbalah and Its Symbolism.* New York:
Schocken

Scholem, G.C. (1971) *The Messianic Idea in Judaism and Other
Essays in Jewish Spirituality.* New York: Schocken

Scholem, G.C. (1973) *Sabbatai Zevi.* London: Routledge

Scholem, G.C. (1978) *Kabbalah.* New York: Meridian

Schooler, C. & Caudill, W. (1964) Symptomatology in Japanese and
American schizophrenics. *Ethnology,* 3, 172–178

Schwartz, L. (1985) Anorexia nervosa as a culture-bound syndrome.
Social Science and Medicine, 20, 725–730

Schwimmer, E. (1972) Symbolic Competition. *Anthropologica,* 14,
117–25

Scott, R.D. (1973) The treatment barrier: Part I and II. *British Journal
of Medical Psychology,* 46, 45–55

Seager, W. (1991) *Metaphysics of Consciousness.* London: Routledge

Sedgwick, P. (1982) *Psycho Politics.* London: Pluto Press

Seidenberg, R. (1974) Images of health, illness and women in drug
advertising. *Journal of Drug Issues,* 4, 264–267

Seligman, C.G. (1928) Anthropological perspectives and psychological
theory. *Journal of the Royal Anthropological Institute,* 62, 193–228

Seligman, M.E.P. (1974) Depression and learned helplessness. In

R.J. Friedman and M.M. Katz (eds.), *The Psychology of Depression: Contemporary Theory and Research*. Washington: Winston Wiley

Sered, S.S. (1994) *Priestess, Mother, Sacred Sister*. New York: Oxford University Press

Shaffir, W. (1974) *Life in a Religious Community: The Lubavitcher Chassidim in Montreal*. Toronto: Toronto University Press

Sharot, S. (1982) *Messianism, Mysticism and Magic: A Sociological Account of Jewish Religious Movements*. Chapel Hill: University of North Carolina Press

Sharot, S. (1991) Hasidism in Modern Society. In G.B. Hundert (ed.), *Essential Papers in Hasidism*. New York: New York University Press

Shirokogoroff, S.M. (1915) *Psychometric Complex of the Tungus*. London: Kegan Paul, Trench and Trubner

Shook, E.V. (1985) *Ho'oponopono: Contemporary Uses of a Hawaiian Problem-Solving Process*. Hawaii: East–West Center

Shore, J.H. and Manson, S. (1983) American Indian psychiatric and social problems. *Transcultural Psychiatric Research* Review, 20, 159–180

Shorter, E. (1983) *A History of Women's Bodies*. London: Allen Lane

Sidel, R. (1973) The role of revolutionary optimism in the treatment of mental illness in the People's Republic of China. *American Journal of Orthopsychiatry*, 43, 732–736

Simons, R.C. and Hughes, C.C. (eds.) (1985) *Culture-Bound Psychiatric Syndromes*. Dordrecht: Reidel

Singer, I.B. (1958) *Satan in Goray*. London: Peter Owen

Singer, I.B.(1976) *Passions*. London: Cape

Singer, K. (1975) Depressive disorders from a transcultural perspective. *Social Science and Medicine*, 9, 289–301

Singer, M. (1990) Reinventing medical anthropology: Towards a critical realignment. *Social Science and Medicine*, 30, 179–187

Skultans, V. (1974) *Intimacy and ritual: A study of spiritualism, mediums and groups*. London: Routledge and Kegan Paul

Smith, R.T. (1988) *Kinship and Class in the West Indies*. Cambridge: Cambridge University Press

Smith-Rosenberg, C. (1972) The hysterical woman: sex roles and conflict in 19th century America. *Social Research*, 39, 652–678

Smith-Rosenberg, C. (1973) Puberty to menopause: The cycle of femininity in 19th-century America. *Feminist Studies*, 1, 58–72

Sobo, E. (1993) *One Blood: The Jamaican Body*. New York: State University of New York Press

Sontag, S. (1979) *Illness as Metaphor*. London: Allen Lane

Southcott, J. (1995) *A Dispute Between The Woman and the Powers of Darkness.* (orig. pub. 1802). Oxford: Woodstock

Spencer, P. (1965) *The Samburu: A Study of Gerontocracy in a Nomadic Tribe.* London: Routledge and Kegan Paul

Sperber, D. (1975) *Rethinking Symbolism.* Cambridge: Cambridge University Press

Sperber, D. (1980) Is symbolic thought pre-rational? In Foster and Brandes, *op. cit.*

Sperber, D. (1985) *On Anthropological Knowledge.* Cambridge: Cambridge University Press

Spero, M.H. (1979) On the Nature of the Therapeutic Encounter Between Hasid and Master. In Bulka *op. cit.*

Spiro, M. (1969) The psychological function of witchcraft belief: the Burmese case. In W. Caudill and T.-Y. Lin (eds.), *Mental Health Research in Asia and the Pacific.* Honolulu: East–West Center Press

Spring, A. (1978) Epidemiology of spirit possession among the Luvale of Zambia. In J. Hoch-Smith and A. Spring (eds.), *Women in Ritual and Symbolic Roles,* New York: Plenum

Stigler, J.W., Shweder, R.A. and Herdt, G. (eds.) (1990) *Cultural Psychology.* Cambridge: Cambridge University Press

Stimson, G. (1975) Women in a doctored world. *New Society,* 32, 265–266

Stirrat, R.L. (1984) Sacred models. *Man* (n.s.), 19, 199–215

Stoller, P. (1984) Sound in Songay cultural experience. *American Anthropologist,* 11, 559–570

Strachey, L. (1981) *Eminent Victorians.* London: Chatto and Windus

Stuart, R.B. and Jacobson, B. (1979) Sex differences in obesity. In E.S. Gomberg and V. Franks (ed.), *Gender and Disordered Behaviour: Sex Differences in Psychopathology.* New York: Brunner/Mazel

Swaan, A. de (1981) The politics of agoraphobia. *Theory and Society,* 10, 359–85

Swartz, L. (1989) Aspects of Culture in South African Psychiatry. PhD Thesis, Cape Town University

Symonds, A. (1971) Phobias after marriage: women's declaration of independence. *American Journal of Psychoanalysis,* 31, 144–52

Szasz, T. (1961) *The Myth of Mental Illness.* New York: Hoeber/ Harper

Tambiah, S.J. (1968) The Magical Power of Words. *Man* (n.s.), 3, 175–208

Tambiah, S.J. (1990) *Magic, Science, Religion and the Scope of Rationality.* Cambridge: Cambridge University Press

Taussig, M. (1987) *Shamanism, Colonialism and the Wild Man: A Study in Terror and Healing.* Chicago: University of Chicago Press

Taussig, M. (1993) *Mimesis and Alterity: A Particular History of the Senses*. New York: Routledge

Teish, L. (1985) *Jambalaya*. San Francisco: Harper and Row

The Bomb (1982) Naked British Professor Lived in Trinidad Bush, Port of Spain, 15 January

The People (1981) Earth People Play Host to English Psychiatrist, Port of Spain, December

Tilt, E.J. (1862) *Ovarian Inflammation and the Physiology and Diseases of Menstruction*. London: Churchill

The Times (1984) The kind and gentle bank robber – aged 70. London: 6 October

Toren, C. (1983) Thinking symbols: a critique of Sperber 1979. *Man* (n.s.), 18, 260–8

Torrey, E.F. (1971) *The Mind Game: Witchdoctors and Psychiatrists*. New York: Emerson Hall

Torrey, E.F. (1972) What Western psychotherapists can learn from witch doctors. *American Journal of Orthopsychiatry*, 42, 69–76

Torrey, E.F. (1980) *Schizophrenia and Civilization*. New York: Aronson

Townsend, J.M. and Carbone, C.L. (1980) Menopausal syndrome: illness or social role – transcultural analysis. *Culture, Medicine and Psychiatry*, 4, 229–248

Trachtenberg, J. (1977) *Jewish Magic and Superstition*. New York: Atheneum (1939)

Trinidad Guardian (1982) Nuisance From the Earth People, leading article, Port of Spain, 9 January

Turner, B. (1984) The Body and Society: *Explorations in Social Theory*. Oxford: Blackwell

Turner, V. (1964) An Ndembu doctor in practice. In A. Kiev (ed.), Magic, *Faith and Healing*. New York: Free Press

Turner, V. (1967) *The Forest of Symbols*. Ithaca: Cornell University Press

Turner, V. (1969) *The Ritual Process*. London: Routledge and Kegan Paul

Turner, V.W. (1986) Dewey, Dilthey and drama: an essay in the anthropology of experience. In V.W. Turner and E.M. Bruner (eds.), *The Anthropology of Experience*. Urbana, Illinois: University of Illinois Press

Tylor, E.B. (1904) *Anthropology*. London: Macmillan

Van Gennep, A. (1960) *The Rites of Passage*. London: Routledge and Kegan Paul

Vonnegut, M. (1976) *The Eden Express*. London: Cape

Wagner, R. (1986) *Symbols That Stand For Themselves*. Chicago: University of Chicago Press

Wallace, A.F.C. (1958) *Revitalisation Movements*. New York: Random House

Wallach, M. (1977) The Chassidism of Stamford Hill. London: *Jewish Chronicle Magazine*, 27 May

Warner, K. (1982) *The Trinidad Calypso*. Heinemann: London

Warner, M. (1983) *Joan of Arc: The Image of Female Heroism*. Harmondsworth: Penguin

Warner, M. (1985) *Monuments and Maidens: The Allegory of the Female Form*. London: Weidenfeld and Nicolson

Waxler, N.E. (1977) Is mental illness cured in traditional societies? *Culture, Medicine and Psychiatry*, 1, 233–253

Weber, M. (1947) The sociology of charismatic authority. In Weber, *Essays in Sociology*. London

Weber, M. (1947) *The Theory of Social and Economic Organisations*. New York: Free Press (1923)

Wedenoja, W. (1989) Mothering and the practice of 'balm' in Jamaica. In C.S. McClain (ed.), *Women as Healers: Cross-Cultural Perspectives*. New Brunswick: Rutgers University Press

Weigle, M. (1989) *Creation and Procreation: Feminist Reflections on Mythologies of Cosmogony and Parturition*. Philadelphia: University of Pennsylvania Press

Weinstein, E.A. (1962) *Cultural Aspects of Delusion*. New York: Free Press

Weisel, E. (1978) *Four Hasidic Masters and Their Struggle Against Melancholy*. London: Notre Dame

Weissman, M.M. and Klerman, A.L. (1977) Sex differences in the epidemiology of depression. *Archives of General Psychiatry*, 34, 98–111

Whiting, J.W.M. and Child, I.L. (1953) *Child-training and Personality*. New Haven: Yale University Press

Wiener, H. (1969) *9½ Mystics: The Kabbala Today*. New York: Collier

Willis, R.G. (1978) Magic and medicine in Ufipa. In Morley, P. and Wallis, P. (eds.), *Culture and Curing*. King's Lynn: Daedalus Press

Wilson, M. (1951) Witch beliefs and social structure. *American Journal of Sociology*, 56, 307–313

Wilson, P.J. (1967) Status ambiguity and spirit possession. *Man* (n.s.), 2, 366–378

Wilson, P.J. (1973) *Crab Antics: The Social Anthropology of English-Speaking Negro Societies of the Caribbean*. New Haven, Conn.: Yale University Press

Wing, J.K. (1978) *Reasoning About Madness*. Oxford: Oxford University Press

Winstanley, G. (1973) *The Law of Freedom and Other Writings* (ed. C. Hill). Harmondsworth: Penguin

Winter, J.A. (1973) The metaphoric parallelist approach to the sociology of theistic beliefs: themes, variations and implications. *Sociological Analysis*, 34, 212–229

Wittgenstein, L. (1958) *Philosophical Investigations*. Oxford: Blackwell

Witztum, E. and D. Greenberg (1990) Mental illness and religious change. *British Journal of Medical Psychology*, 63, 33–41

Wolpe, J. (1970) Identifying the antecedents of an agoraphobic reaction. *Behaviour Therapy and Experimental Psychiatry*, 1, 299–309

Woocher, J.S. (1979) The Kabbalah, Hasidism and the life of unification. In Bulka *op. cit.*

Wootton, B. (1959) *Social Science and Social Pathology*. London: Allen and Unwin

Young, A. (1975) Why Amhara get kureynya: sickness and possession in an Ethiopian zar cult. *American Ethnologist*, 567–584

Young, A. (1976) Some implications of medical beliefs and practices for social anthropology. *American Anthropologist*, 78, 5–24

Young, A. (1980) An anthropological perspective on medical knowledge. *Journal of Medicine and Philosophy*, 5, 102–111

Young, I.M. (1984) Pregnant embodiment: subjectivity and alienation. *Journal of Medicine and Philosophy*, 9, 45–62

Zapperi, R. (1991) *The Pregnant Man*. Char: Harwood

Zborowski, M. and E. Herzog (1962) *Life Is With People: The Culture of the Shtetl*. New York: Schocken (1952)

Zigler, E. and Phillips. L. (1960) Social effectiveness and symptomatic behaviours. *Journal of Abnormal Psychology*, 61, 231–8

The Zohar (1934) (Selections translated by H. Sperling, M. Simon and P. Levertoff), London: Soncino

Index

Index compiled by
Sue Carlton

New Titles for 1998

CONTEMPORARY PERSPECTIVES ON PSYCHOTHERAPY AND HOMOSEXUALITIES
Edited by Christopher Shelley

Most psychotherapy training programmes don't incorporate elements which examine the special needs of the gay and lesbian populations. It is therefore questionable whether practitioners possess the basic necessary skills for assessing and employing interventions based on sexually sensitive material. An unexamined and untrained approach to working with homosexual populations can no longer be tolerated.
This book address some of the incoherence that exists in this field. The contributors address theories and models of practice that will be more beneficial to the therapeutic needs of homosexual clients. Their accounts represent a significant step towards a better understanding of the needs of this client group.

JOHN BOWLBY: HIS EARLY LIFE
A Biographical Journey into the Roots of Attachment Theory
Suzan van Dijken

In an insightful treatment of the early years of John Bowlby's life and work, Suzan van Dijken sheds light on a number of events that are very much linked to the eventual creation of Attachment Theory but have not been known about or published to date. In addition, she provides much new information about topics that Bowlby was quite reluctant to discuss in detail, whether in public or in private, and yet are clearly connected to his later life and theoretical pursuits.

This biographical portrait covers in great depth Bowlby's family of origin, his upbringing, schooling and later education, his little-known work with Cyril Burt, his introduction to psychoanalysis, and his involvement in some of the major events in that world, including the Controversial Discussions between Anna Freud and Melanie Klein.

MIDWIFERY OF THE SOUL
A Holistic Perspective on Psychoanalysis

Margaret Arden

Early on in her career, Margaret Arden became fascinated by the problem of the gap between theory and practice. She came to realise that what she relied on in her work was not the theory she had been taught but her sense of the truth of what was going on in the consulting room. The process of psychoanalysis, the work of transference and counter transference, enables the analyst to meet one of the patient's basic needs by recognising the truth of who he or she is.

This book takes the reader on an intellectual journey. Each chapter represents a stage in the exploration of ideas which have influenced the author's view of psychoanalysis. The book is remarkable for the coherance of her thinking and the clarity of presentation of ideas which connect Jung with Freud, science with religion and the emerging science of consciousness with Goethe's scientific views. Anyone who has felt the need to explore the unrealised possibility of psychoanalytic theory will find this book rewarding.

THE PSYCHOANALYTIC MYSTIC

Michael Eigen

Most psychoanalysts tend to be anti-mystical or, at least, non-mystical. Psychoanalysis is allied with science and, if anything, is capable of deconstructing mystical experience. Yet some psychoanalysts tend to be mystical or make use of the mystical experience as an intuitive model for psychoanalysis. Indeed, the greatest split in the psychodynamic movement, between Freud and Jung, partly hinged on the way in which mystical experience was to be understood.

Michael Eigen has often advocated and encouraged a return to the spiritual in psychoanalysis - what Freud called the 'oceanic feeling'. Here he expands on his call to celebrate and explore the meaning of mystical experience within psychoanalysis, illustrating his writing with the work of Bion, Milner and Winnicott.

DEVELOPMENT AND DIVERSITY
New Applications in Art Therapy
Edited by Doug Sandle

This new collection represents some of the best and most interesting examples of the widening application of art therapy. The contributors - all experienced art therapists - cover such topics as family trauma, work with children with learning difficulties and with autism, with criminal offenders, anorexics, the sexually abused and with people who stammer.

The new developments represented in this book have implications not just for the profession of Art Therapy but also for methods of practice. They point up the challenge of new methodologies which focus on process rather than on the finished image. They remind practitioners how stylistic and aesthetic elements, as well as content, can provide therapeutic insights.

Providing a rich diversity of approach, this collection will be essential reading for all students and practitioners requiring the broadest and most up-to-date statement of the current status of Art Therapy.

THE ELUSIVE HUMAN SUBJECT
A Psychoanalytic Theory of Subject Relations
Roger Kennedy

'This is a major work on the nature of human subjectivity. Kennedy argues that we need to conceptualize the human subject differently in psychoanalysis, and he proposes a complex yet lucid theory of what that would be. I have no doubt that it will establish itself as one of the major works of contemporary psychoanalysis.' **Christopher Bollas**

'There is something essentially elusive about our subjective life, which makes it difficult to capture'. From this position of uncertainty, Kennedy pursues his exploration of how we can gain access to the human subject, through what we experience as individuals and also through the multiple and complex interactions between individuals in the social field.

This is an outstanding book in which Roger Kennedy has succeeded in a major re-evaluation of how we describe the Self, and what that means for psychoanalysis.

Also published by FAB

THE DIALECTICS OF SCHIZOPHRENIA
Philip Thomas
'Thomas may become the new Clare in the eyes of the Psychiatrists... for the non-medical readership interested in mental health, this book is a gem.'
Open Mind
'Undoubtedly one of the most readable accounts of schizophenia research to be published in recent years.'
Mental Health Care

SOMATIC ILLNESS AND THE PATIENT'S *OTHER* STORY
A practical Integrative Mind/Body Approach to Disease for Doctors and Psychotherapists
Brian Broom
'A must for those working in the field of mind/body medicine.'
Counselling News
This is an unusual book that integrates Internal Medicine and Psychotherapy. Although conceptually informed, its principal provision is an in-depth, holistic approach to those illnesses that present physical symptoms but whose underlying cause may be psychological.

THE POLITICS OF ATTACHMENT
Towards a Secure Society
Edited by Sebastian Kraemer and Jane Roberts
Preface by Patricia Hewitt
'The theme of the book is the usefulness and limits of attachment theory placed within a constructive and critical exchange with other perspectives. The book as a whole furnishes a welcome antidote to soundbite politics. It discusses ideas about family and community, about youth crime and insecurity, about identity and political process.'
New Times

The contributors to *The Politics of Attachment* - all distinguished authorities from a variety of backgrounds in public, professional and academic life - share a common conviction that we all have a powerful need to belong, to be attached to people, places and projects, and that social and political processes must reflect that. The writers draw on recent research and debate in developmental psychology and political science to provide a unique dialogue between the psychological and the social - a political grasp of ordinary human needs.